DEAD
STYLE

AF531076

EDITOR:
GARRETT MCGRATH

DESIGNER:
HEESANG LEE

PRODUCTION MANAGER:
ALISON GERVAIS

LIBRARY OF CONGRESS CONTROL NUMBER: 2019939883

ISBN: 978-1-4197-4291-0
EISBN: 978-1-68335-885-5

PRINTED AND BOUND IN CHINA
10 9 8 7 6 5 4 3 2 1

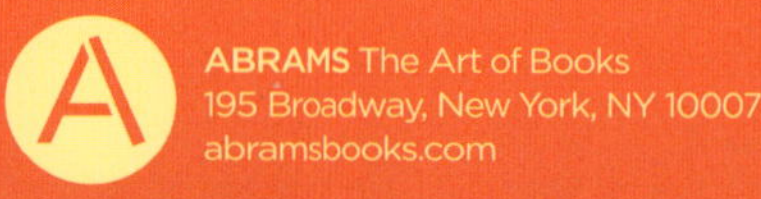
ABRAMS The Art of Books
195 Broadway, New York, NY 10007
abramsbooks.com

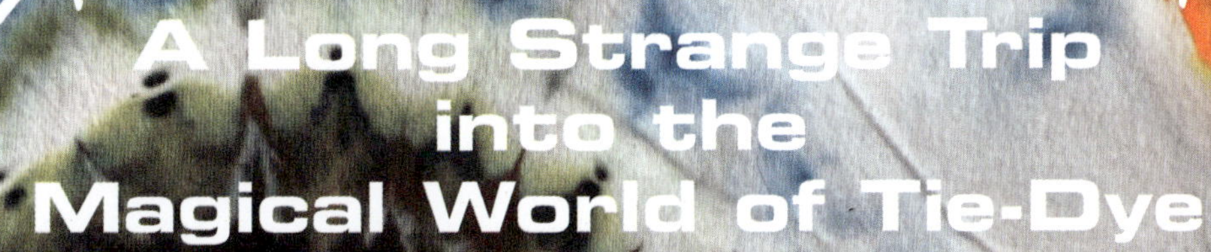

DEAD STYLE

Mordechai
"MISTER MORT"
Rubinstein

ABRAMS IMAGE, NEW YORK

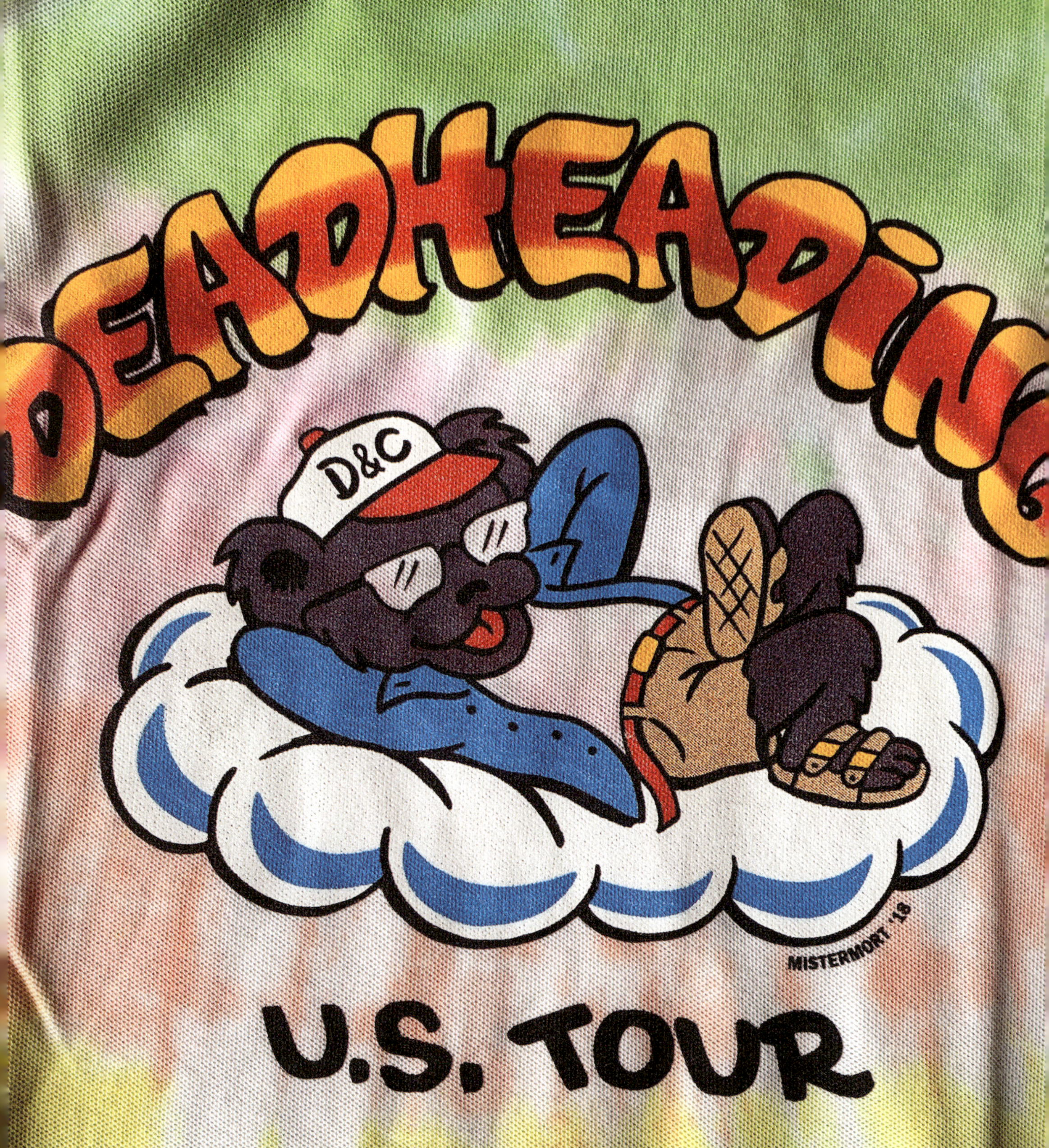
DEADHEADING
D&C
MISTERMORT '18
U.S. TOUR

TABLE OF CONTENTS

Introduction: Here It Comes Again by Will Welch 6

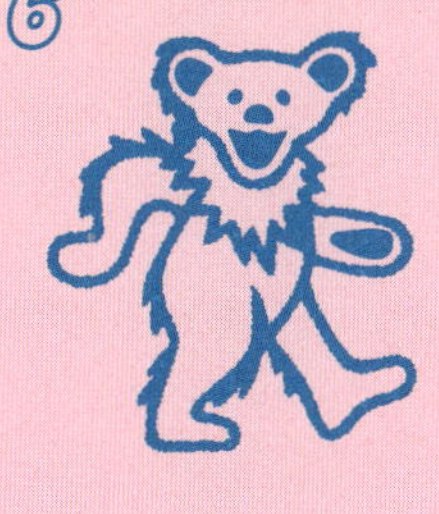

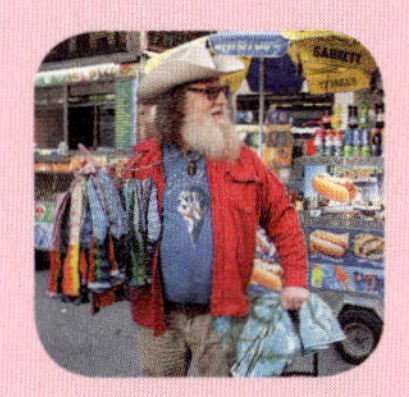

11
MADISON SQUARE GARDEN
New York City, New York
Sunday, November 12th, 2017, &
Tuesday, November 14th, 2017

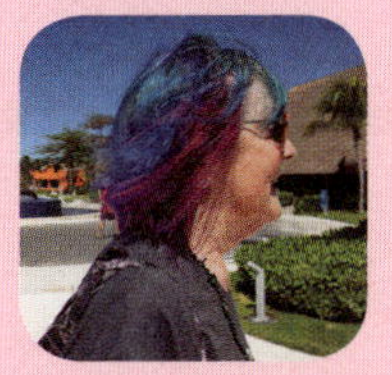

25
PLAYING IN THE SAND/ BARCELÓ MAYA
Riviera Maya, Mexico
Thursday, February 15th, 2018,
Saturday, February 17th, 2018, &
Sunday, February 18th, 2018

55
SARATOGA PERFORMING ARTS CENTER
Saratoga Springs, New York
Monday, June 11th, 2018

73
XFINITY THEATRE
Hartford, Connecticut
Wednesday, June 13th, 2018

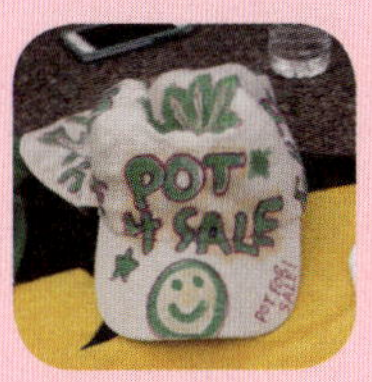

83
CITI FIELD
Flushing, New York
Friday, June 15th, 2018, &
Saturday, June 16th, 2018

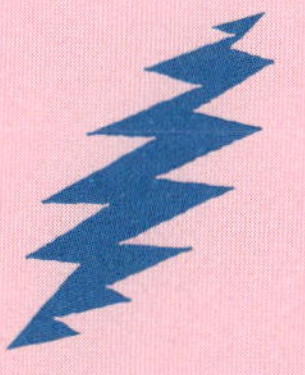

111
ALPINE VALLEY MUSIC THEATRE
East Troy, Wisconsin
Friday, June 22nd, 2018, &
Saturday, June 23rd, 2018

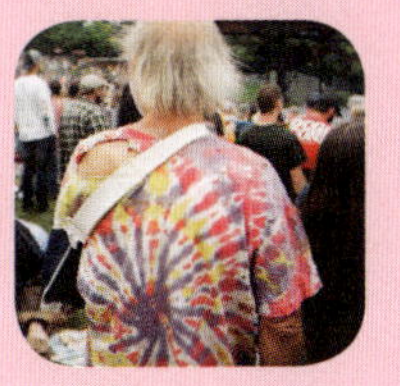

143
FOLSOM FIELD
Boulder, Colorado
Friday, July 13th, 2018, &
Saturday, July 14th, 2018

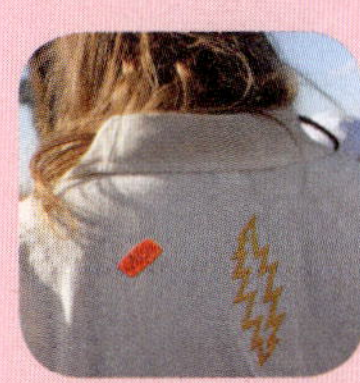

157
THE GORGE AMPHITHEATRE
George, Washington
Friday, June 7th, 2019, &
Saturday, June 8th, 2019

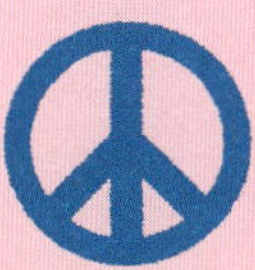

Here It Comes Again

By Will Welch

Naturally, my favorite description of what it's like to be a **Deadhead** comes from the **Grateful Dead** itself. I'm specifically talking about the fifth verse of "The Music Never Stopped," which goes like this:

> They're a band beyond description
> Like Jehovah's favorite choir
> People joining hand in hand while
> The music played the band
> Lord they're setting us on fire!

That's the feeling.

When Jerry Garcia passed away in August 1995, I was over at my friend Ben's house. I was fourteen years-old. Ben's dad was a committed **Deadhead**. He's the one who turned us on to the music. There was always a show playing at their house—a bootleg CD, or one of countless Maxell XLII-S 90s. That weekend, Ben's dad was despondent. Like the fire was out. What is a **Deadhead** without Jerry? There are any number of bands that play music, but where else can you go if you want that feeling? Where can you go to hear the music play the band?

Fast-forward two decades. Without really talking about it, my **Deadhead** friend Gabe and I had committed ourselves to pretty much always going when the various post-Jerry incarnations of the **Grateful Dead** came to town. There were good nights and there were bad nights. Between the **Dead**, Further, and Phil Lesh and Friends, I saw plenty of both over the years. What was more consistent than the music was the opportunity to fellowship with what had become a slightly threadbare yet still intensely dedicated community of **heads**. Some shows we danced our faces off; others we went home early in the second set. But our commitment never wavered.

We didn't know to expect anything different from **Dead & Company**. I remember seeing the band's first run—on November 1, 2015, at Madison Square Garden. It was fun. They sounded good. The very fact of John Mayer in the Jerry spot brought a different level of energy and curiosity to the proceedings. But there was no expectation that this would somehow drastically eclipse the good-natured nostalgia of all the other post-Jerry formations.

I didn't see **Dead & Company** again until almost exactly two years later: November 14, 2017. Madison Square Garden again. I had no expectations. But as the band worked through a smoking first set, and a second set that featured a bittersweet, sparkling "China Doll" sung by Oteil and a heavy "St. Stephen" → "NFA" closer, we could all feel it. The music played the band that night. Suddenly it was obvious that this lineup was transcending the whole reunion thing. It was becoming its own beast. If not a band beyond description, then at least a band all its own. And the word from both Bob Weir and John Mayer was that they were sticking with it.

And that's why this book is here: The whole three-ring traveling **Deadhead** circus—the miracle we'd all been looking for—has kicked back into gear. High gear. Even Shakedown Street—the impromptu bootleg bazaar out in the parking lot—has become more than just a nostalgic tribute to the glorious lot scenes of yore. It's all happening in its own new way. Everybody's dancing. If you're looking for proof, just flip through these pages.

From that fall tour on, it really started getting trippy. The spirit of what was happening at **Dead & Company**'s shows—both in the arenas and out in the lots—started to ripple out into the larger culture. Suddenly being a **Deadhead** no longer felt like being a Trekker or whatever people who are into model trains call themselves. It got, like, cool. Old heads were pulling their tie-dyes out of storage. New heads were born every day. In my capacity as the editor of the magazine GQ Style, I started asking Mordechai to go document the scene at the shows for our website. I felt certain that Mordechai—who has spent his life spotting, photographing, and celebrating people on the street who have exactly the kind of unself-consciously expressive style that is a hallmark of **Grateful Dead** culture—was born to be a **Deadhead**. It just took a little while for him to discover that facet of himself. Once he fell into it, he fell hard.

Meanwhile, the shows kept getting better—Lord, they're setting us on fire!—and the scene kept growing—people joining hand in hand!—and Mordechai kept shooting.

This June, I booked myself a ludicrous travel itinerary so that I could finally catch a show at the Gorge, the almost mythical venue that hangs off the side of a river canyon in Washington. The plan was to meet up with my friends Alix Ross and Elijah Funk, whose tie-dye T-shirt brand Online Ceramics has become the foremost signifier of the new, youthful energy around the ongoing **Grateful Dead** revival. I had arrived several hours ahead of them, so I found my way to Shakedown. I dropped my bags behind the table that their crew had already set up, and I walked the lot a few times. I bought an Americano (organic fair trade beans from Ethiopia). And a plate of vegan pad Thai. I met Jerry Jaspar (!!), and got him to sign one of his tie dye bandanas. I overpaid for a WHARF RAT ring (worth it) that still hangs from my keychain. I had some heady conversations, and took some photos, and bumped into Mordechai, who took my photo. We were a long way from New York but altogether unsurprised to see each other.

Later my friends texted to say they were now in a brutally long line to park their RV, and that it would be another while longer before they'd make it to the lot. So I lay down in a patch of grass just off Shakedown and stared up at the fat, fast-moving clouds high up in the blue summer sky. The show was still a few hours away. There was nothing to do, and nowhere to go. I took a deep breath of clean Oregonian air. It smelled of fresh-cut grass. It felt like summer. It was a moment beyond description. It was a miracle.

October 2019
New York City

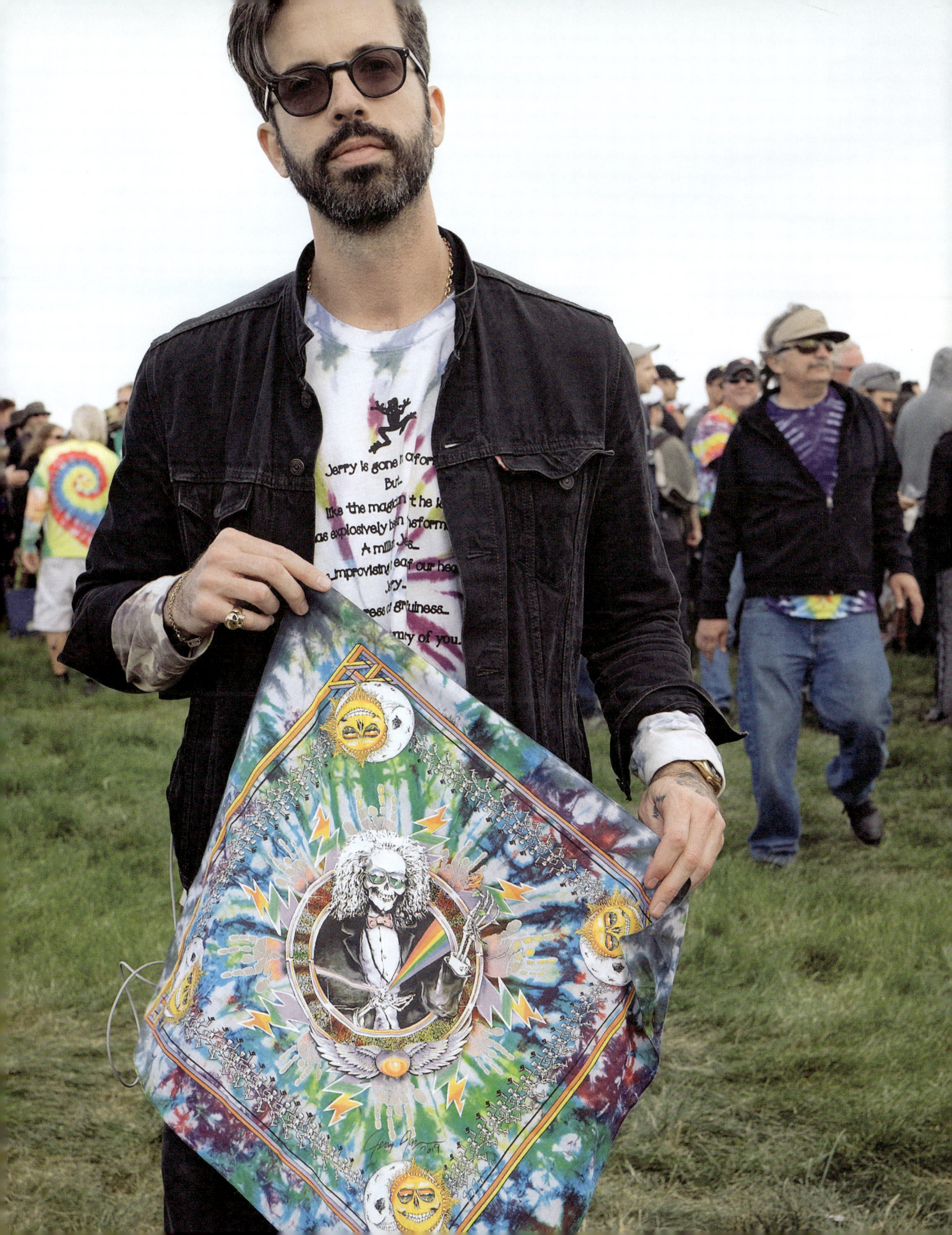

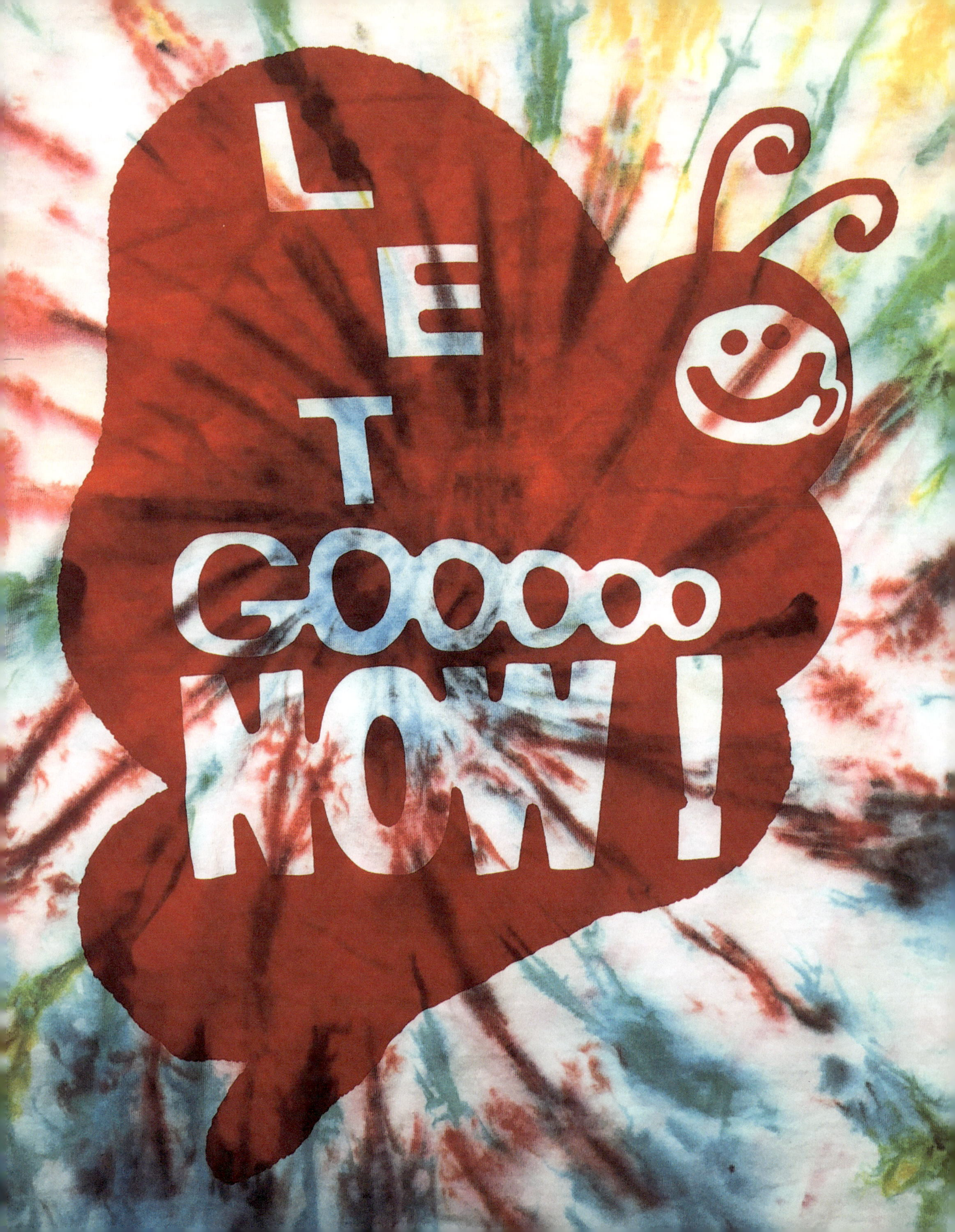
LET
GOOOOO
NOW!

MADISON SQUARE GARDEN

New York City, New York

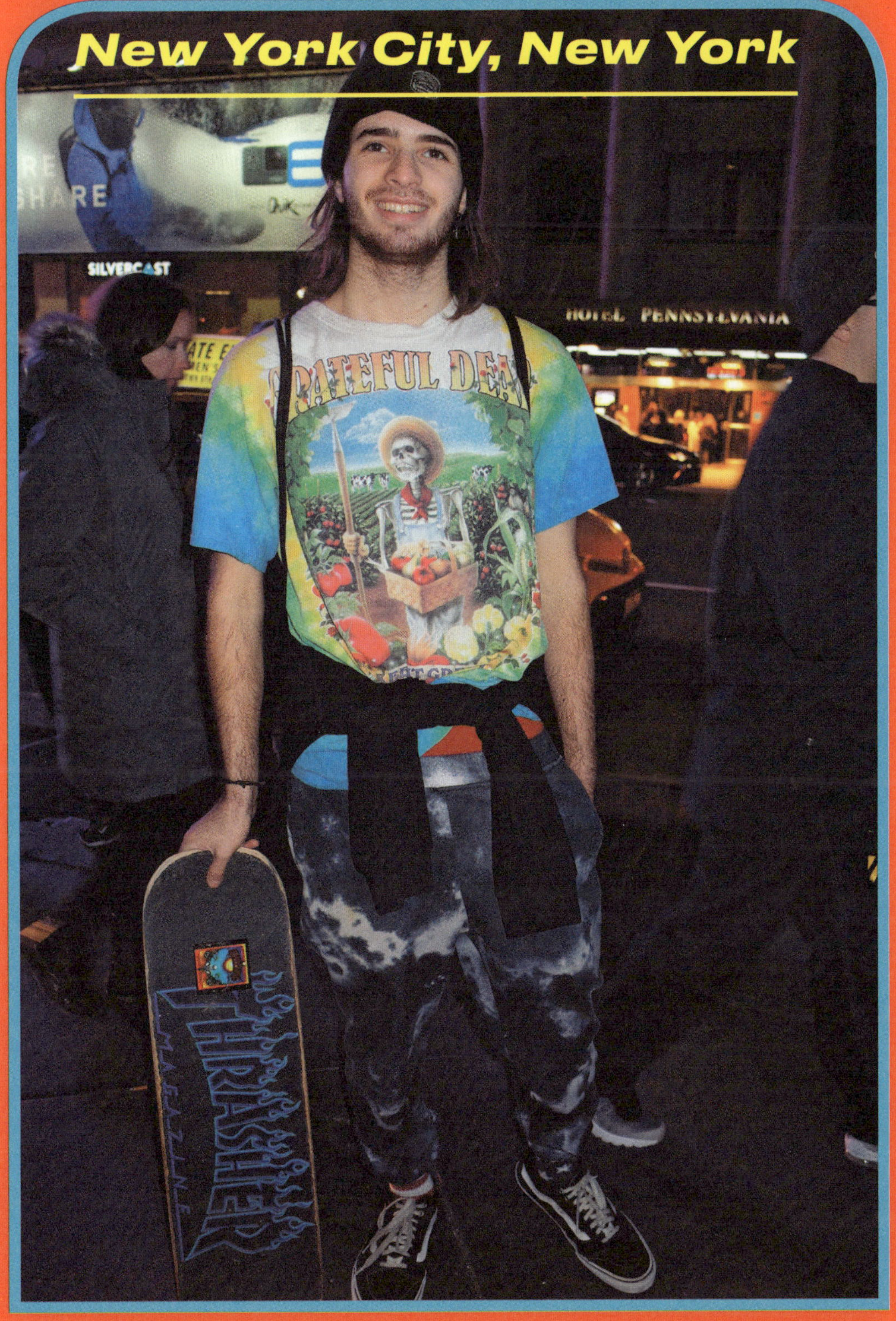

Sunday, November 12th, 2017, &
Tuesday, November 14th, 2017

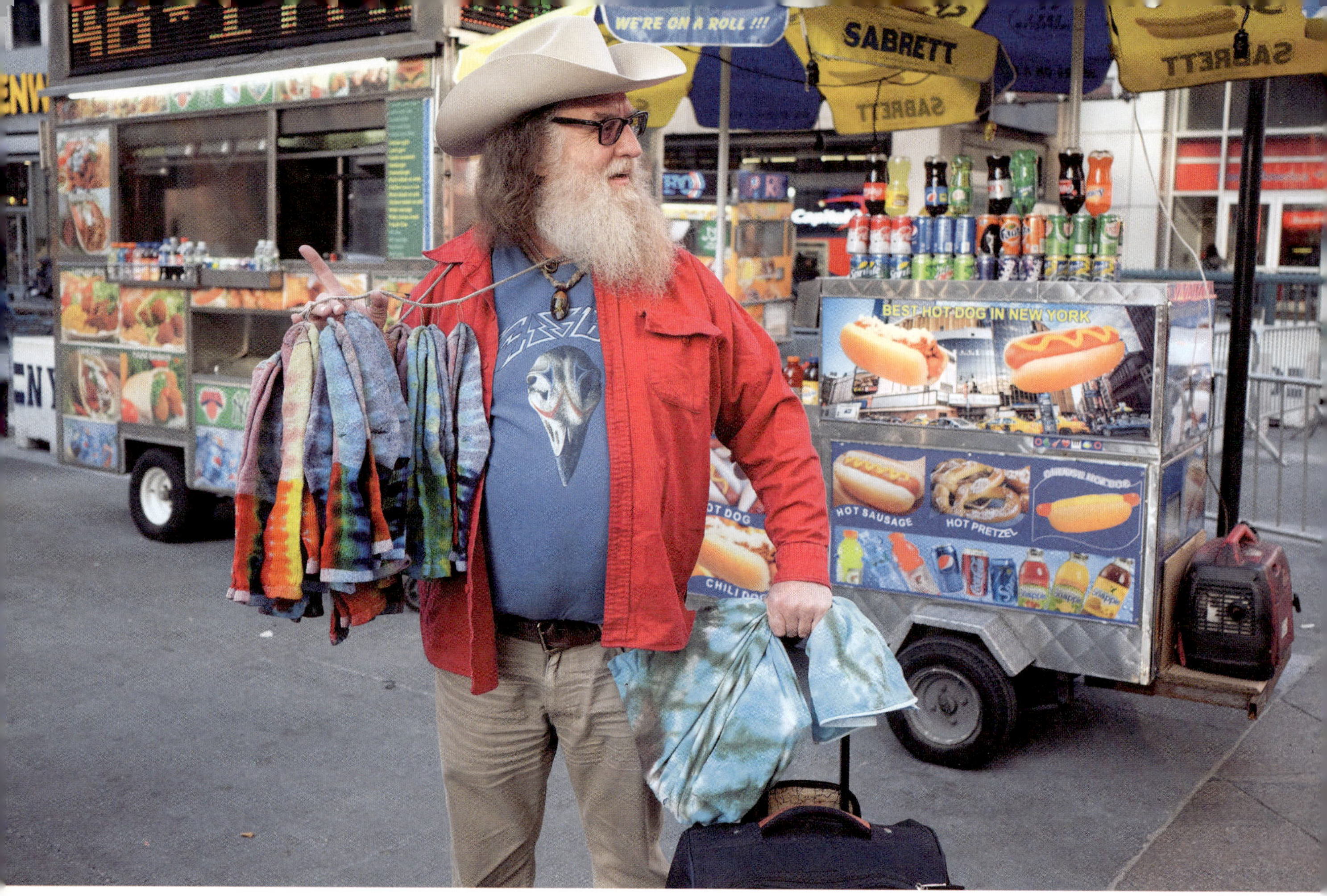

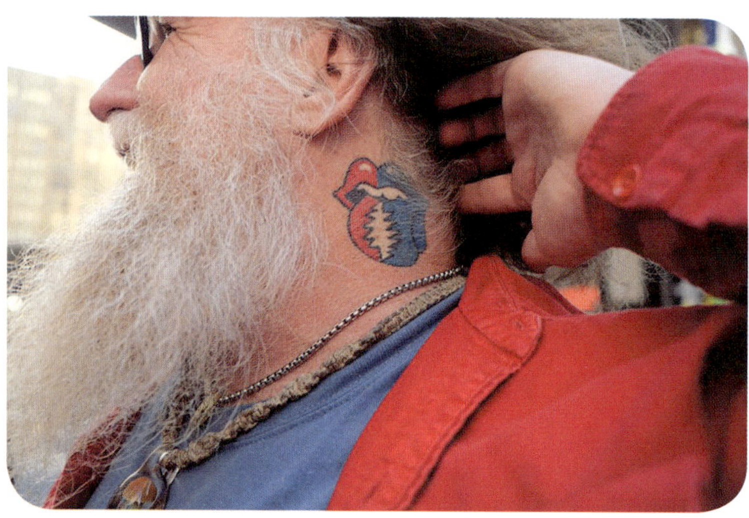

Two of the first pics
I took at MSG. Rad to
see a cowboy hat-wearing
vendor slinging socks
in Midtown Manhattan—
a real taste of lots to come.

THE CLASSIC "WHO'S GOT MY MIRACLE?"

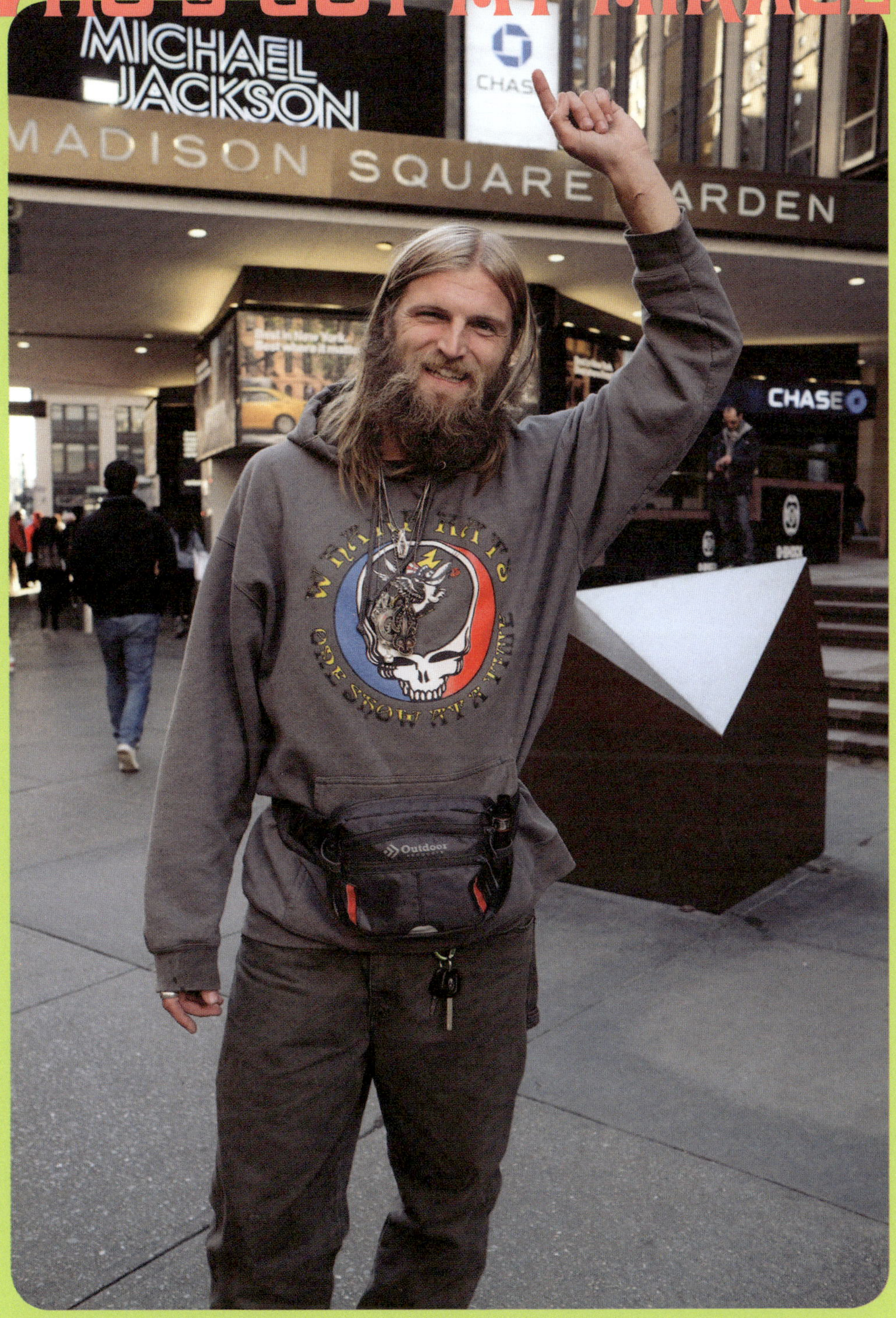

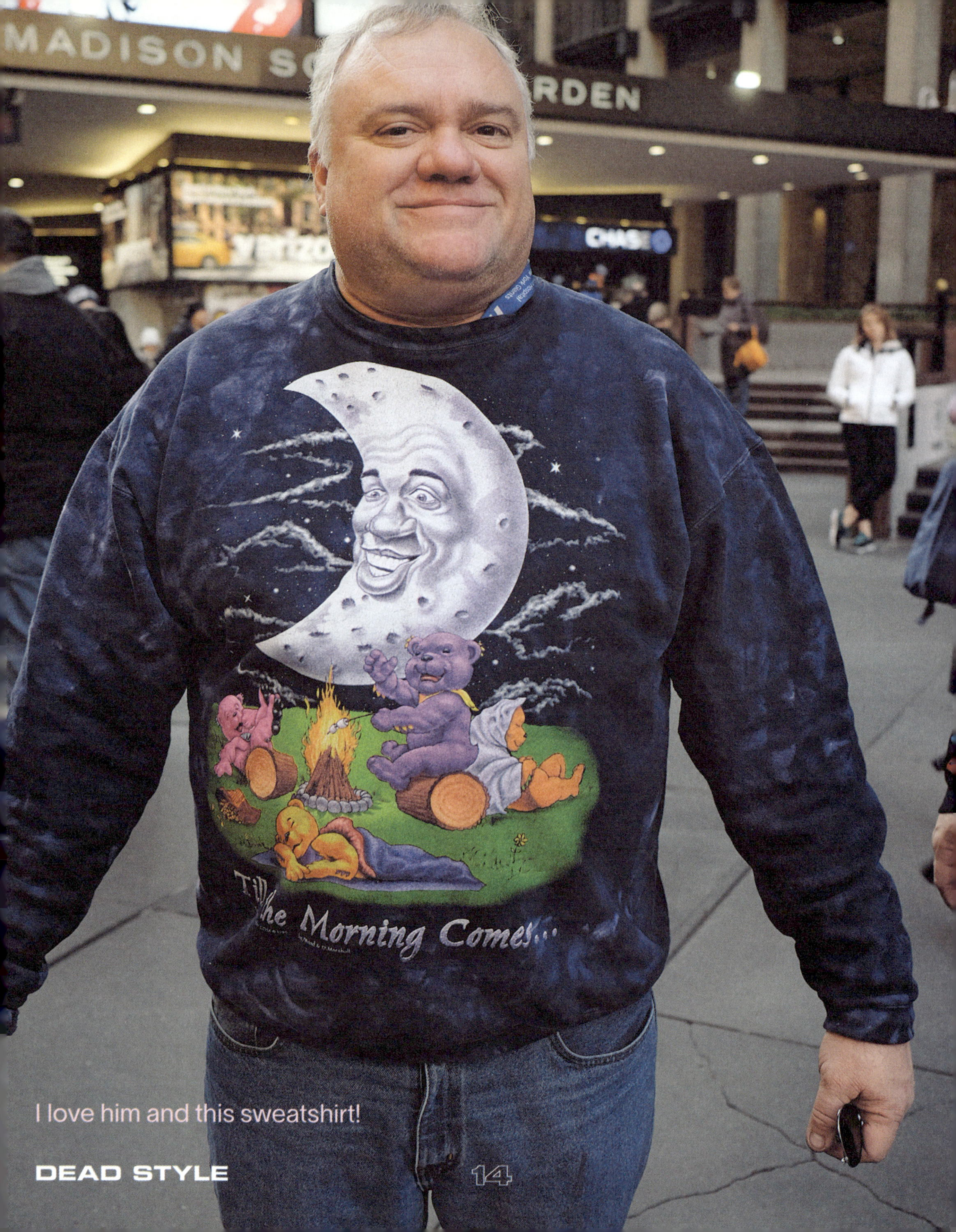

I love him and this sweatshirt!

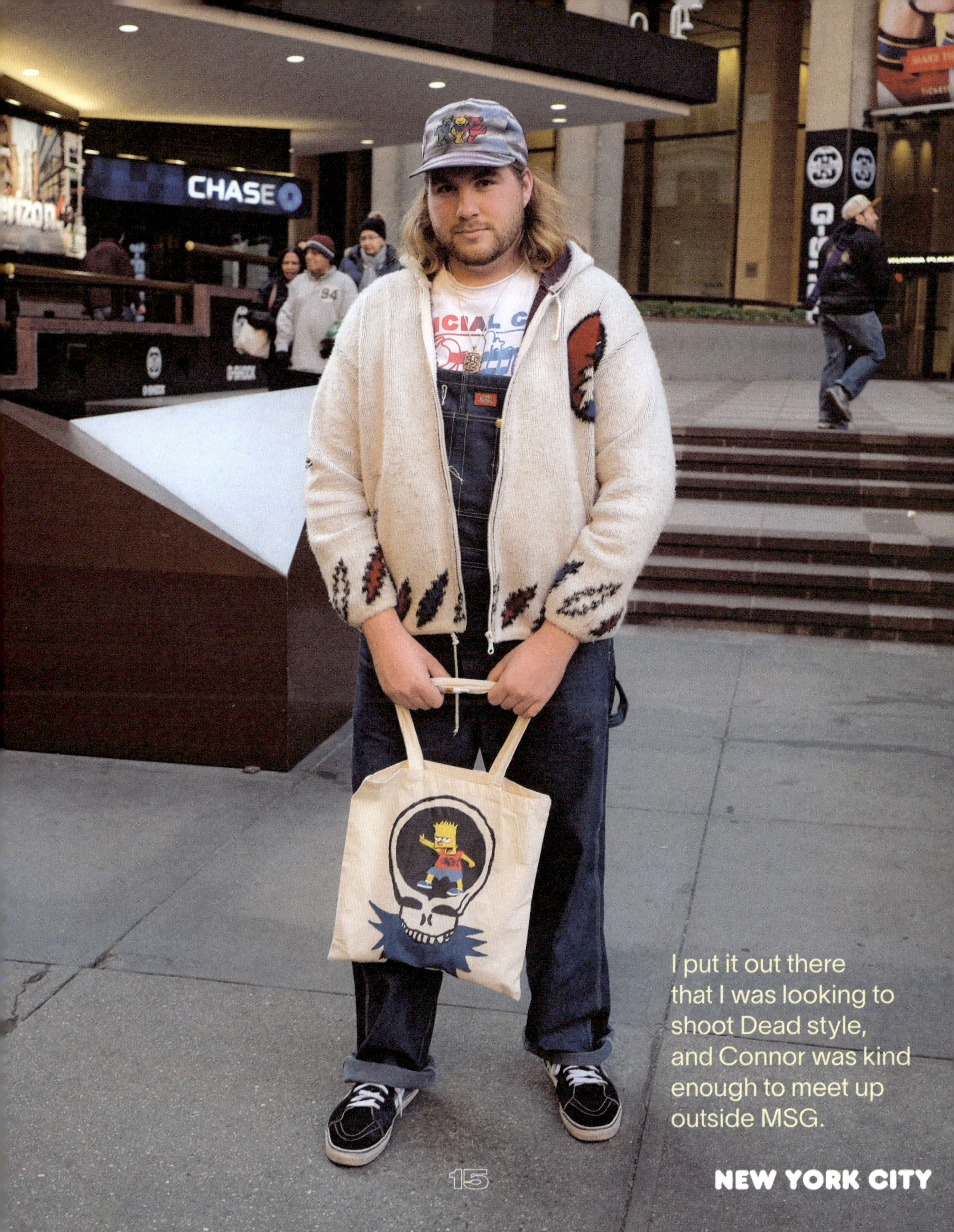

I put it out there that I was looking to shoot Dead style, and Connor was kind enough to meet up outside MSG.

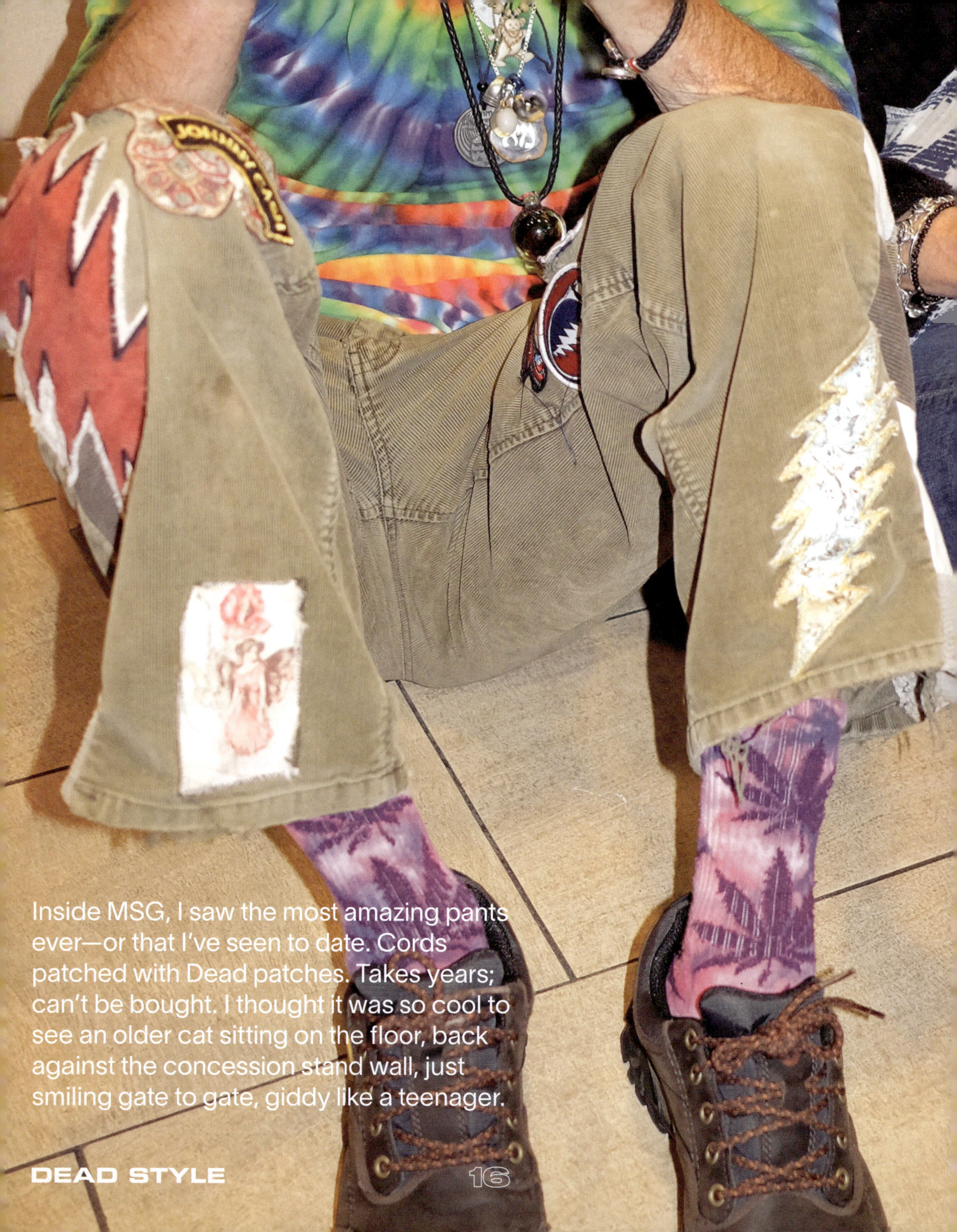

Inside MSG, I saw the most amazing pants ever—or that I've seen to date. Cords patched with Dead patches. Takes years; can't be bought. I thought it was so cool to see an older cat sitting on the floor, back against the concession stand wall, just smiling gate to gate, giddy like a teenager.

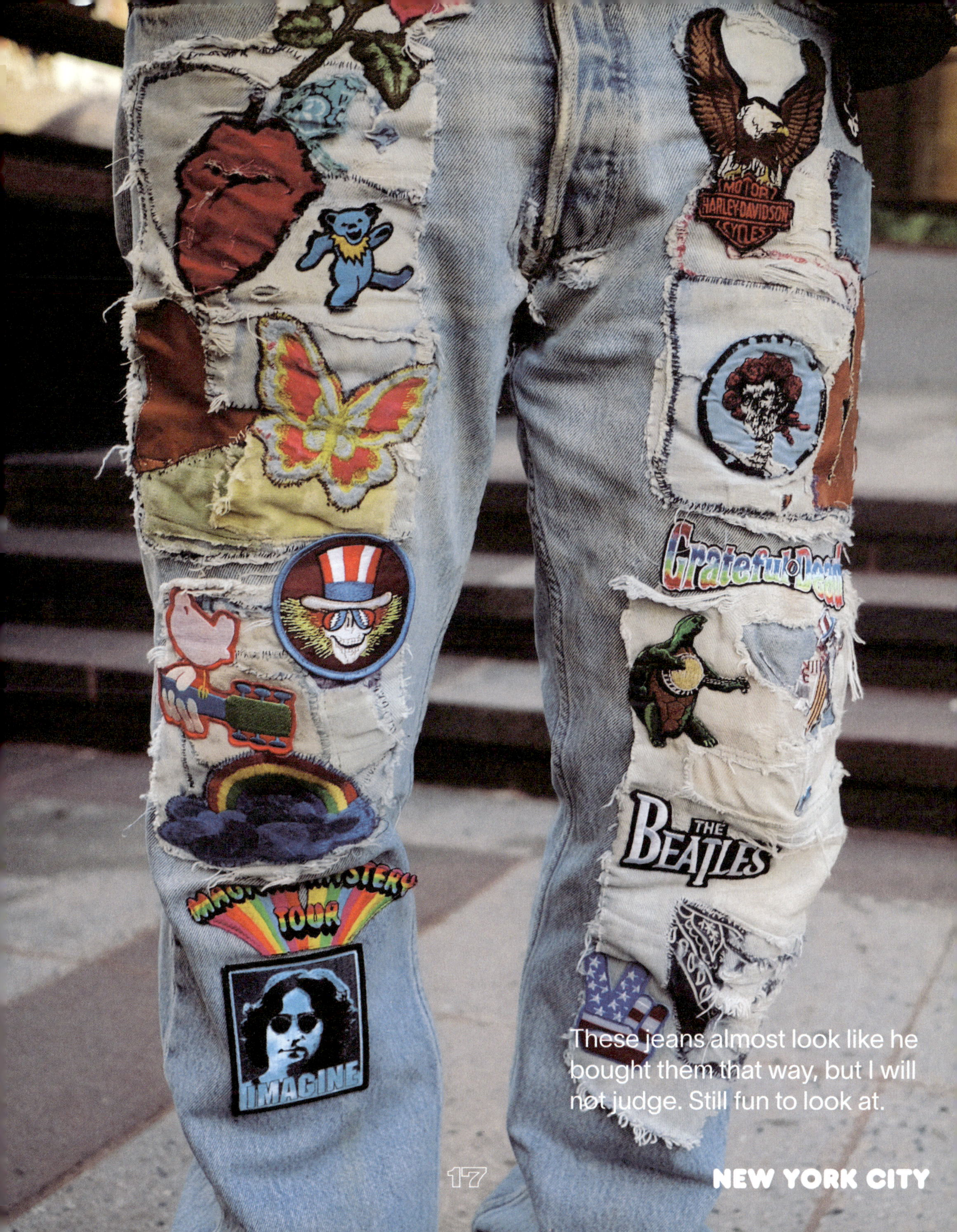

These jeans almost look like he bought them that way, but I will not judge. Still fun to look at.

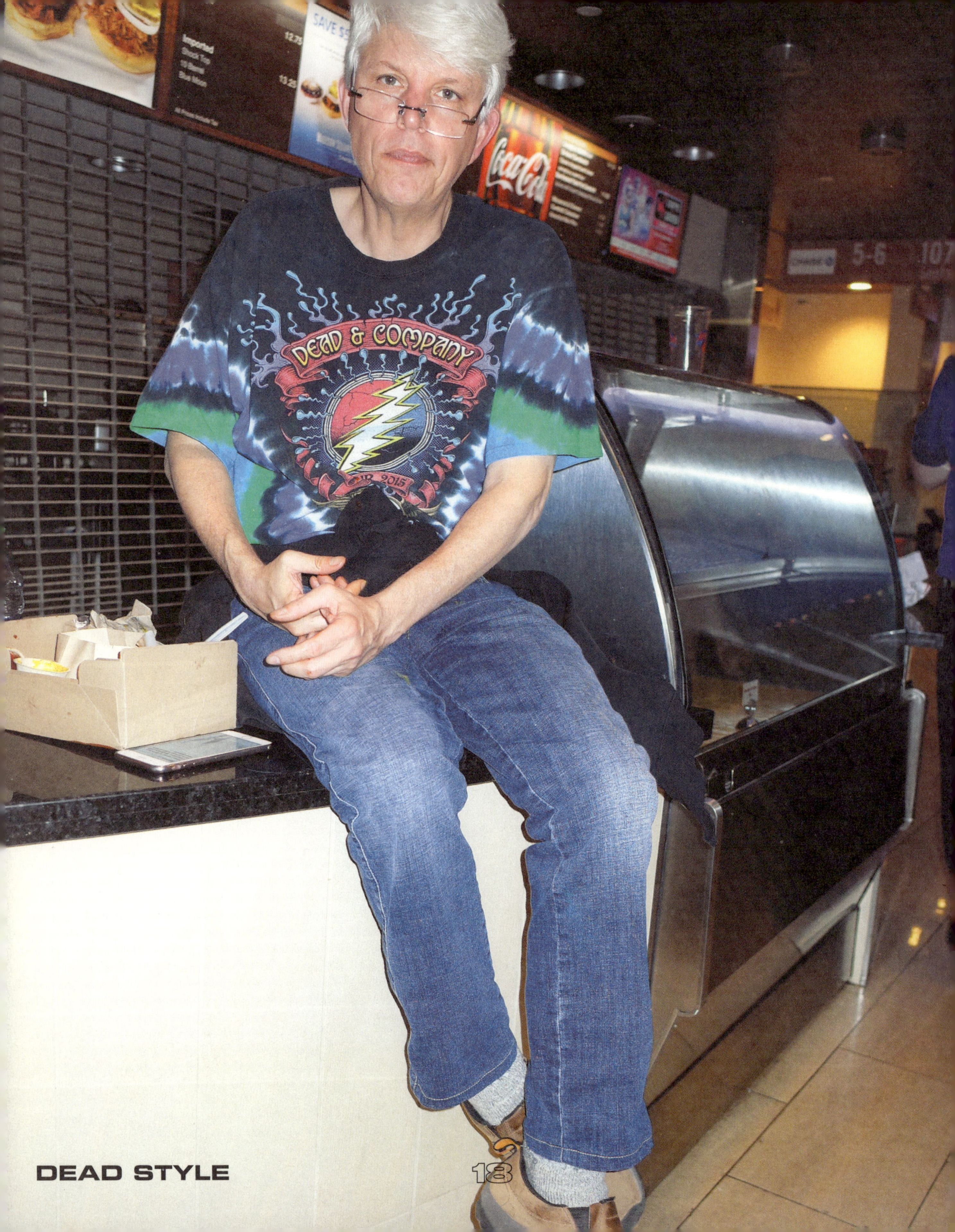
DEAD & COMPANY
Coca-Cola
5-6

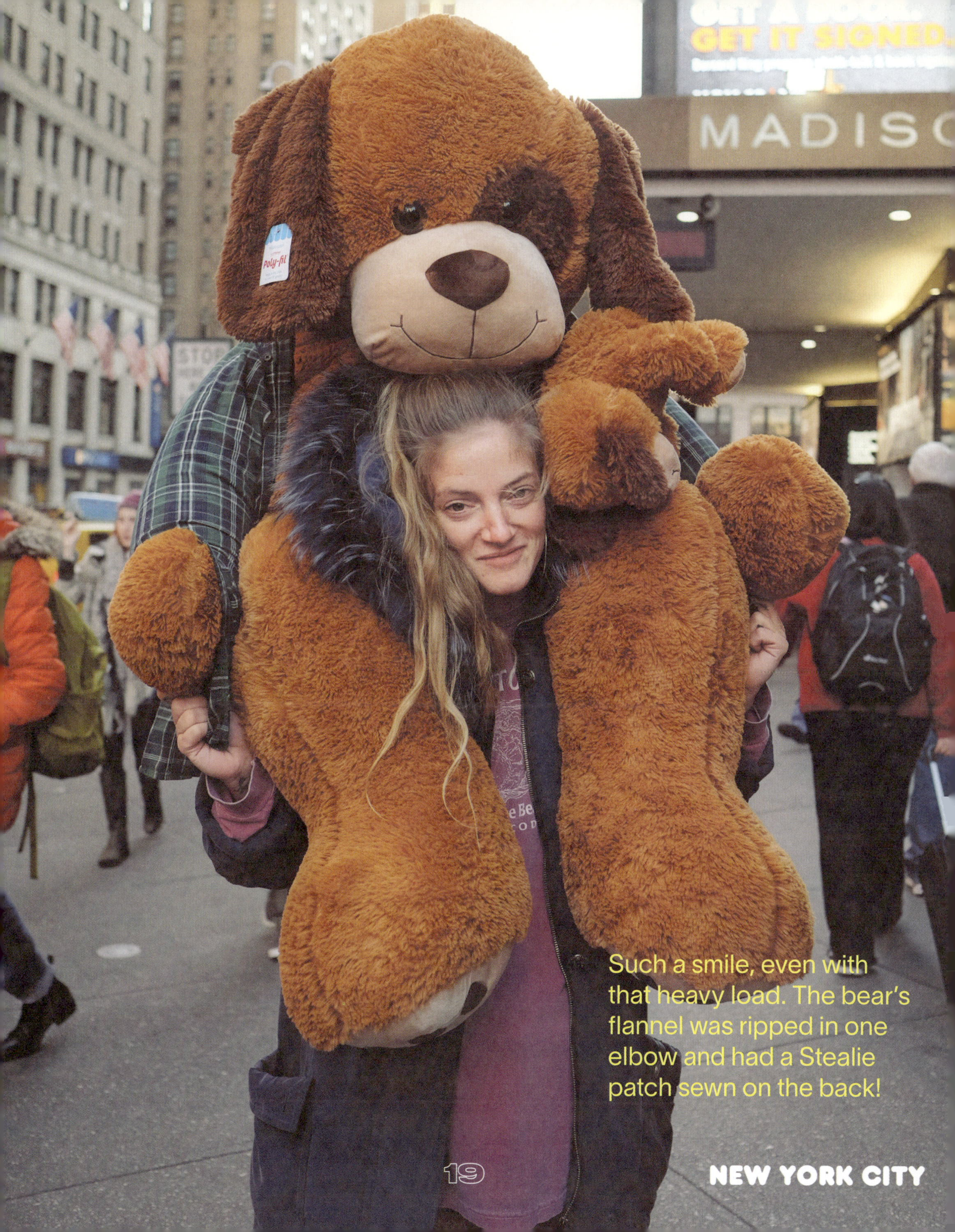

Such a smile, even with that heavy load. The bear's flannel was ripped in one elbow and had a Stealie patch sewn on the back!

NEW YORK CITY

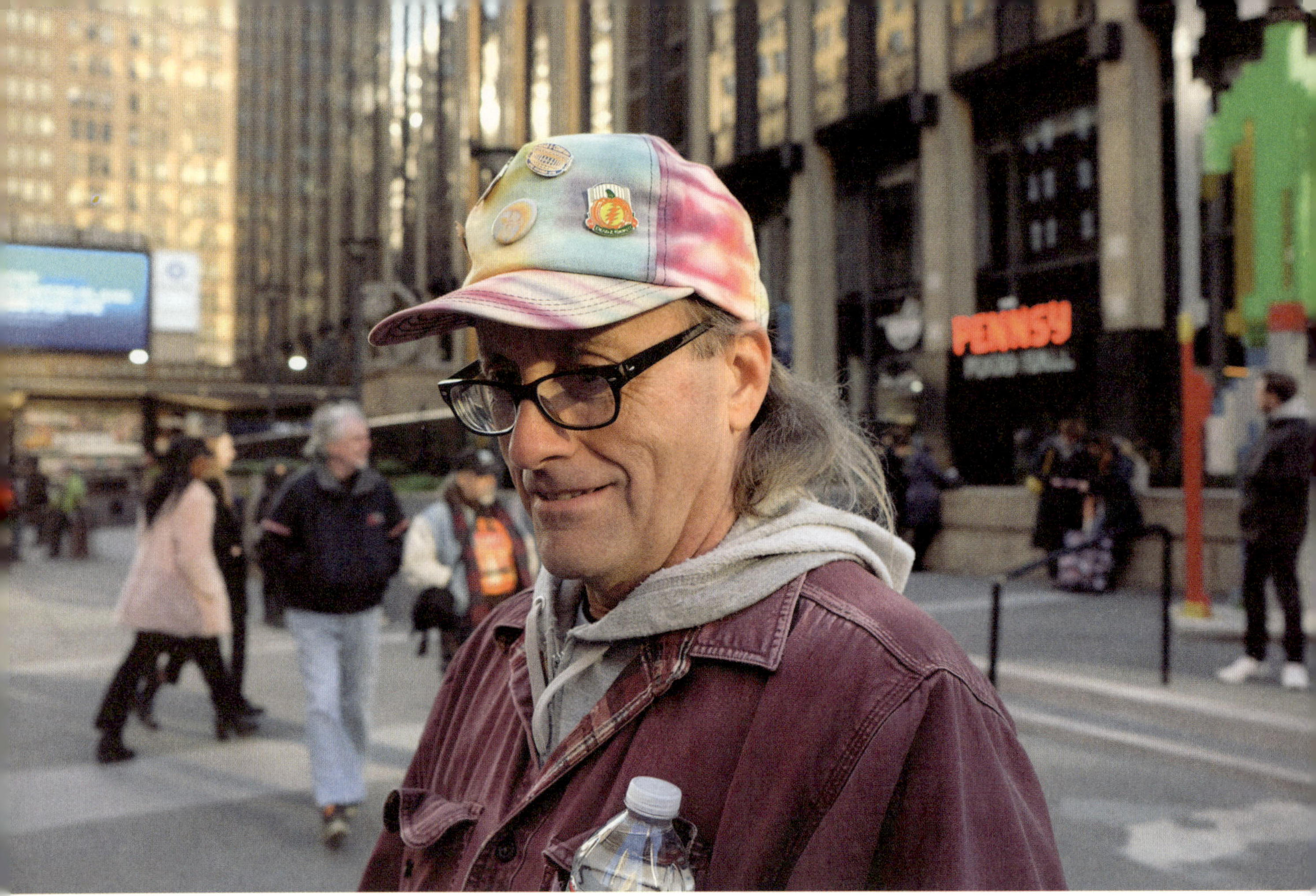

I love lived-in clothes, but his cap faded so beautifully. It's so rad that he's wearing it. It may sit on a special shelf at home, but it's rad to see it on someone who's clearly owned it from its birth. I buy so much secondhand Dead stuff and see so much for sale, it's special to see a cap like this on the head of its original owner.

Dead in the streets

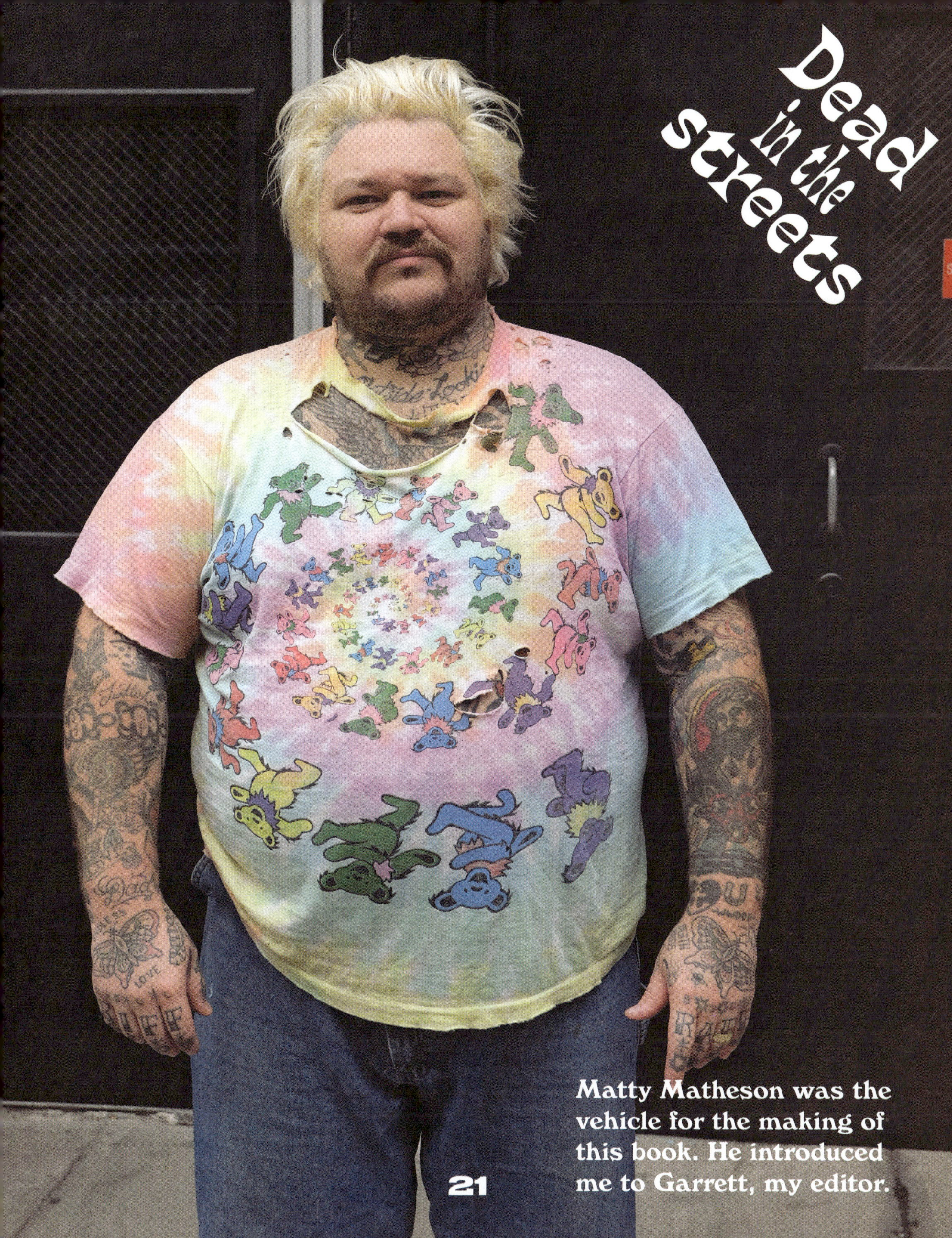

Matty Matheson was the vehicle for the making of this book. He introduced me to Garrett, my editor.

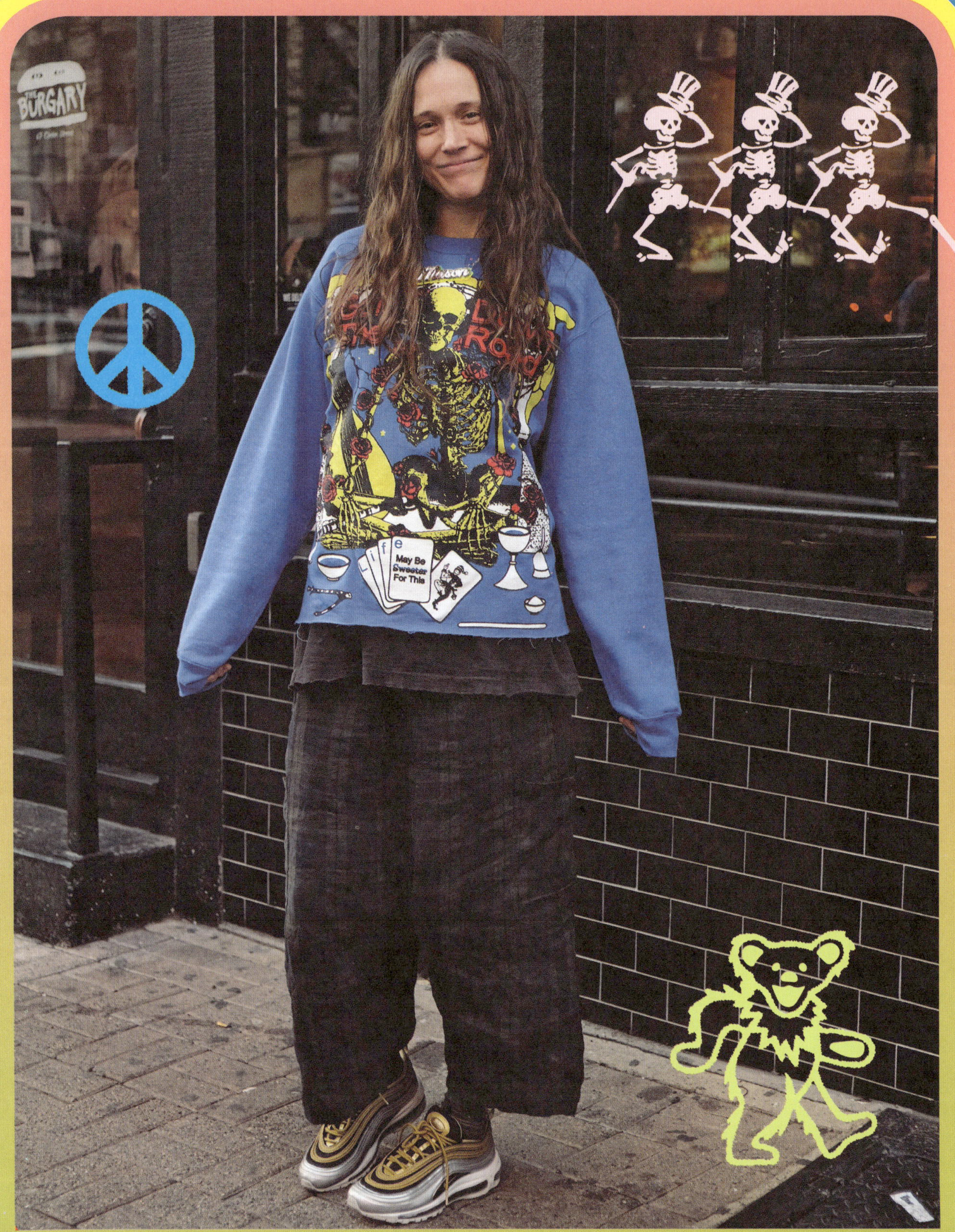
BURGARY
Life
May Be
Sweeter
For This

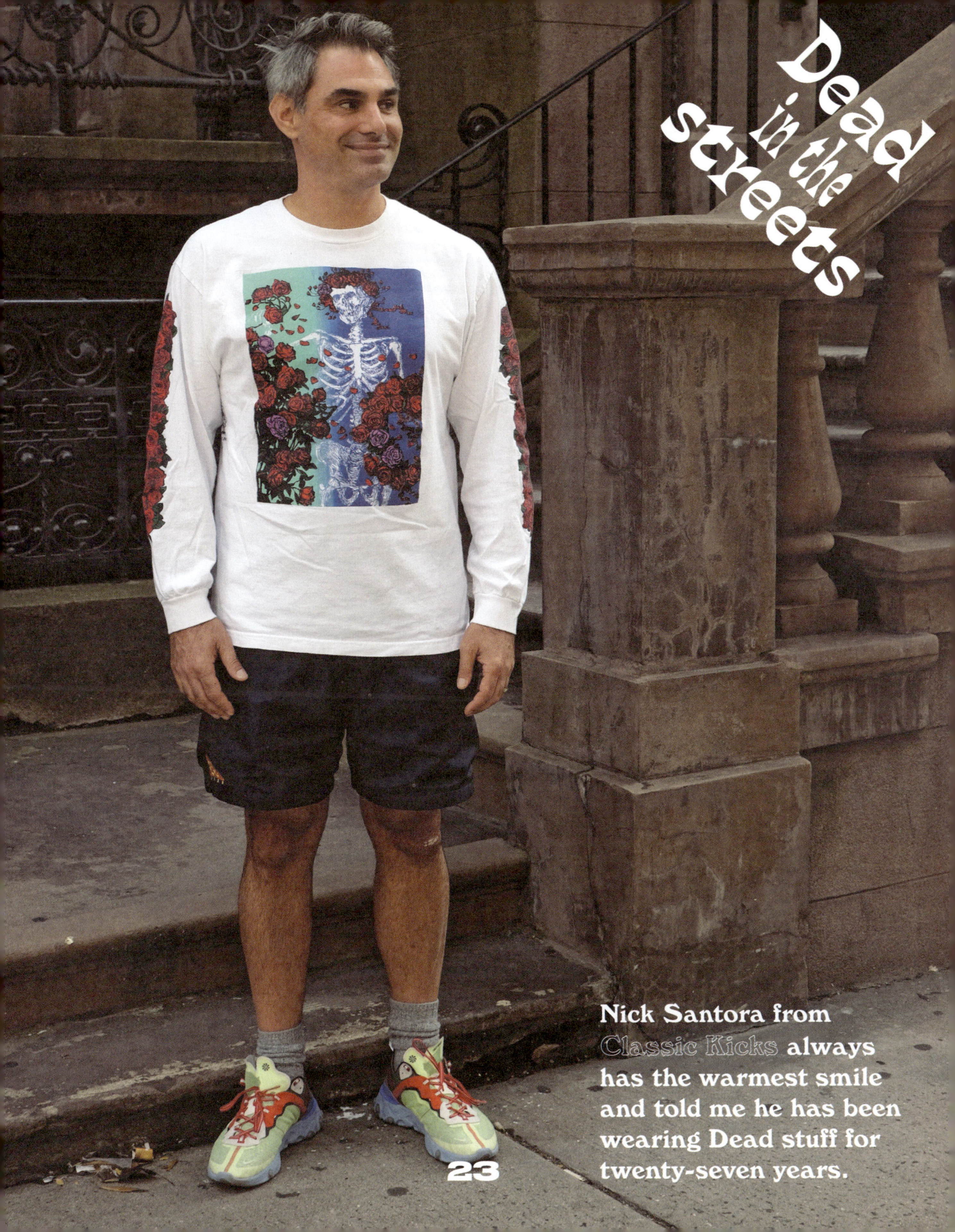

Dead in the streets

Nick Santora from Classic Kicks always has the warmest smile and told me he has been wearing Dead stuff for twenty-seven years.

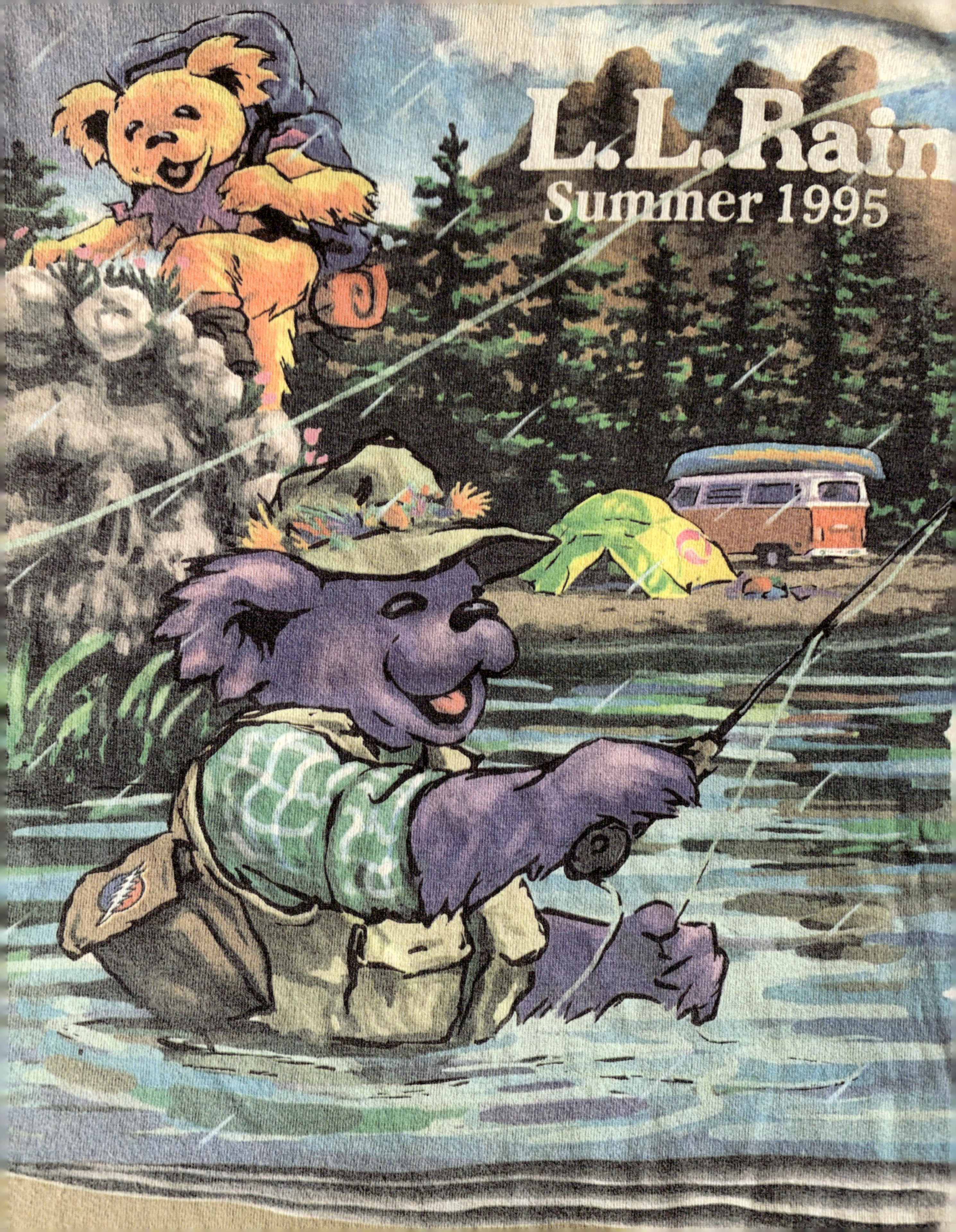
L.L.Rain
Summer 1995

PLAYING IN THE SAND/ BARCELÓ MAYA

Riviera Maya, Mexico

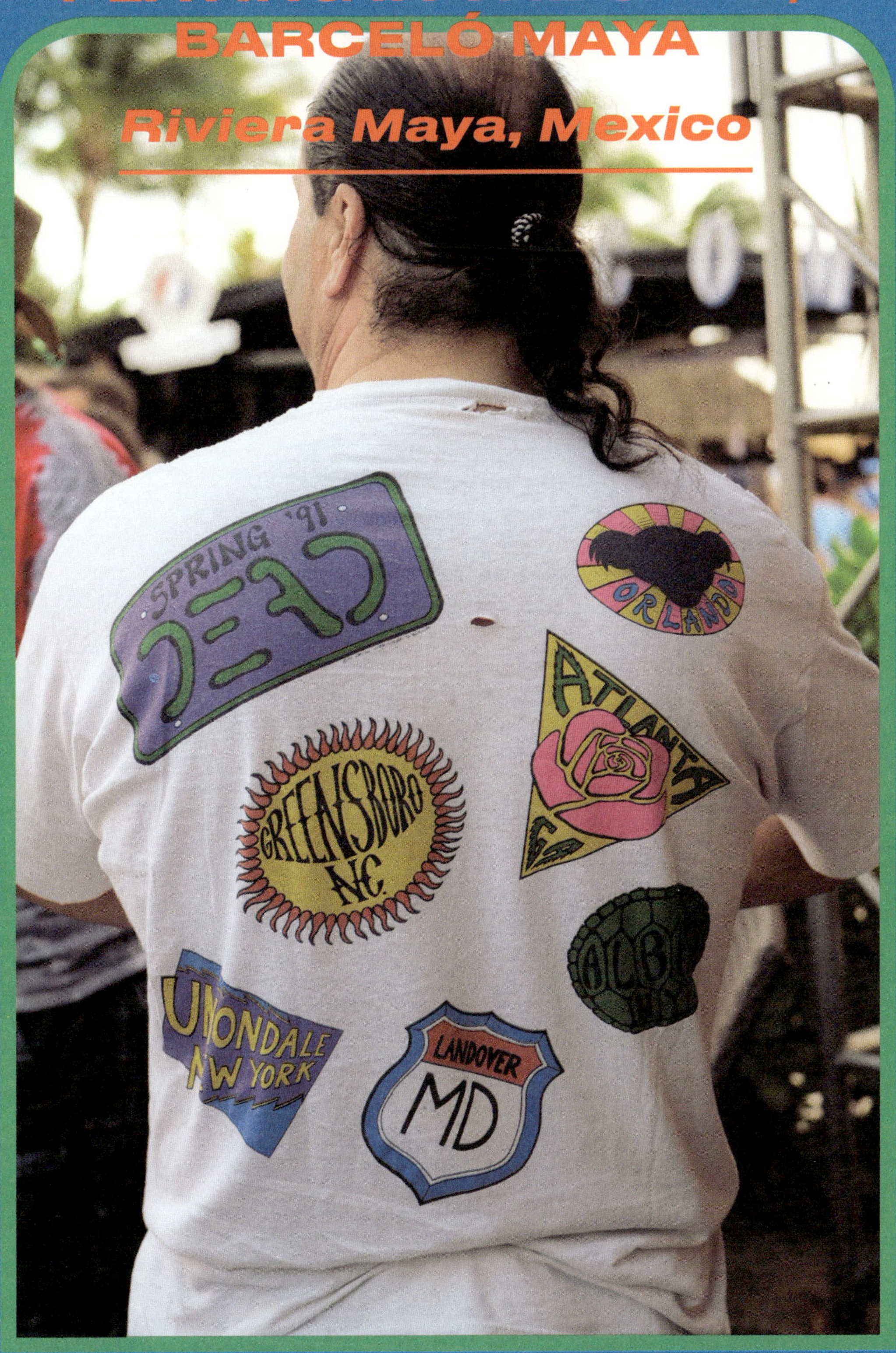

Thursday, February 15th, 2018,
Saturday, February 17th, 2018, &
Sunday, February 18th, 2018

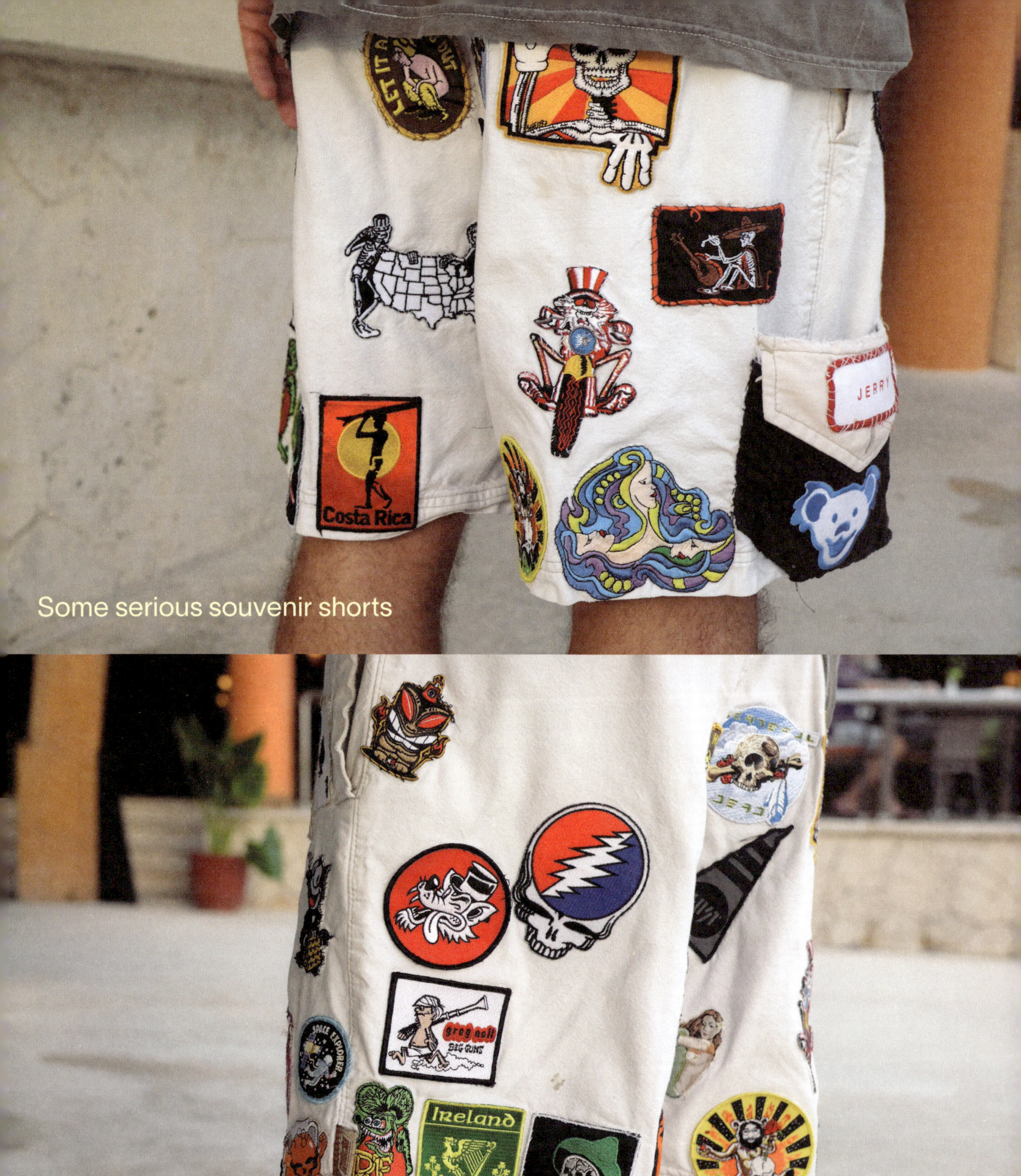

Some serious souvenir shorts

TUCKED AND READY TO PARTY

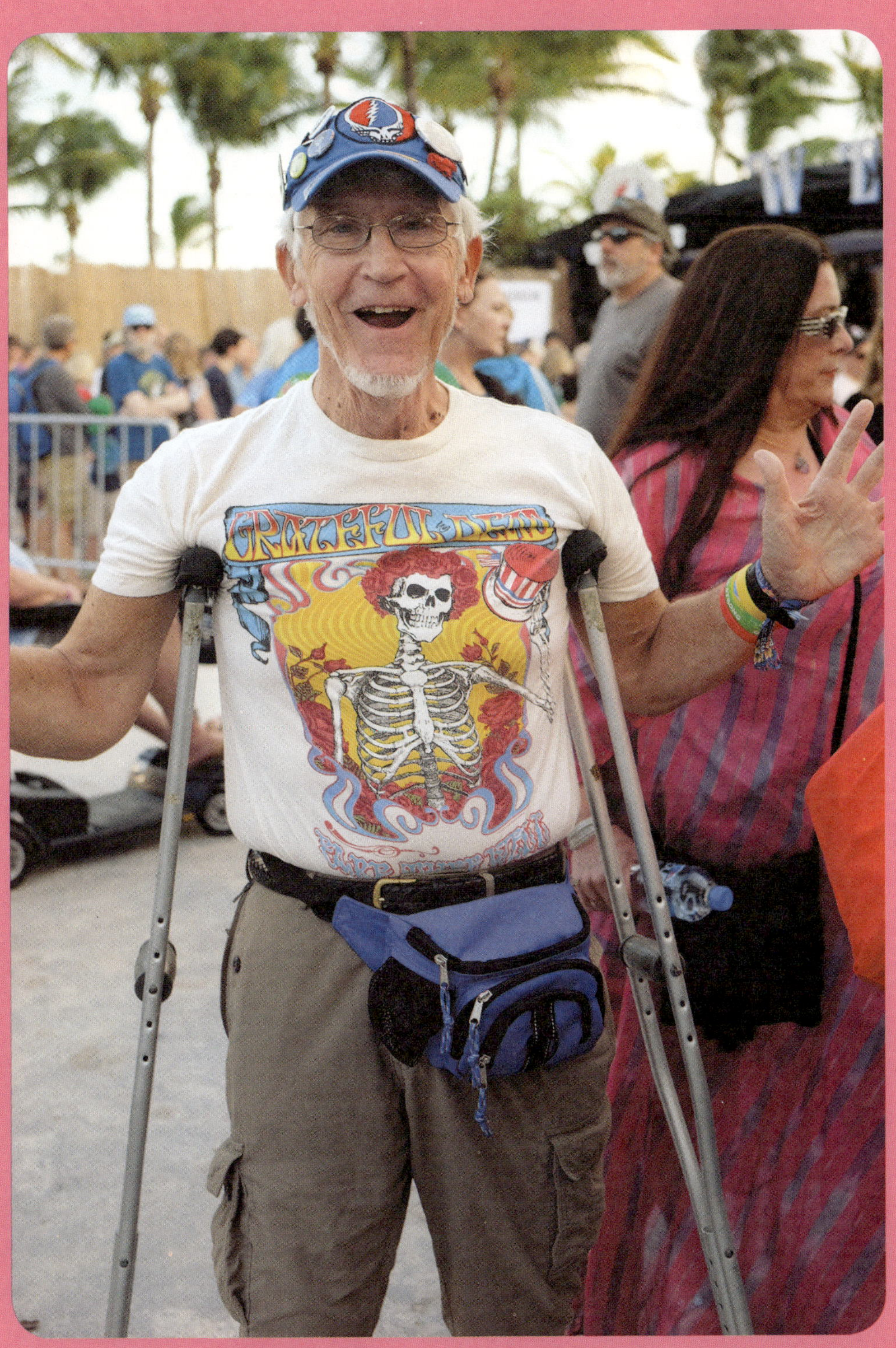

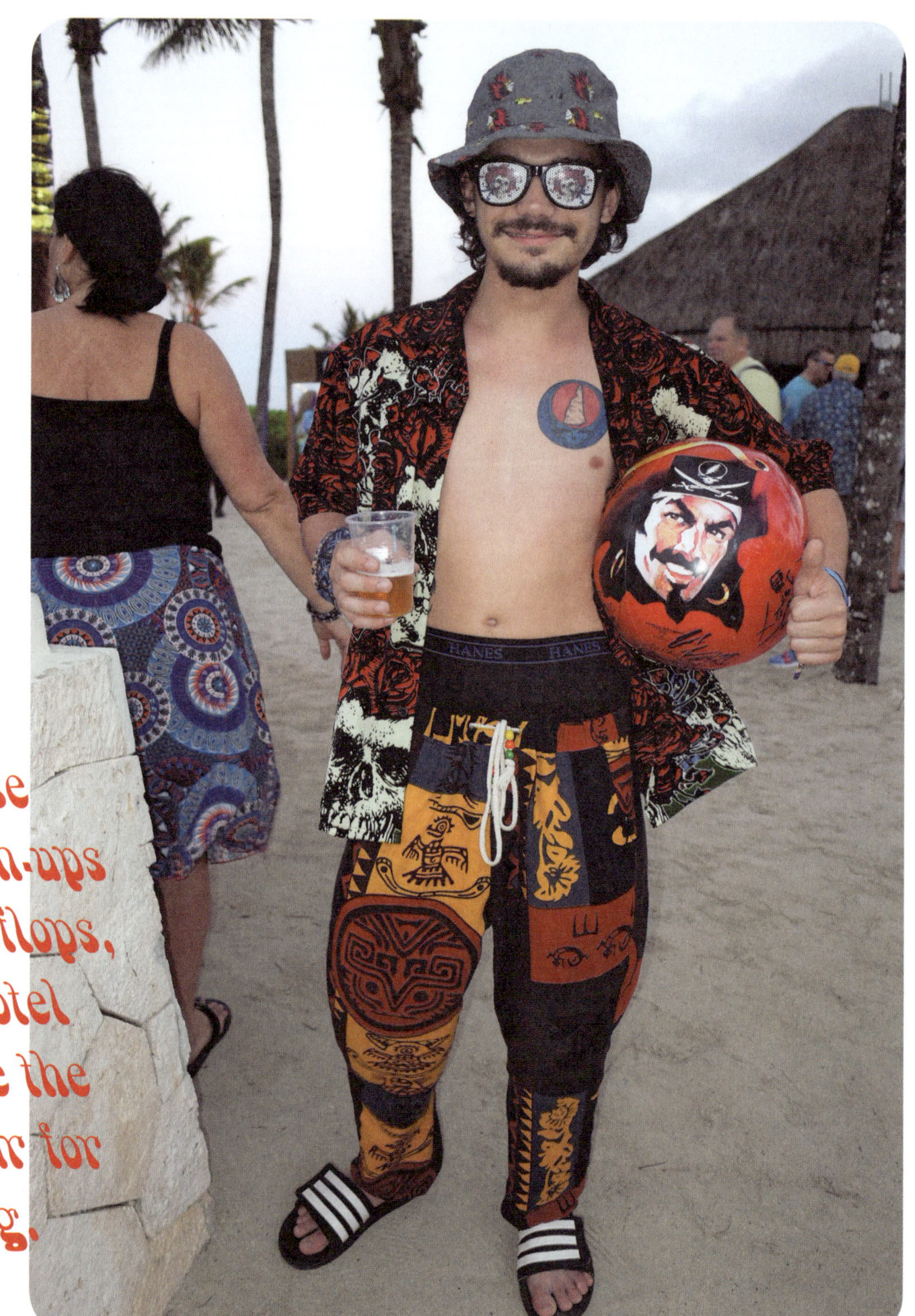

I love those graphic button-ups so much. Flip-flops, slides, or hotel slippers were the choice footwear for the evening.

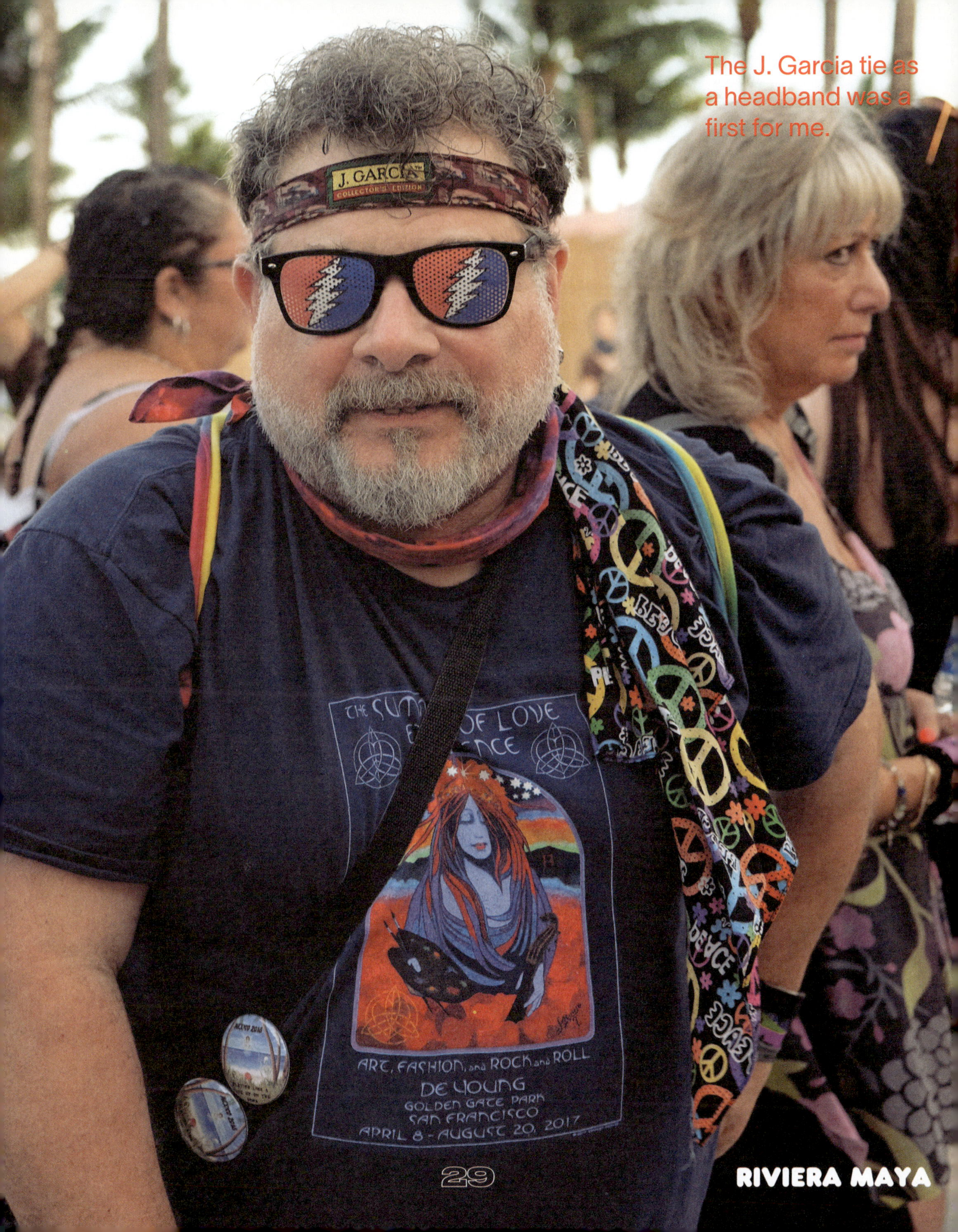

The J. Garcia tie as a headband was a first for me.

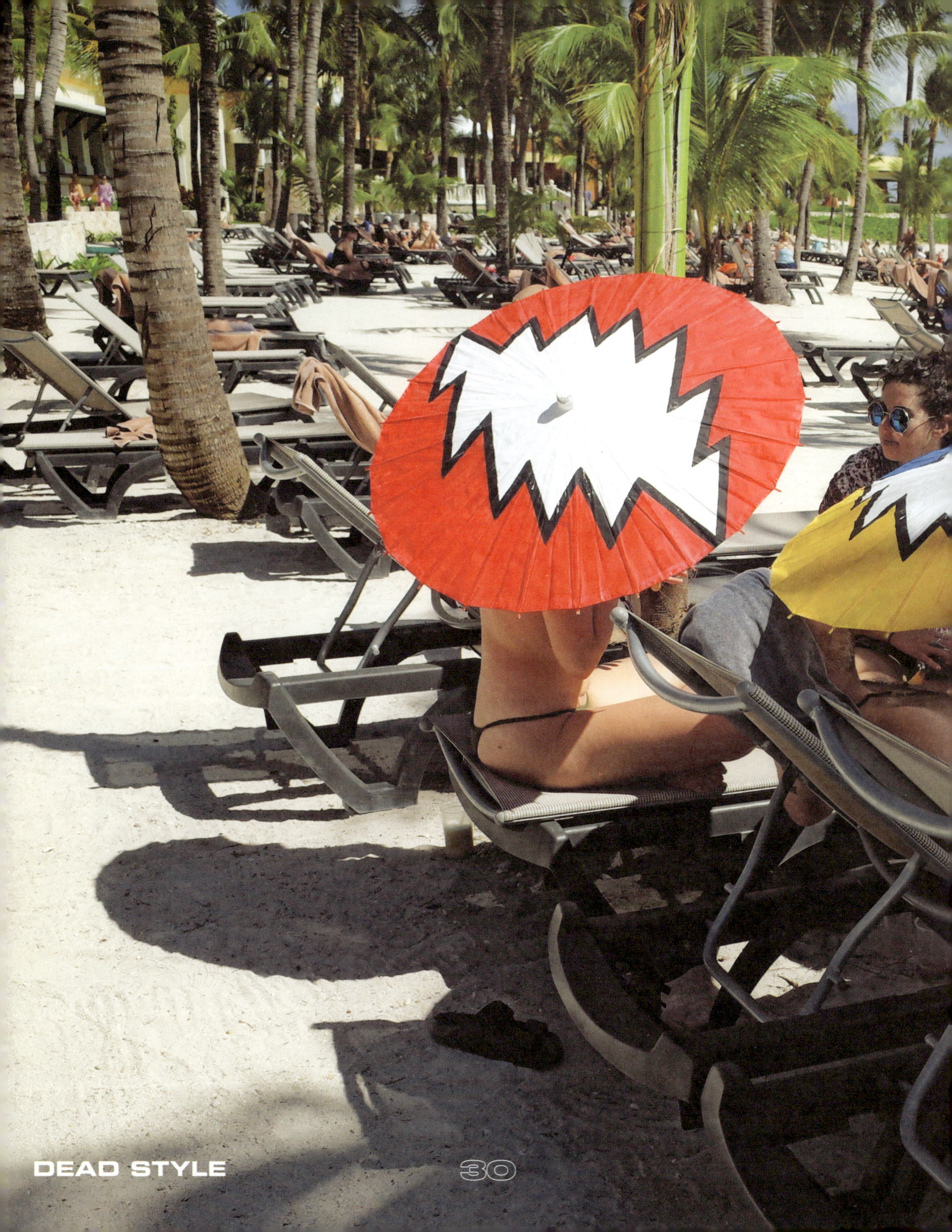

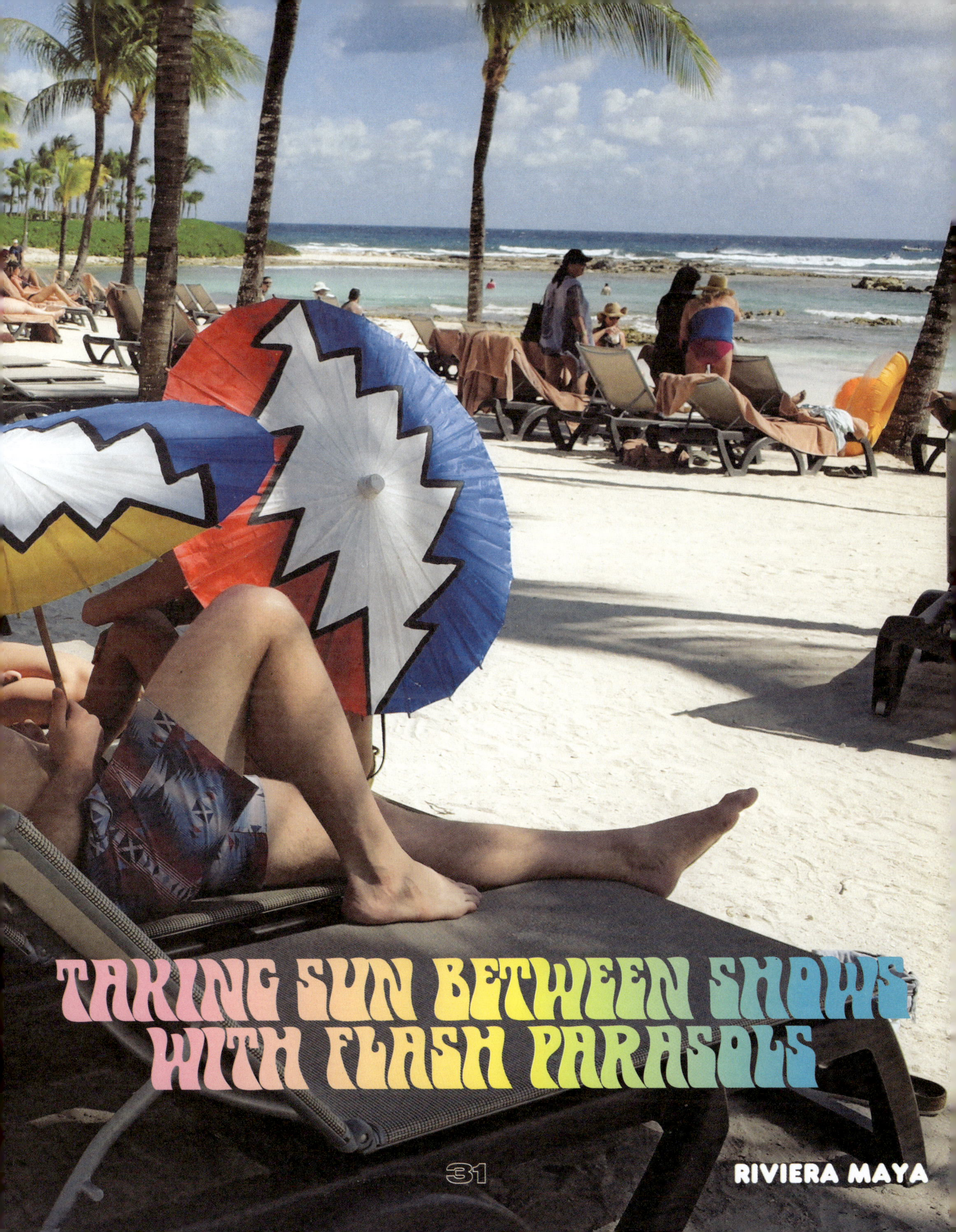
TAKING SUN BETWEEN SHOWS
WITH FLASH PARASOLS

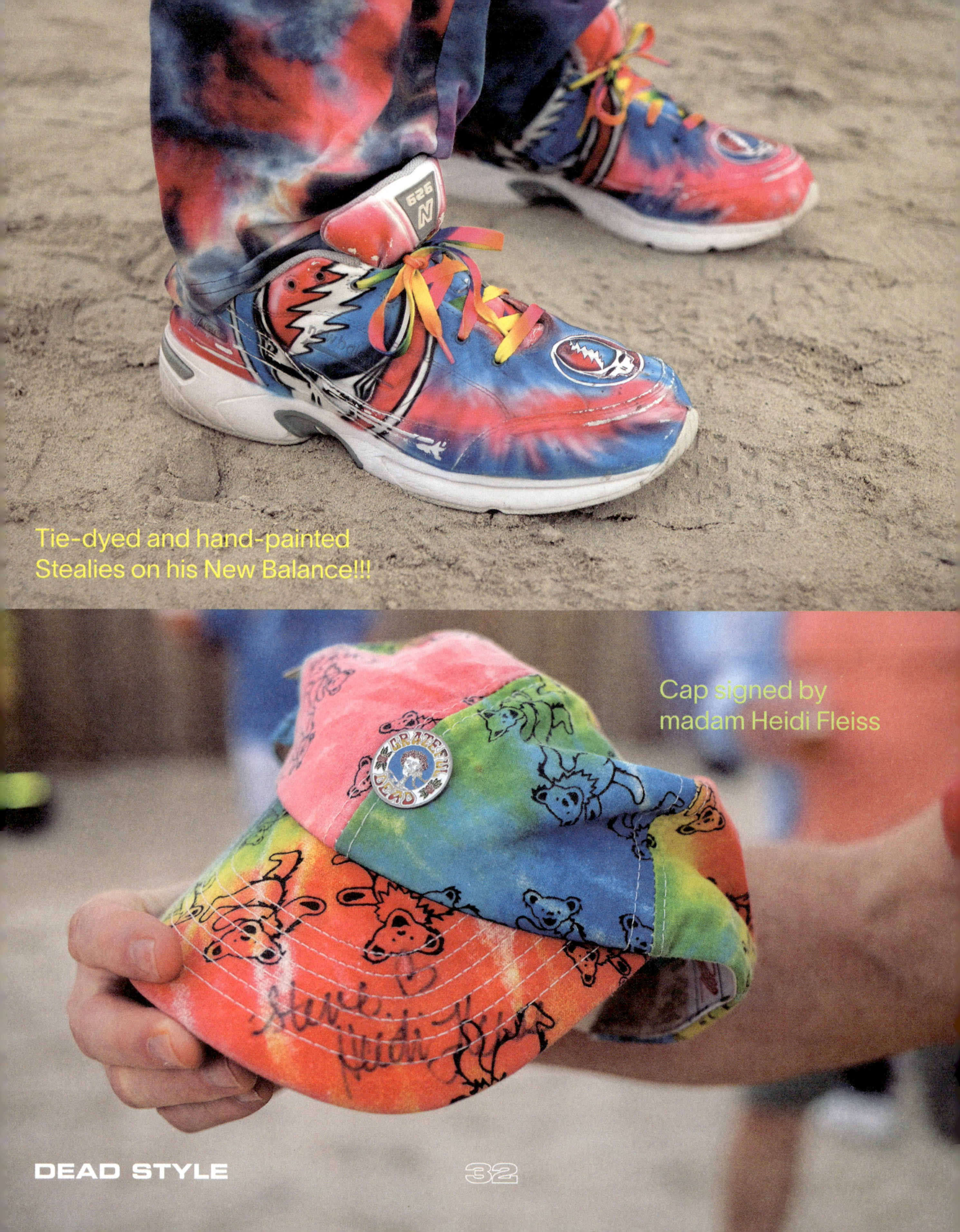

Tie-dyed and hand-painted
Stealies on his New Balance!!!

Cap signed by
madam Heidi Fleiss

SEEN LOTS
OF O'ALLS
ON THE LOTS,
BUT THESE
JUST LOOKED
GREAT WITH
THE SNOOPY TEE
AND THE COLORS
OF THE DYE.

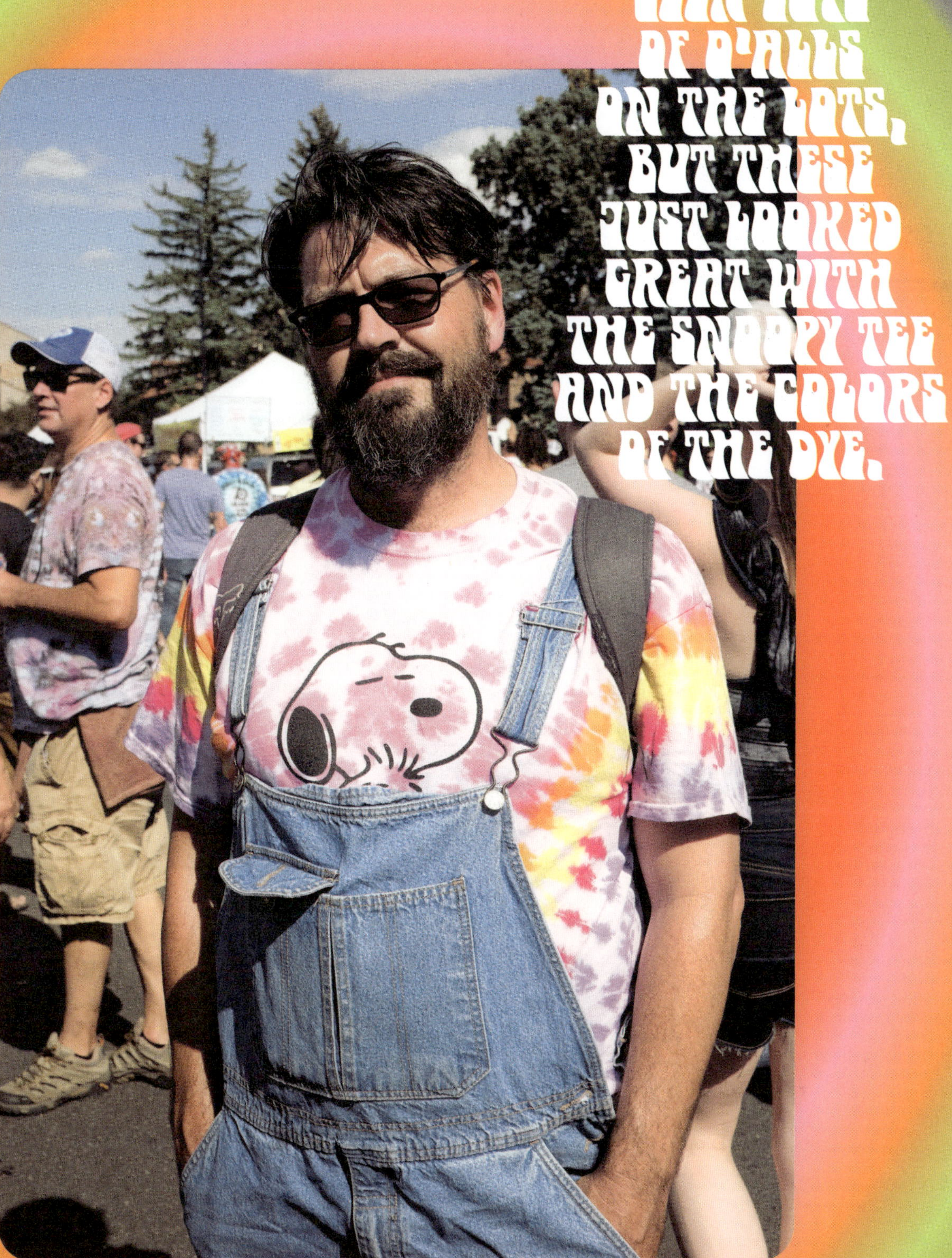

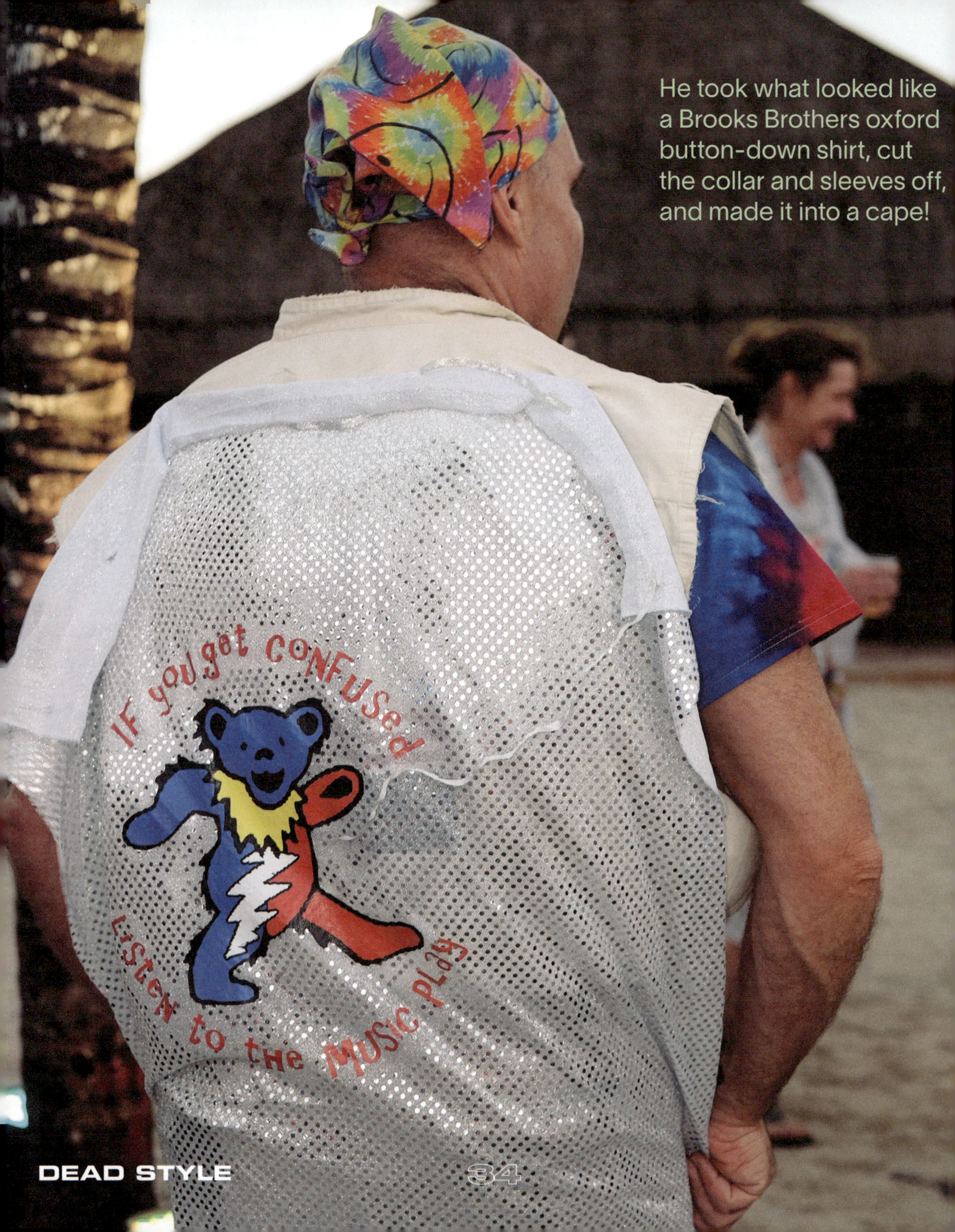

He took what looked like a Brooks Brothers oxford button-down shirt, cut the collar and sleeves off, and made it into a cape!

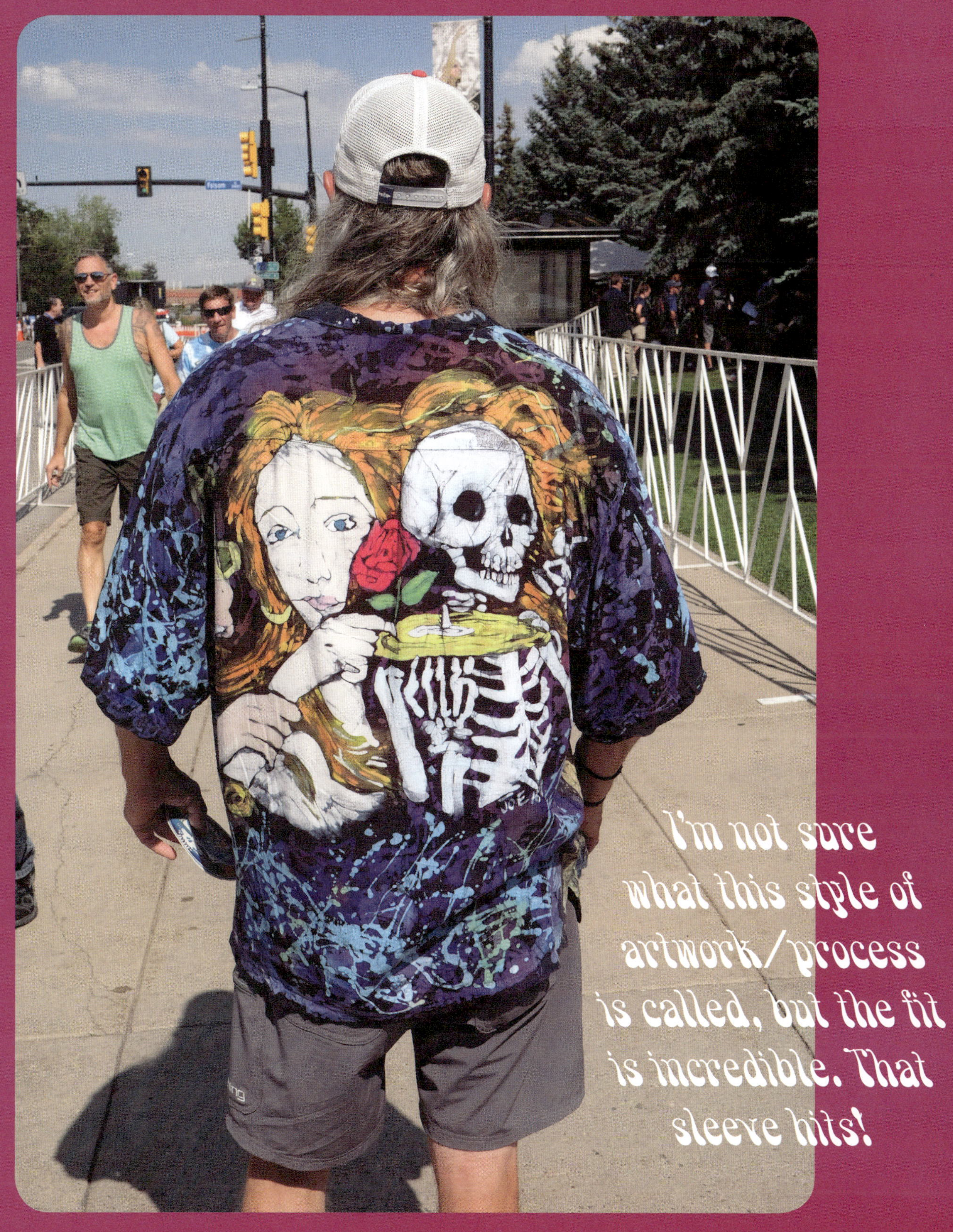

I'm not sure what this style of artwork/process is called, but the fit is incredible. That sleeve hits!

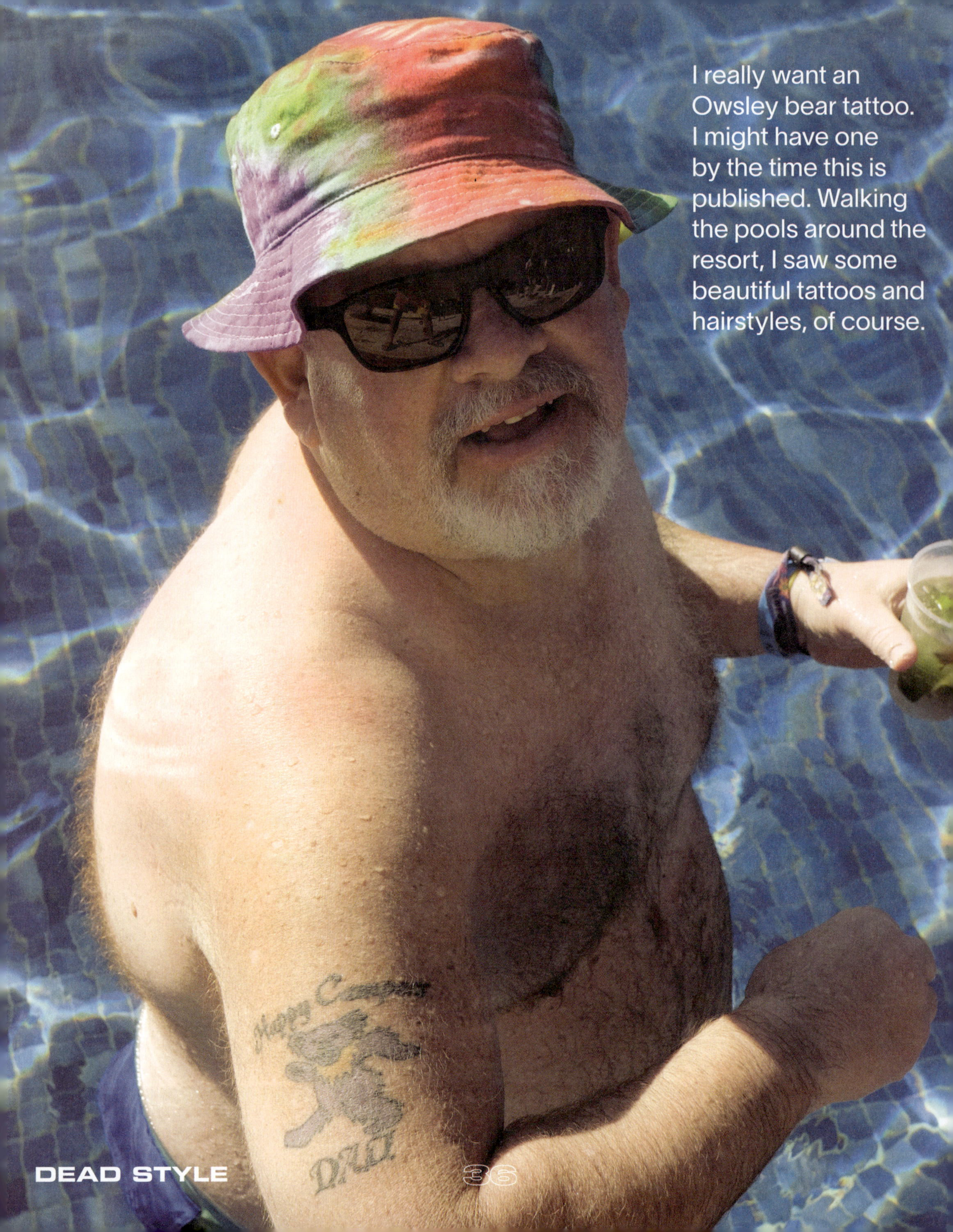

I really want an Owsley bear tattoo. I might have one by the time this is published. Walking the pools around the resort, I saw some beautiful tattoos and hairstyles, of course.

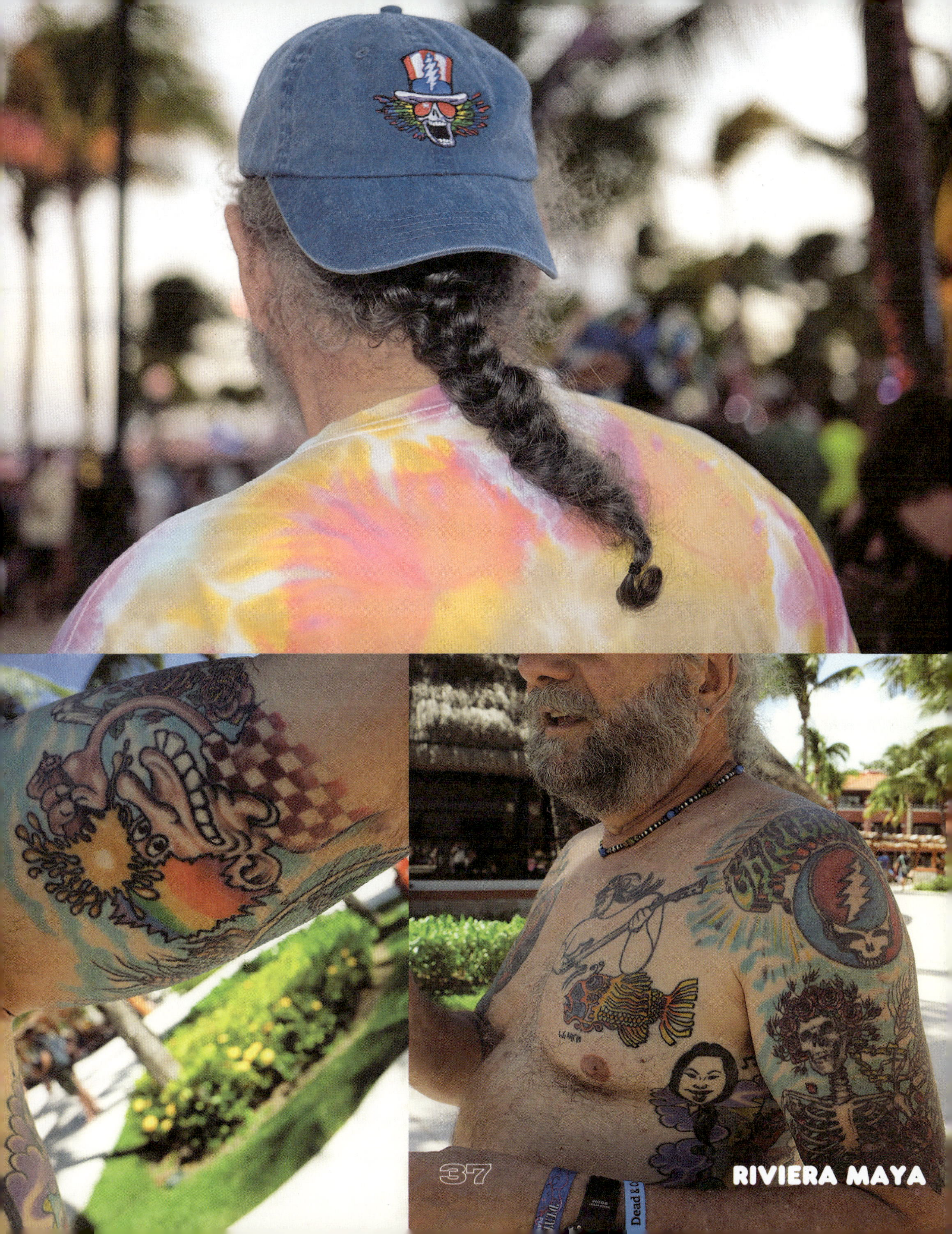

SOME RISE, SOME FALL, SOME CLIMB TO GET TO TERRAPIN TUCKED INTO A DRAWSTRING.

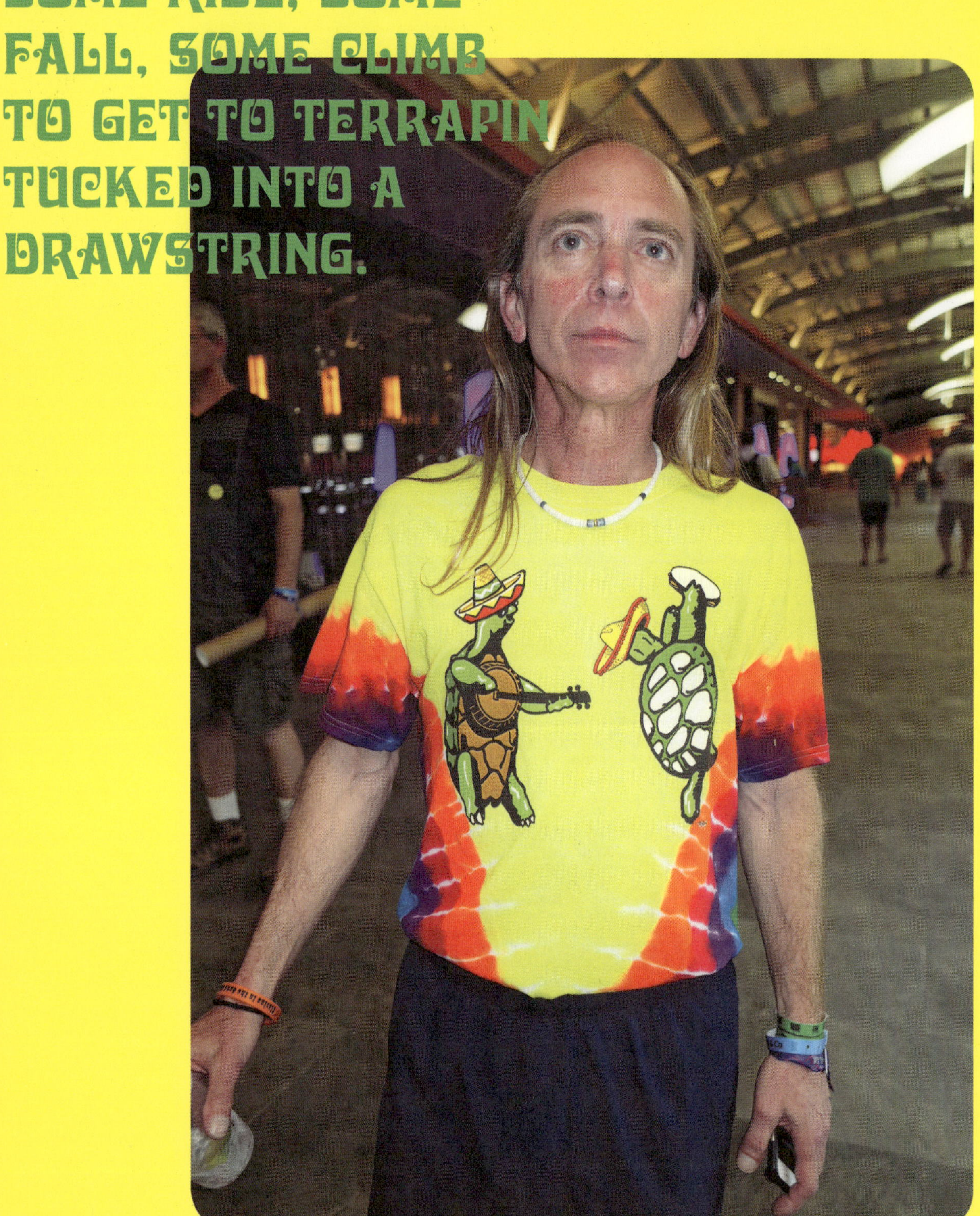

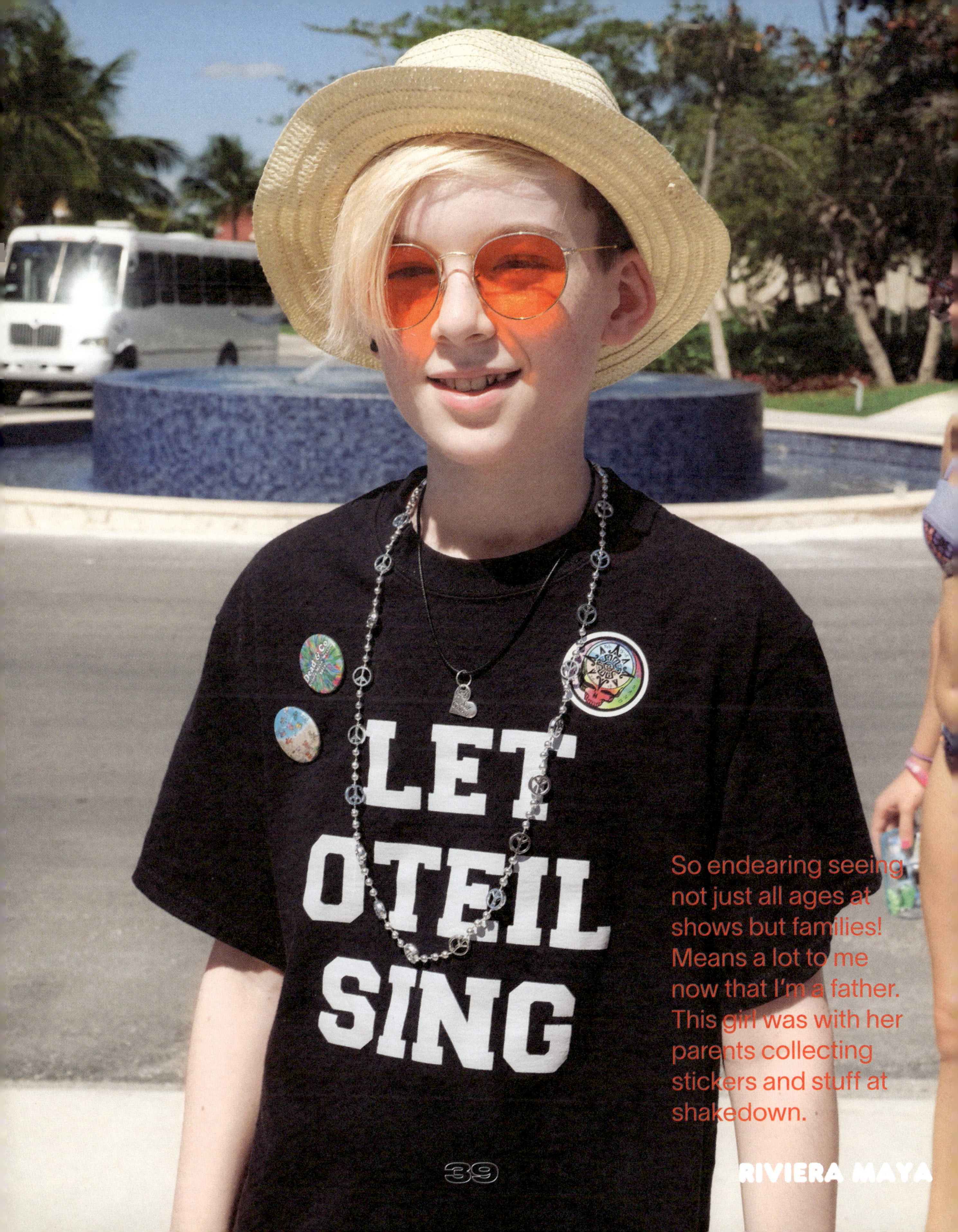

So endearing seeing not just all ages at shows but families! Means a lot to me now that I'm a father. This girl was with her parents collecting stickers and stuff at shakedown.

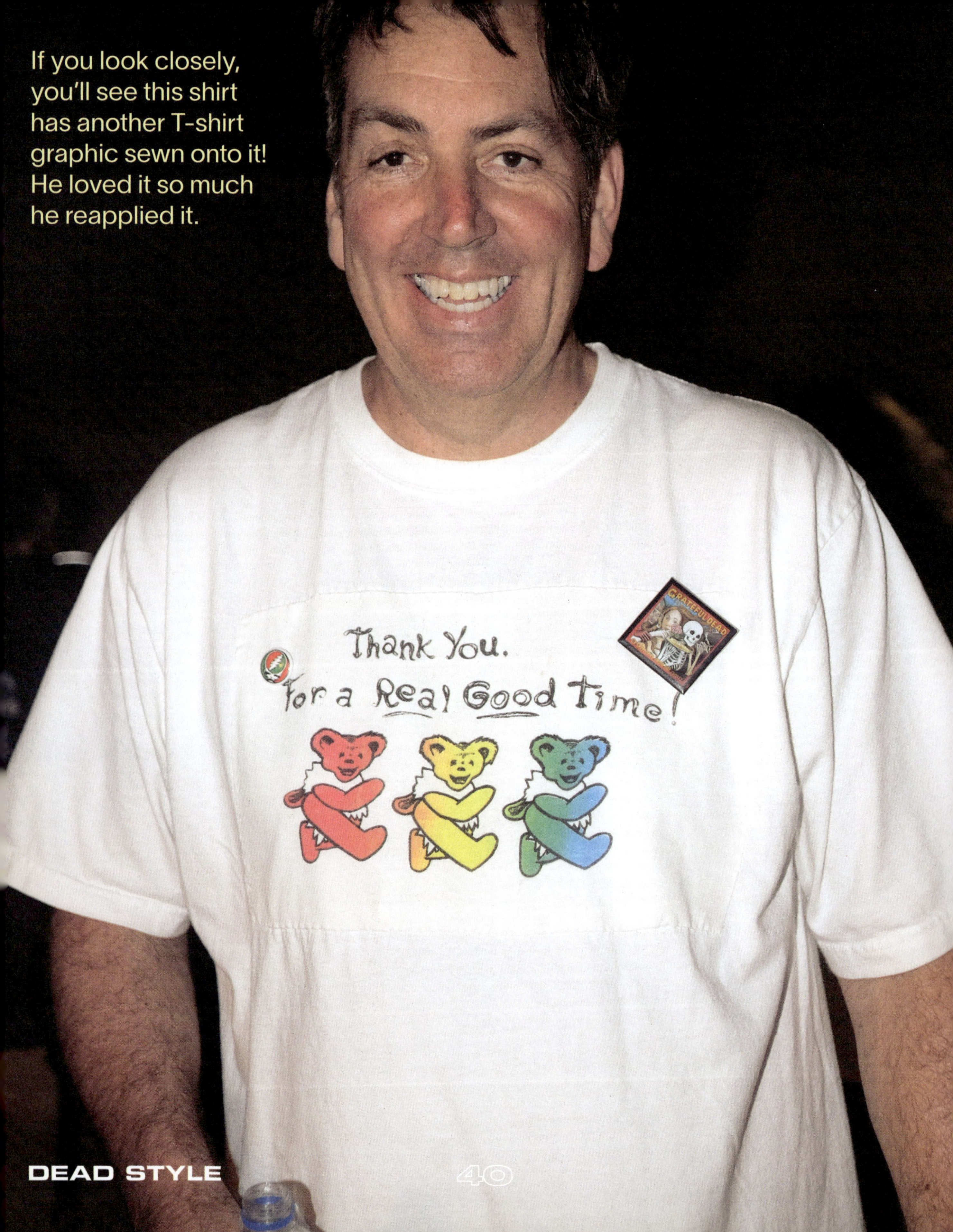

If you look closely, you'll see this shirt has another T-shirt graphic sewn onto it! He loved it so much he reapplied it.

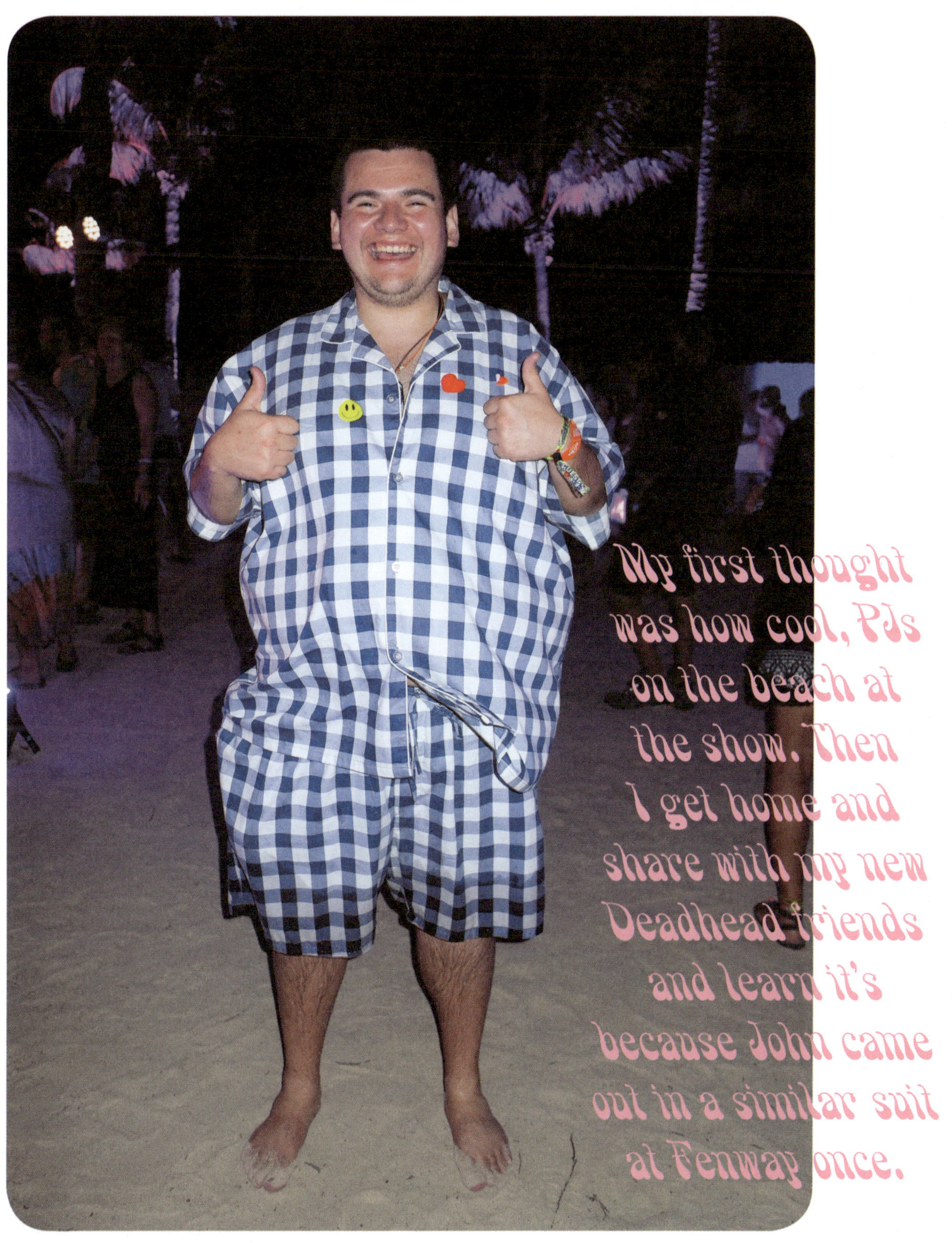

My first thought was how cool, PJs on the beach at the show. Then I get home and share with my new Deadhead friends and learn it's because John came out in a similar suit at Fenway once.

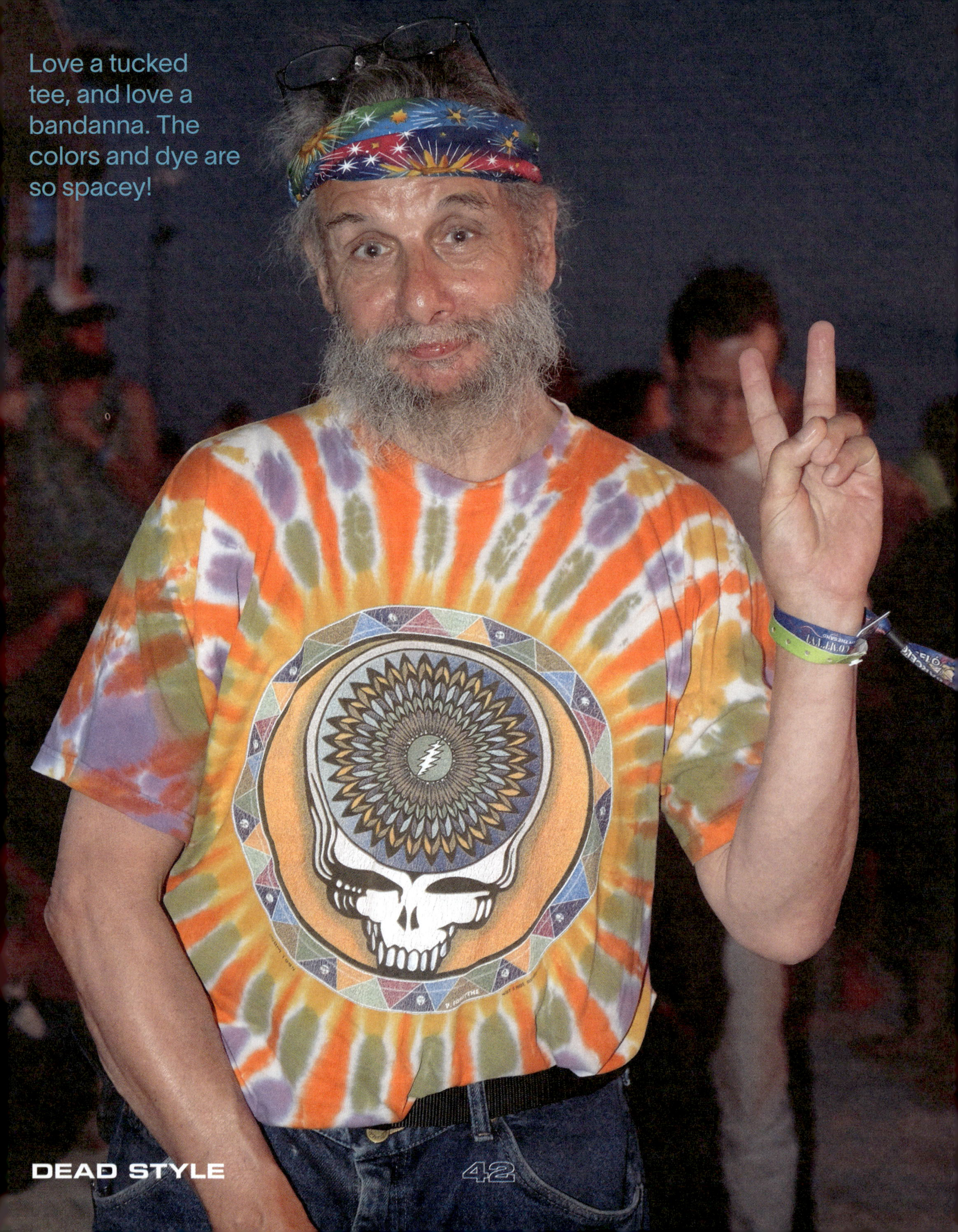

Love a tucked tee, and love a bandanna. The colors and dye are so spacey!

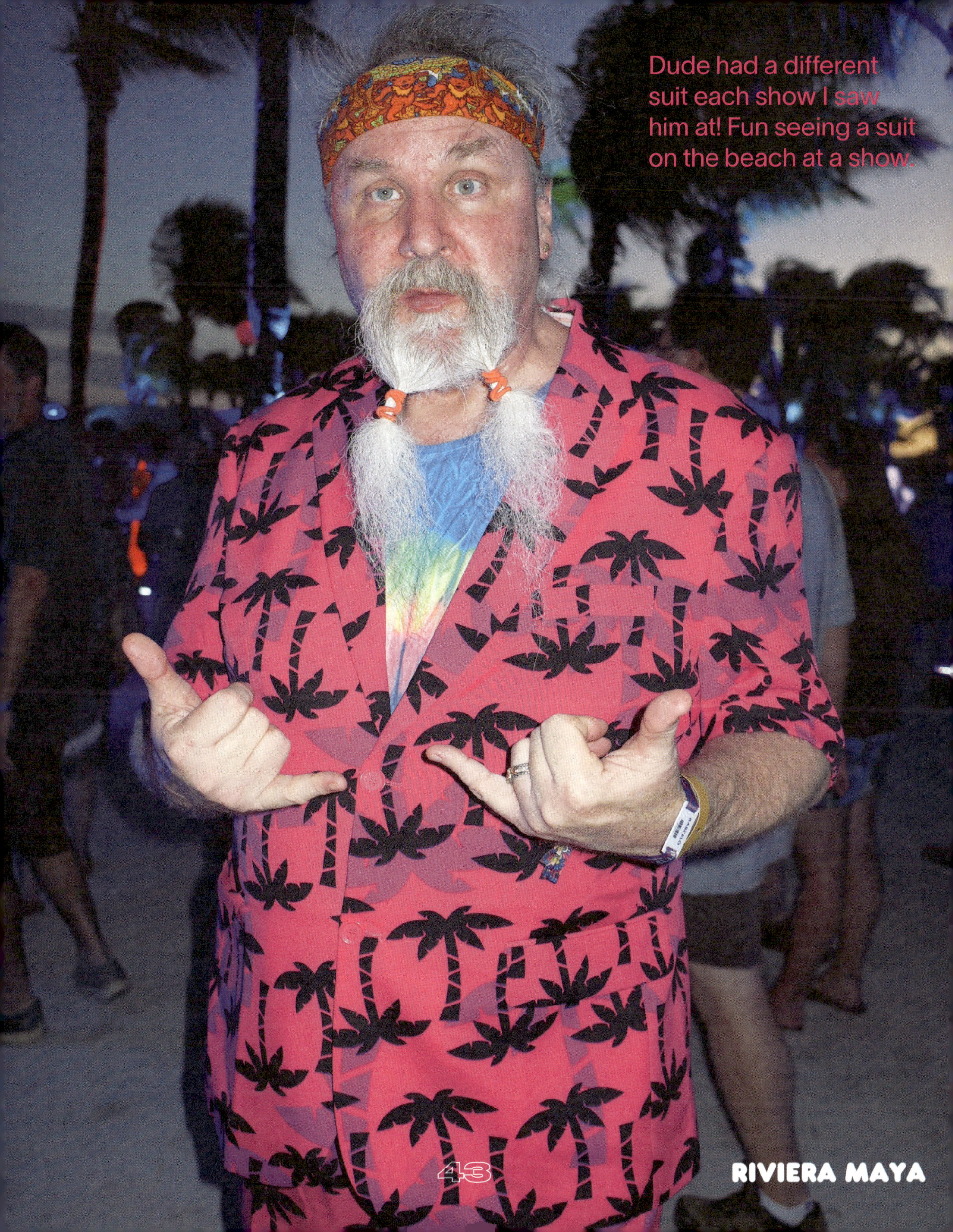

Dude had a different suit each show I saw him at! Fun seeing a suit on the beach at a show.

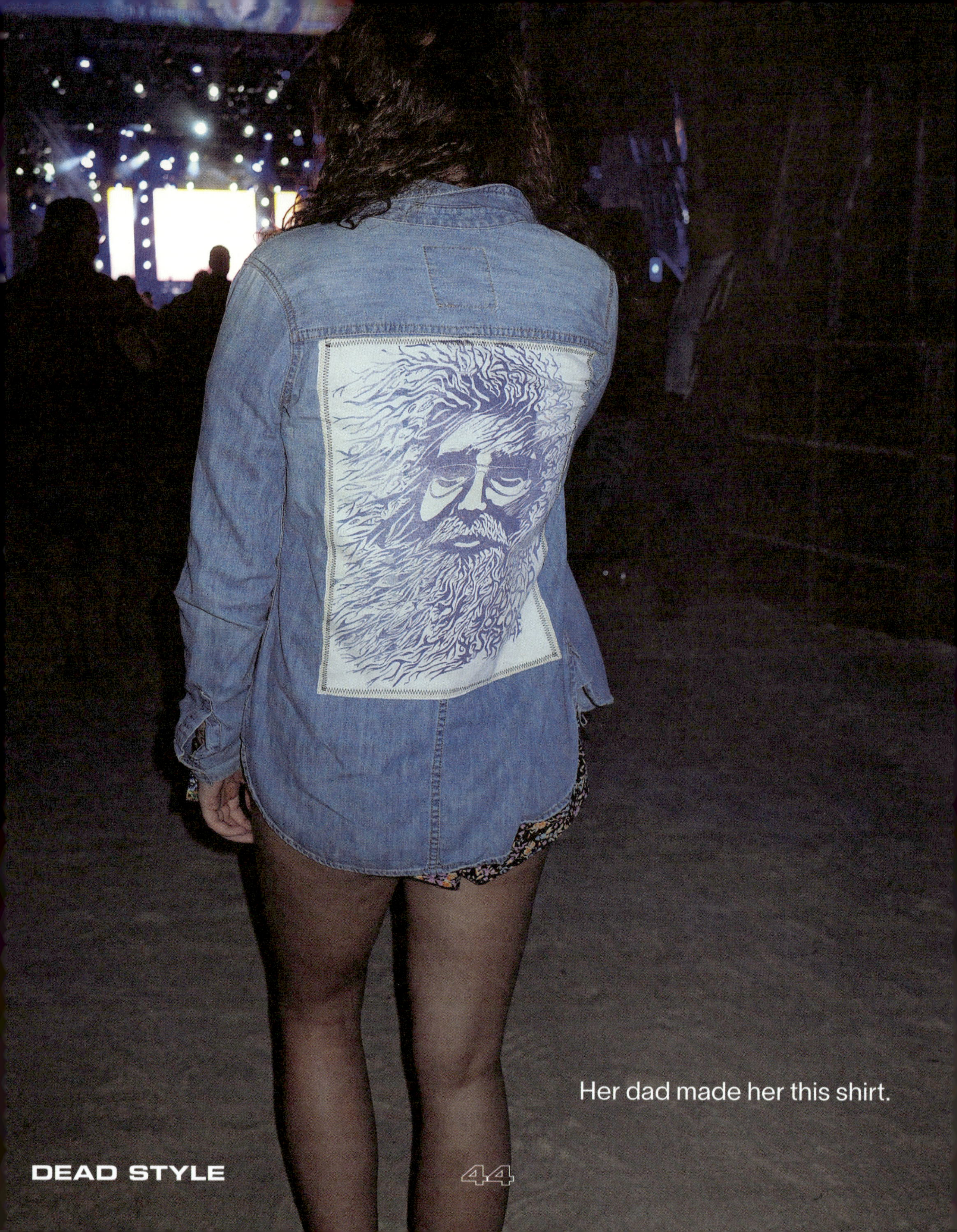

Her dad made her this shirt.

That's a hand-painted Stealie on the bucket's crown.

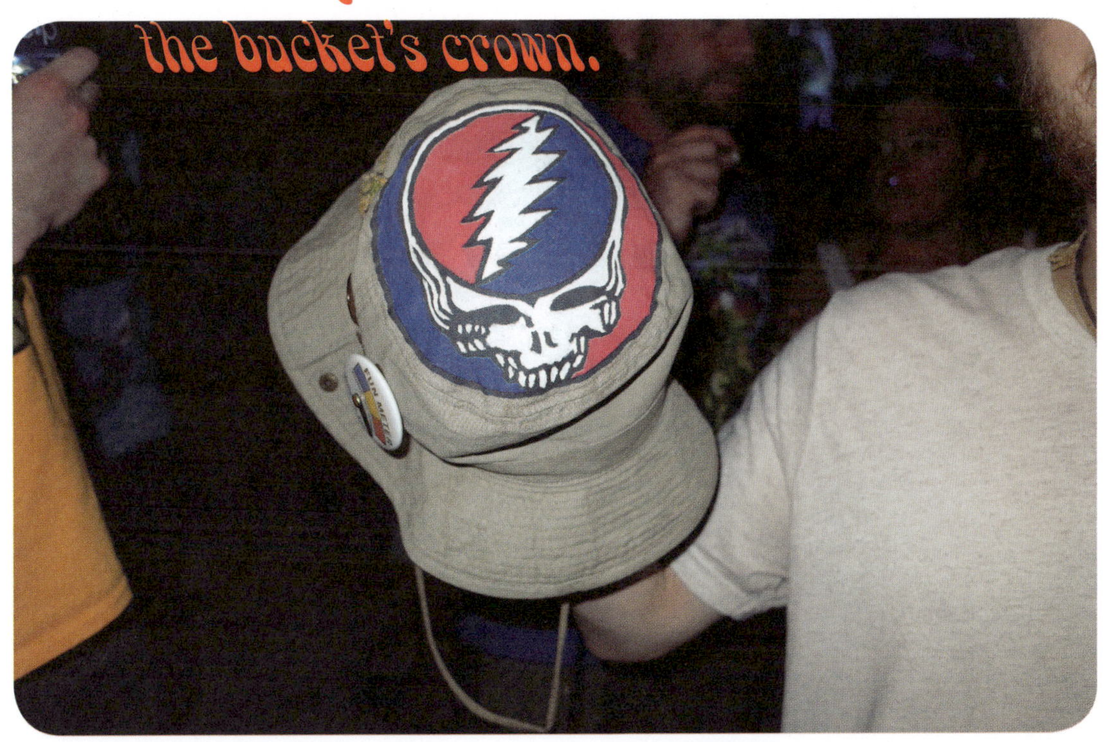

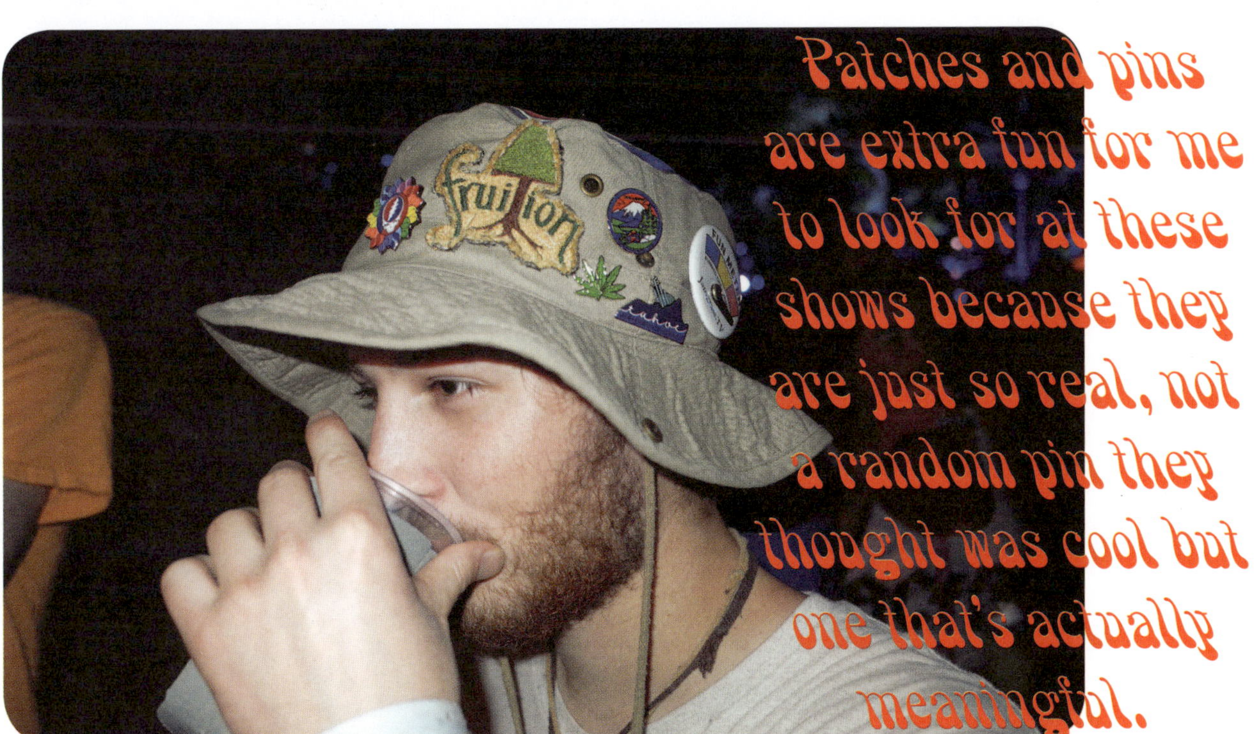

Patches and pins are extra fun for me to look for at these shows because they are just so real, not a random pin they thought was cool but one that's actually meaningful.

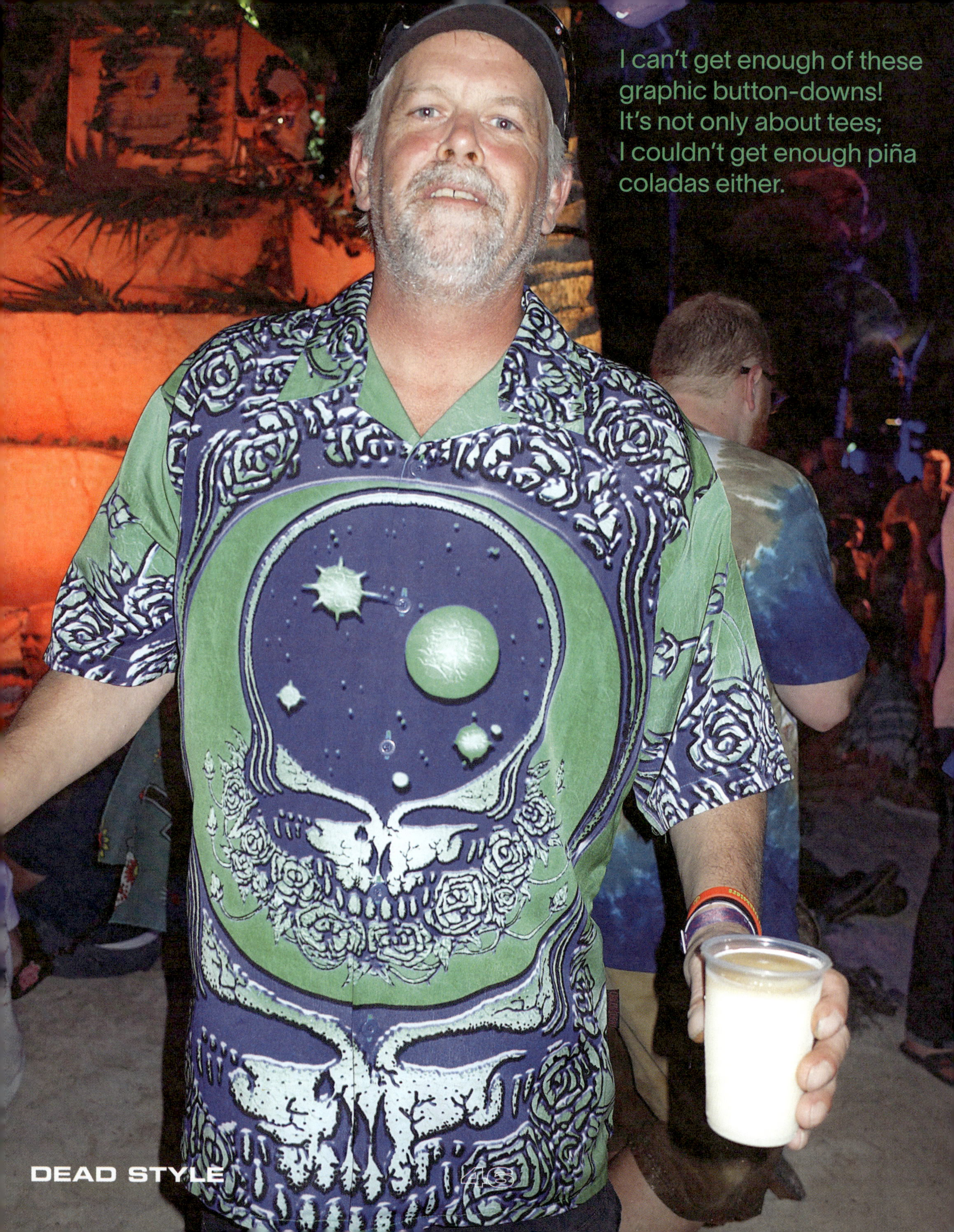

I can't get enough of these graphic button-downs! It's not only about tees; I couldn't get enough piña coladas either.

HIS FAVORITE TEE? FROM '84. WHAT I LIKE IS THAT IT'S SORTA SMALL; IT'S JUST HIM. THAT'S BEAUTIFUL.

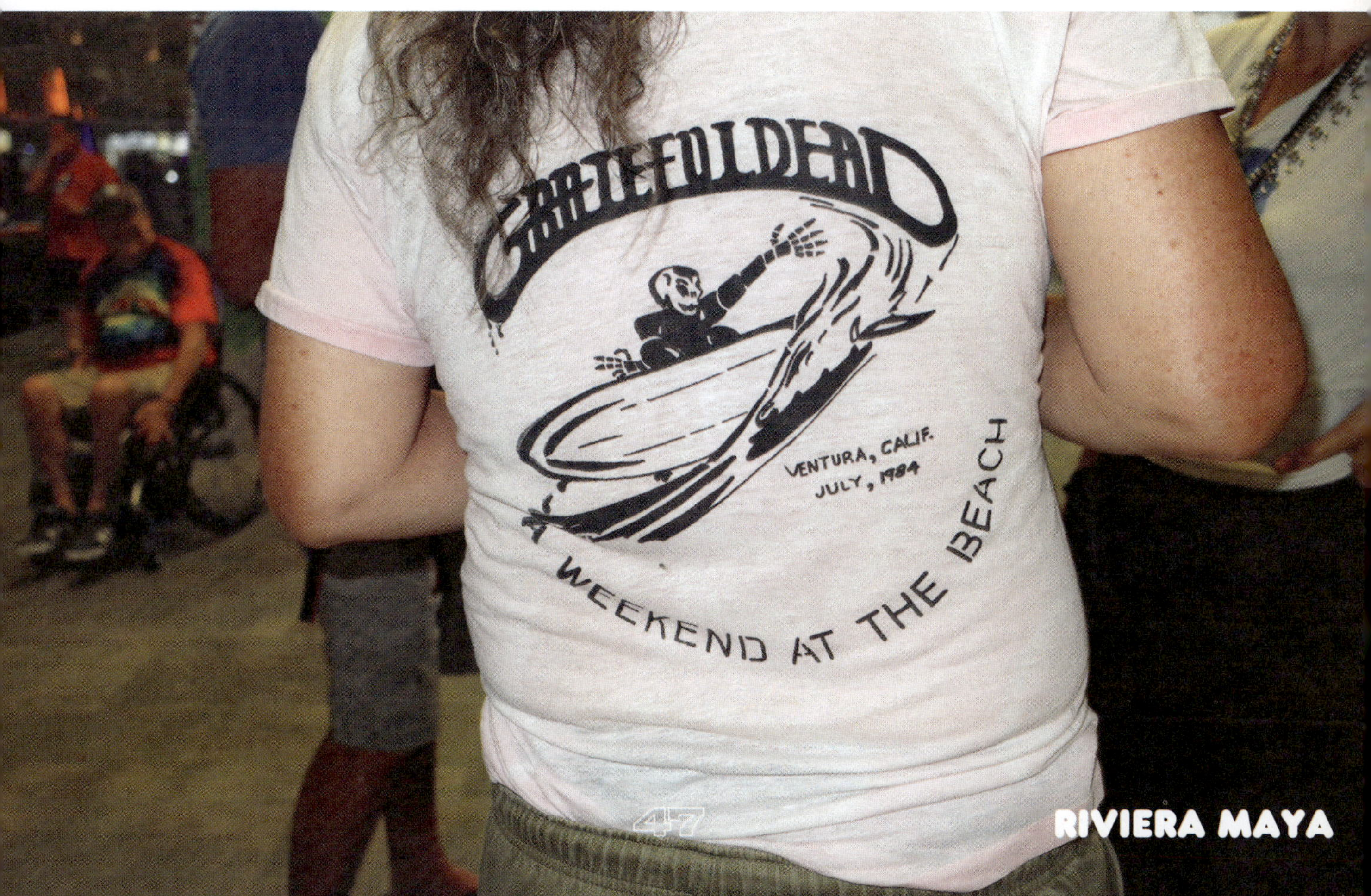

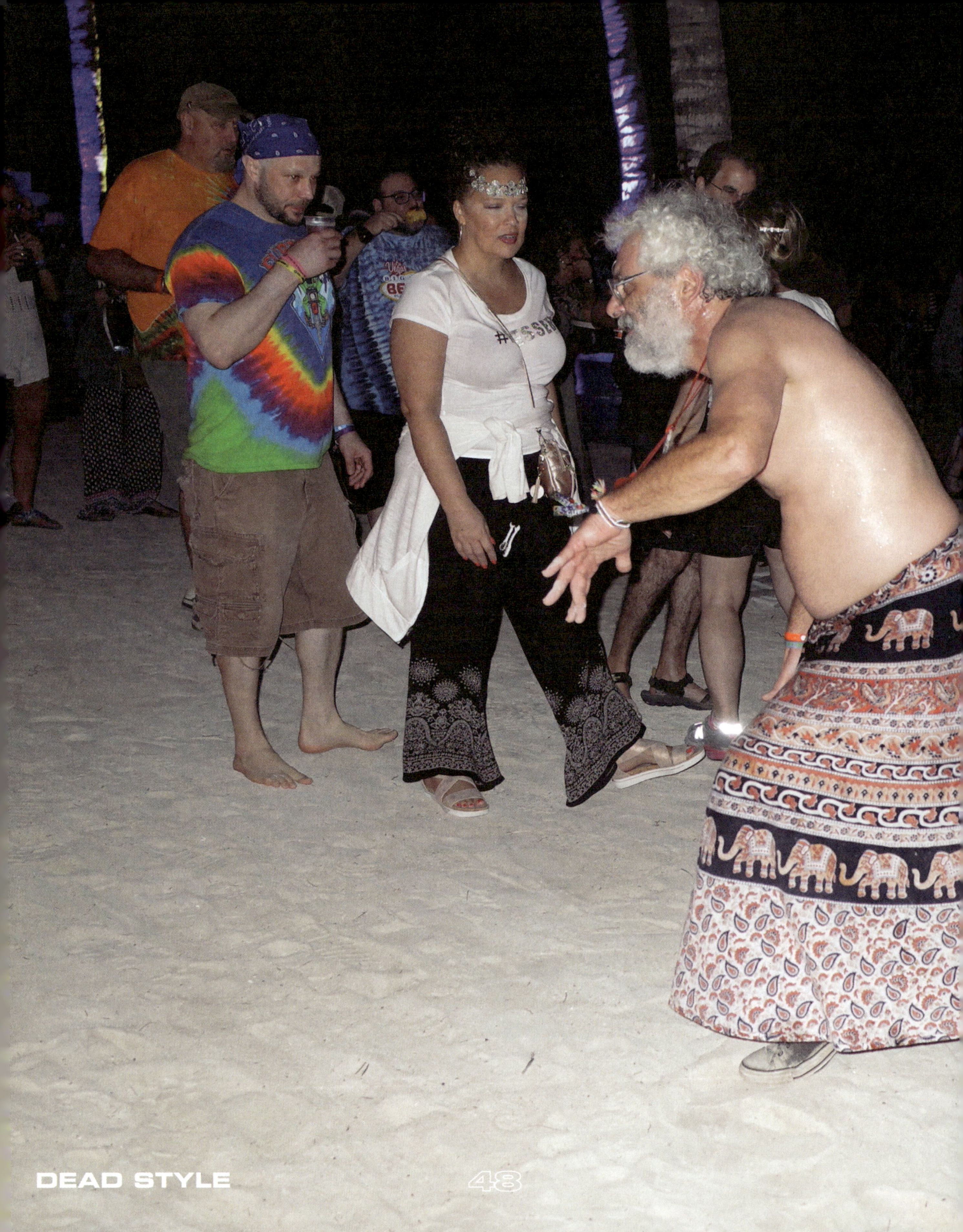

I watched this dude dance for at least one song before I tried asking for a photo. When I mustered the courage to ask, he did what so many people do and simply smiled and gave me the international signal for "Go ahead, man." I watched him dance for a long time.

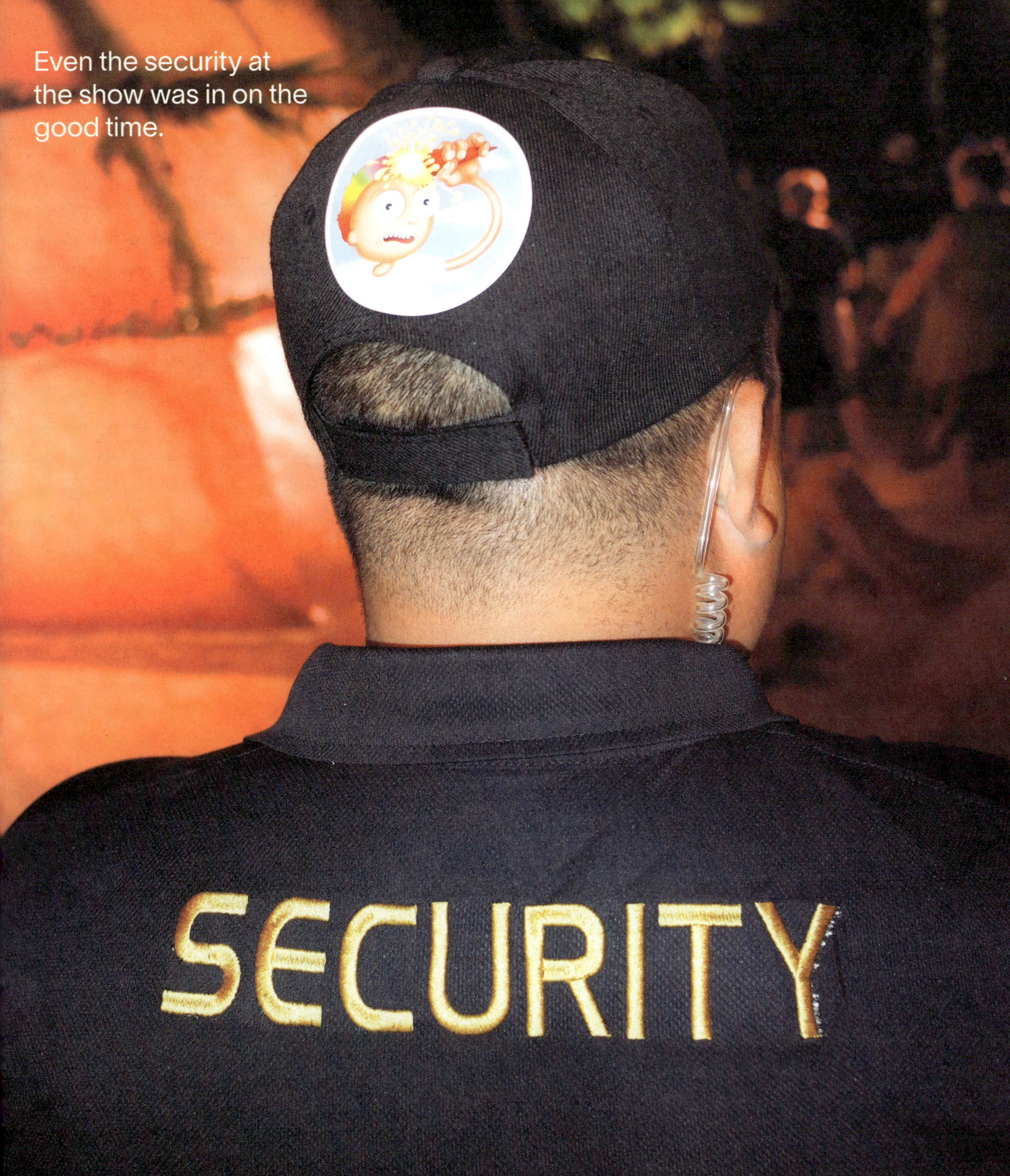

Even the security at the show was in on the good time.

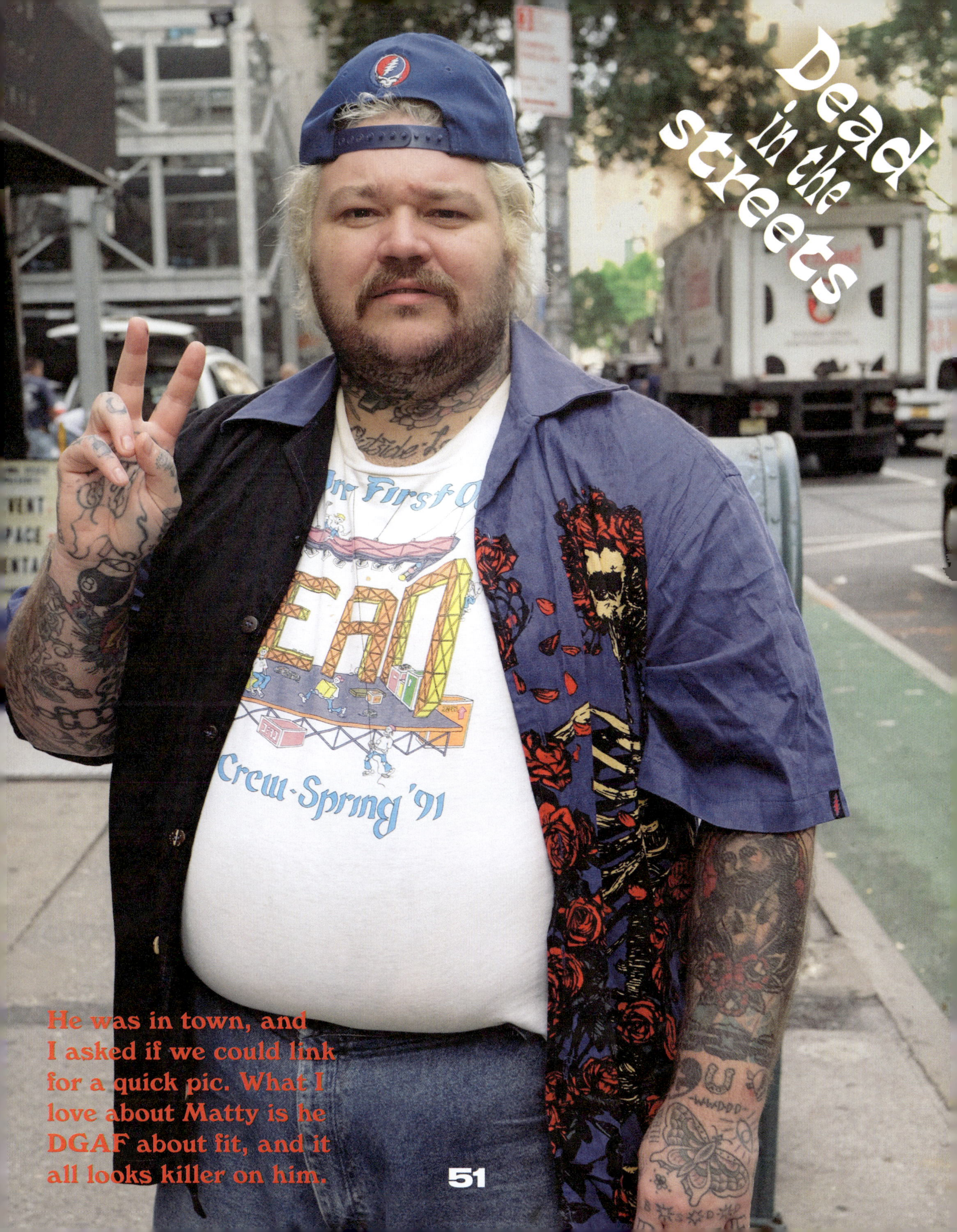

He was in town, and I asked if we could link for a quick pic. What I love about Matty is he DGAF about fit, and it all looks killer on him.

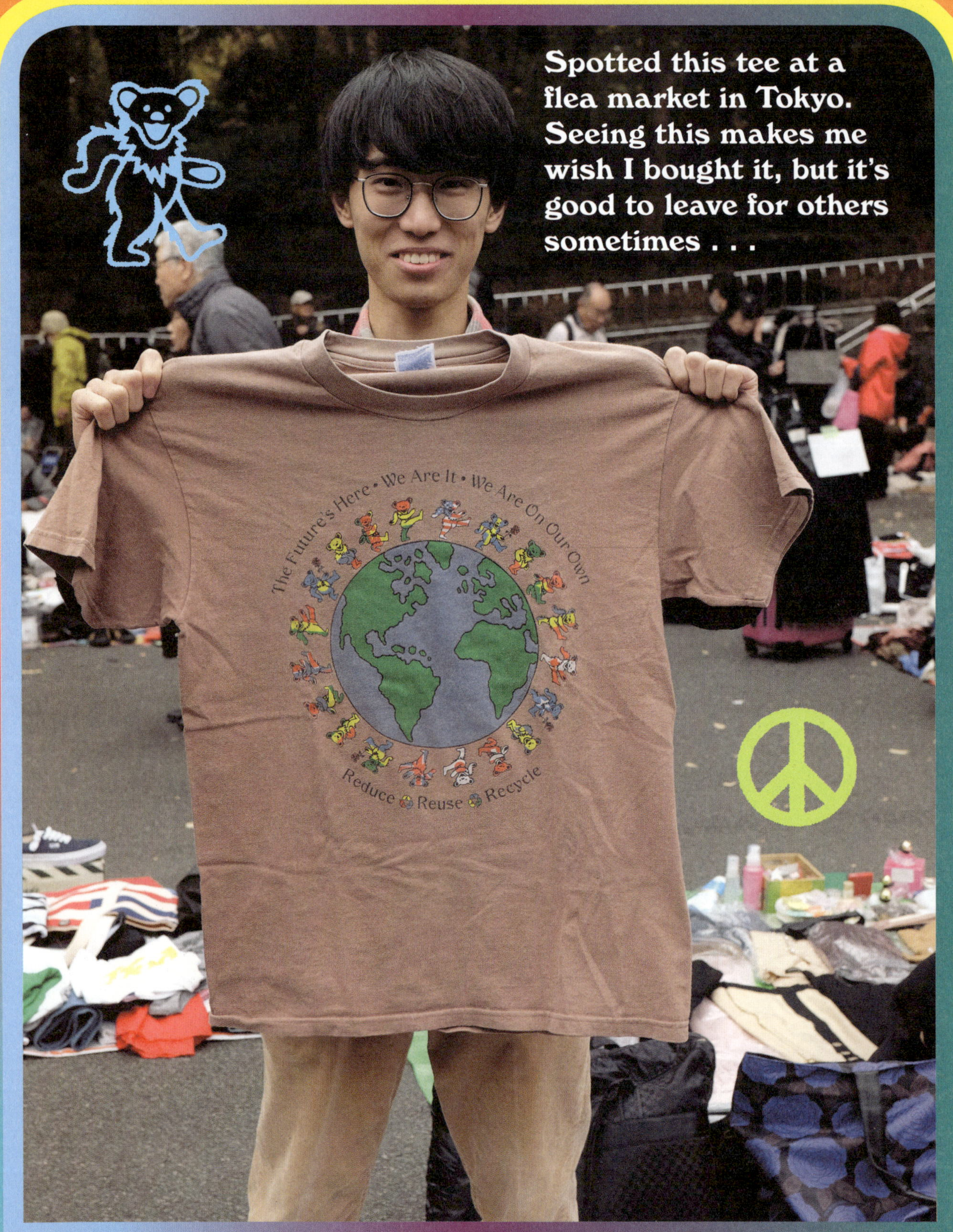

Spotted this tee at a flea market in Tokyo. Seeing this makes me wish I bought it, but it's good to leave for others sometimes . . .

Dead in the streets

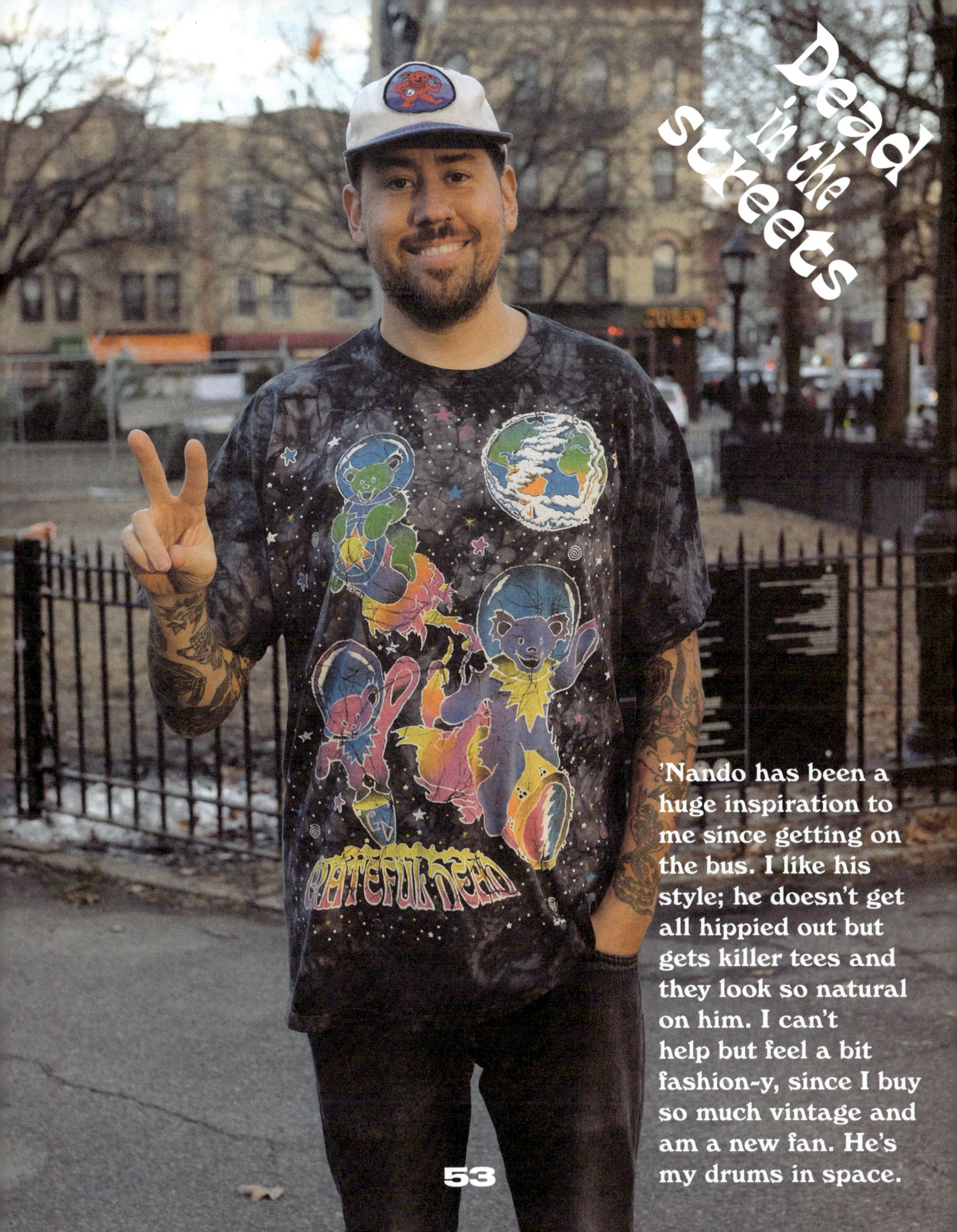

'Nando has been a huge inspiration to me since getting on the bus. I like his style; he doesn't get all hippied out but gets killer tees and they look so natural on him. I can't help but feel a bit fashion-y, since I buy so much vintage and am a new fan. He's my drums in space.

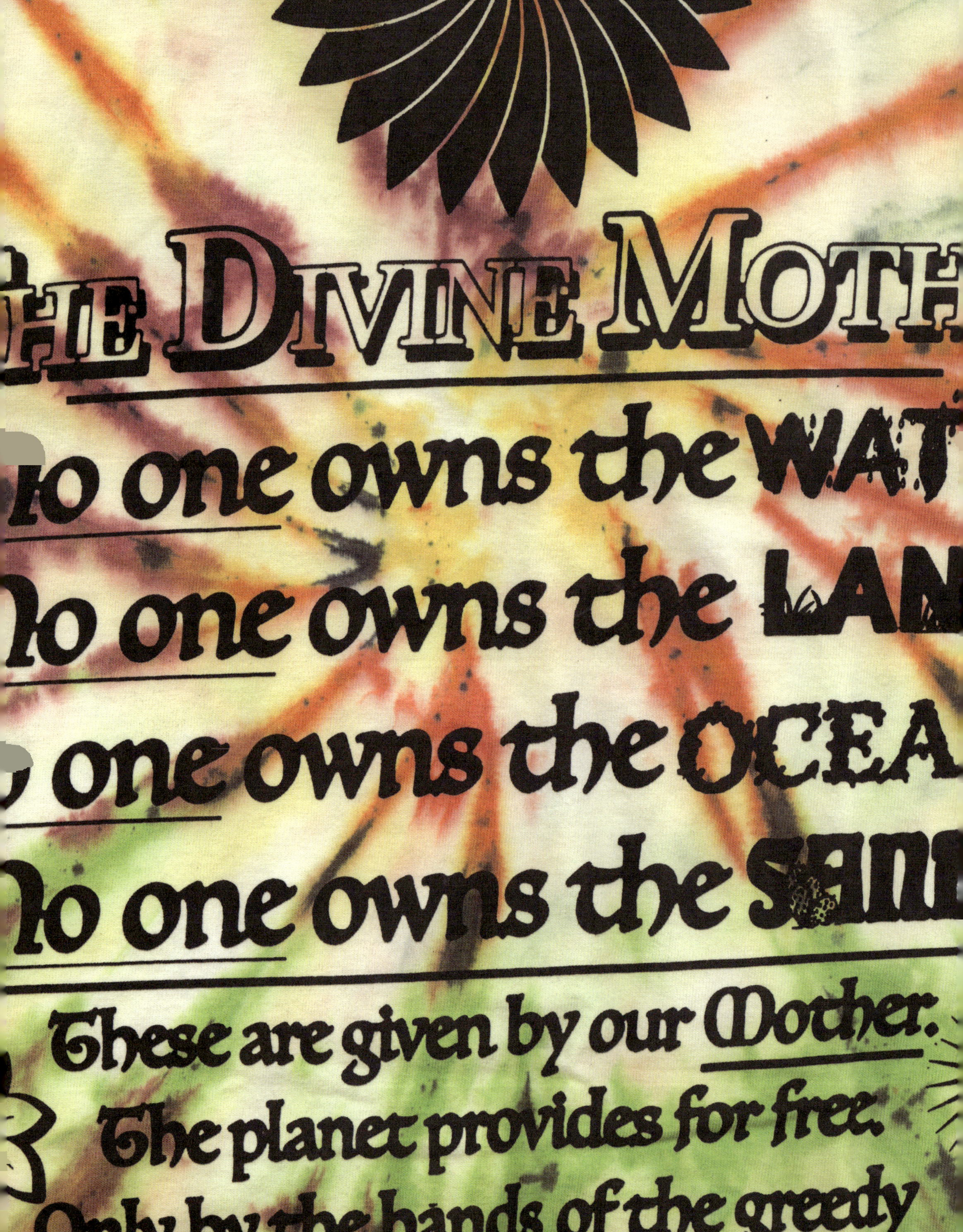
HE DIVINE MOTH
o one owns the WAT
o one owns the LAN
one owns the OCEA
o one owns the
These are given by our Mother.
The planet provides for free.
hands of the greedy

SARATOGA PERFORMING ARTS CENTER

Saratoga Springs, New York

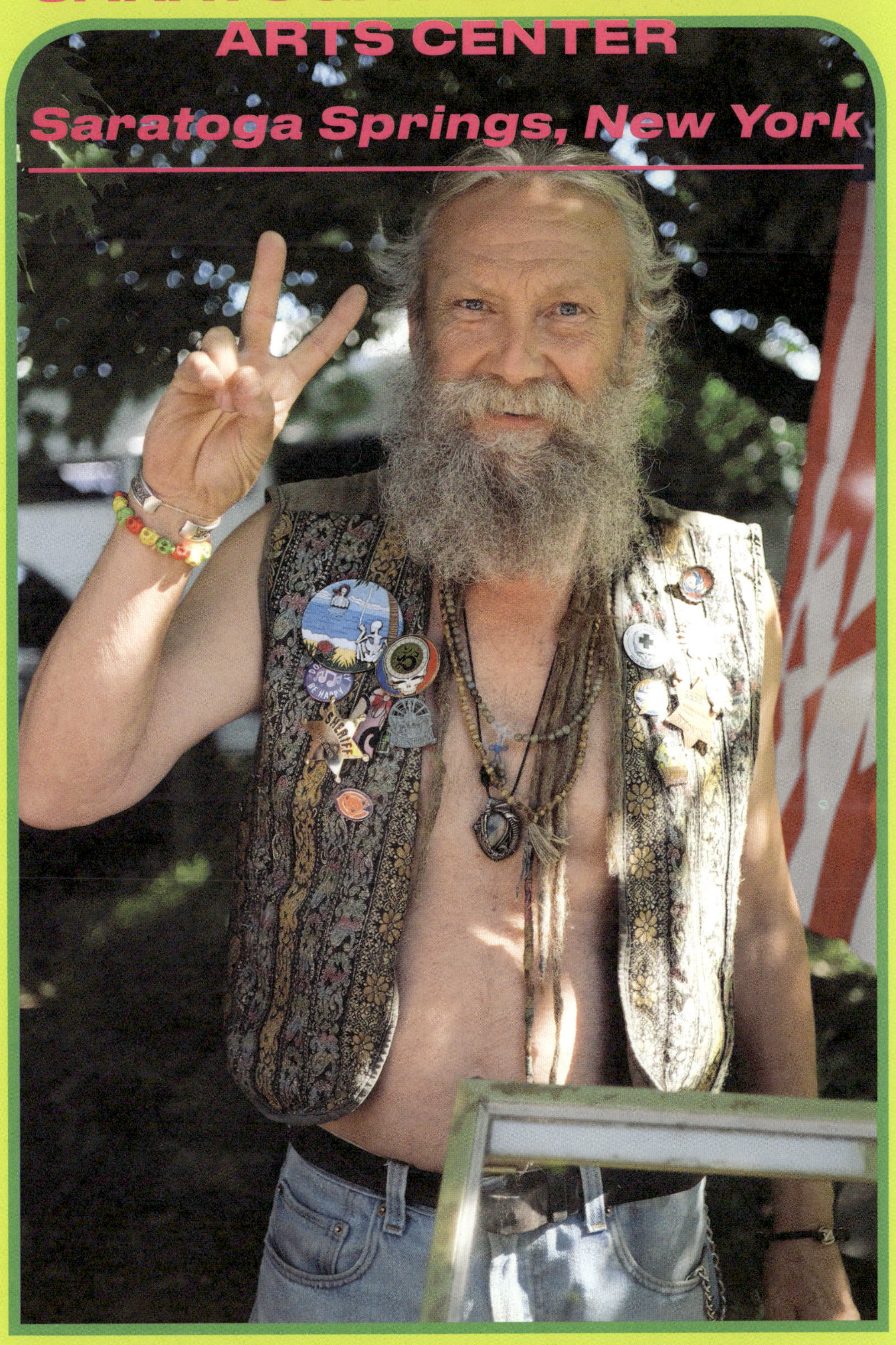

Monday, June 11th, 2018

The skinny jean with Chucks and oversized tee is just perfect. A very musician look, but the Chucks fade and the tee has me thinking it could be his older brother's or dad's! I like to dream.

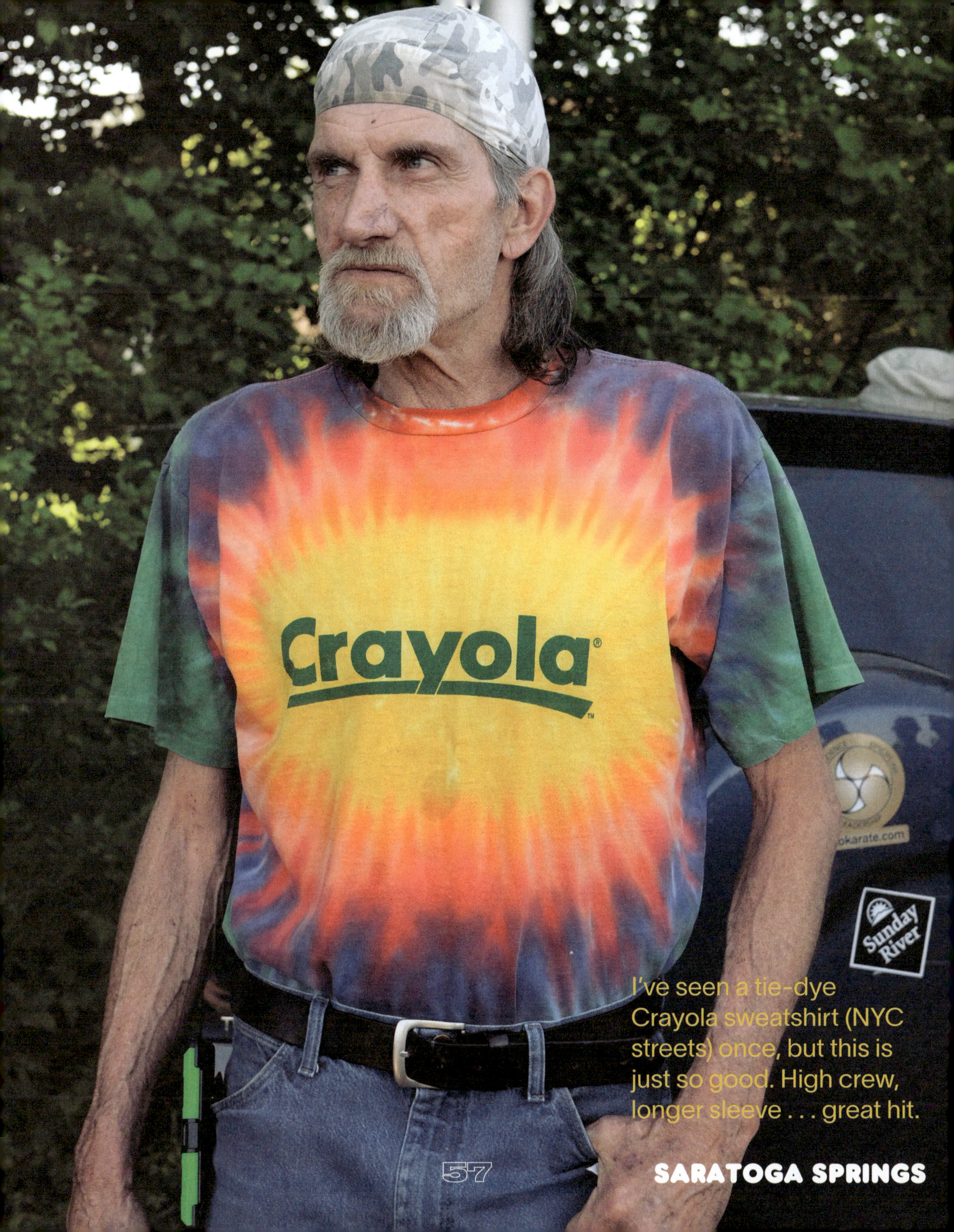

I've seen a tie-dye Crayola sweatshirt (NYC streets) once, but this is just so good. High crew, longer sleeve . . . great hit.

SARATOGA SPRINGS

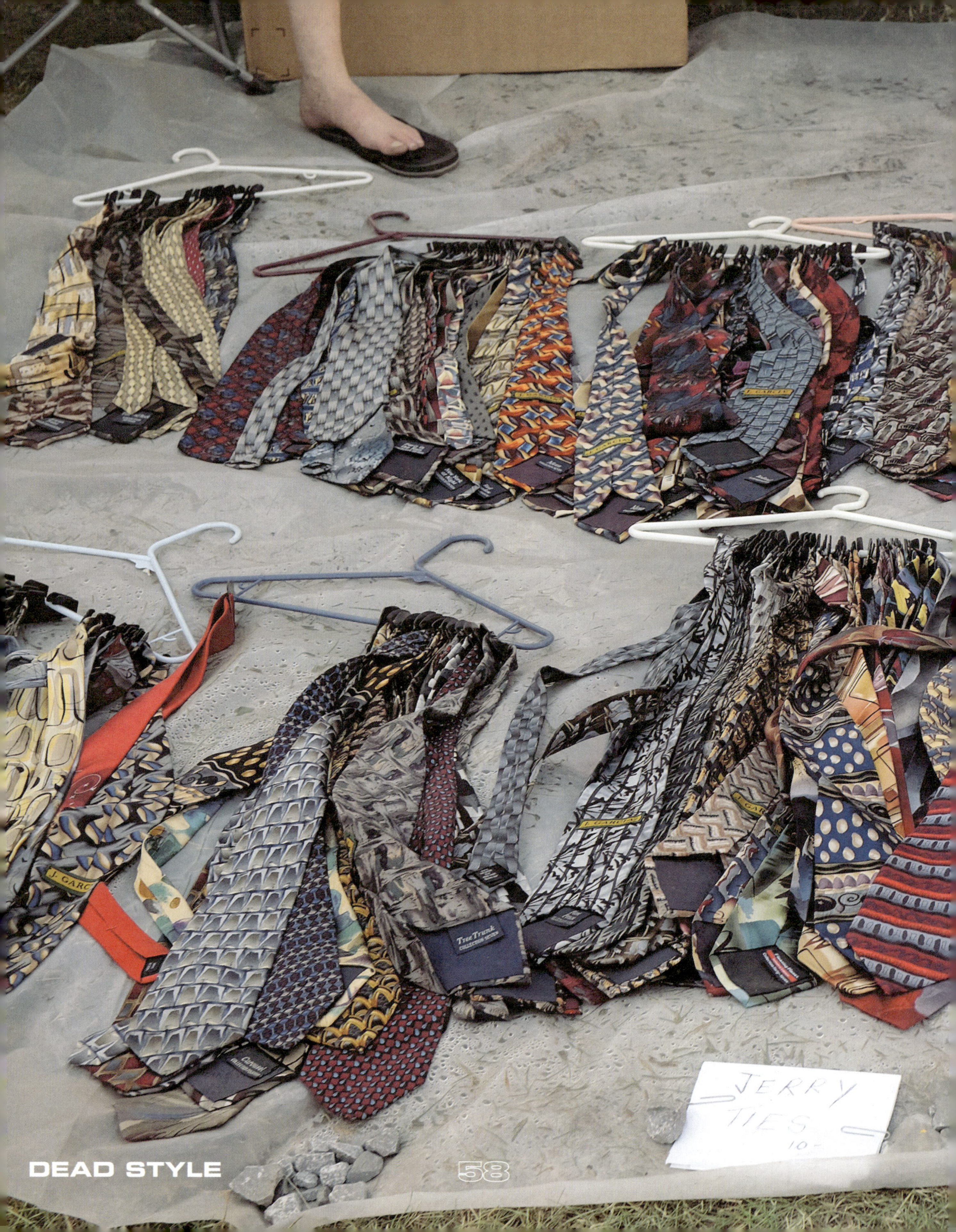
JERRY
TIES
10-

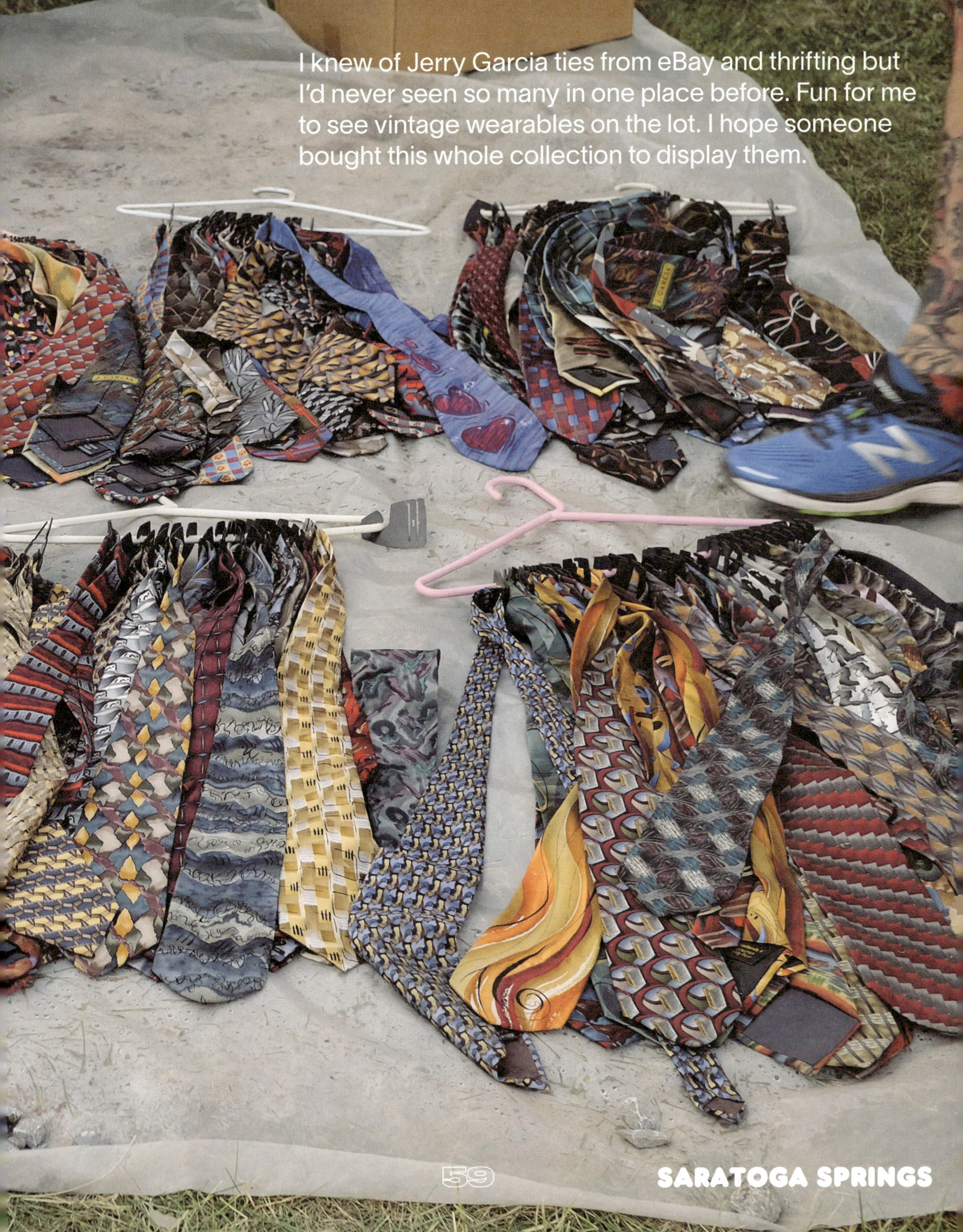

I knew of Jerry Garcia ties from eBay and thrifting but I'd never seen so many in one place before. Fun for me to see vintage wearables on the lot. I hope someone bought this whole collection to display them.

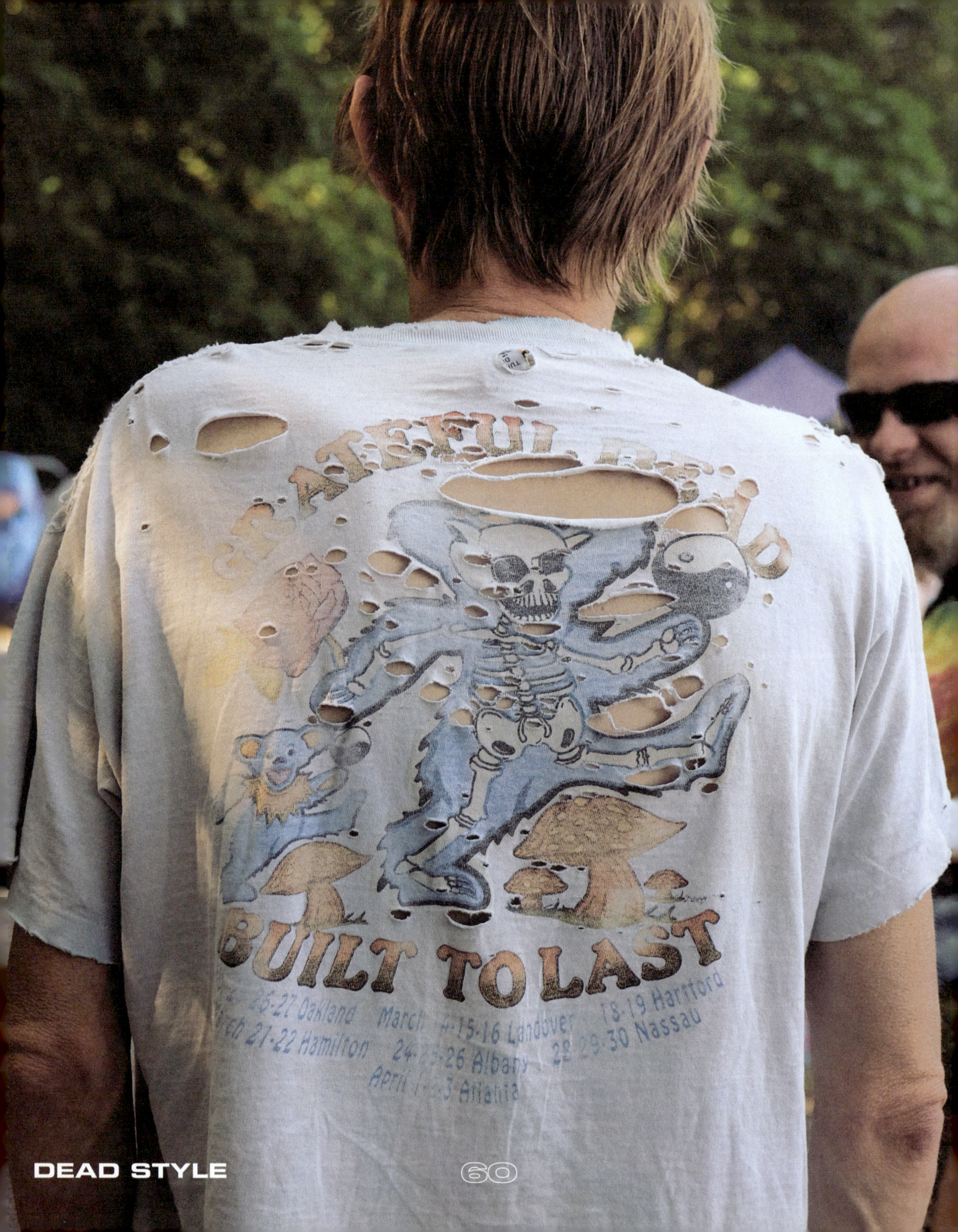
BUILT TO LAST

The writing does not lie! Definition of worn in, not worn out.

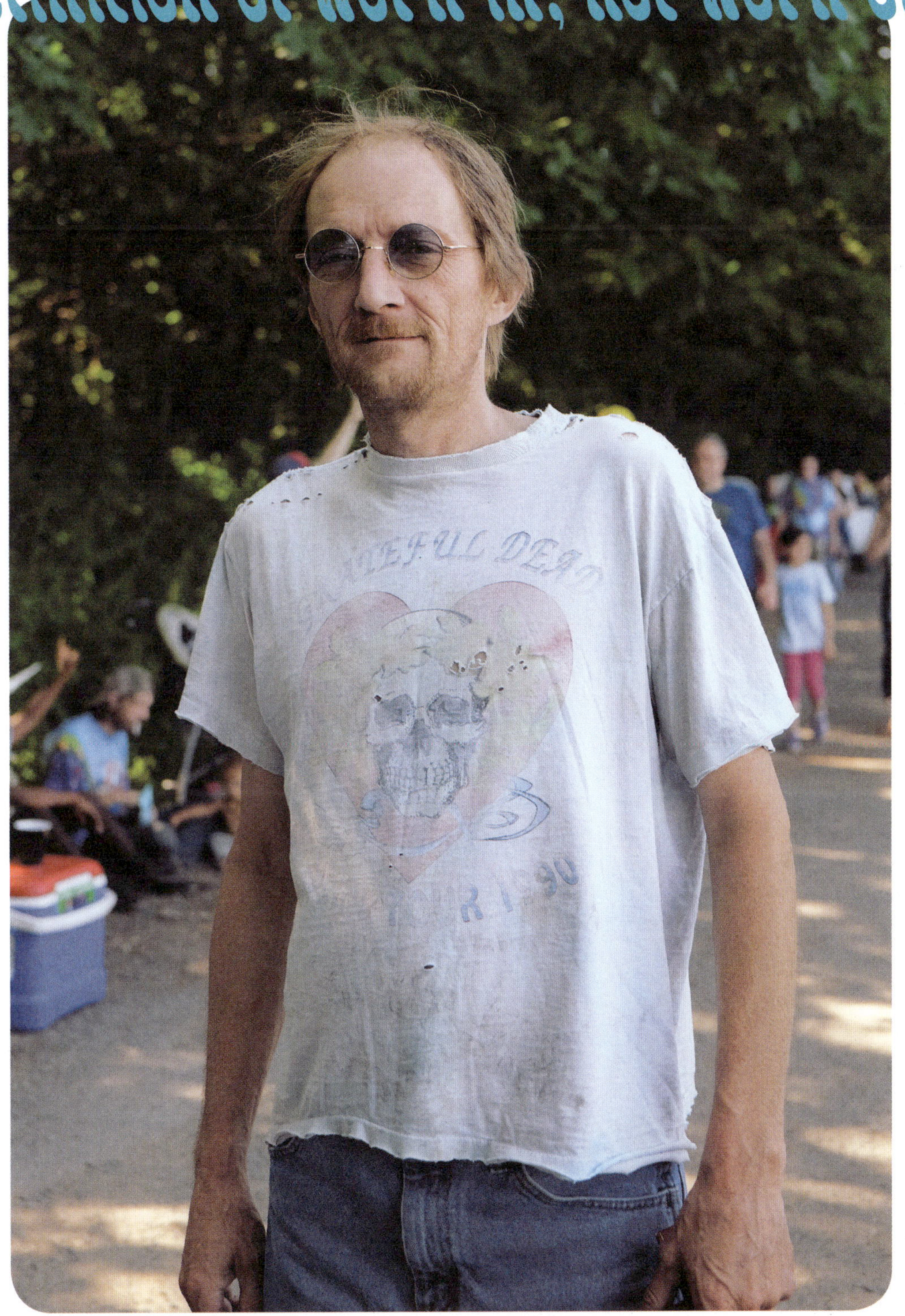

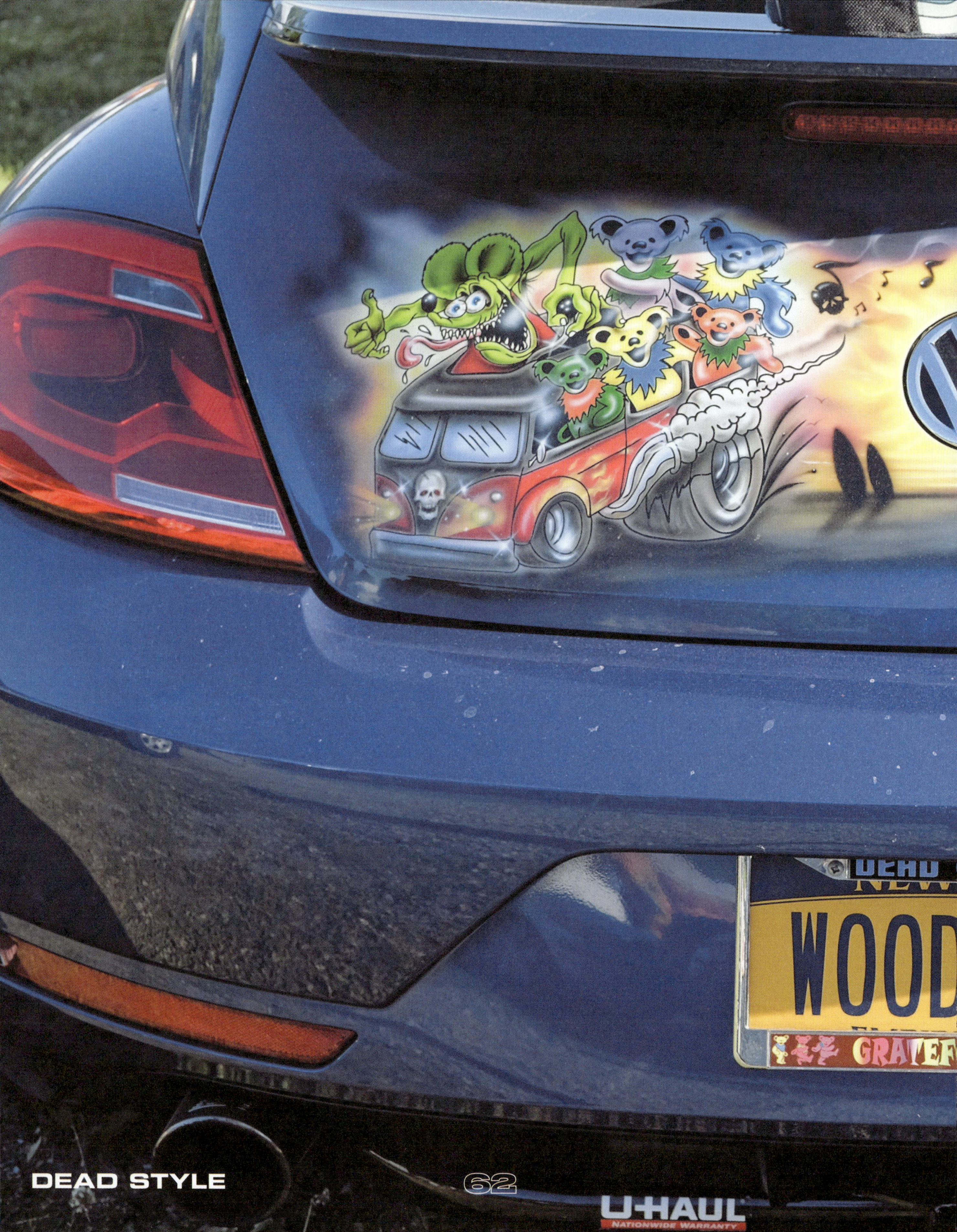
WOOD
U-HAUL
NATIONWIDE WARRANTY

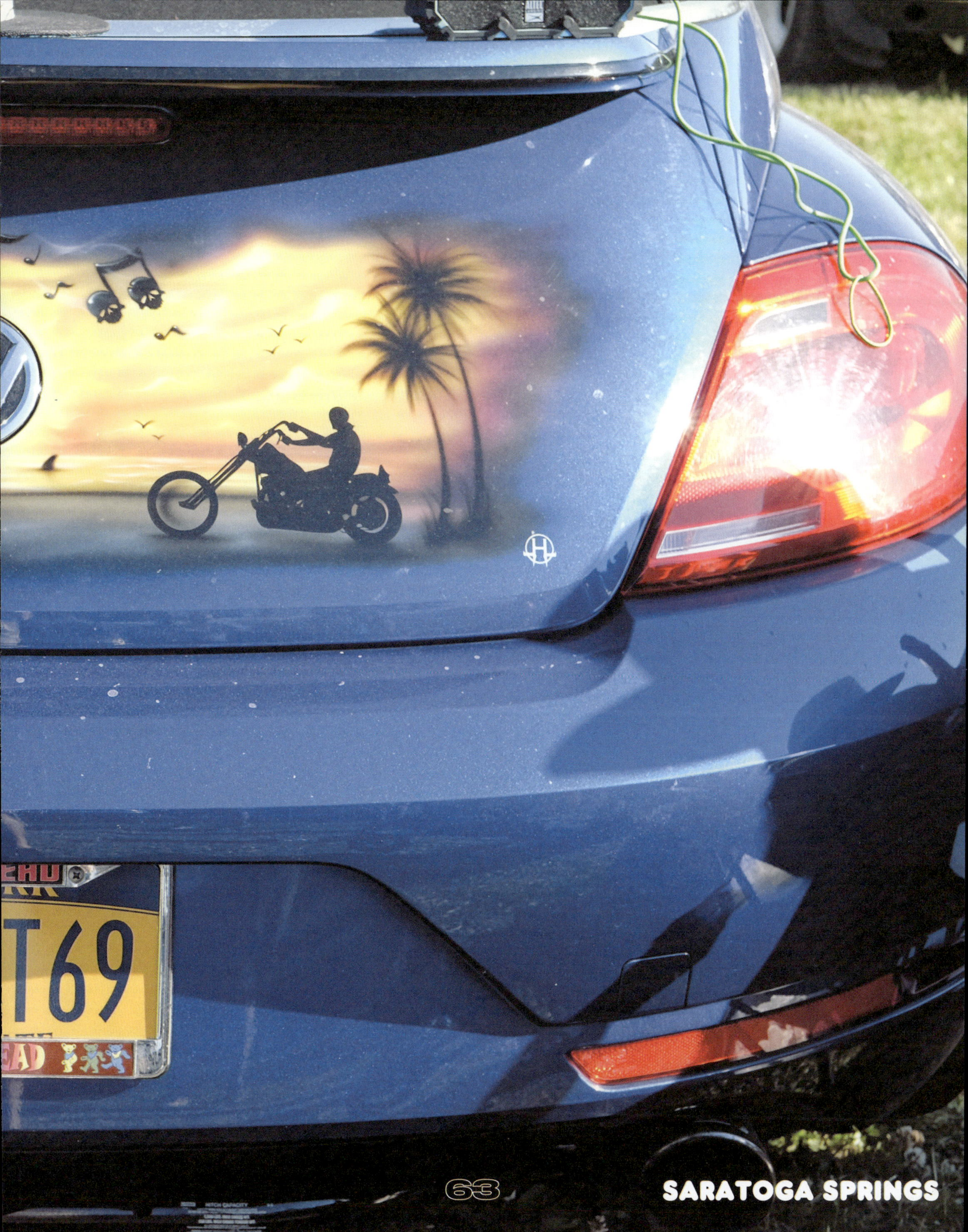
T69

HAND-PAINTED AND I HOPE WILL NEVER FADE, BECAUSE THIS SHOULD END UP IN A MUSEUM.

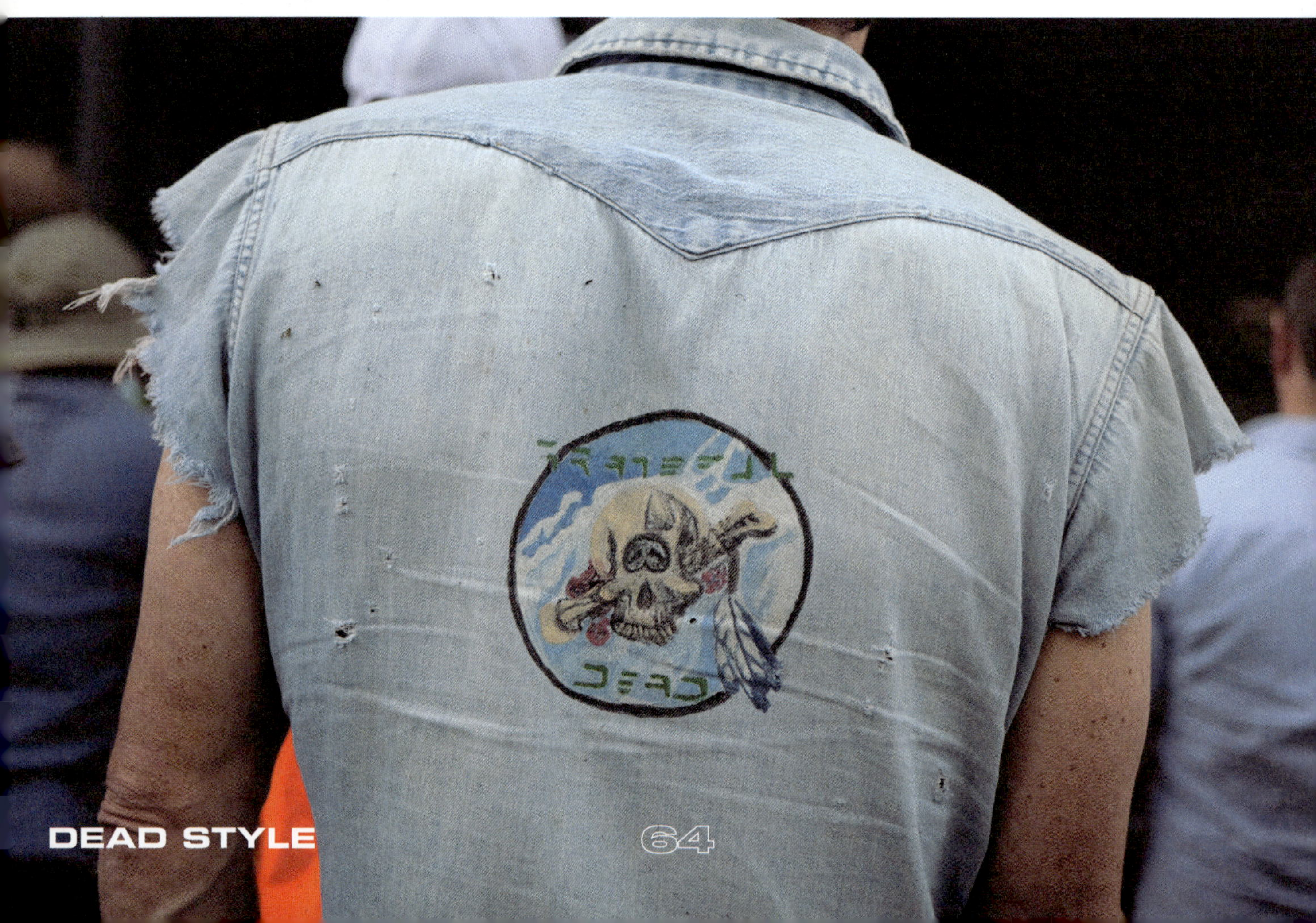

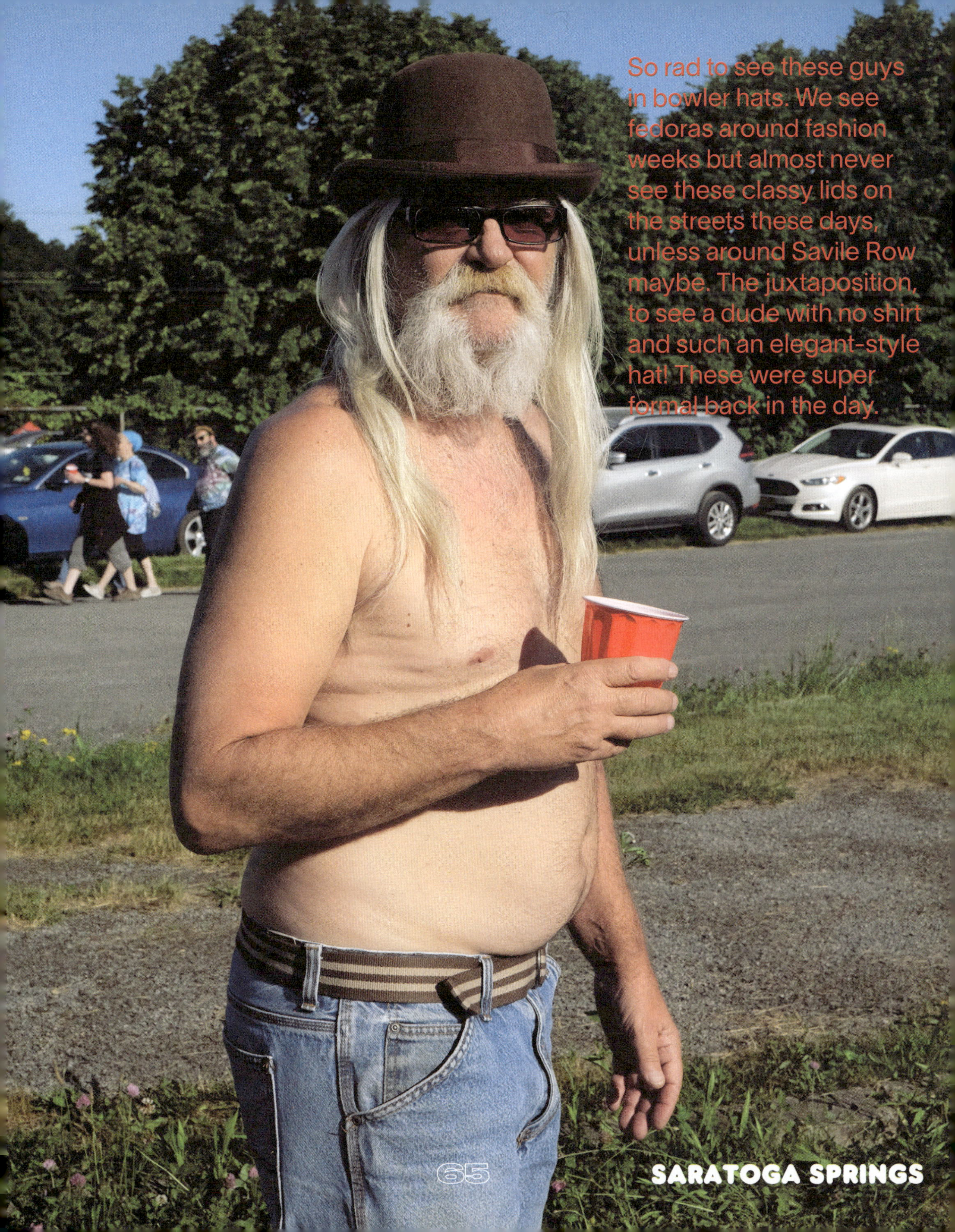

So rad to see these guys in bowler hats. We see fedoras around fashion weeks but almost never see these classy lids on the streets these days, unless around Savile Row maybe. The juxtaposition, to see a dude with no shirt and such an elegant-style hat! These were super formal back in the day.

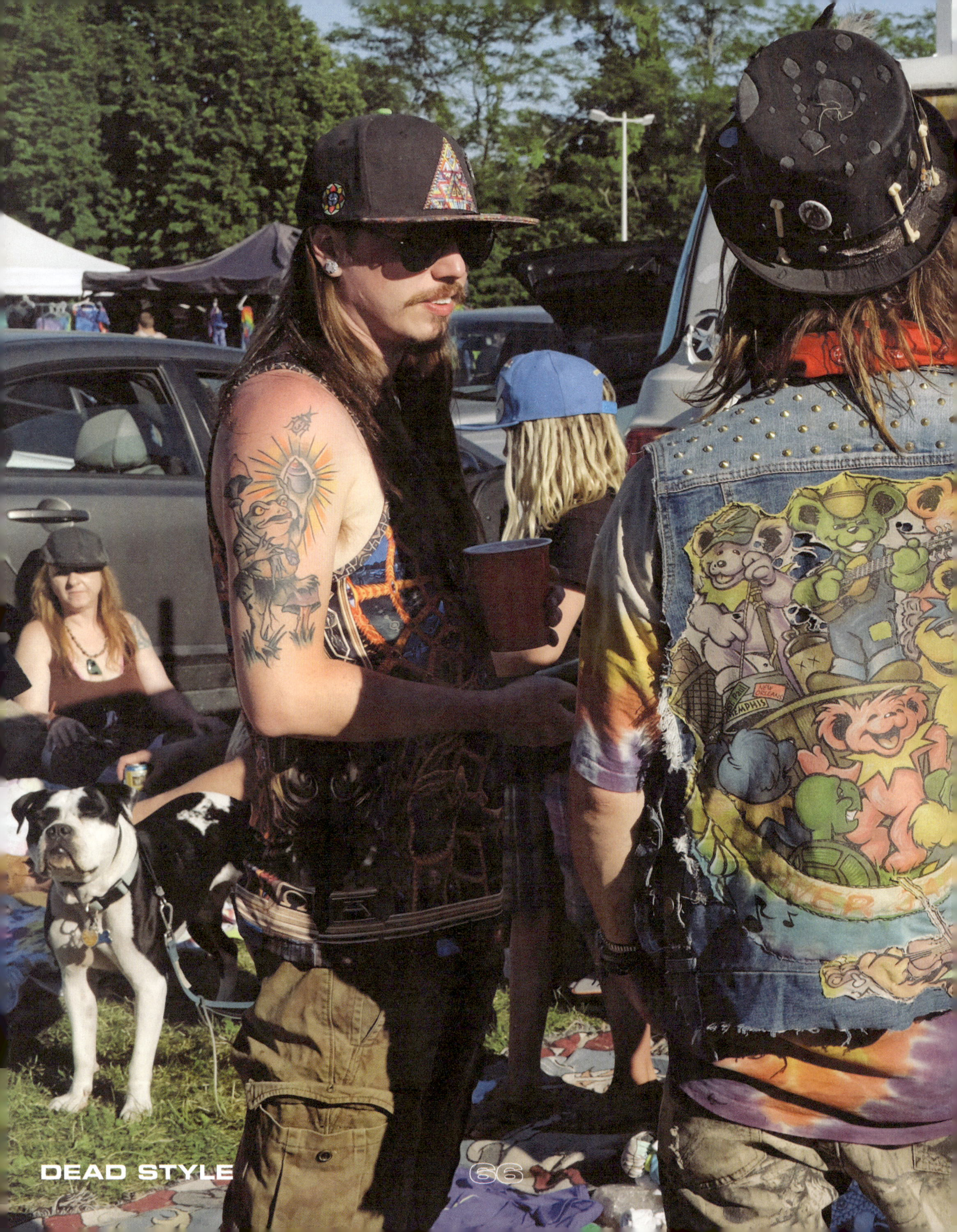

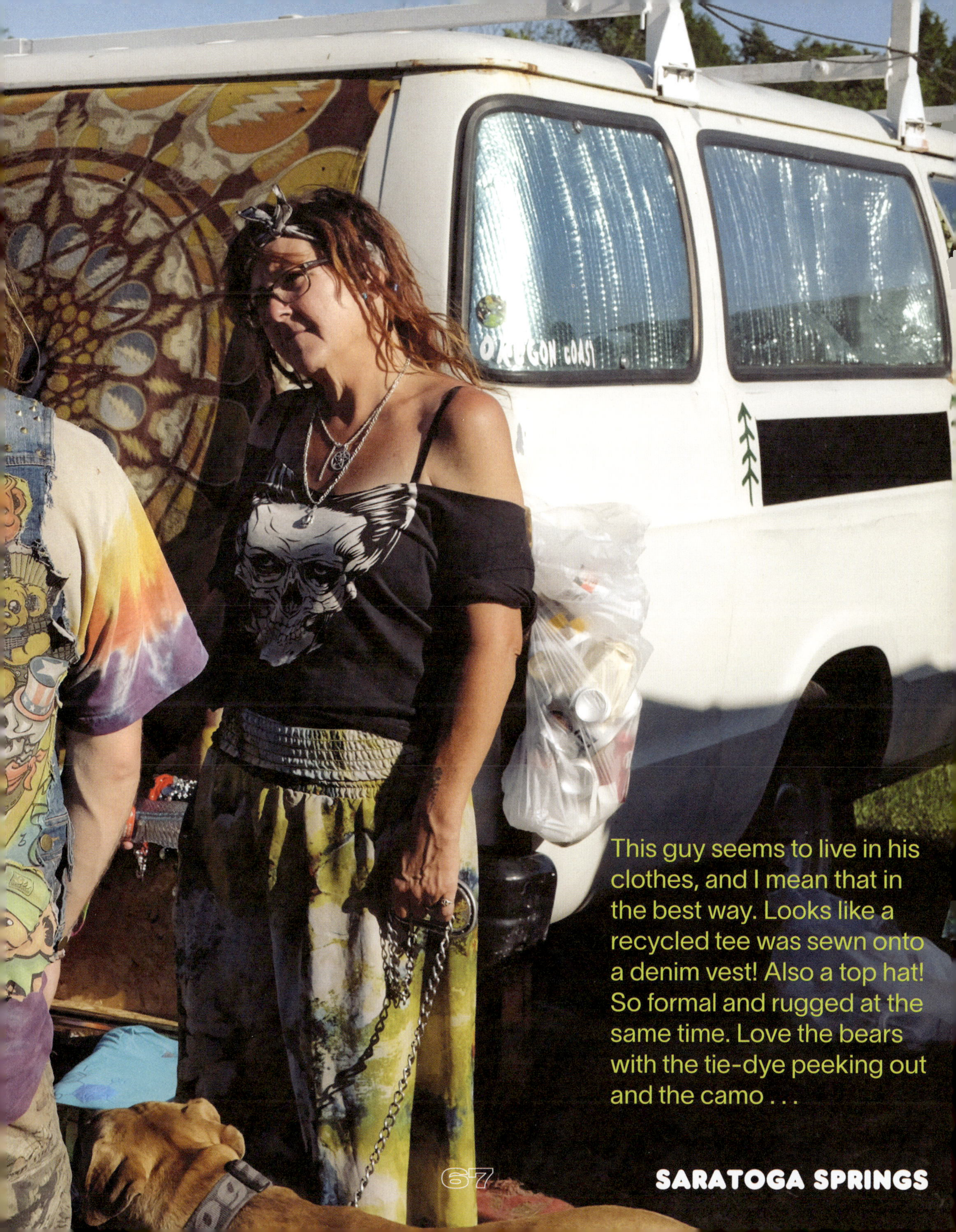

This guy seems to live in his clothes, and I mean that in the best way. Looks like a recycled tee was sewn onto a denim vest! Also a top hat! So formal and rugged at the same time. Love the bears with the tie-dye peeking out and the camo . . .

LOOKING OUT FOR THE WHOLE FAMILY

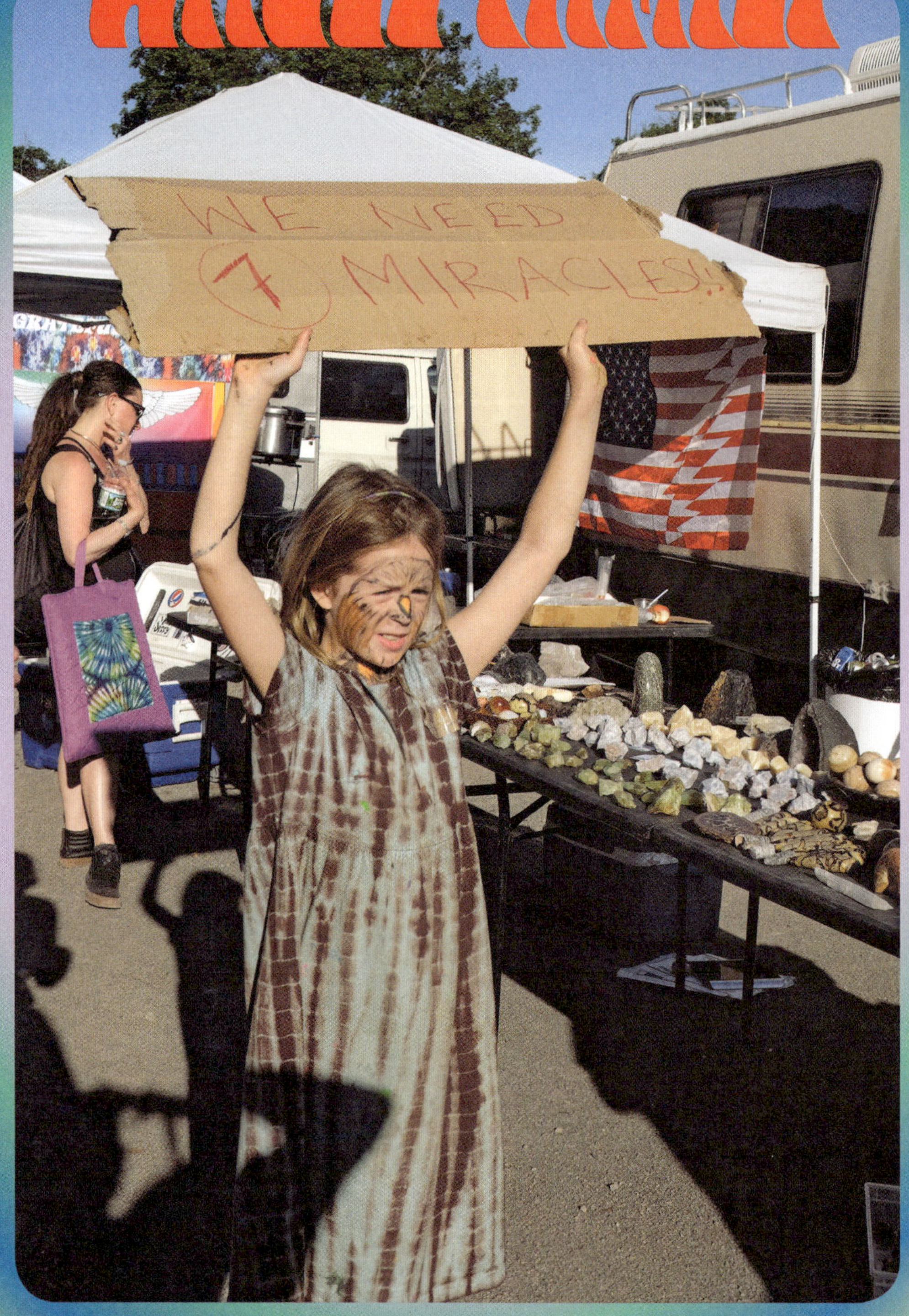

Dead in the streets

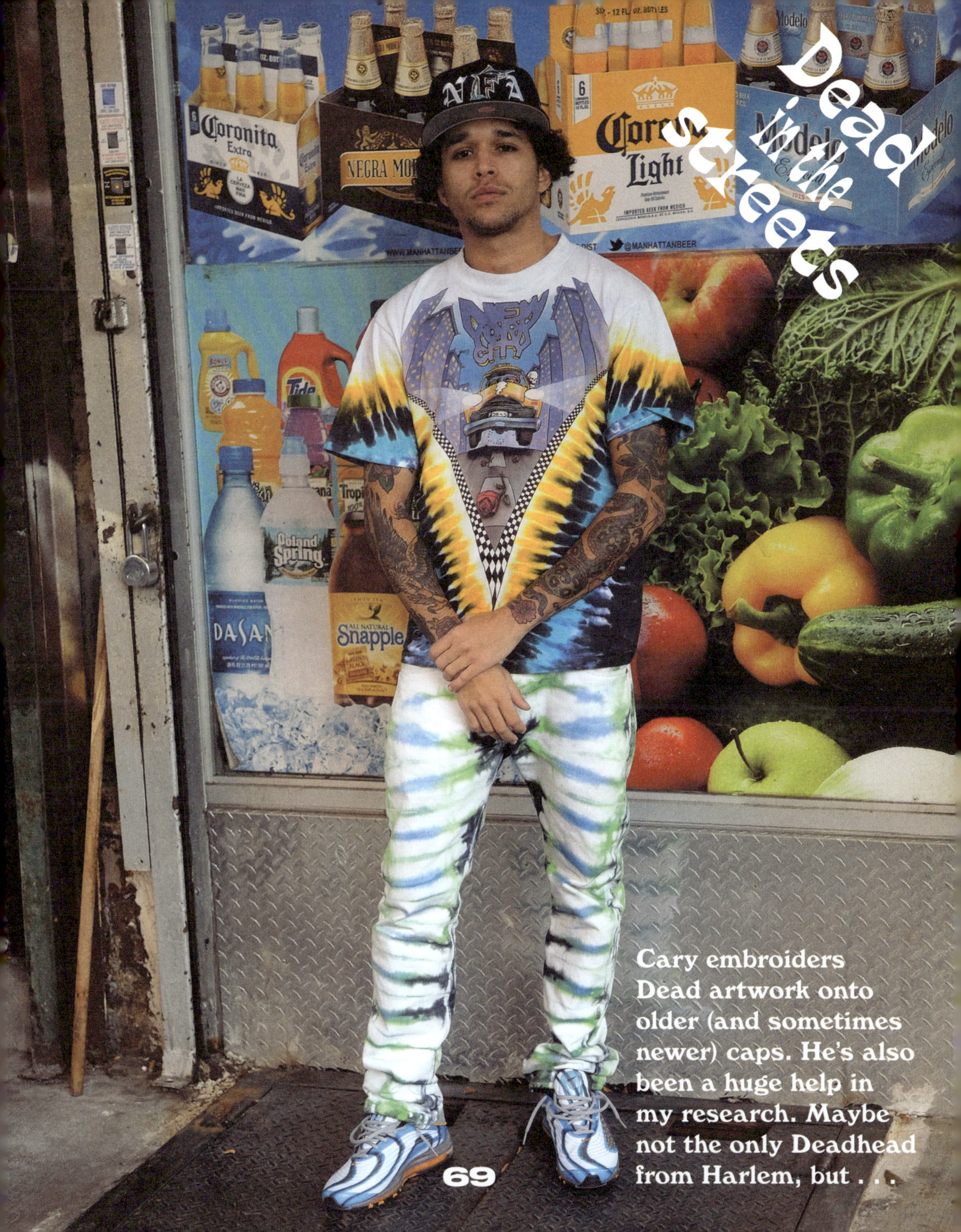

Cary embroiders Dead artwork onto older (and sometimes newer) caps. He's also been a huge help in my research. Maybe not the only Deadhead from Harlem, but . . .

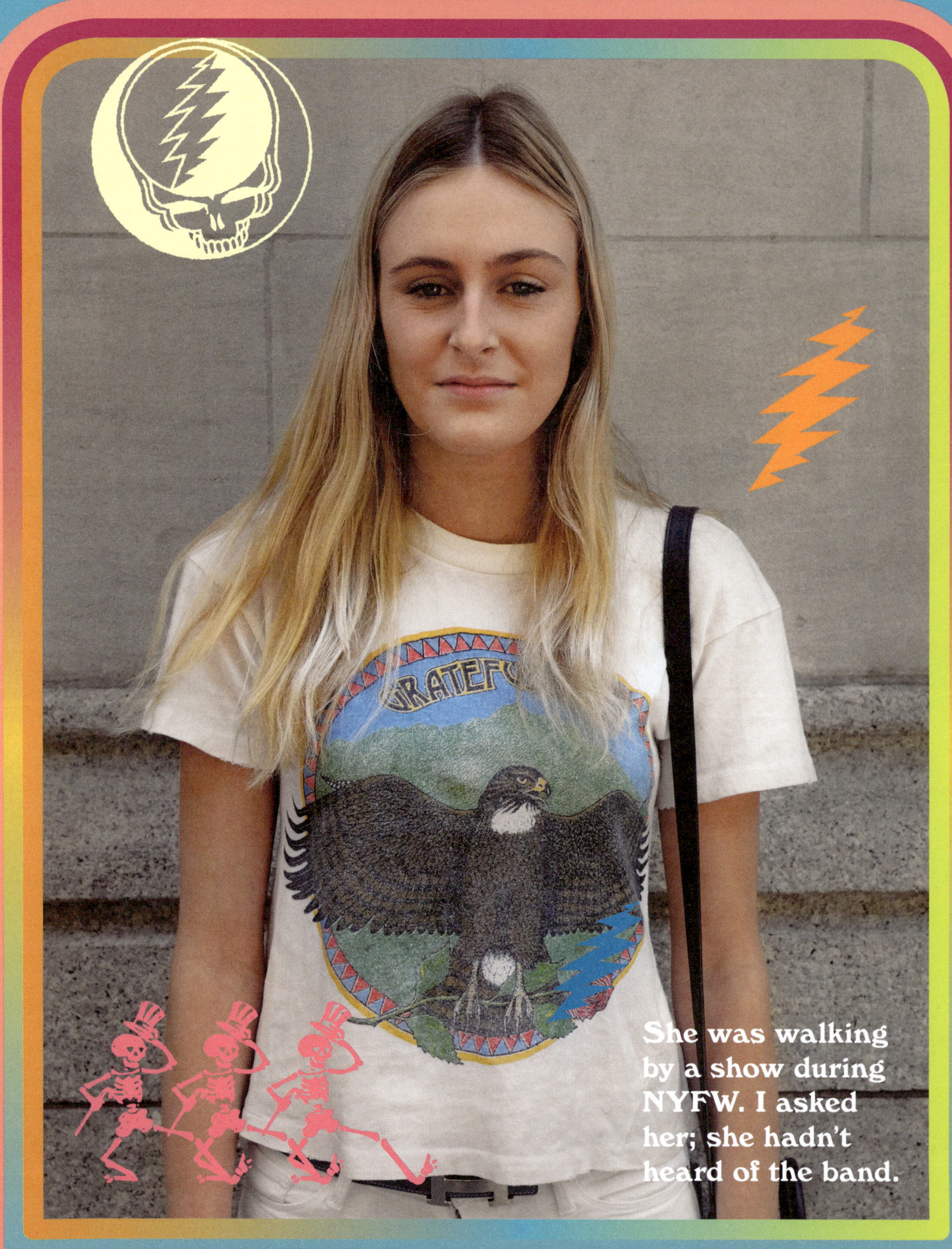

She was walking by a show during NYFW. I asked her; she hadn't heard of the band.

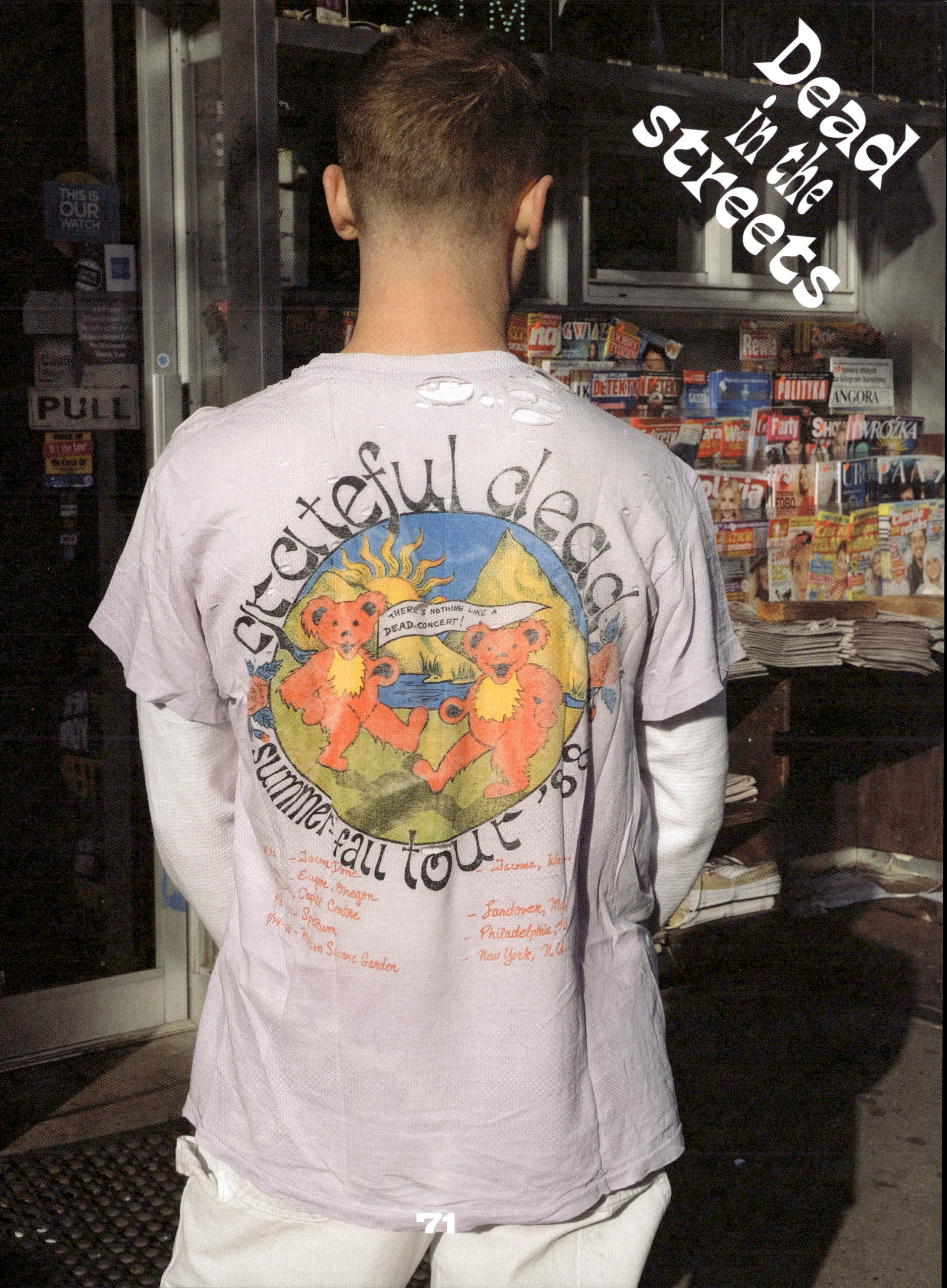

Dead in the streets

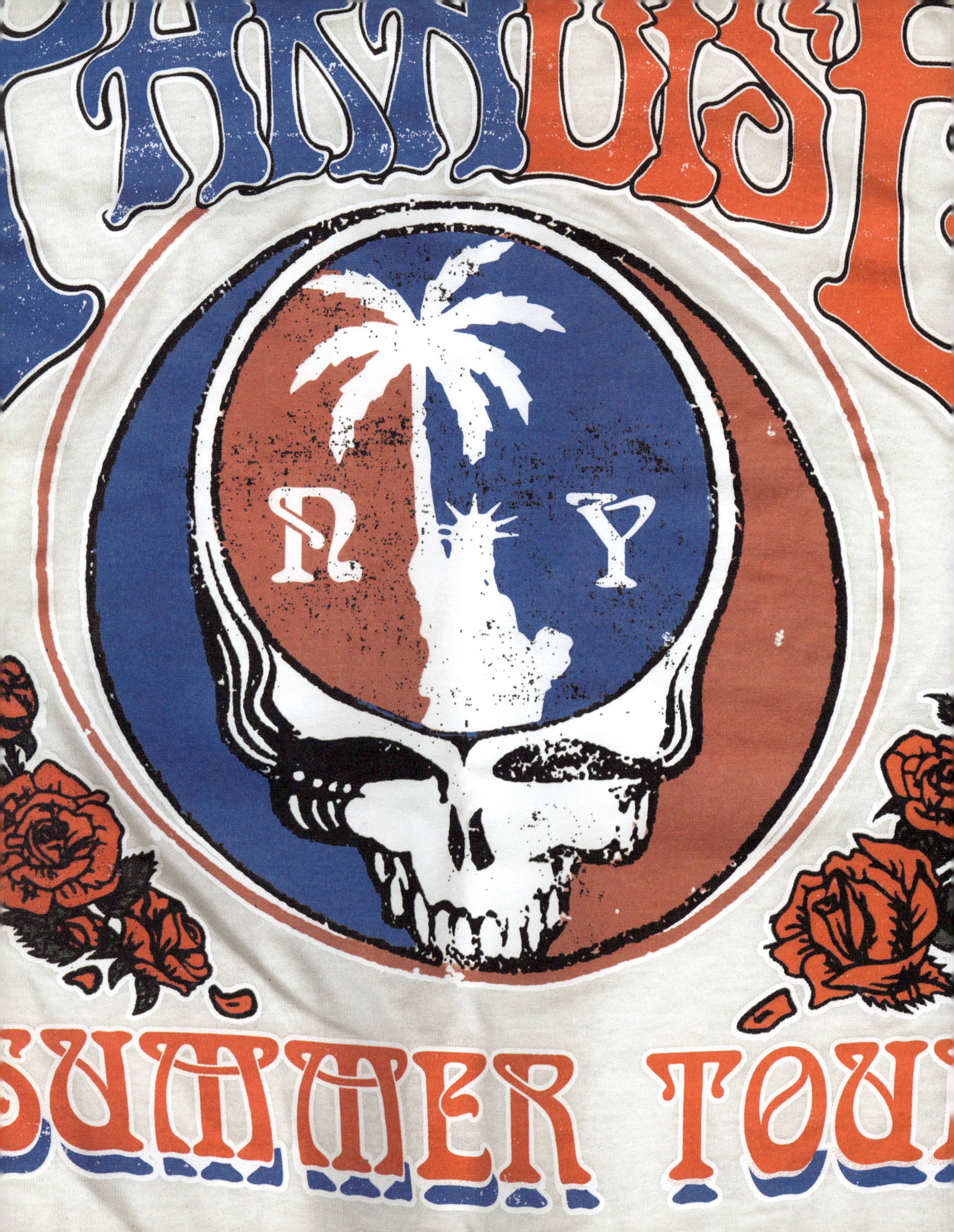
N Y
SUMMER

XFINITY THEATRE

Hartford, Connecticut

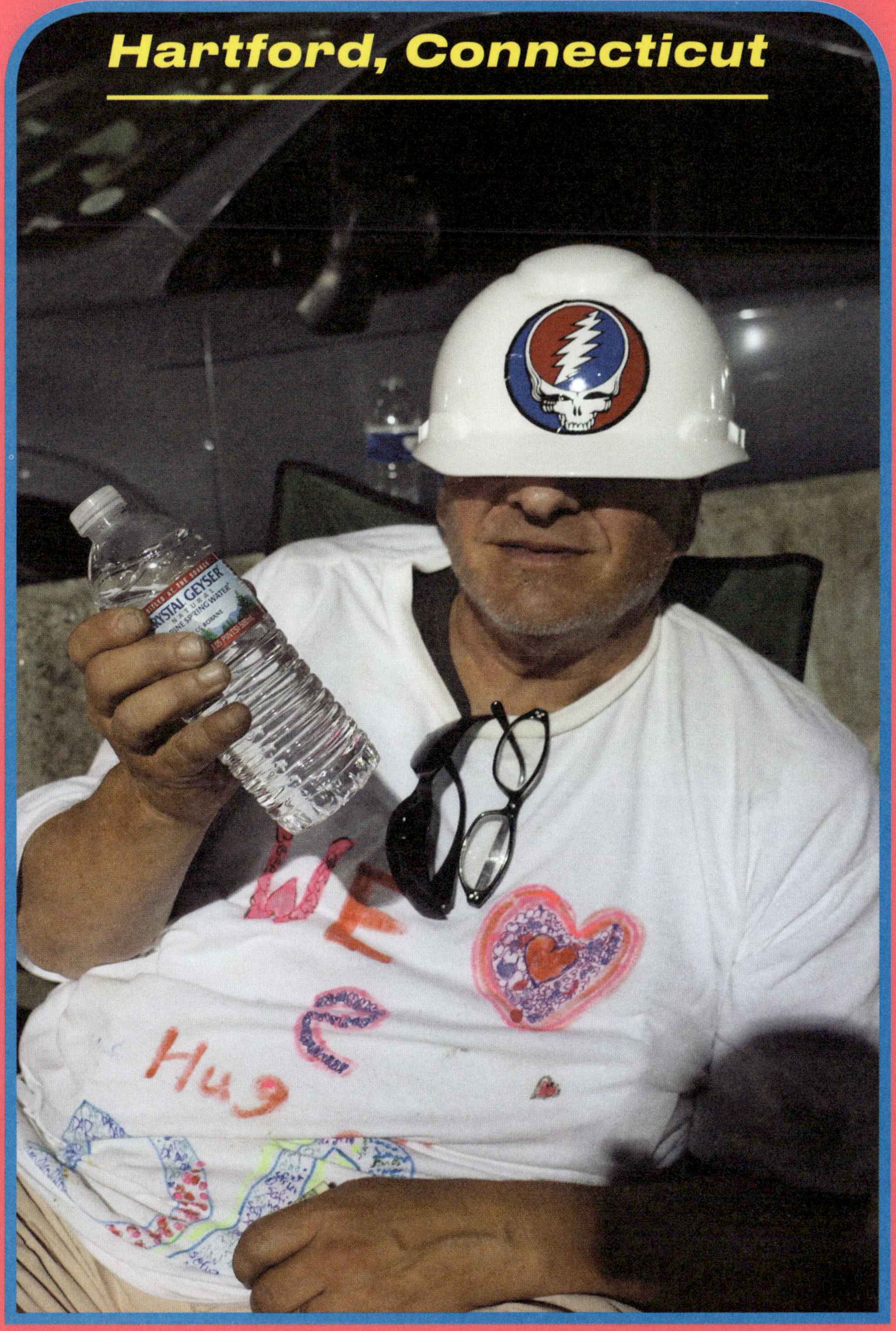

Wednesday, June 13th, 2018

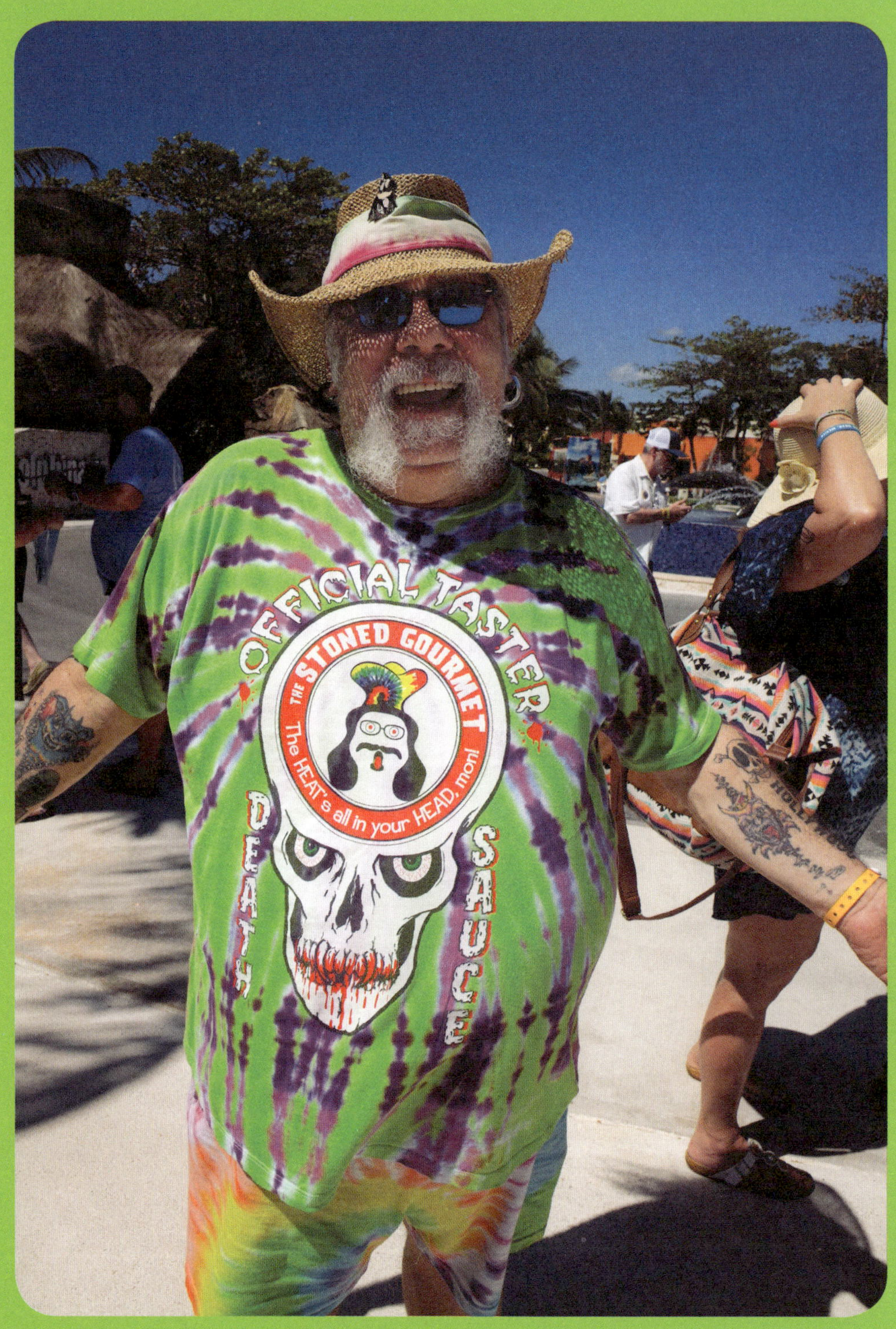
OFFICIAL TASTER
THE STONED GOURMET
The HEAT's all in your HEAD, mon!
DEATH
SAUCE

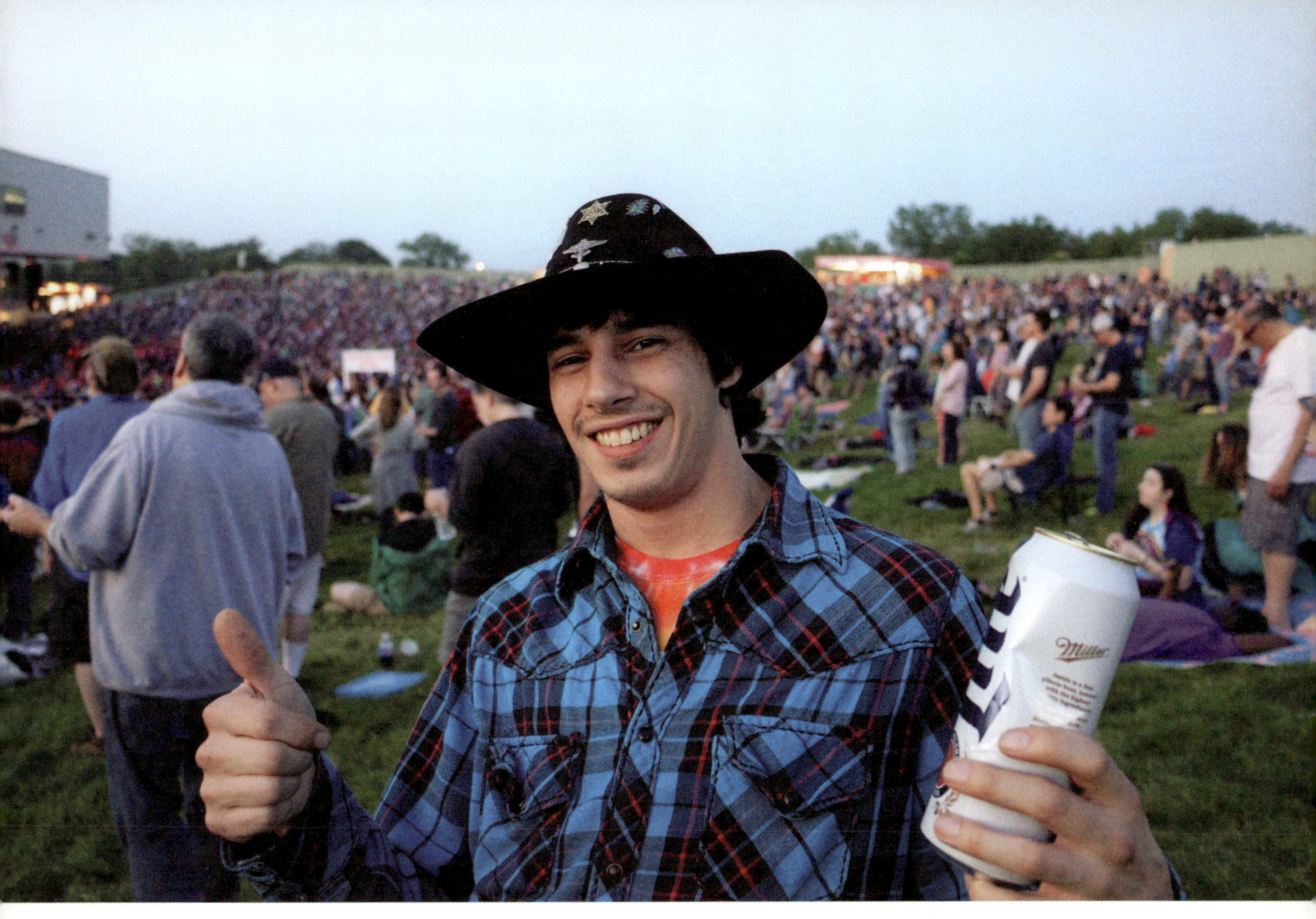

This was the first time I'd seen a cowboy hat with pins all over it! I've seen patches glued on at the rodeo, but this was so awesome.

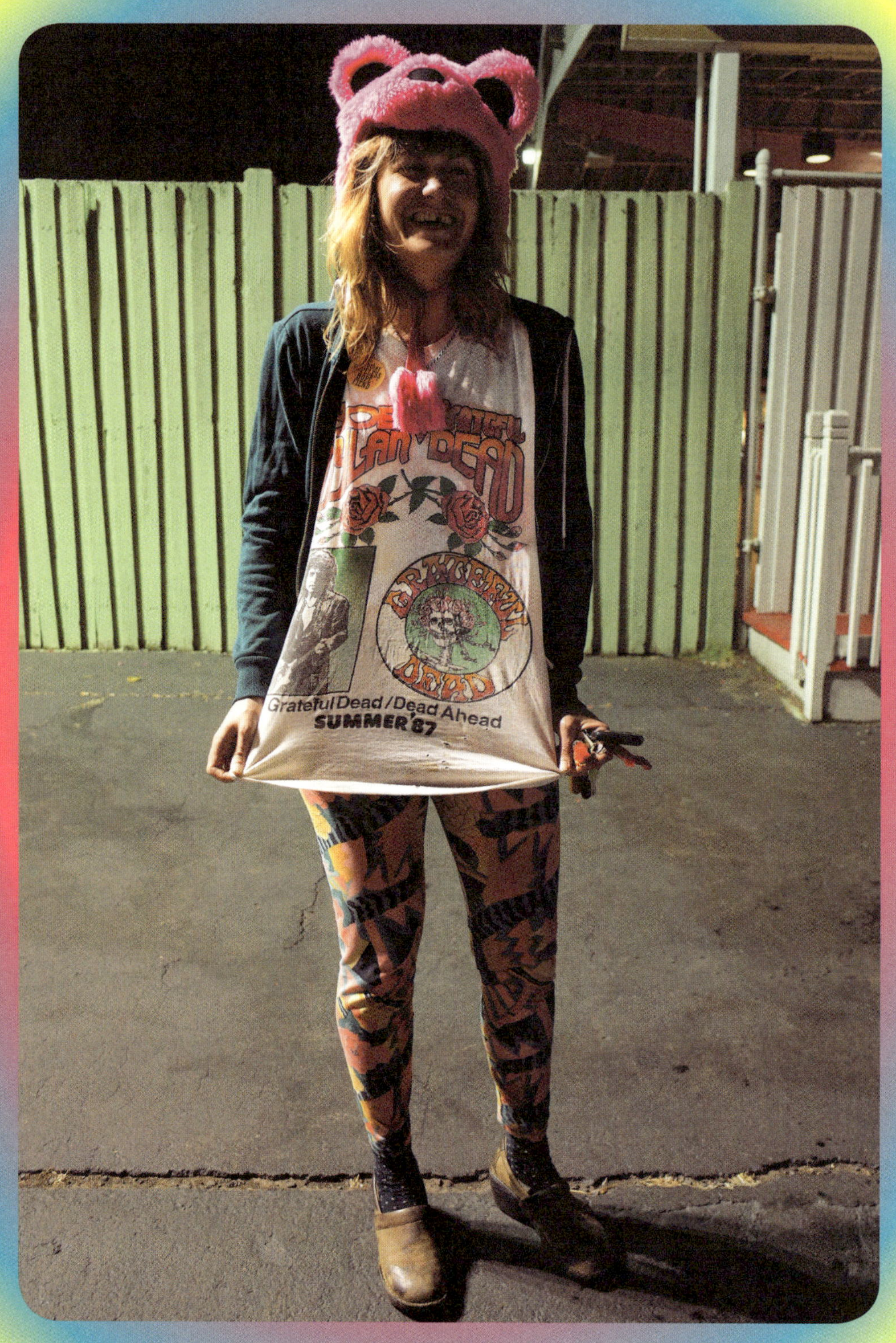
Grateful Dead / Dead Ahead
SUMMER '87

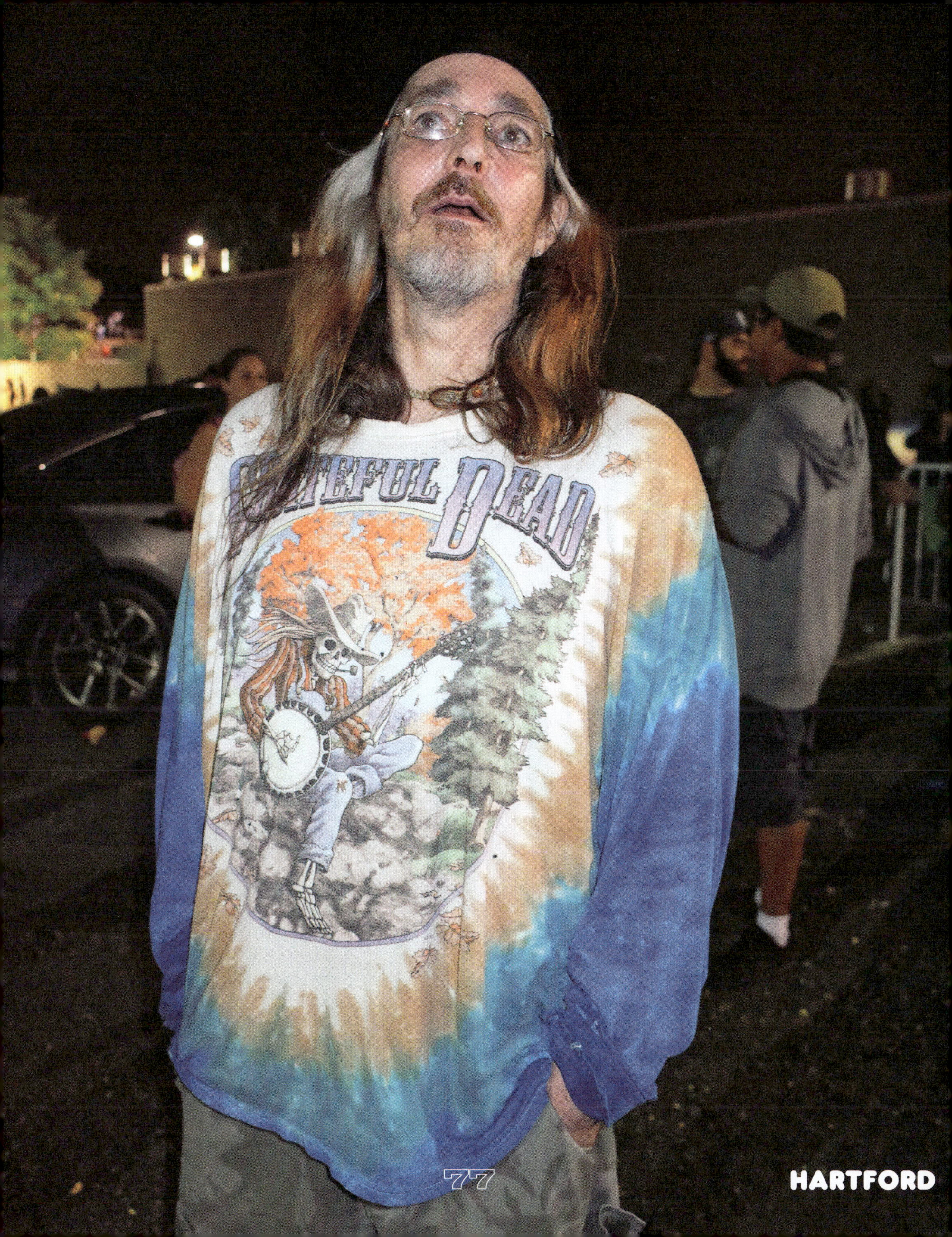

HARTFORD

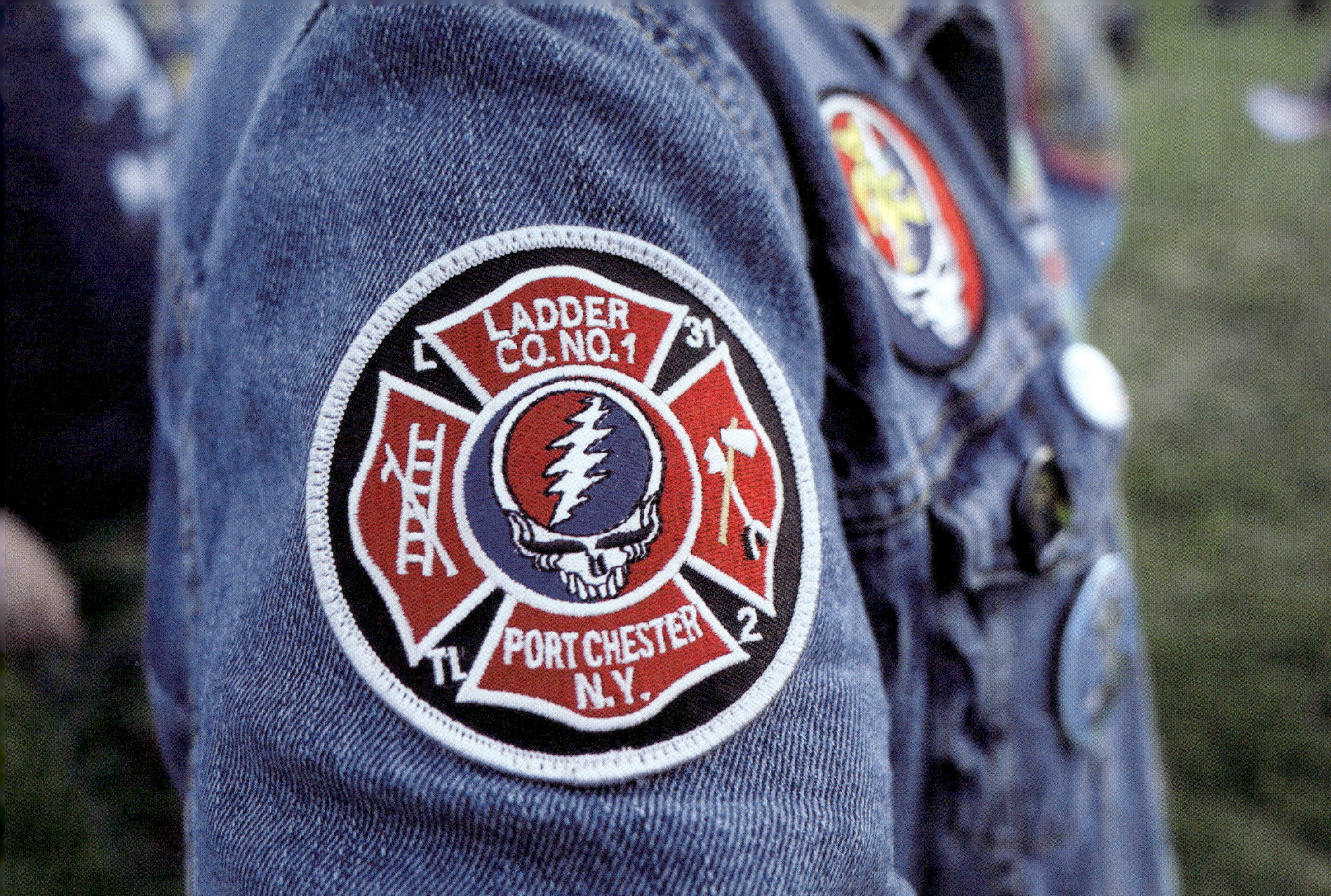
LADDER
CO. NO.1
31
2
TL
PORT CHESTER
N.Y.

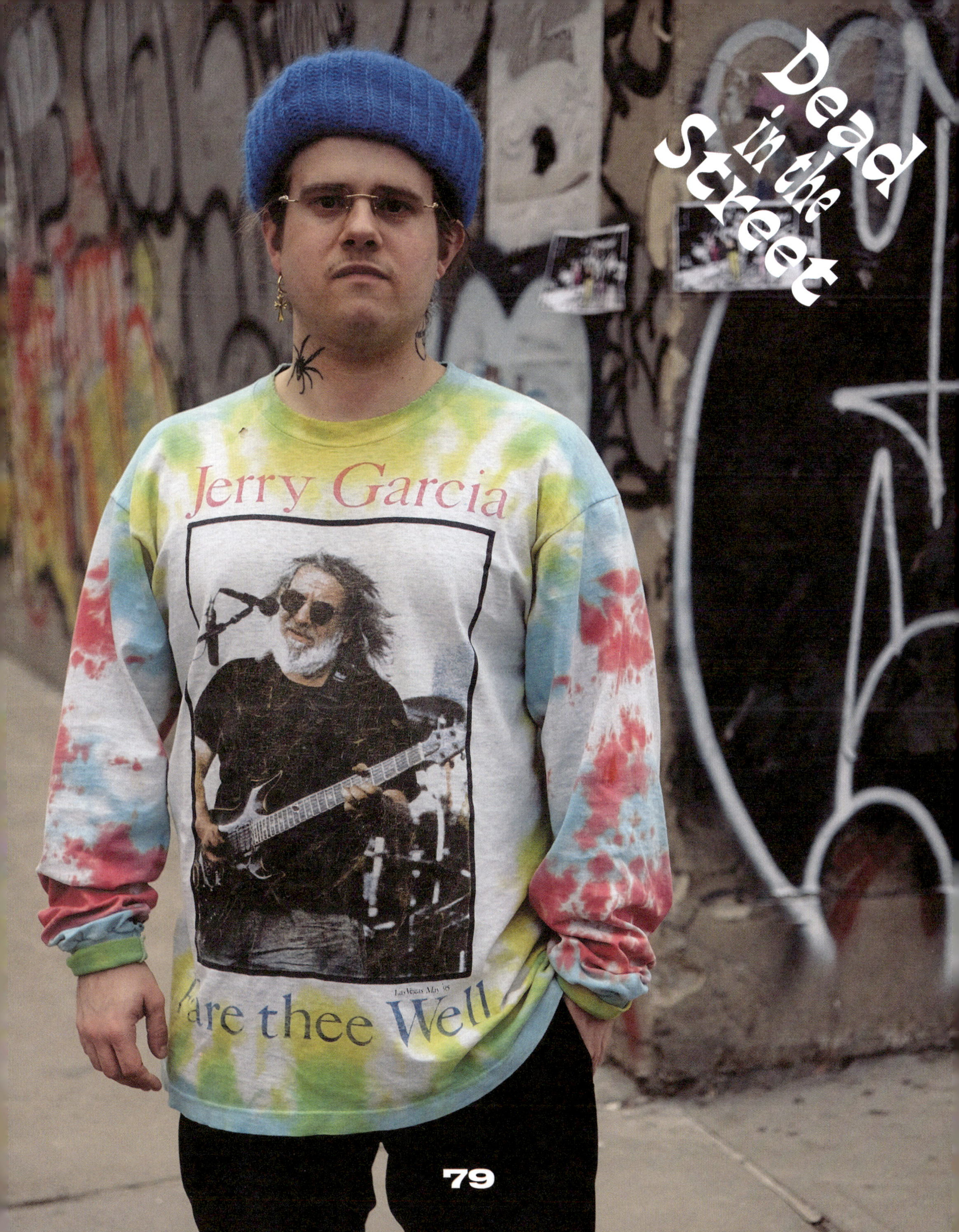
Dead in the Street
Jerry Garcia
Fare thee Well
Las Vegas May '95

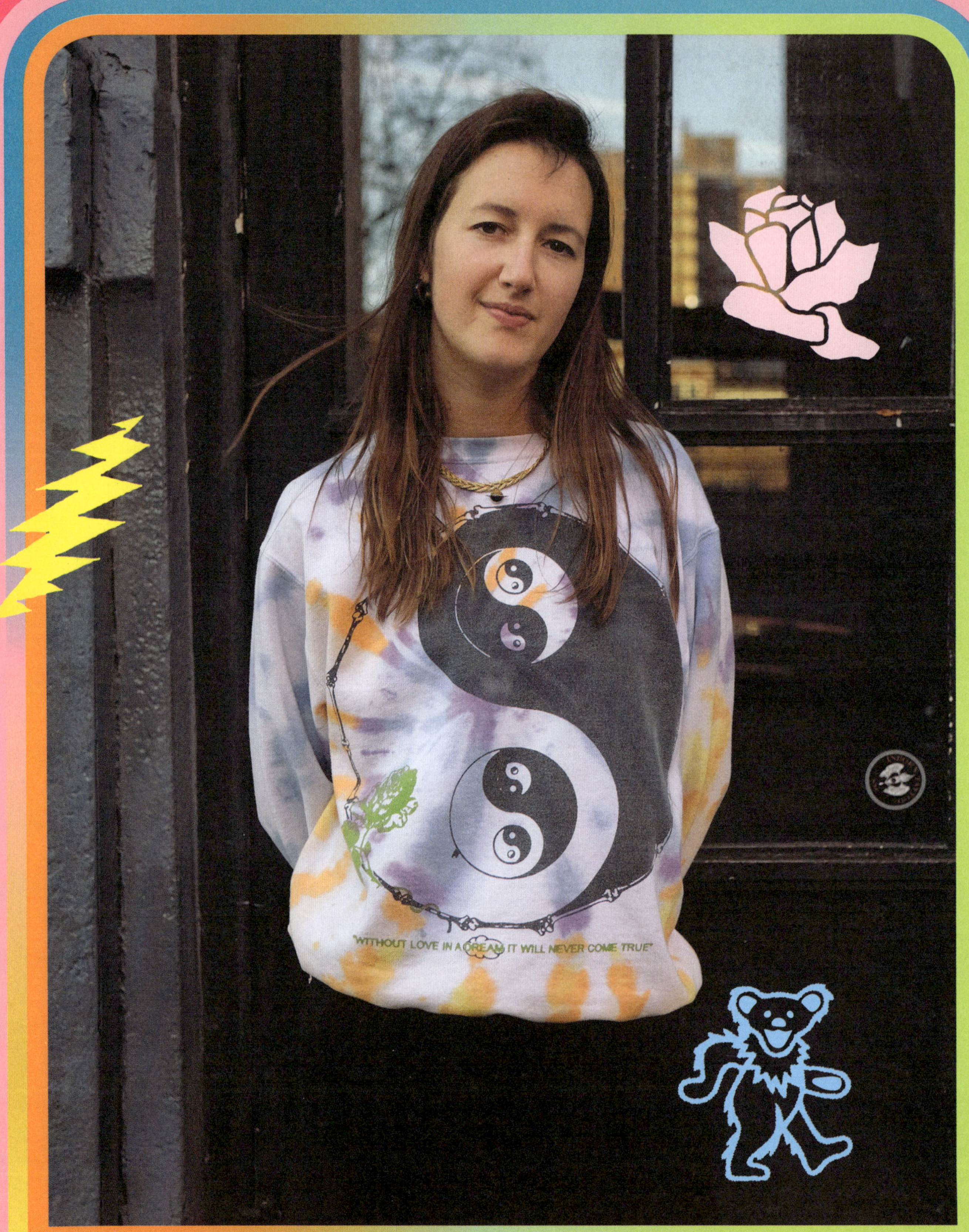
"WITHOUT LOVE IN A DREAM IT WILL NEVER COME TRUE"

Dead in the streets

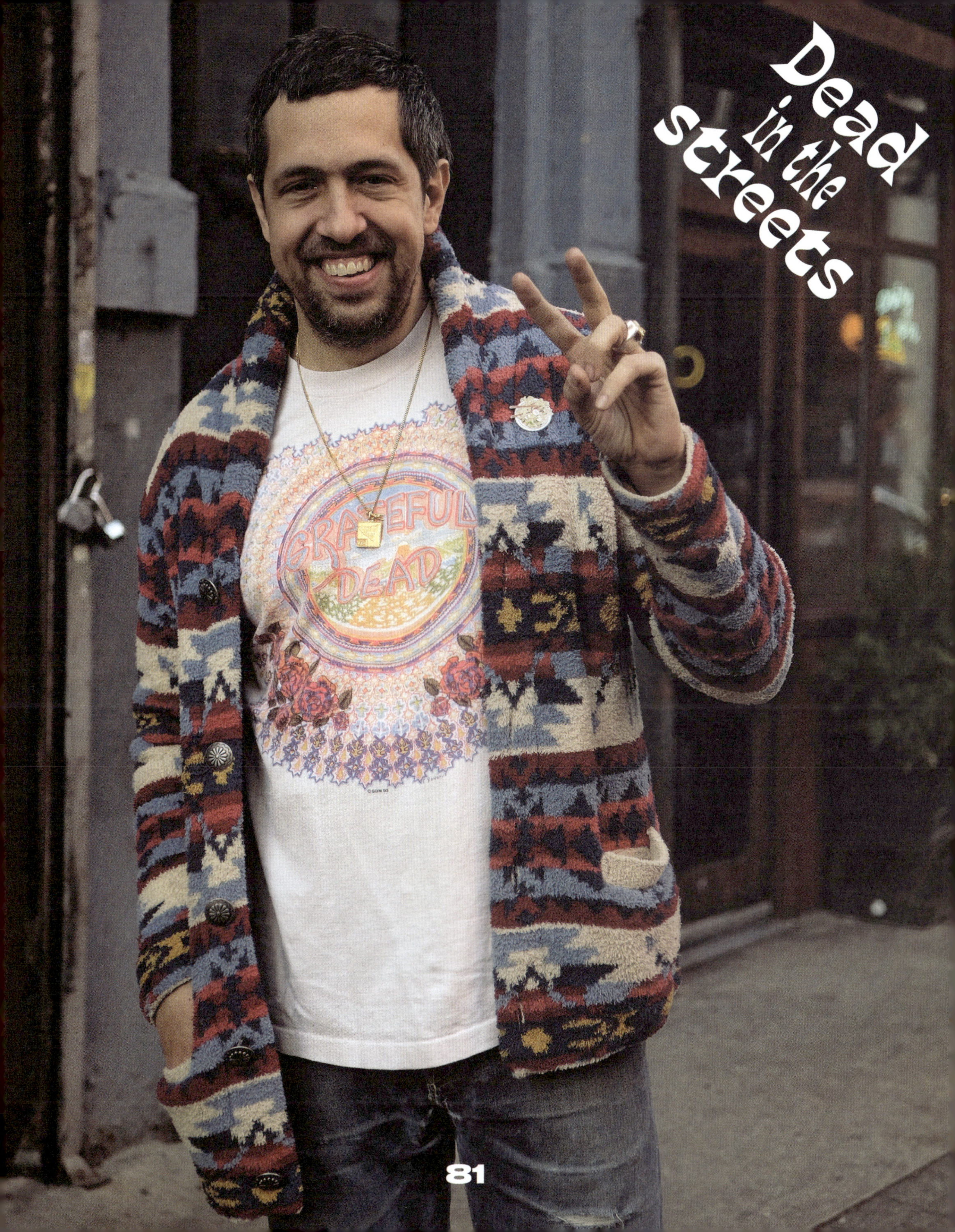

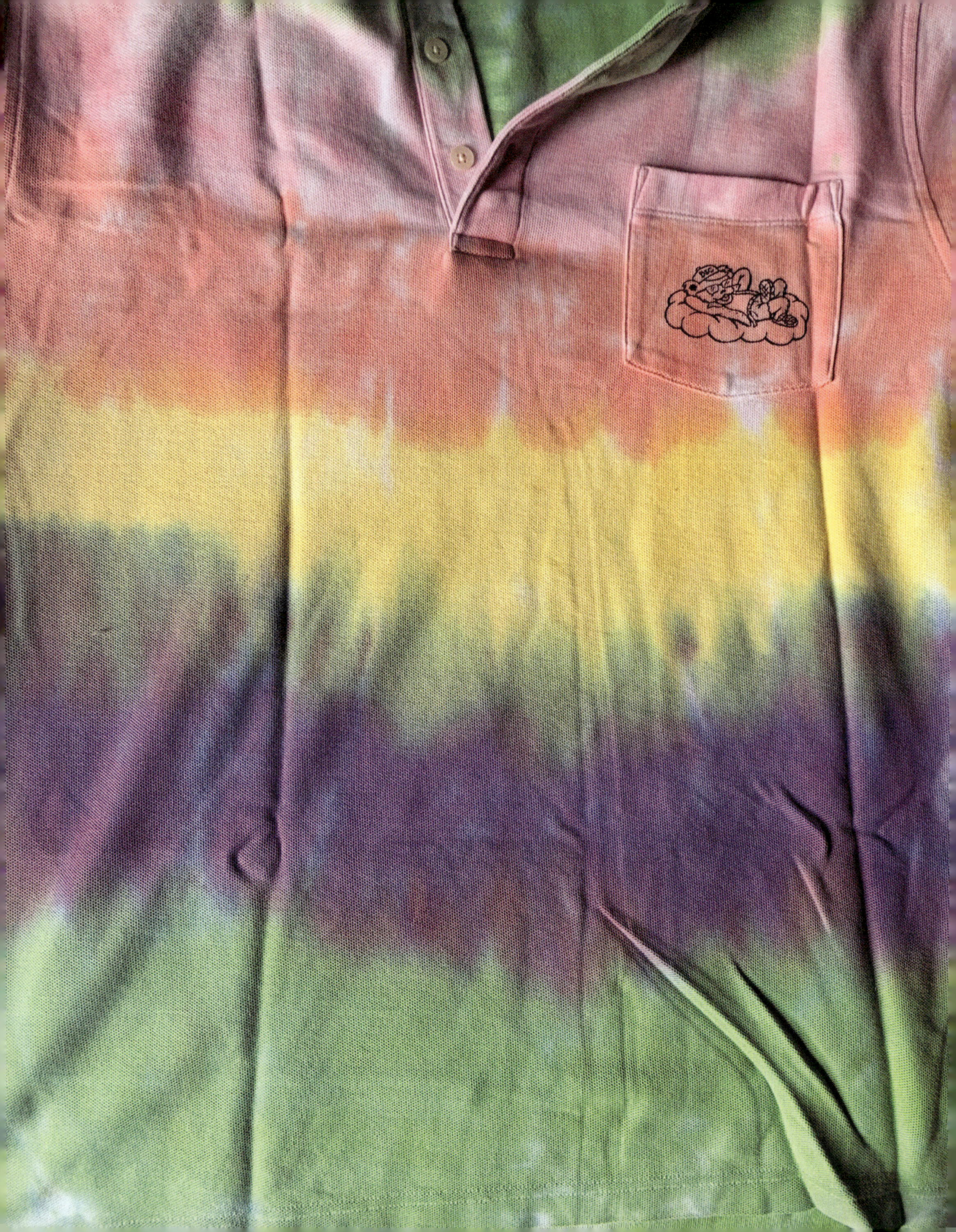

CITI FIELD

Flushing, New York

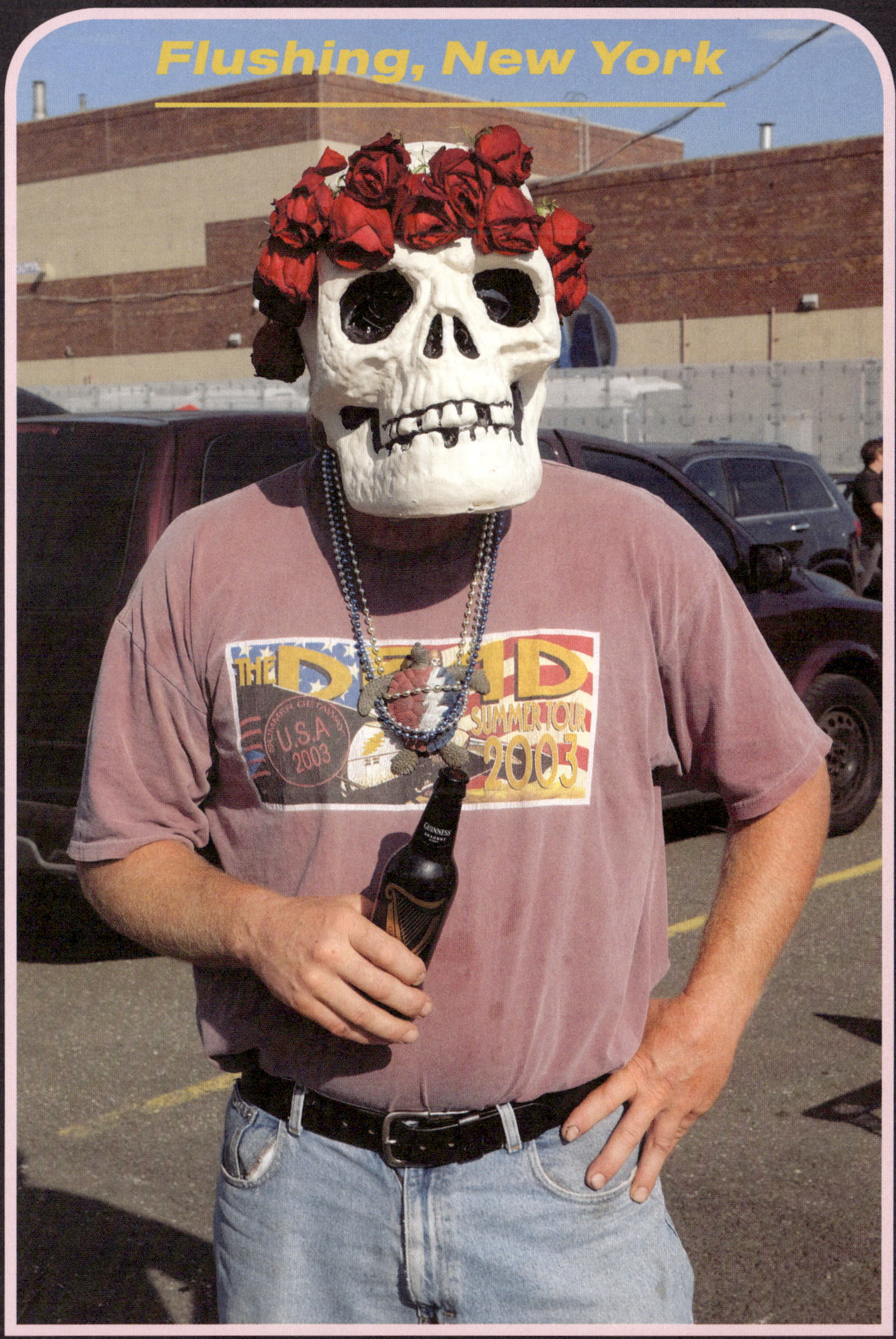

Friday, June 15th, 2018, &
Saturday, June 16th, 2018

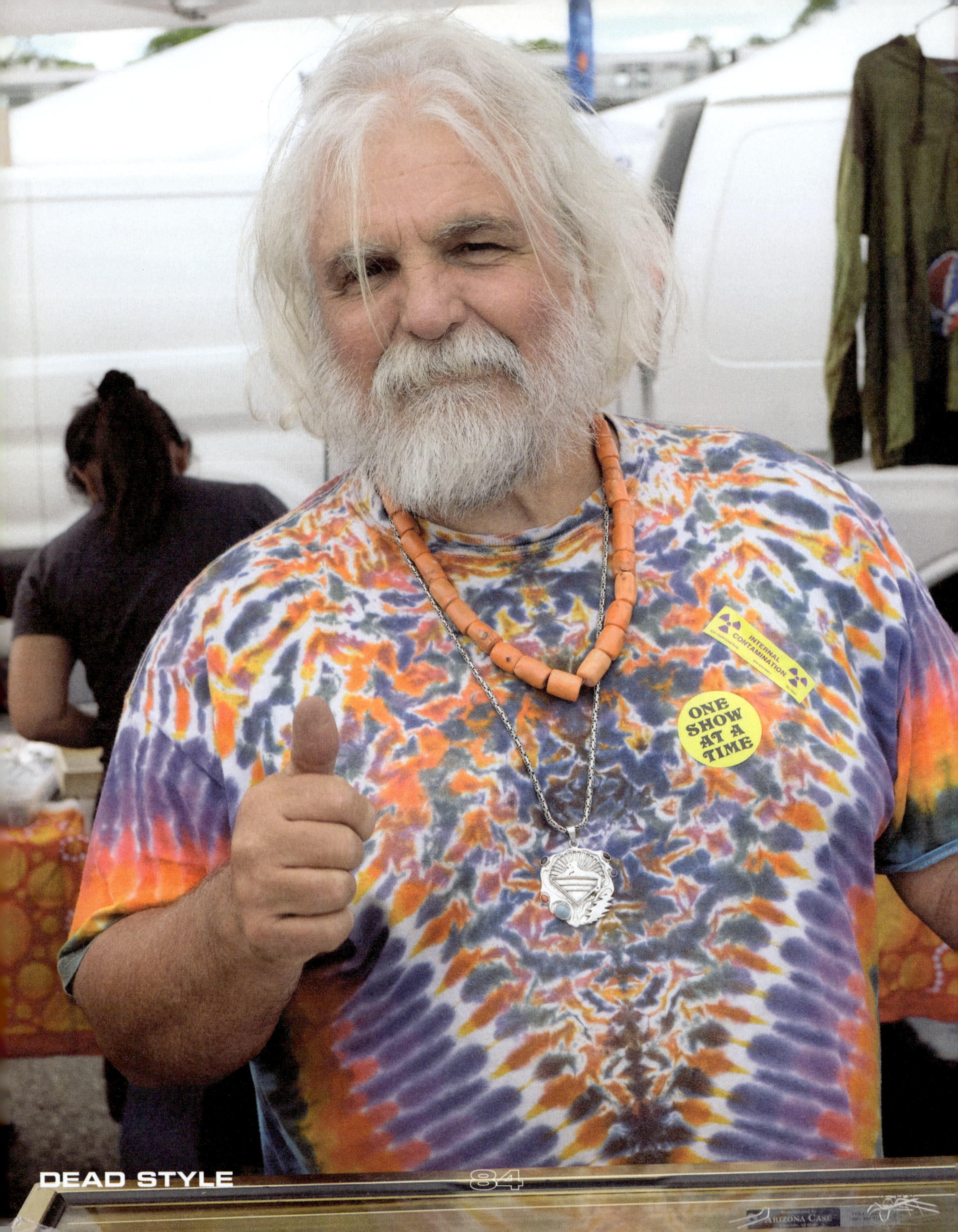
INTERNAL CONTAMINATION
ONE SHOW AT A TIME

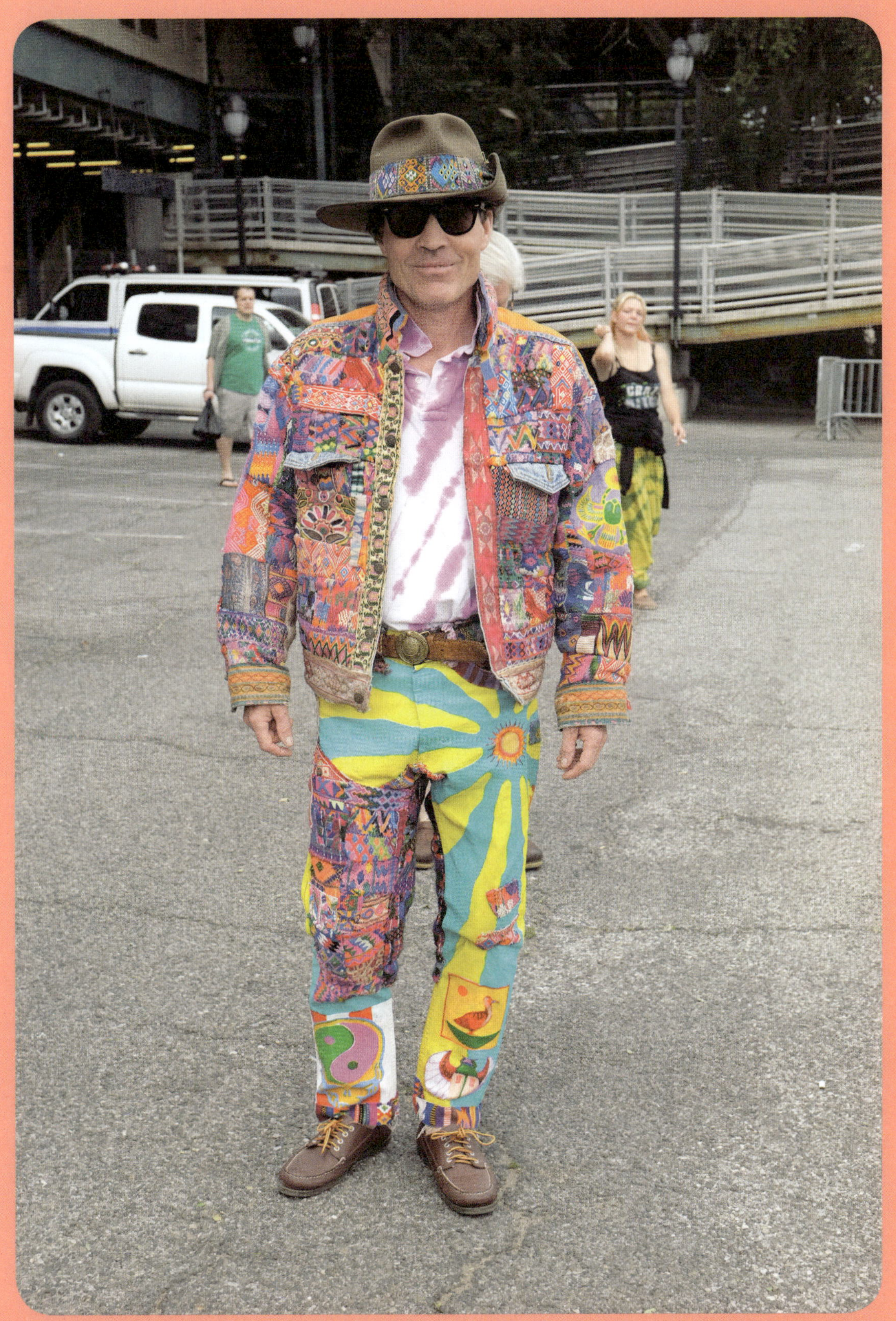

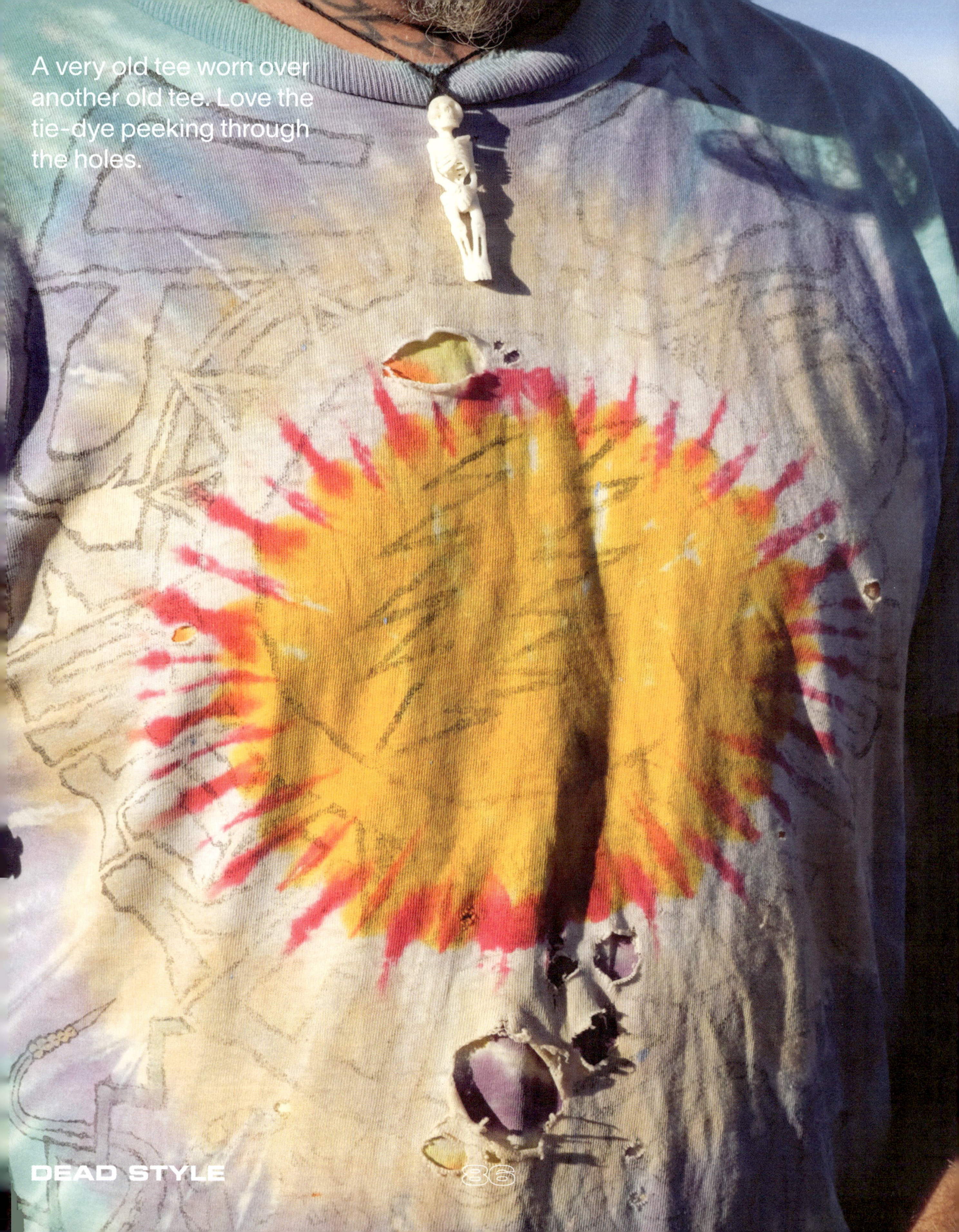

A very old tee worn over another old tee. Love the tie-dye peeking through the holes.

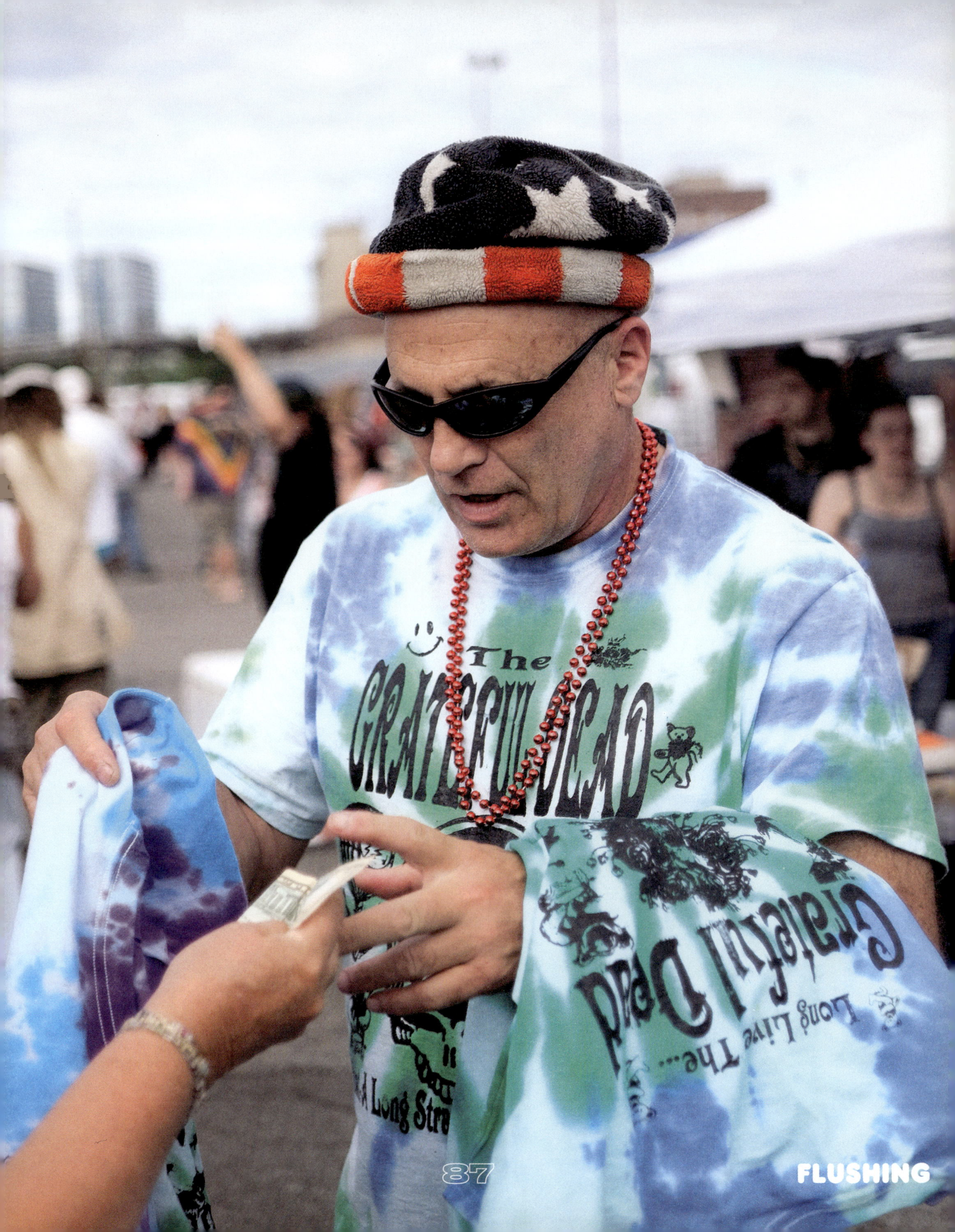
The
Grateful Dead
Long Live The....

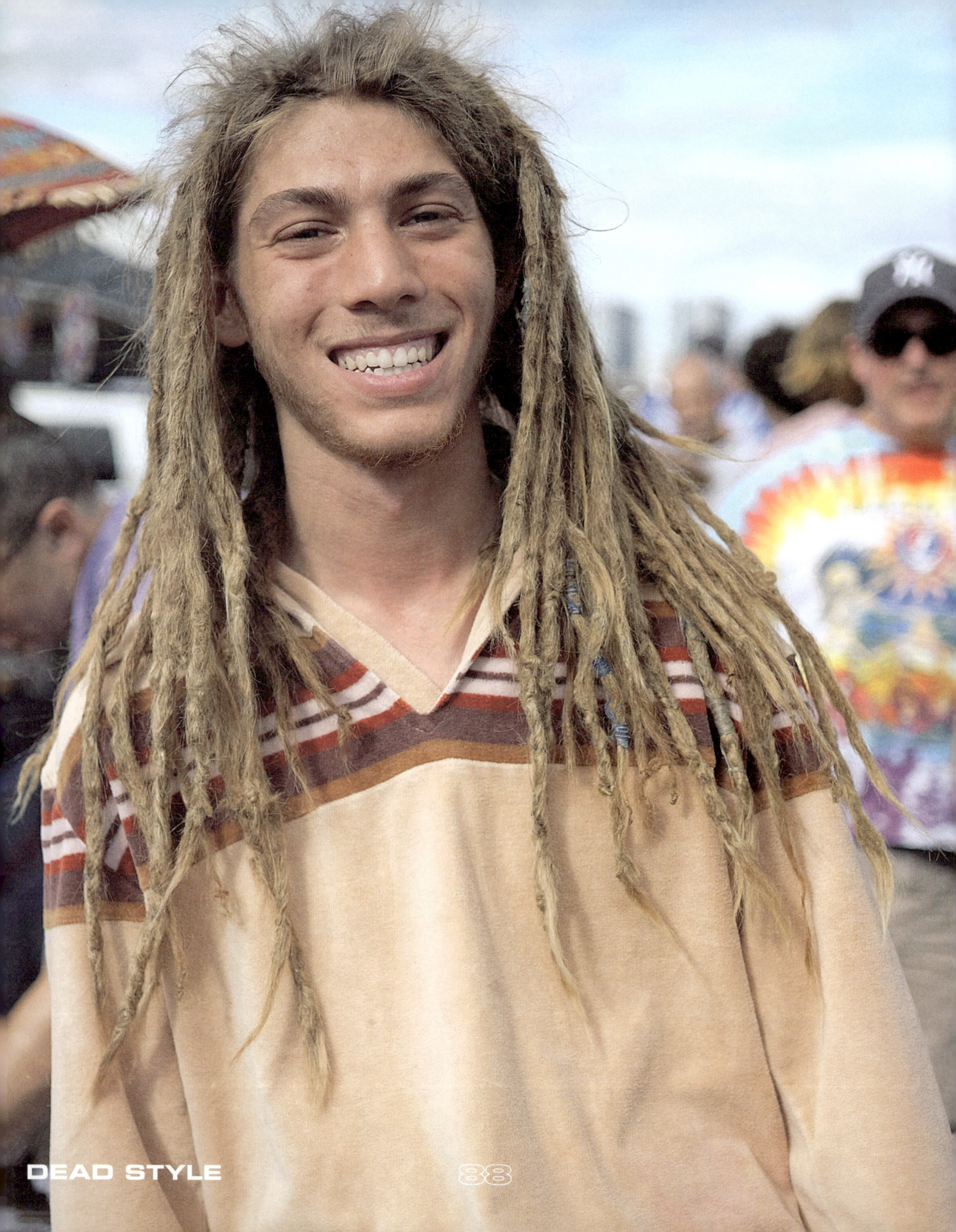

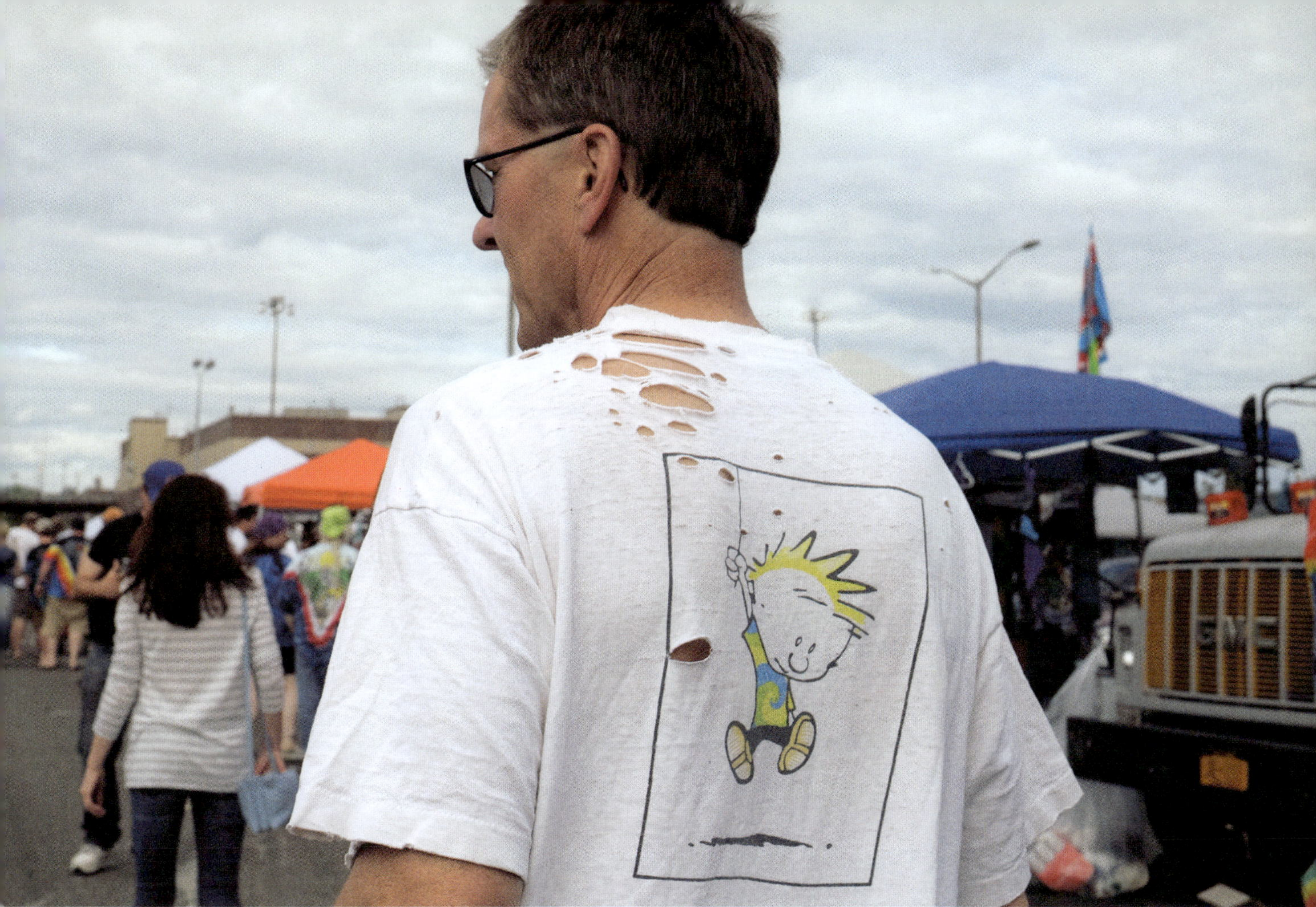
GMC

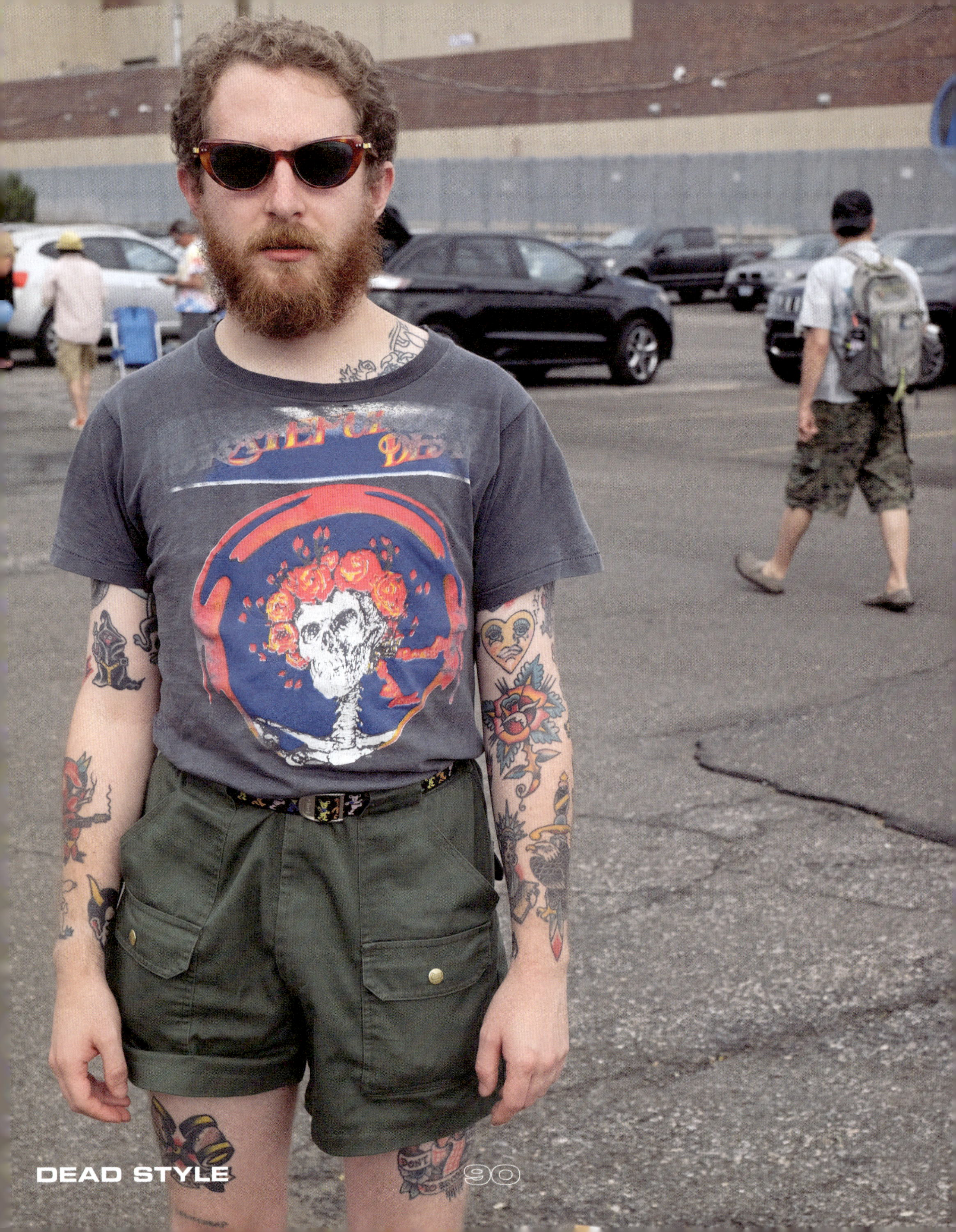

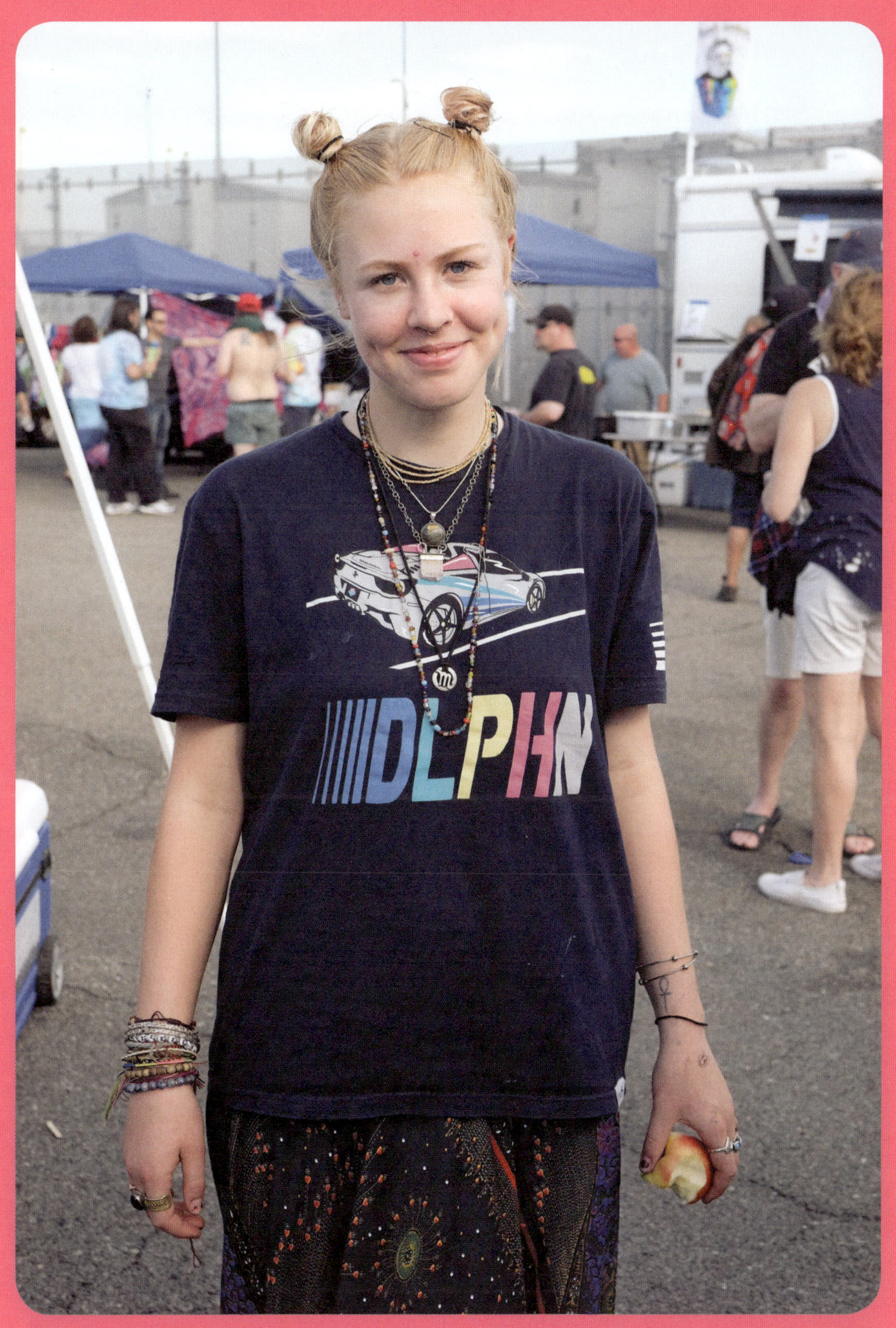
DLPHN

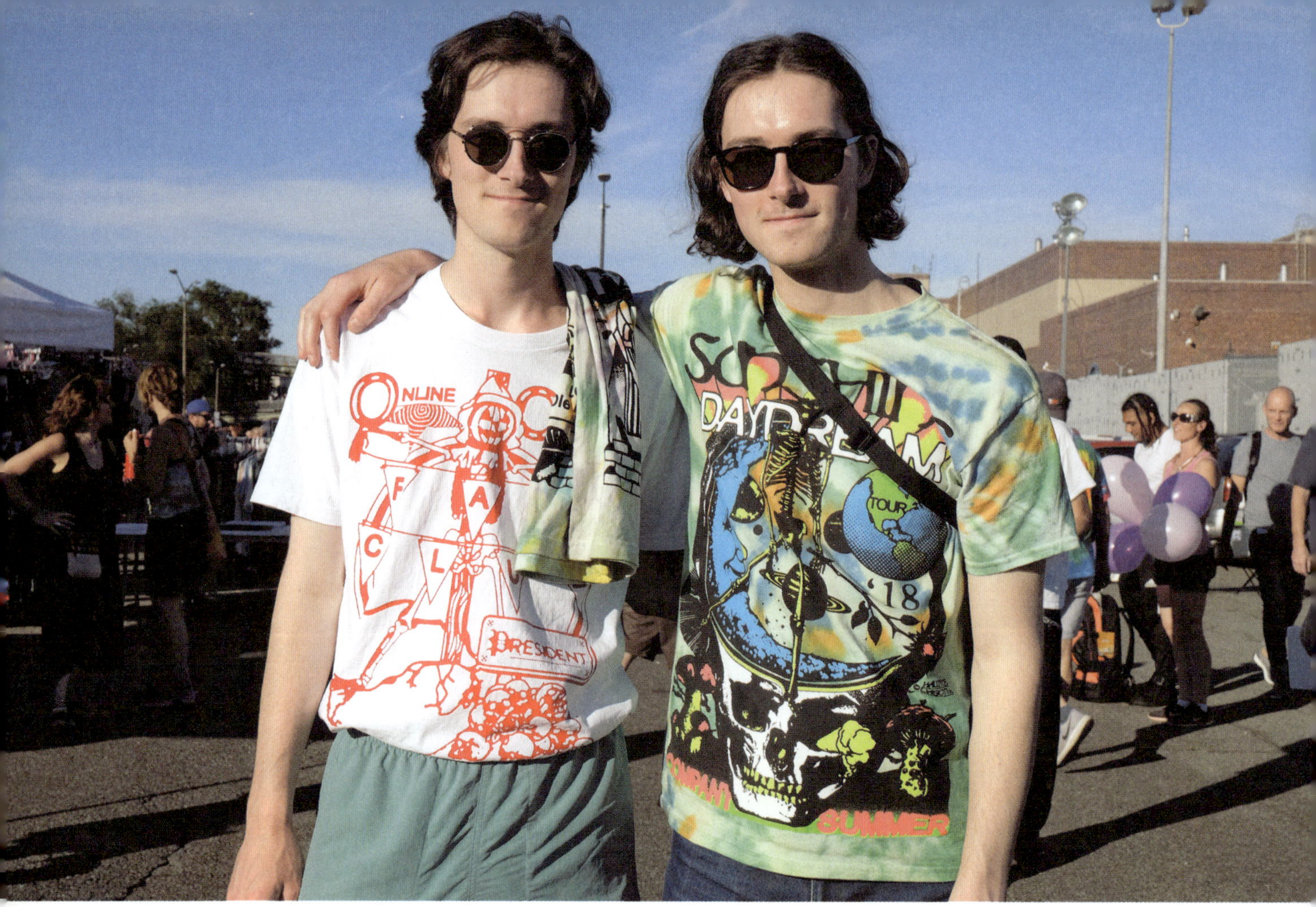

SEASON FOR TWINNING

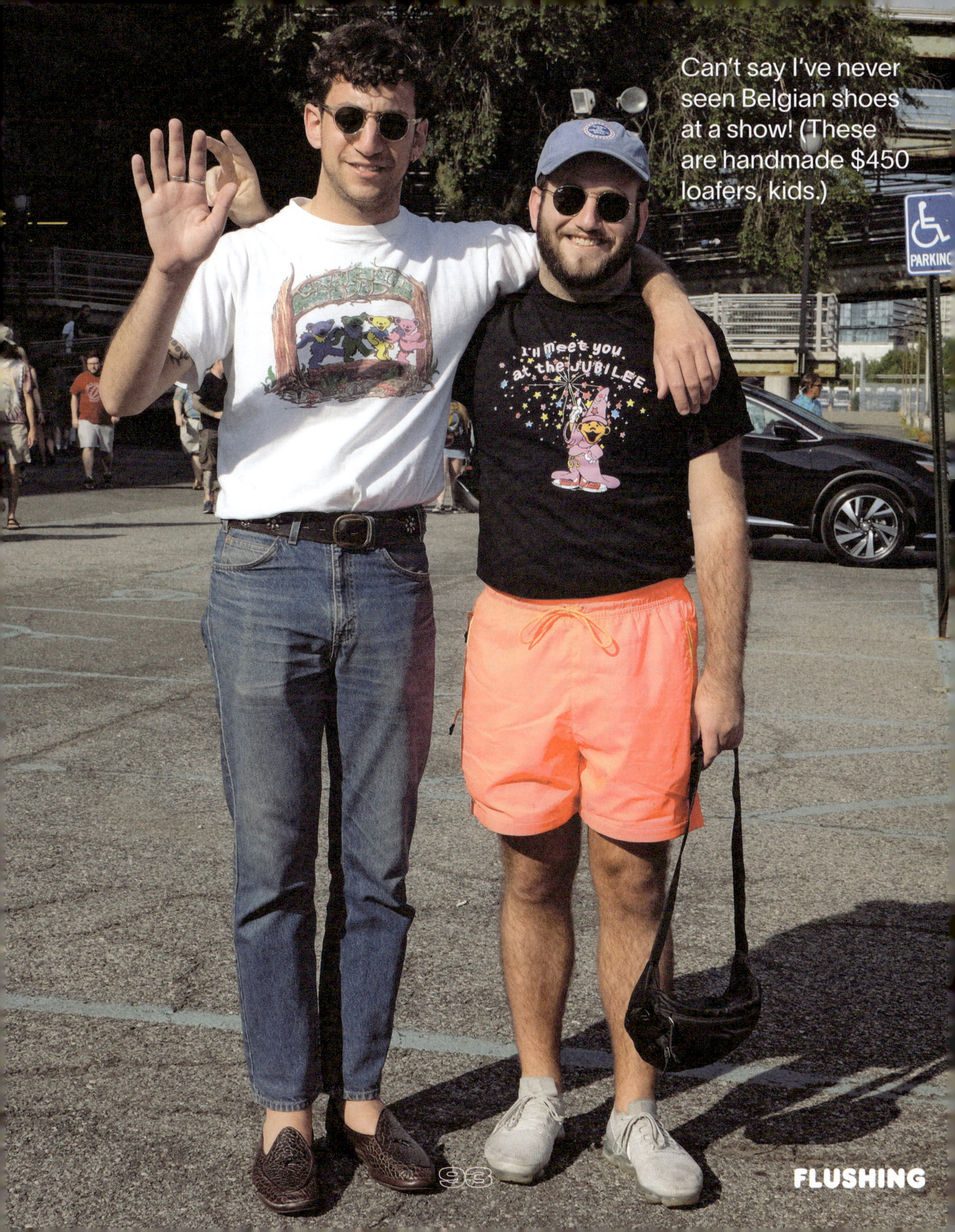

Can't say I've never seen Belgian shoes at a show! (These are handmade $450 loafers, kids.)

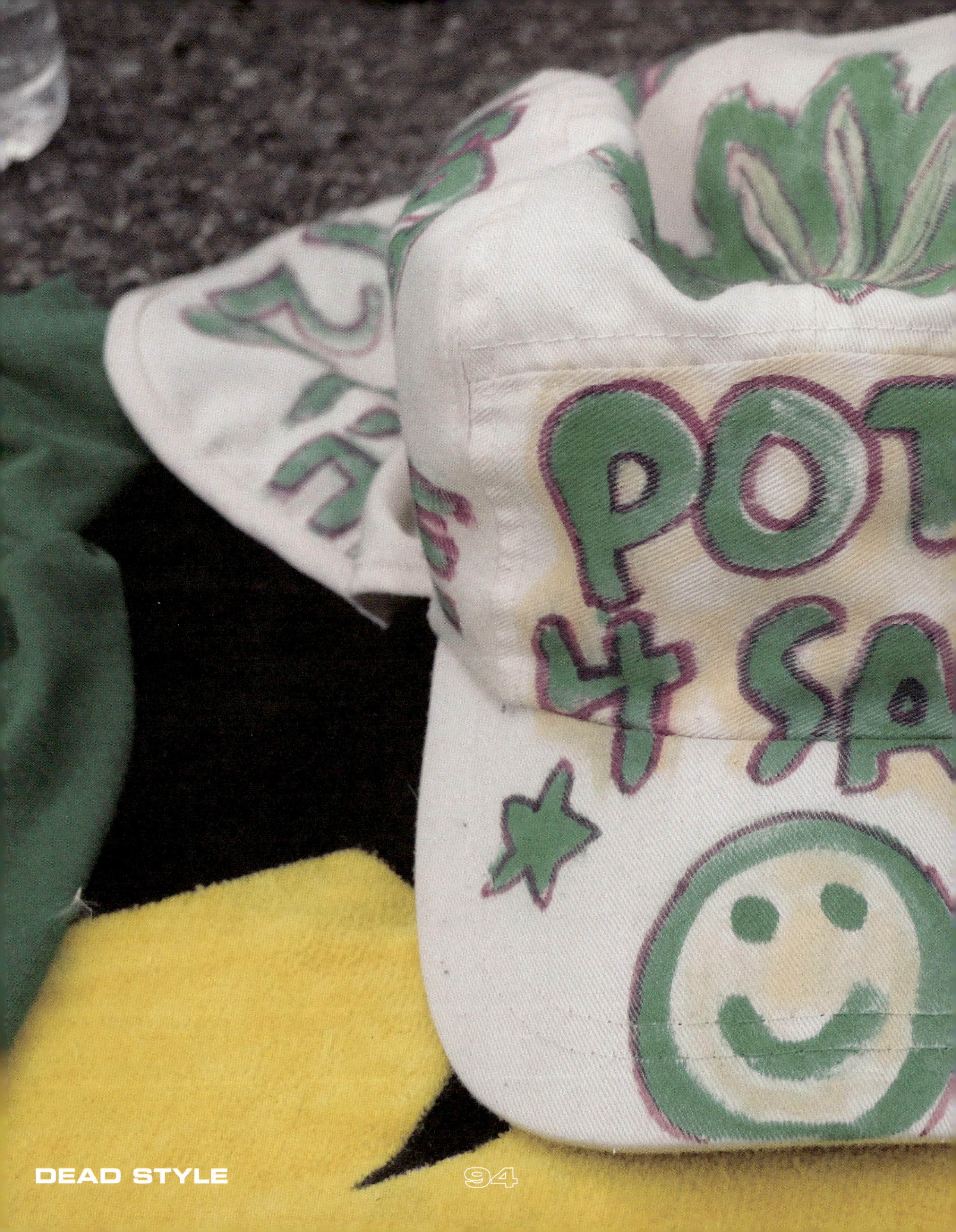

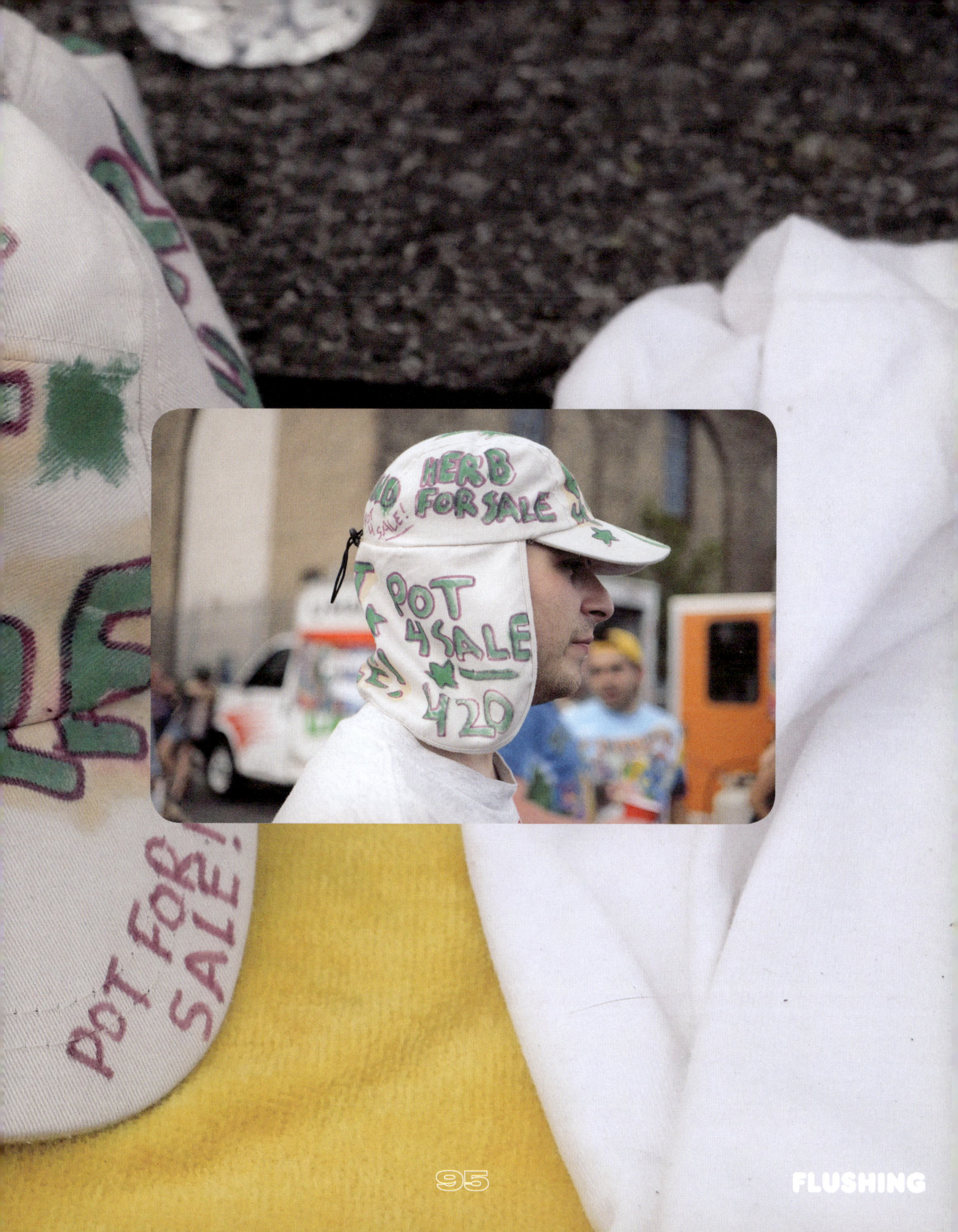
HERB
FOR SALE
POT
4 SALE!
POT
4SALE
420
POT FOR
SALE!

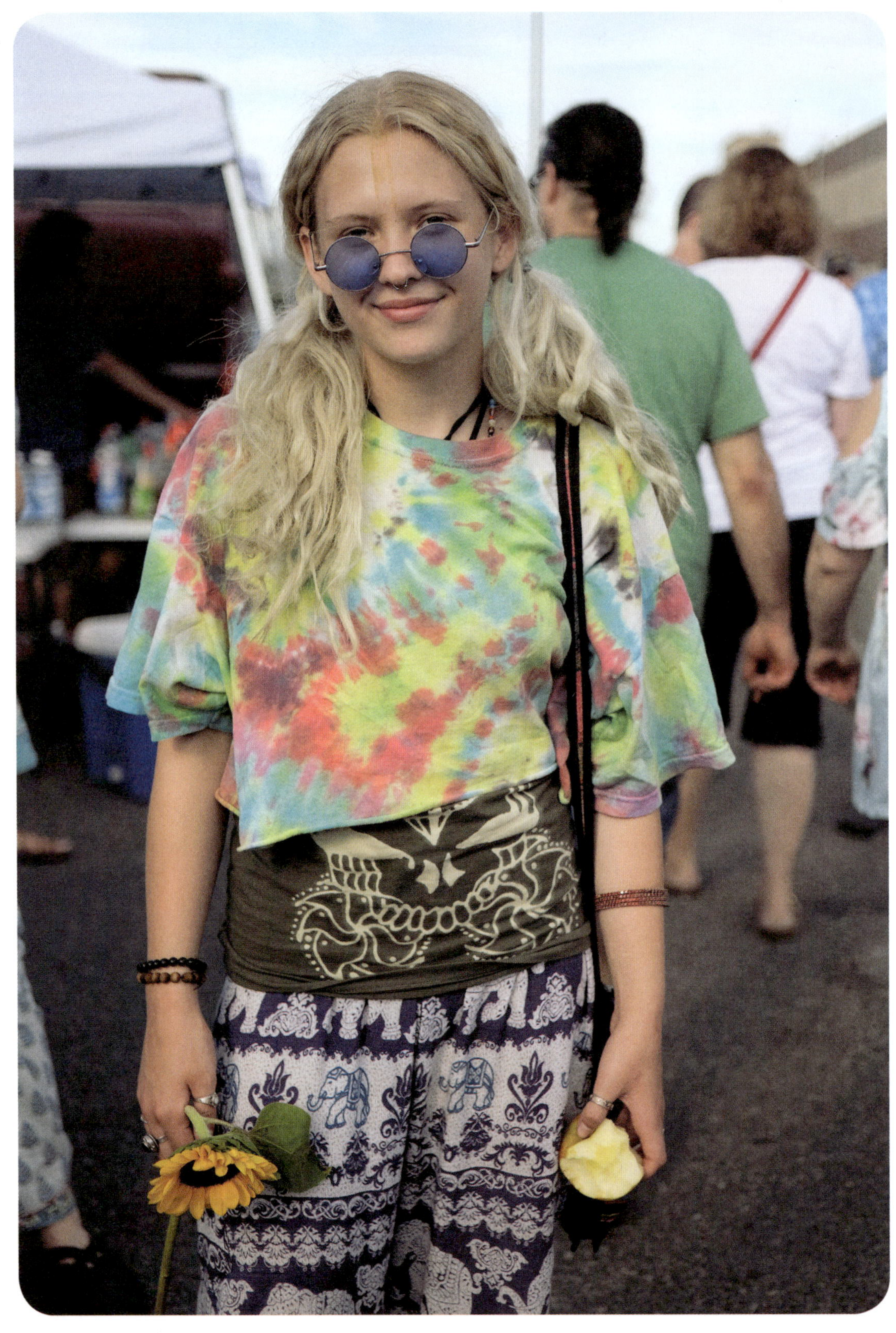

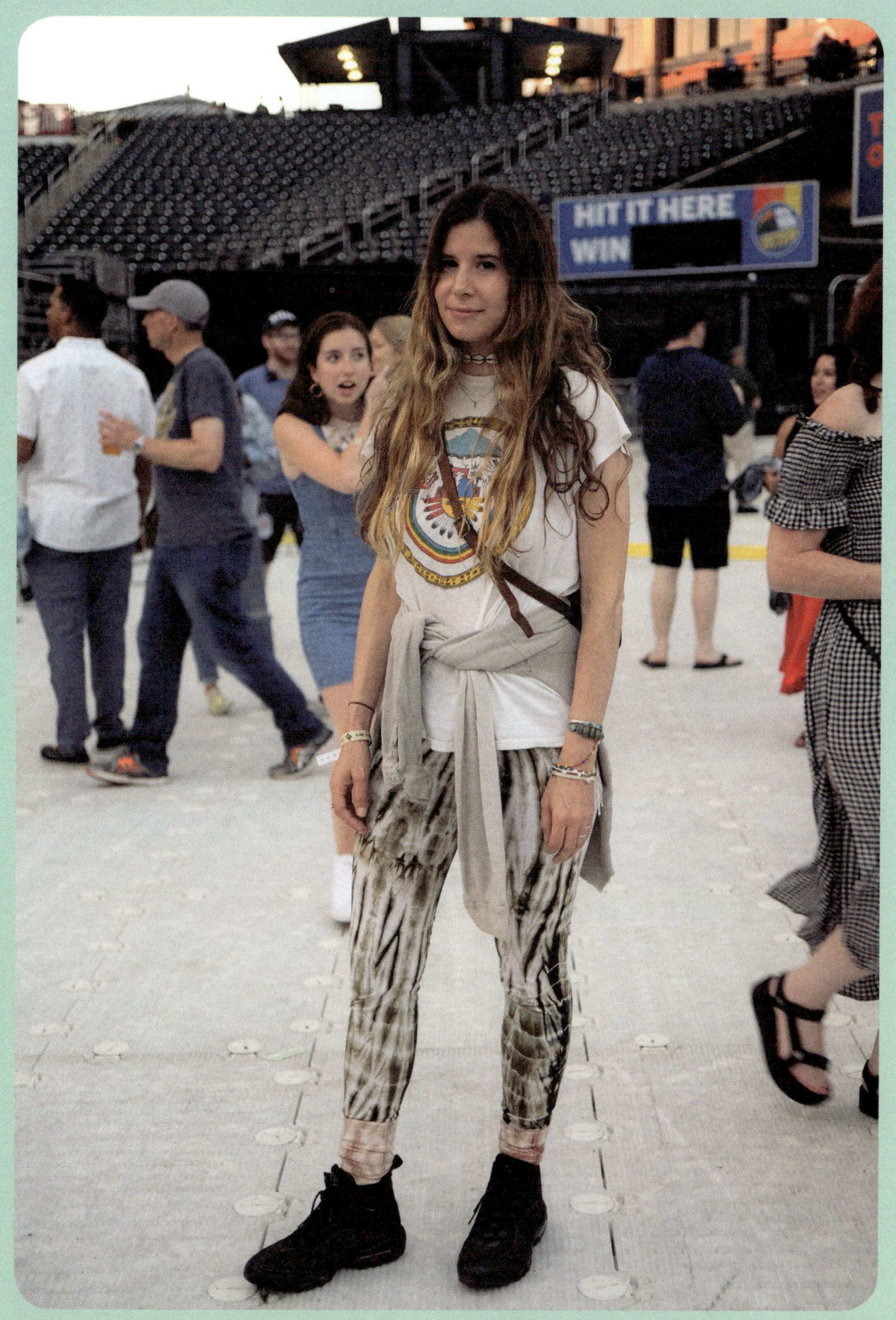
HIT IT HERE
WIN

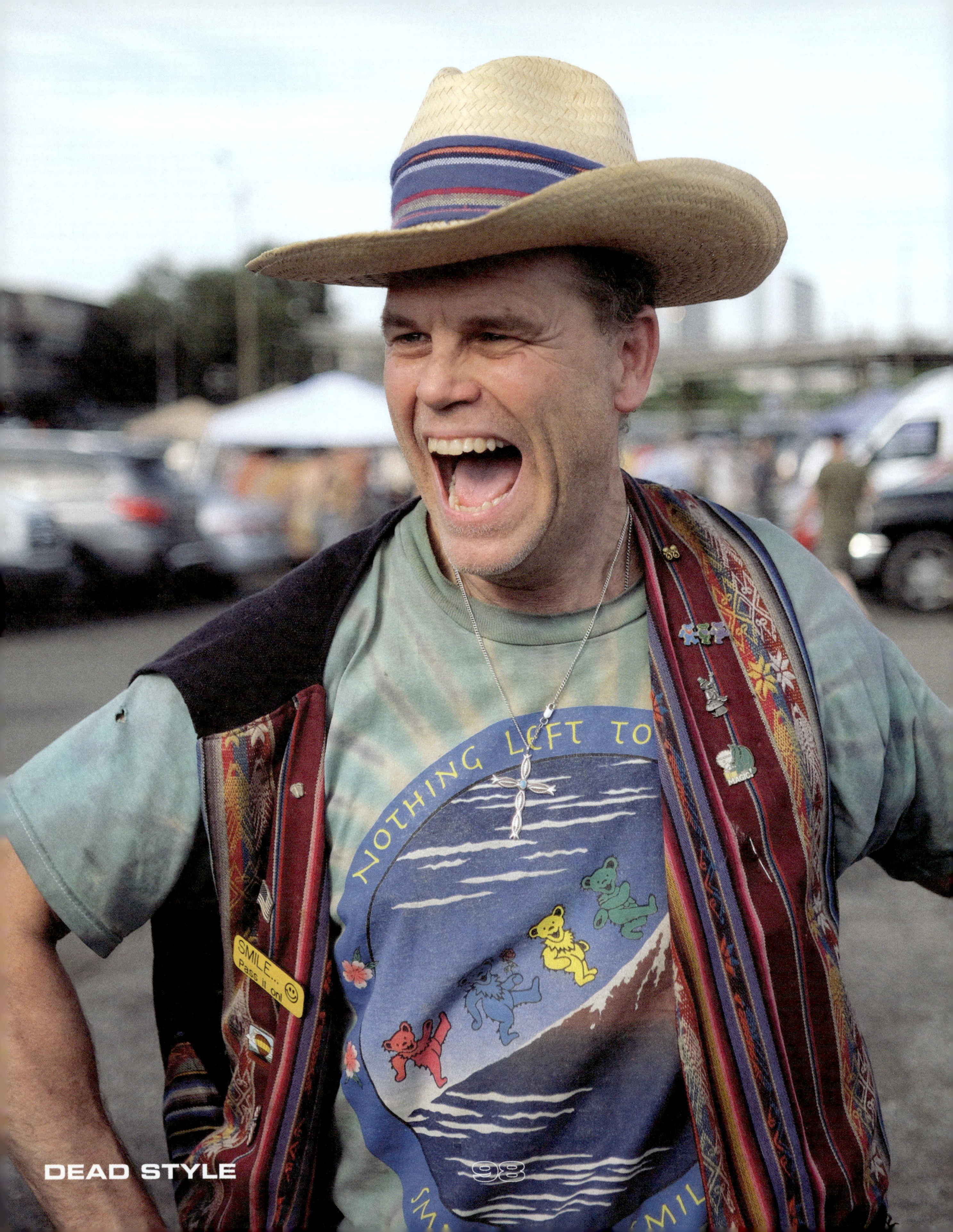
NOTHING LEFT TO
SMILE...
Pass it on!

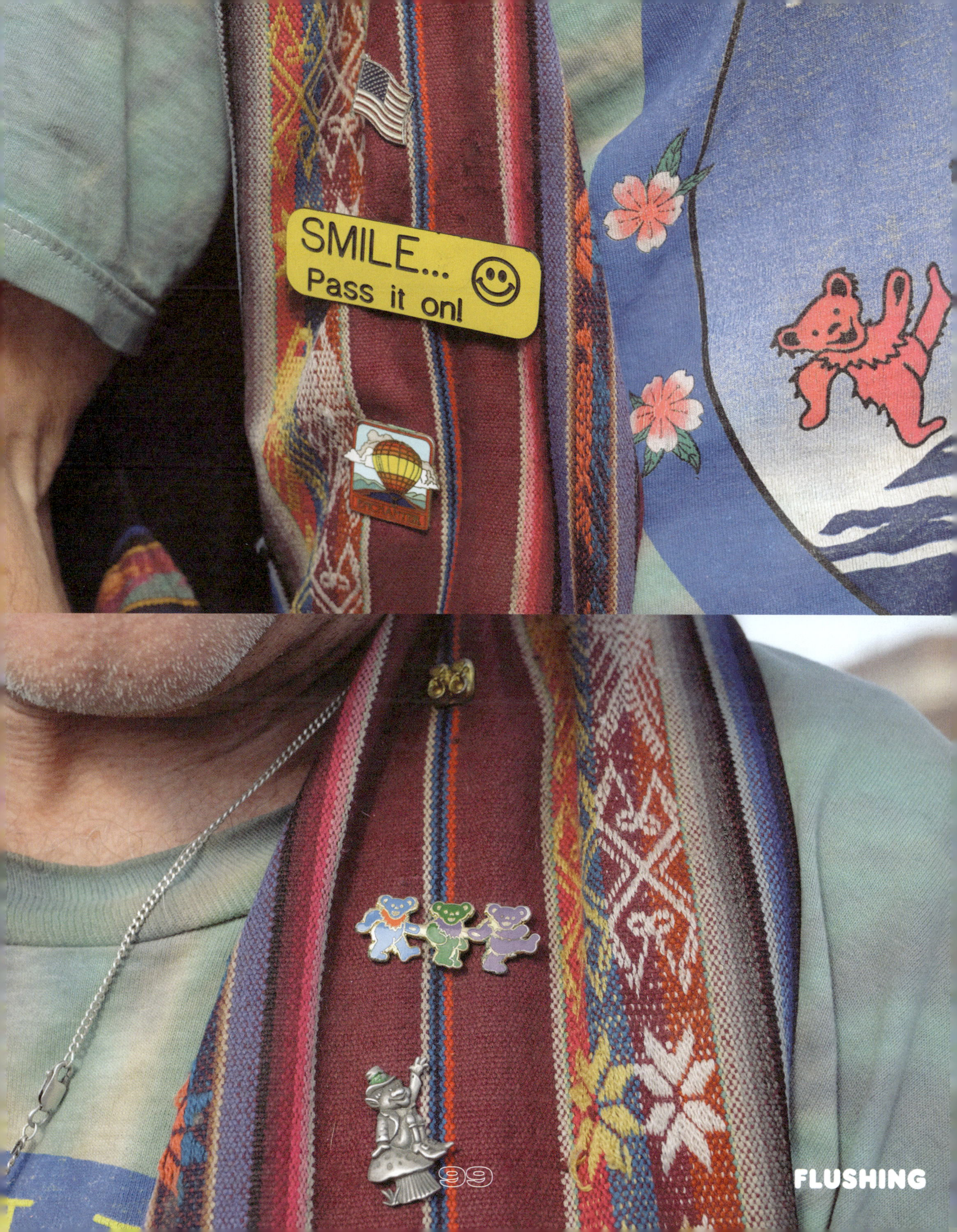
SMILE...
Pass it on!

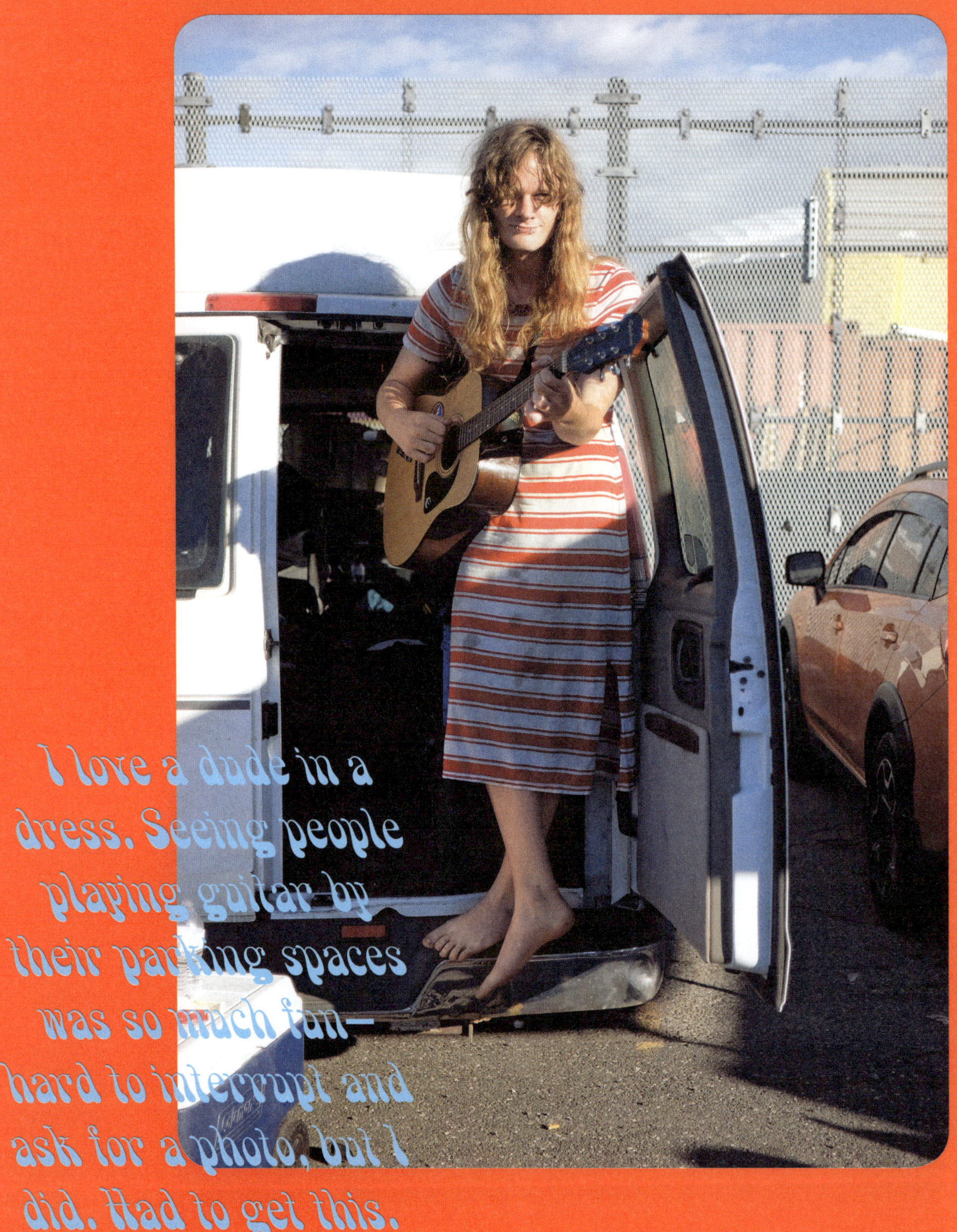

I love a dude in a dress. Seeing people playing guitar by their parking spaces was so much fun—hard to interrupt and ask for a photo, but I did. Had to get this.

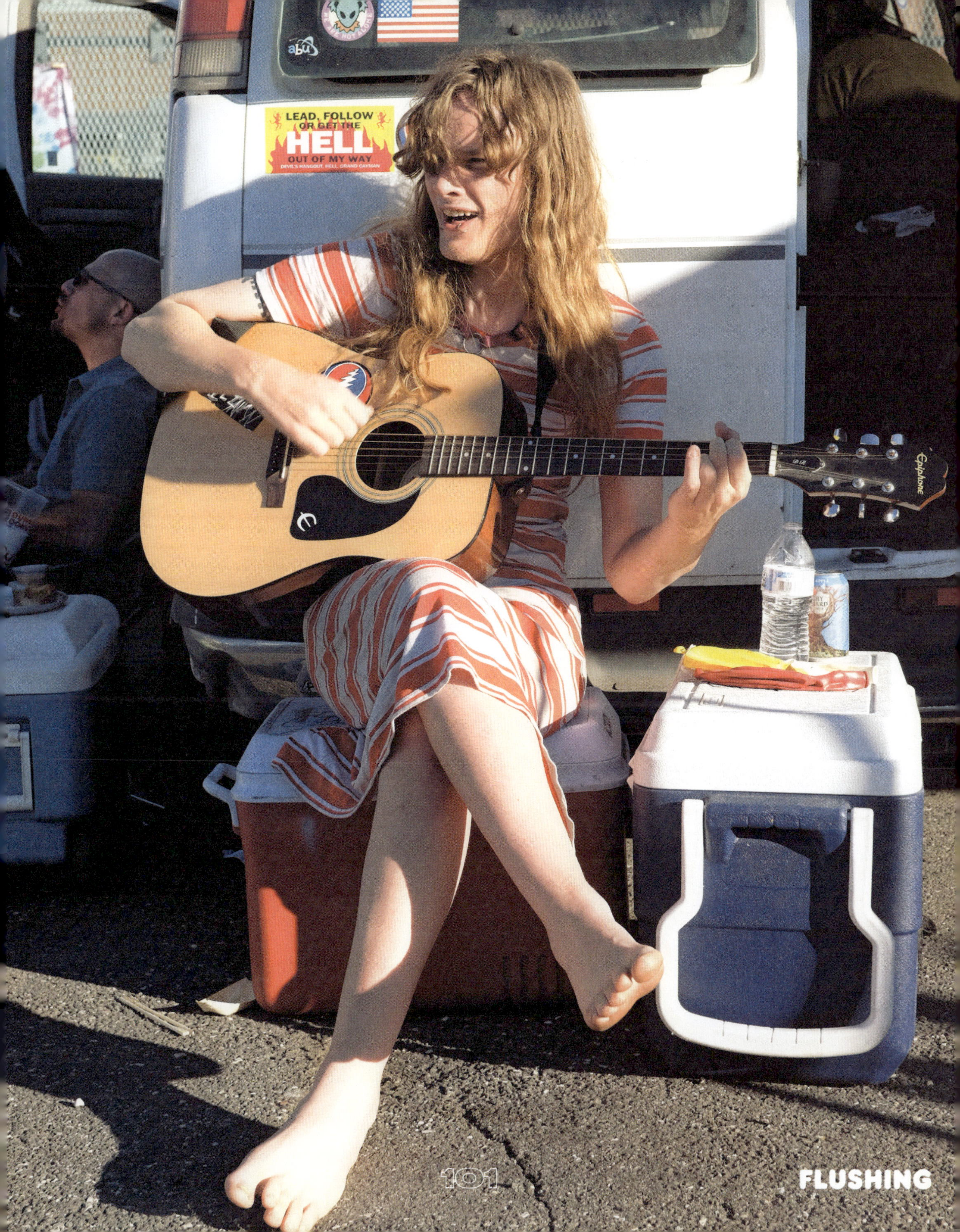
LEAD, FOLLOW
OR GET THE
HELL
OUT OF MY WAY

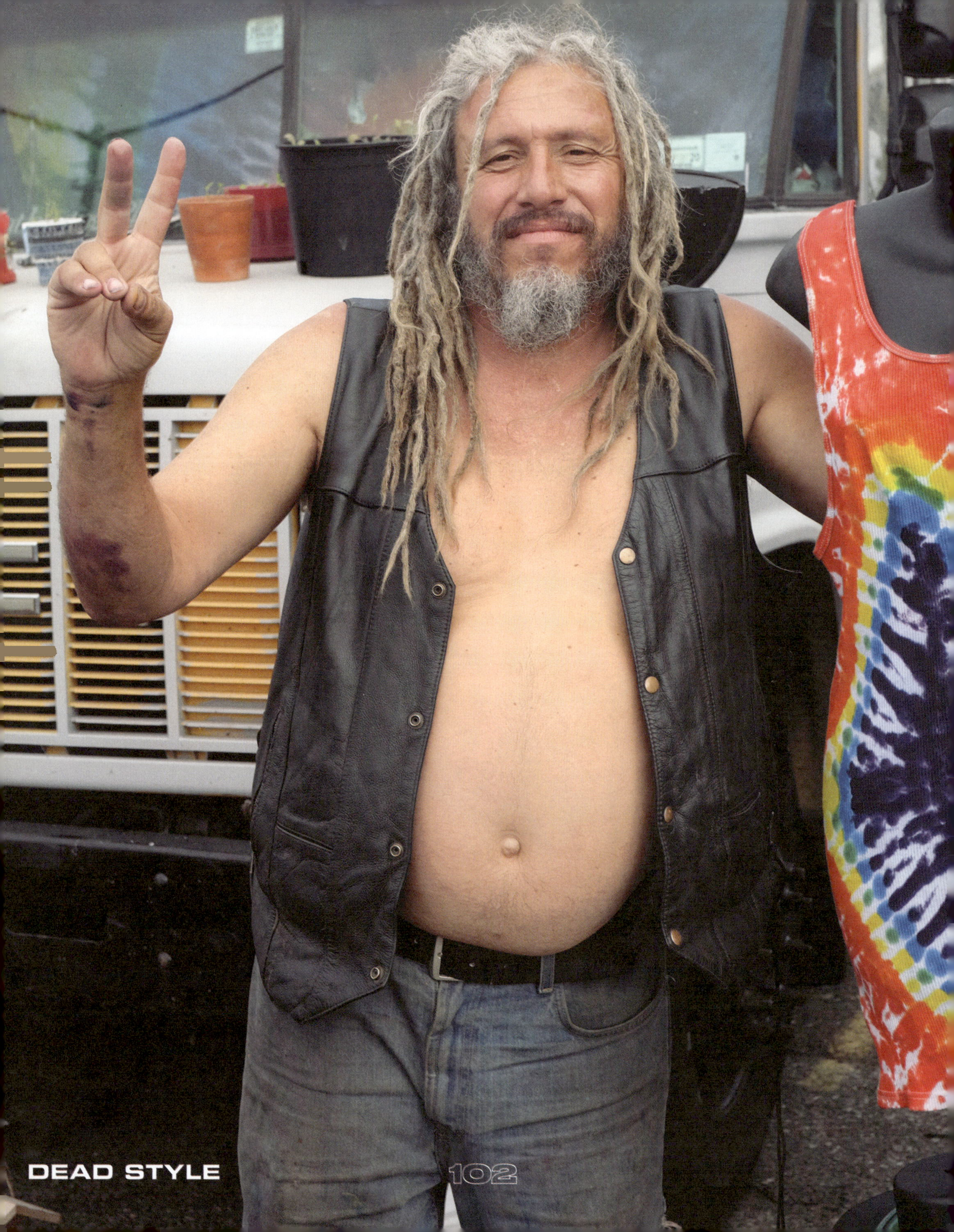

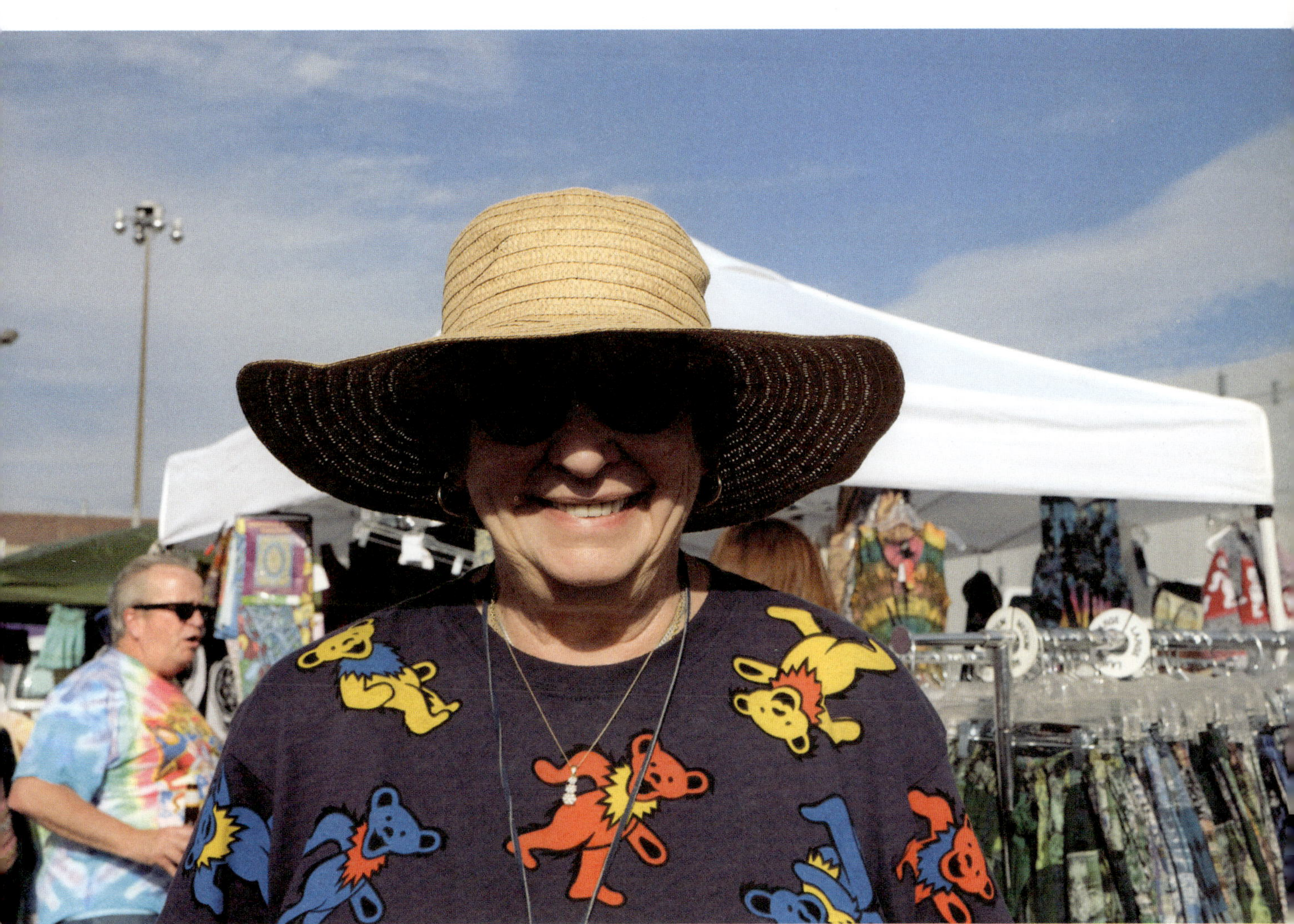

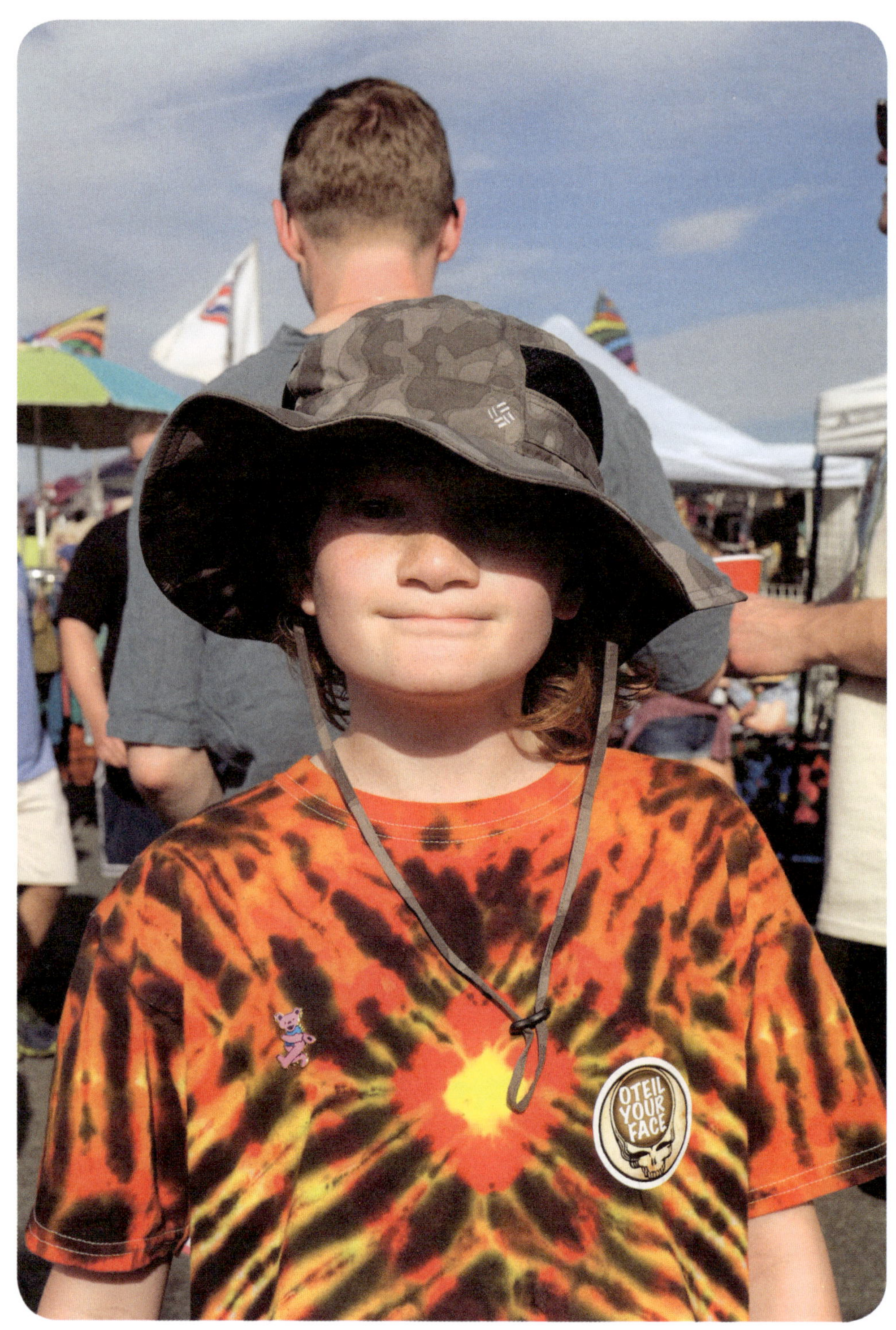
OTEIL
YOUR
FACE

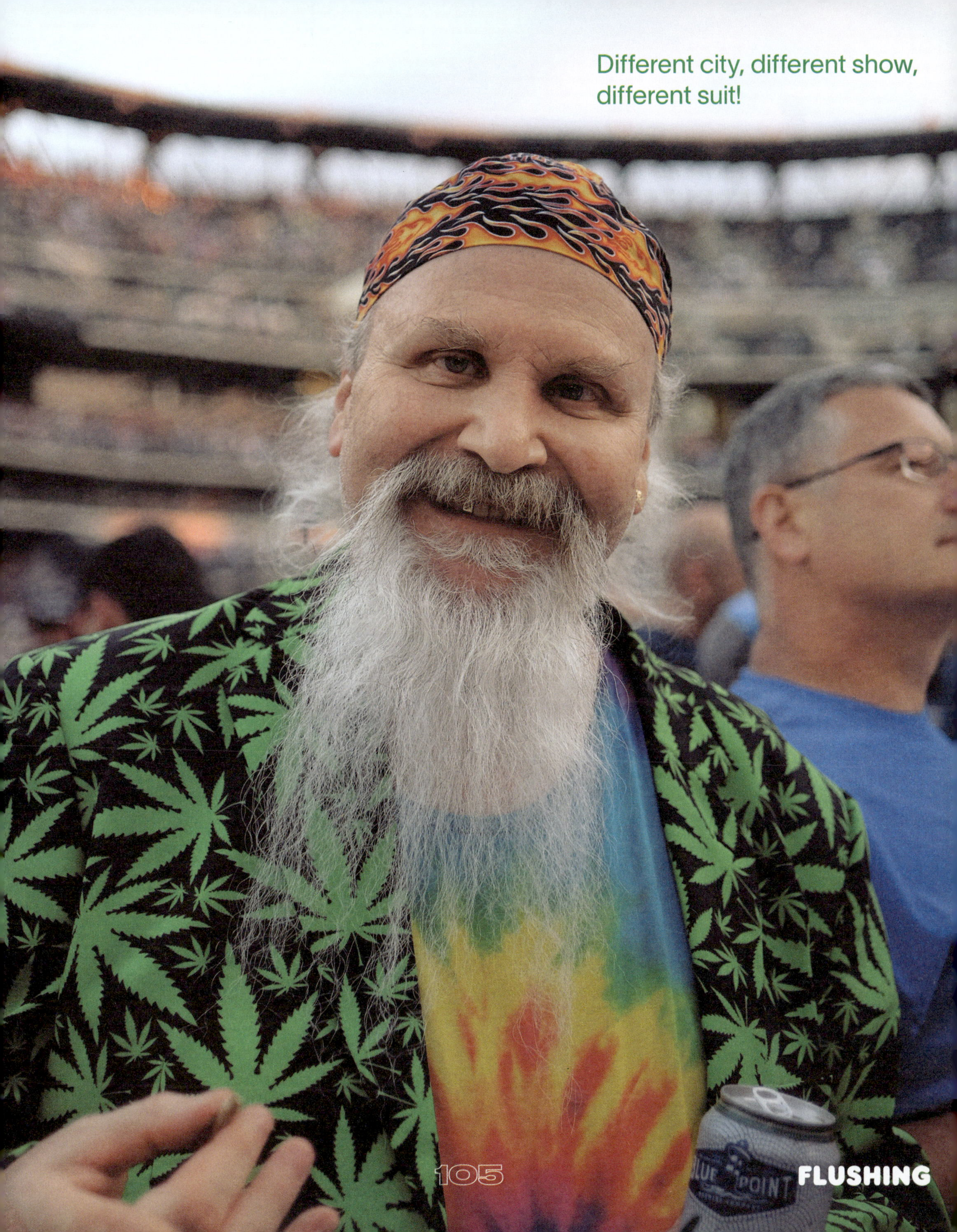

Different city, different show, different suit!

HIS HAT LOOKS TO BE HAND-PAINTED.

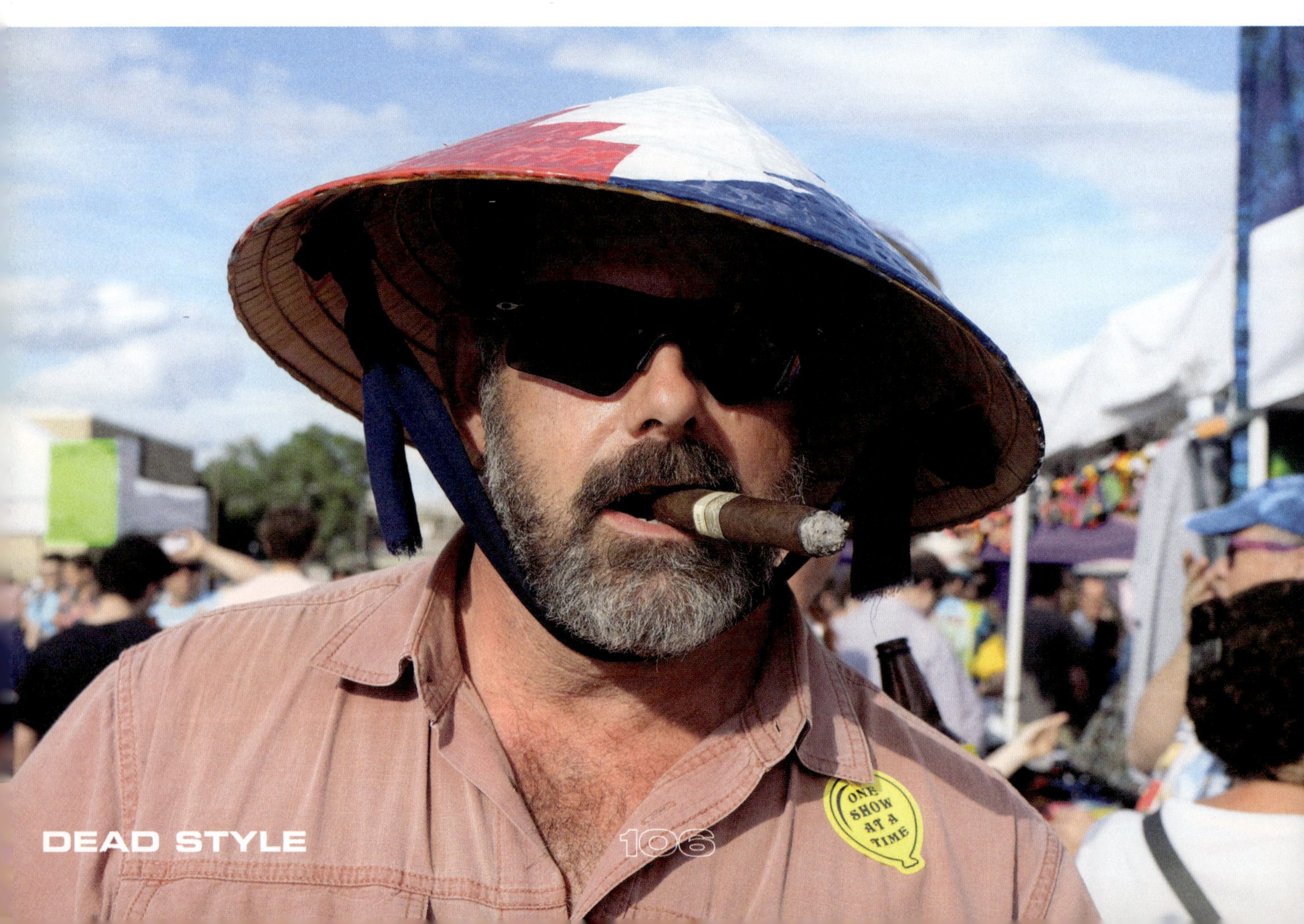

Dead in the streets

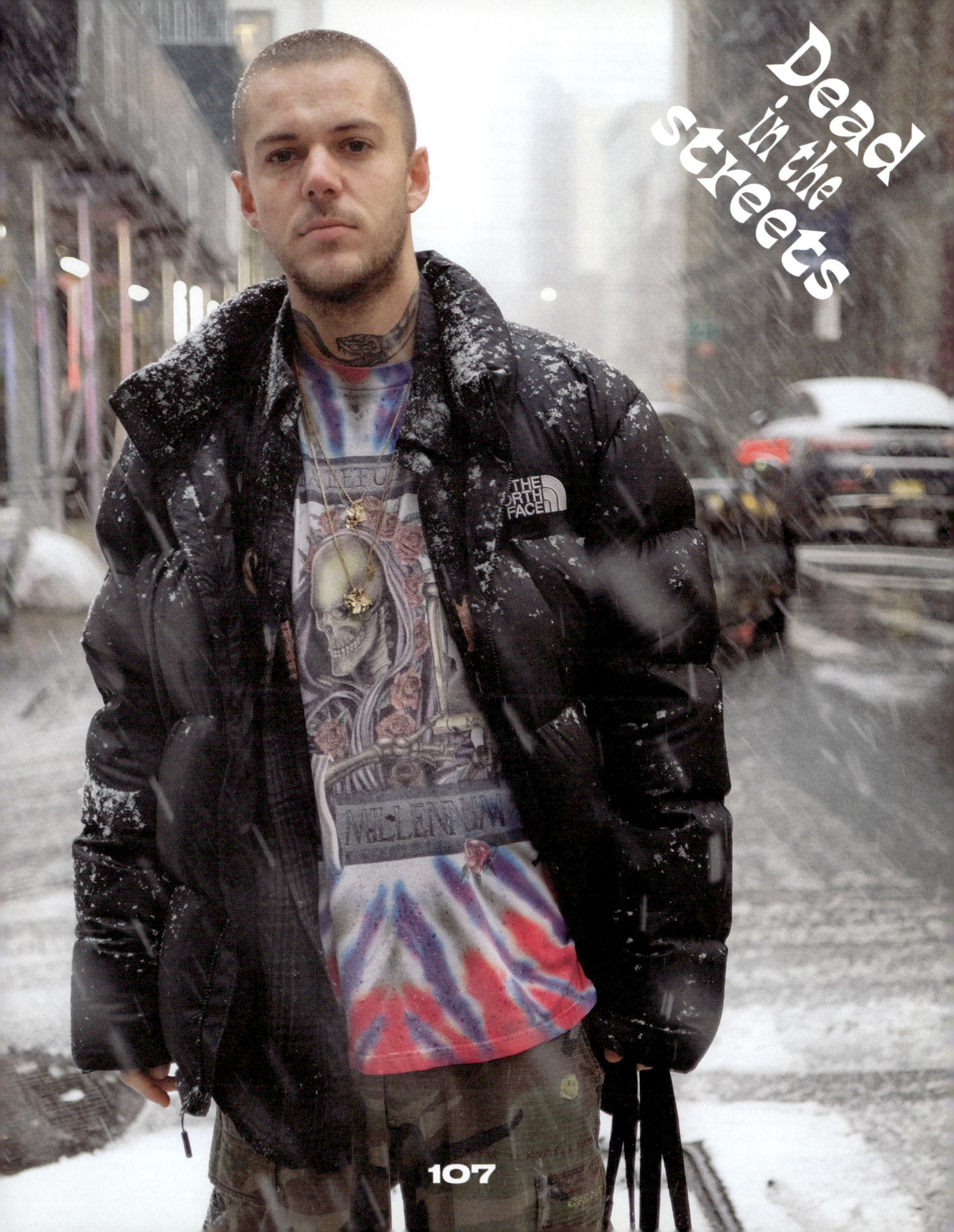

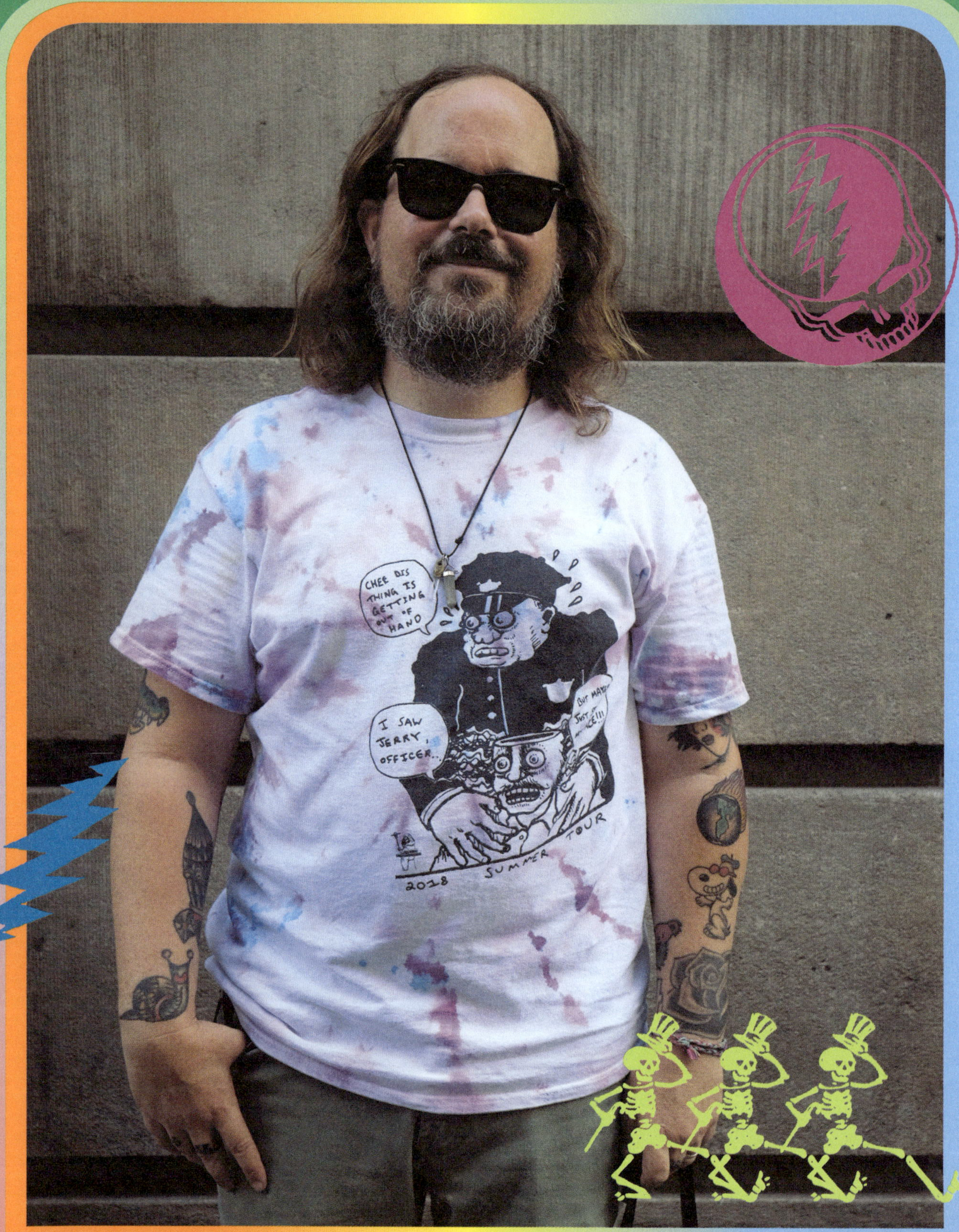
CHEE DIS THING IS GETTING OUT OF HAND
I SAW JERRY, OFFICER...
2018 SUMMER TOUR

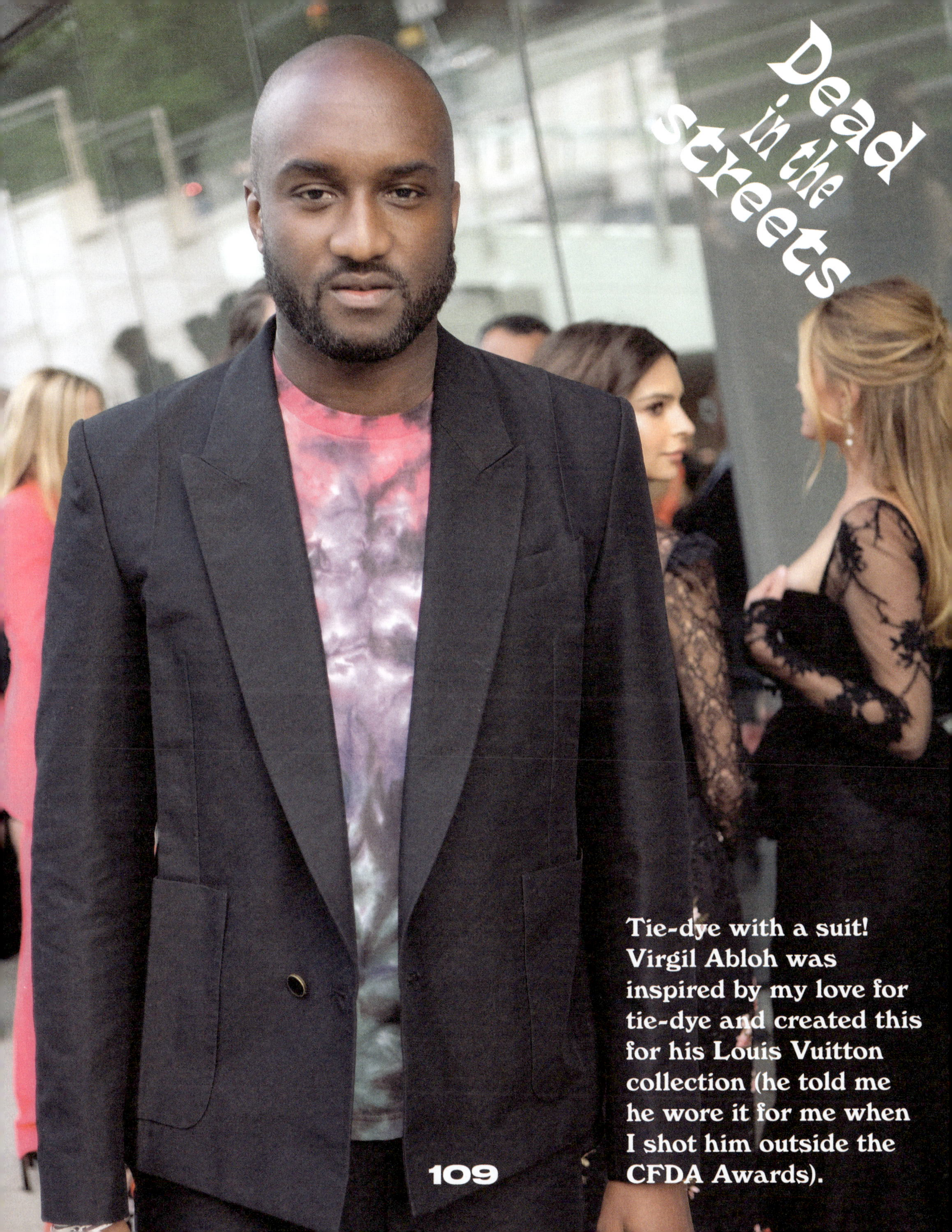

Dead in the streets

Tie-dye with a suit! Virgil Abloh was inspired by my love for tie-dye and created this for his Louis Vuitton collection (he told me he wore it for me when I shot him outside the CFDA Awards).

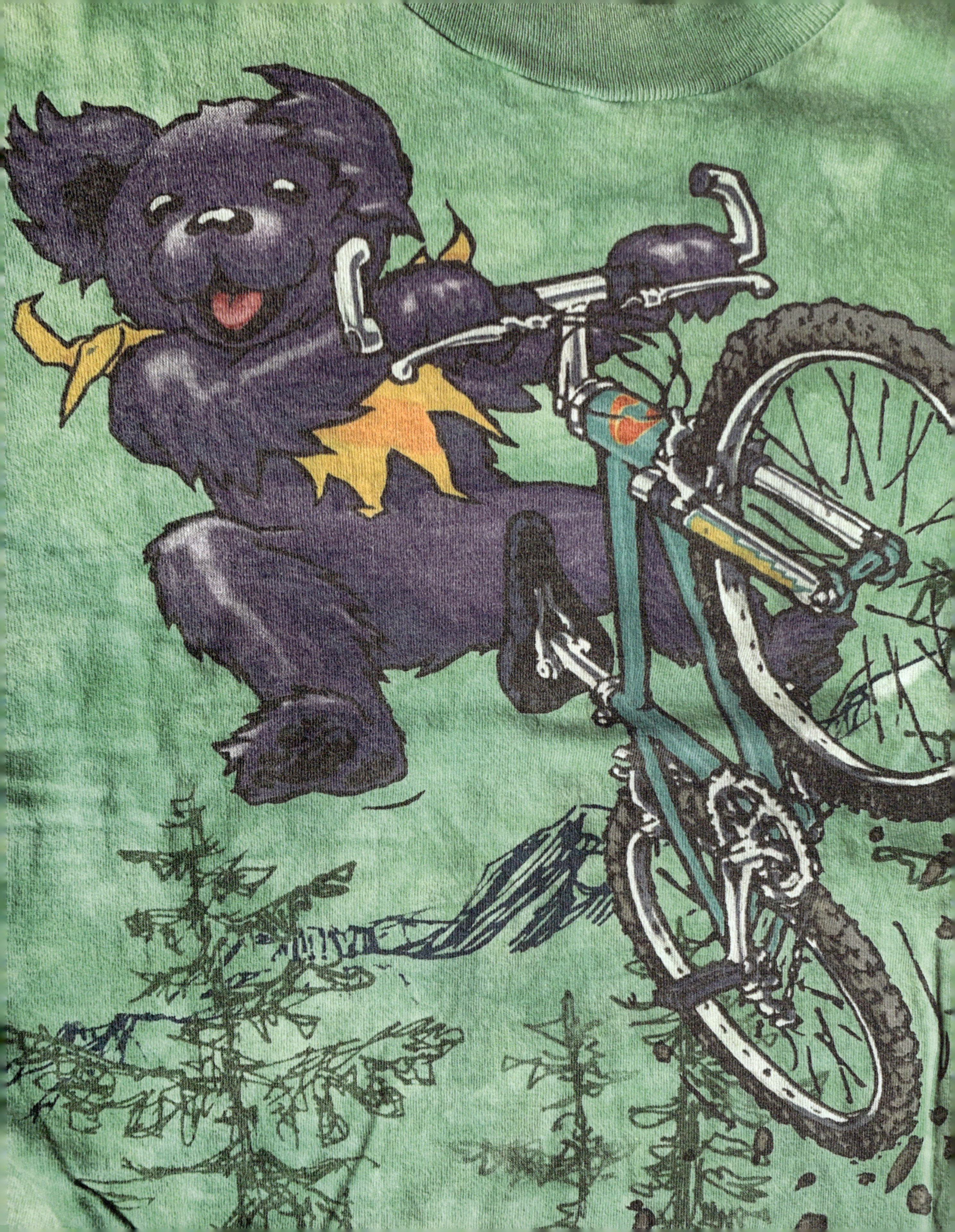

ALPINE VALLEY MUSIC THEATRE

East Troy, Wisconsin

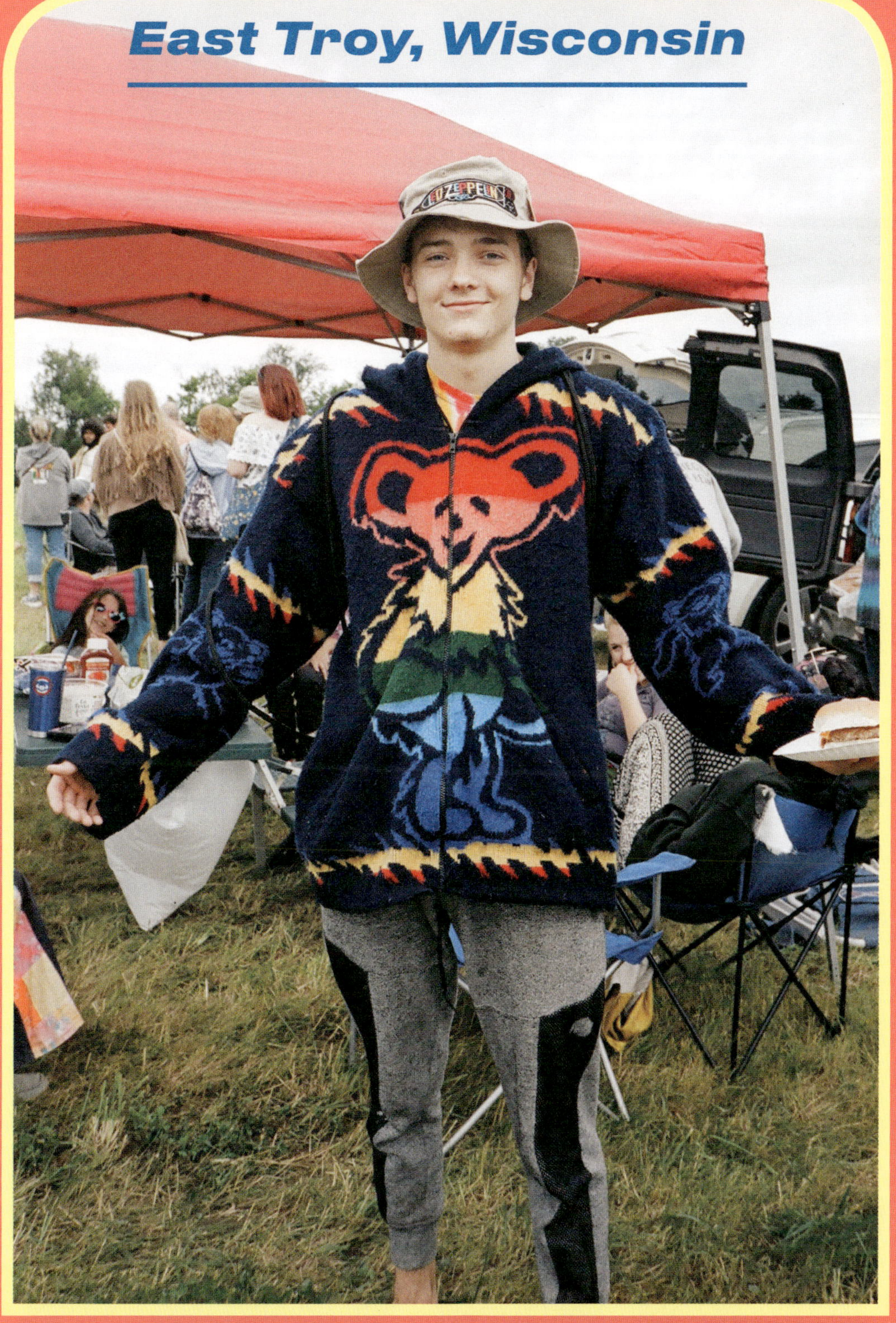

Friday, June 22nd, 2018, &
Saturday, June 23rd, 2018

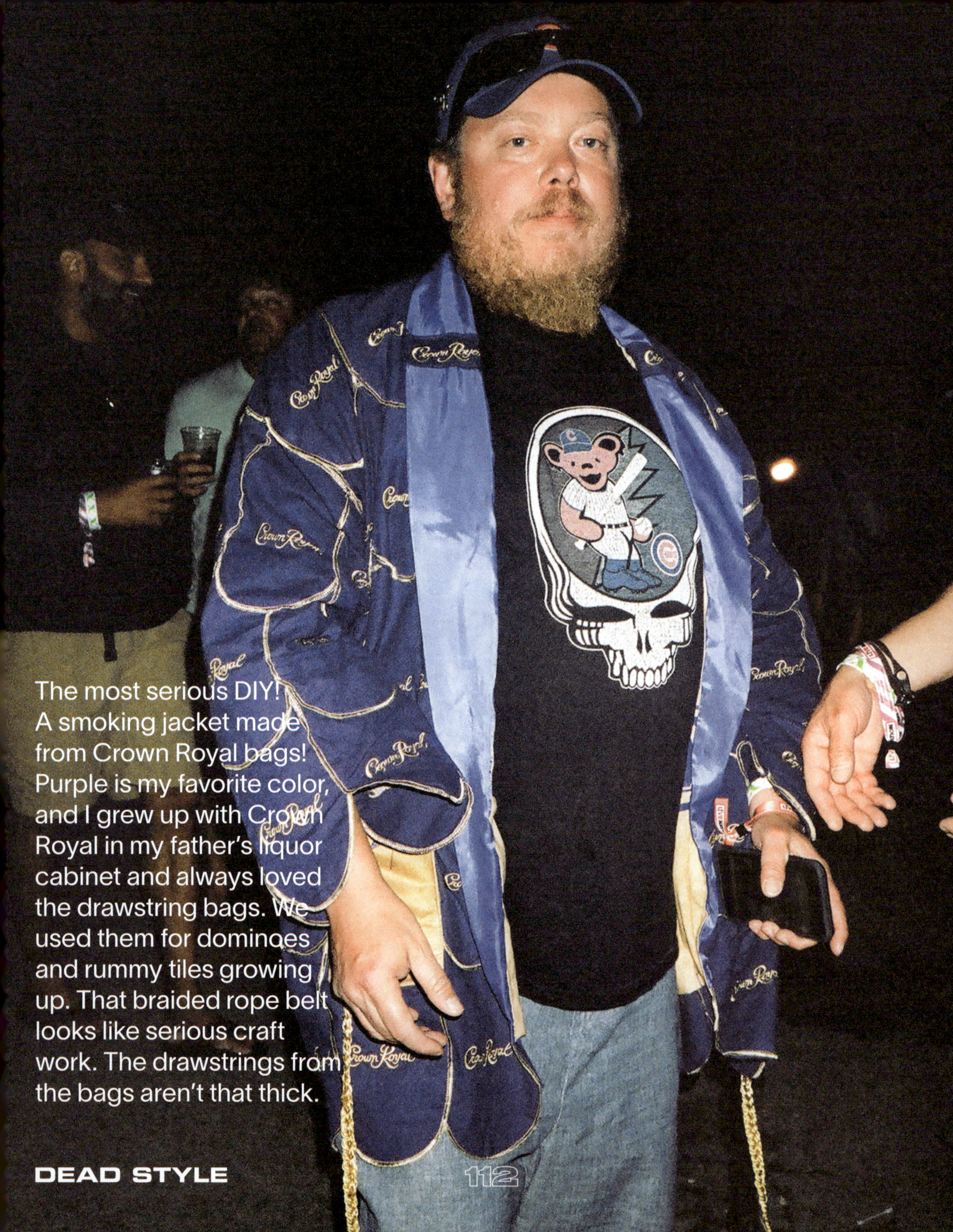

The most serious DIY! A smoking jacket made from Crown Royal bags! Purple is my favorite color, and I grew up with Crown Royal in my father's liquor cabinet and always loved the drawstring bags. We used them for dominoes and rummy tiles growing up. That braided rope belt looks like serious craft work. The drawstrings from the bags aren't that thick.

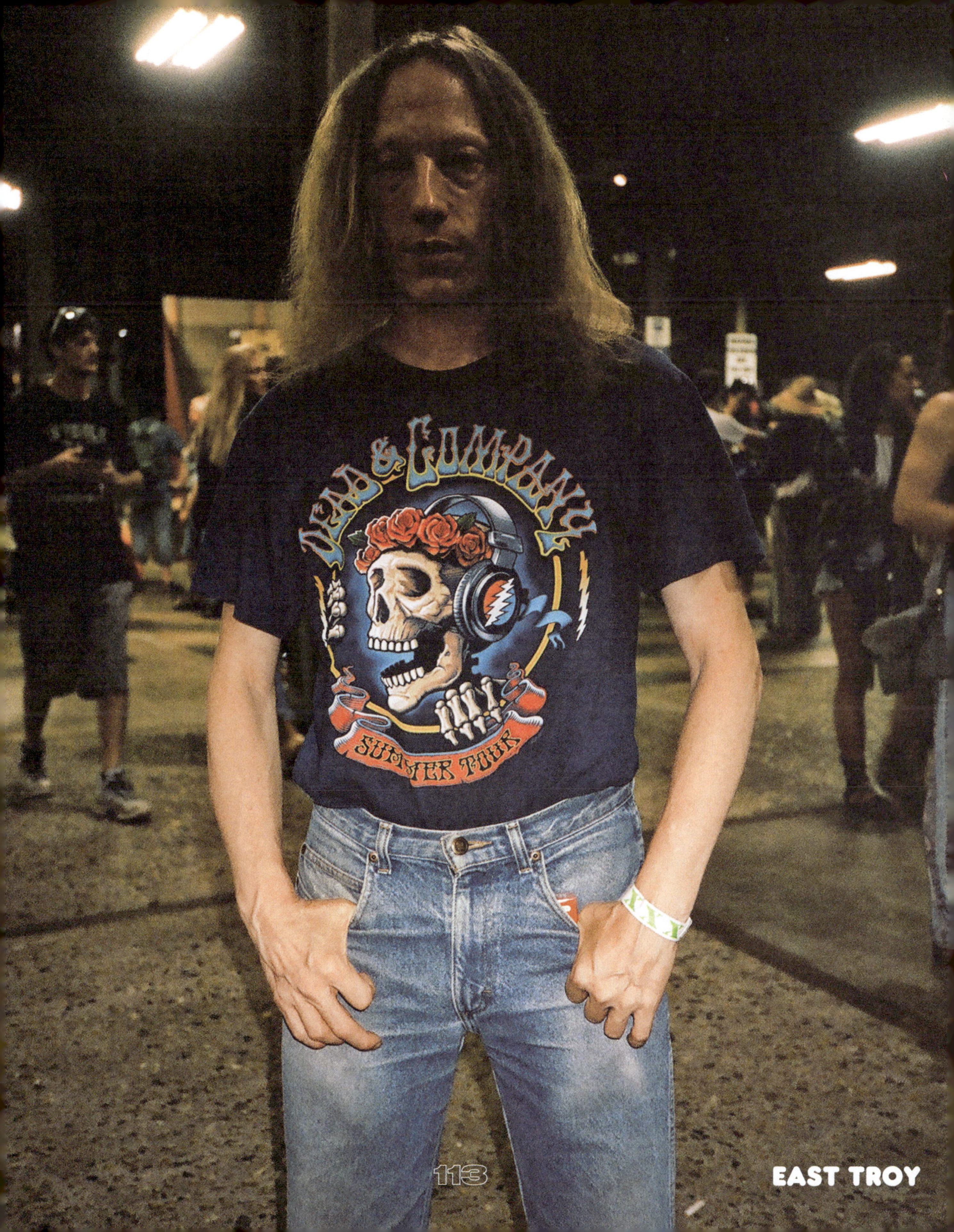

EAST TROY

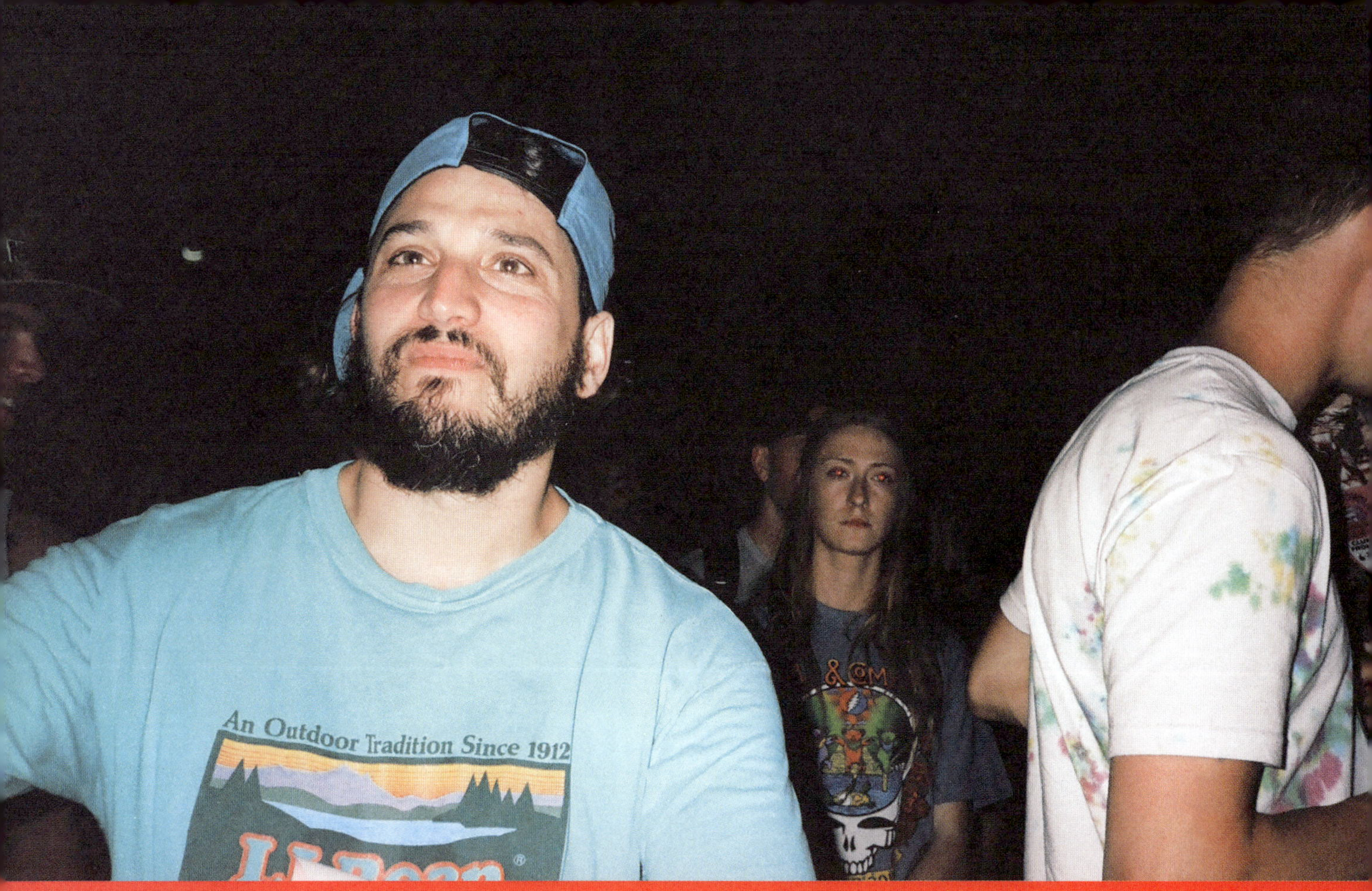

My brother, Moshe, met me for the Alpine Valley shows, and I asked him to not bring clothes so I could dress him. Not so I could style him—he needs no help—but because I typically overpack and wanted to share. On this day I asked him to wear the tee so we could match. I had it in a coral color. He wasn't all too excited, but he owned the look.

Jerry said the phrase "always a hoot" to Bob when they left the stage at Soldier Field on July 9th, 1995. It would be the last show the Grateful Dead would ever play, as Jerry died exactly one month later, on August 9th.

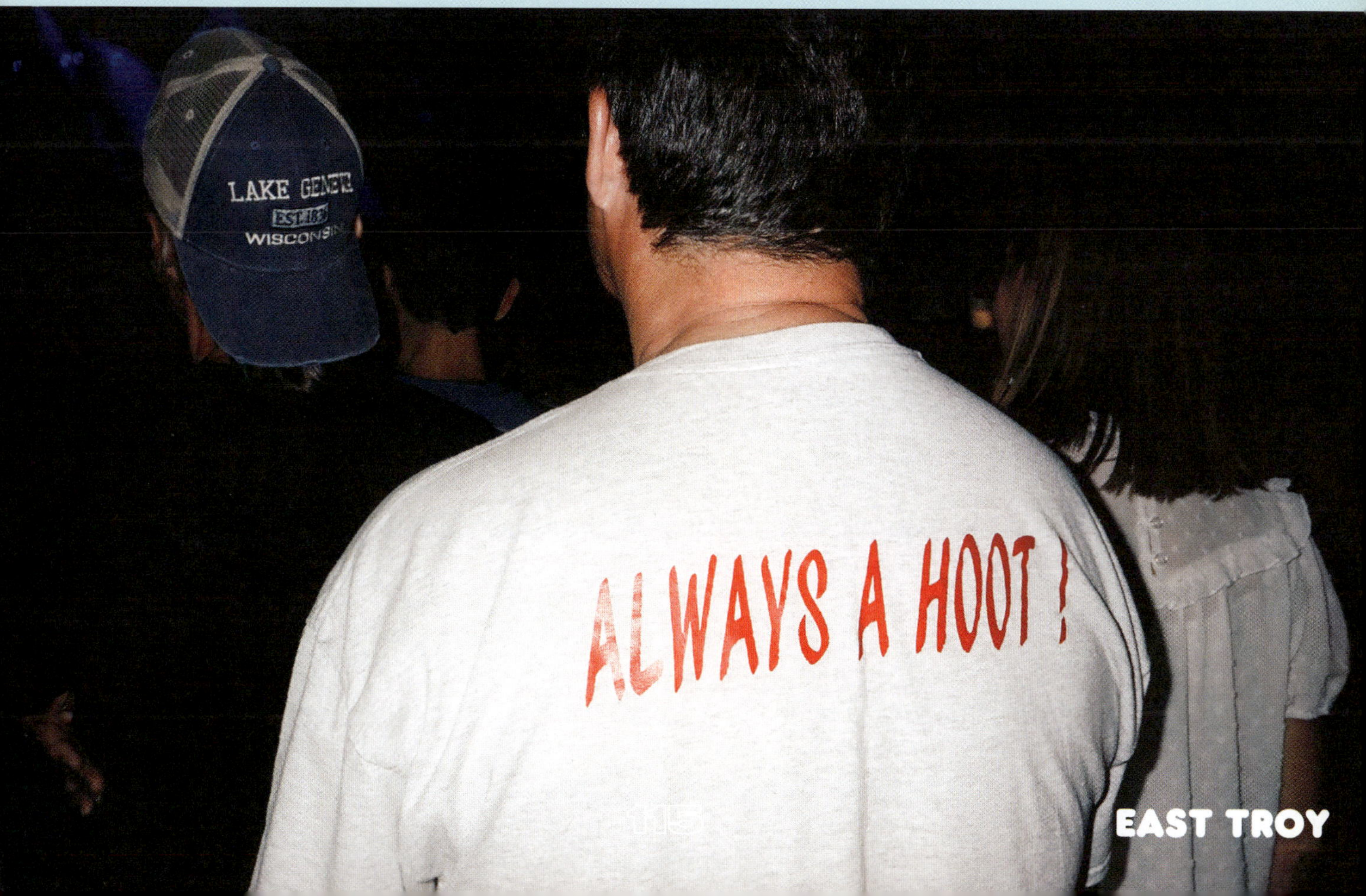

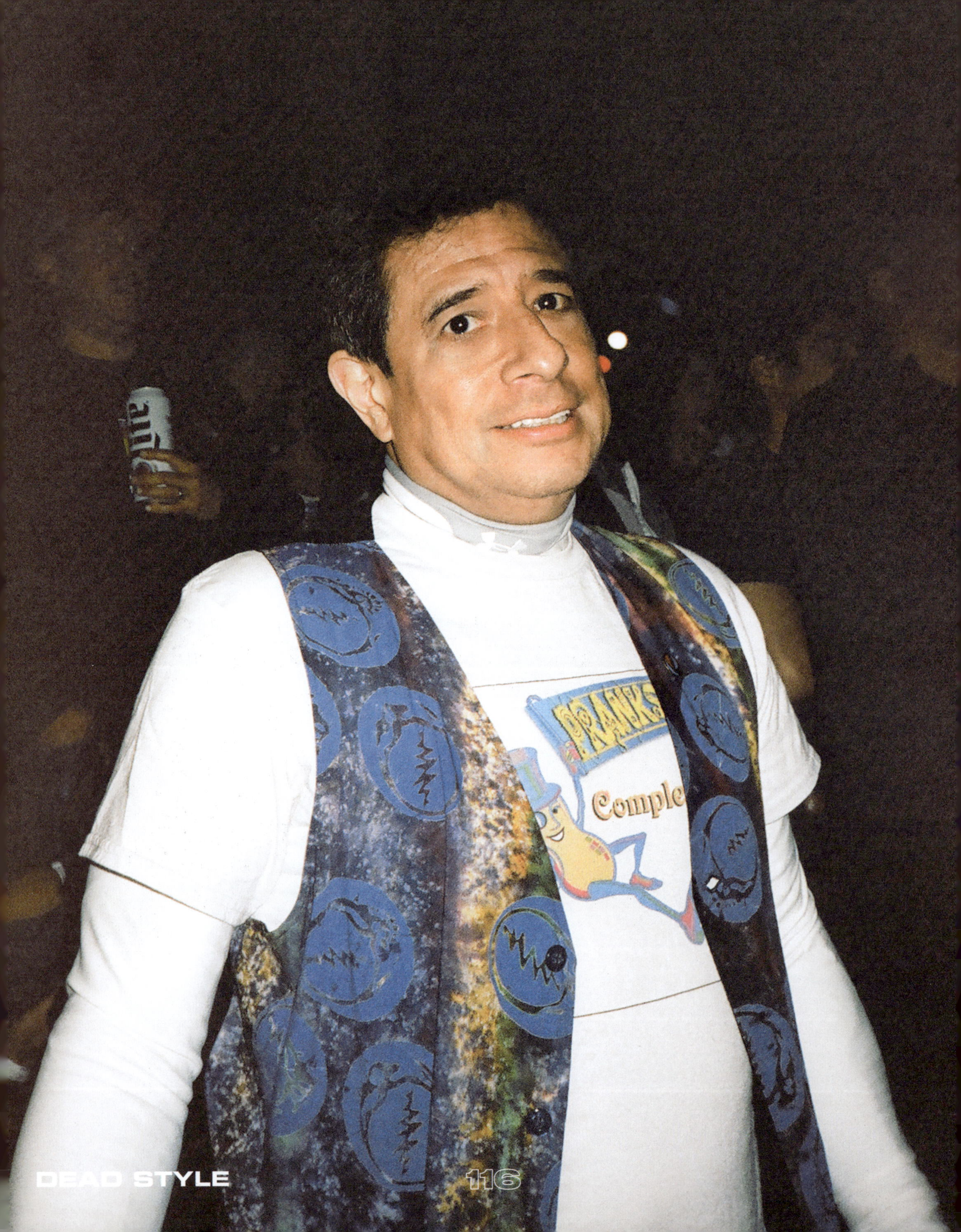

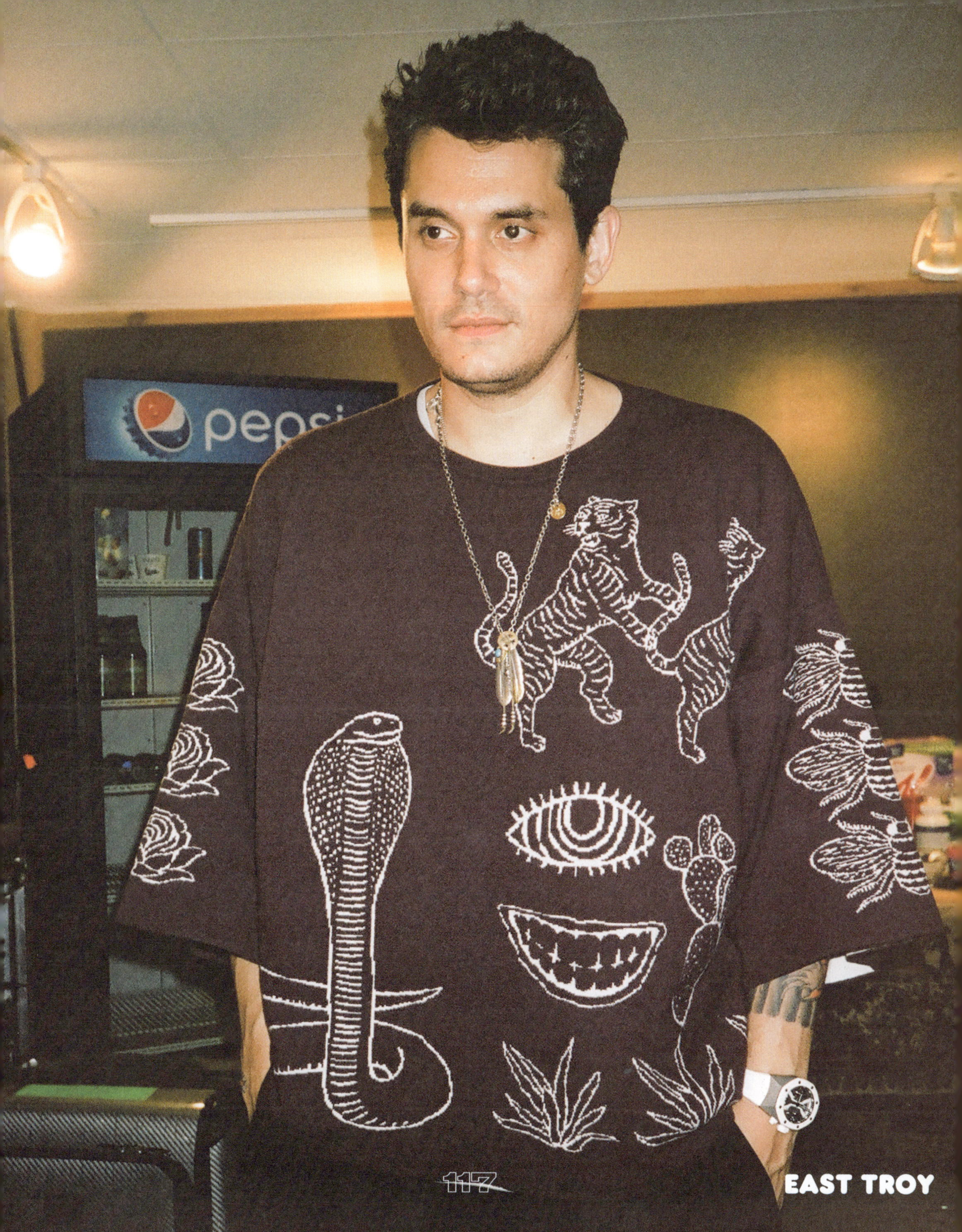
pepsi

TALK ABOUT TYING ONE ON! I NEVER IMAGINED SEEING A TIE ON LOT, BUT HE'S WEARING A TIE OVER A COLLARED STONES FLEECE!

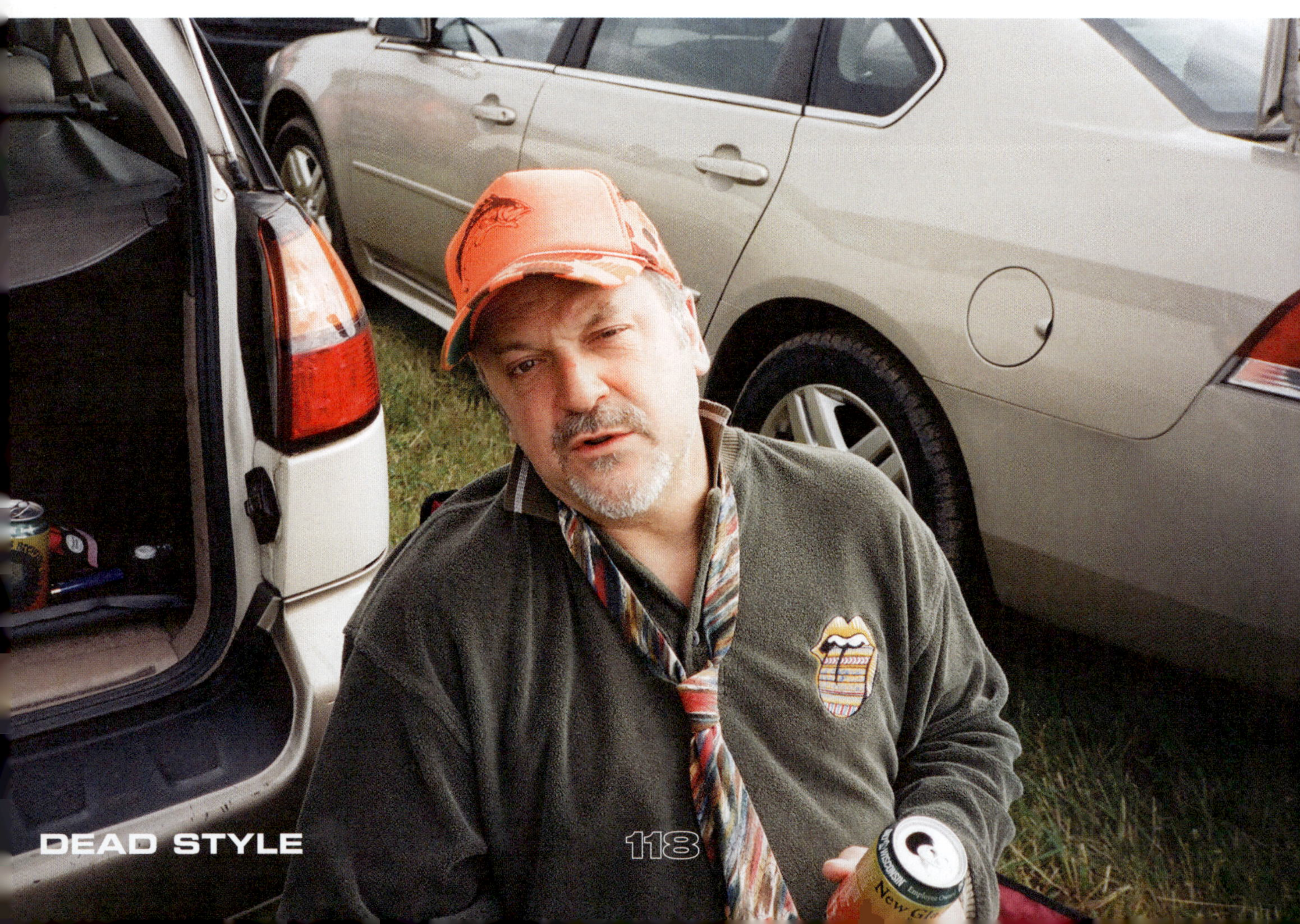

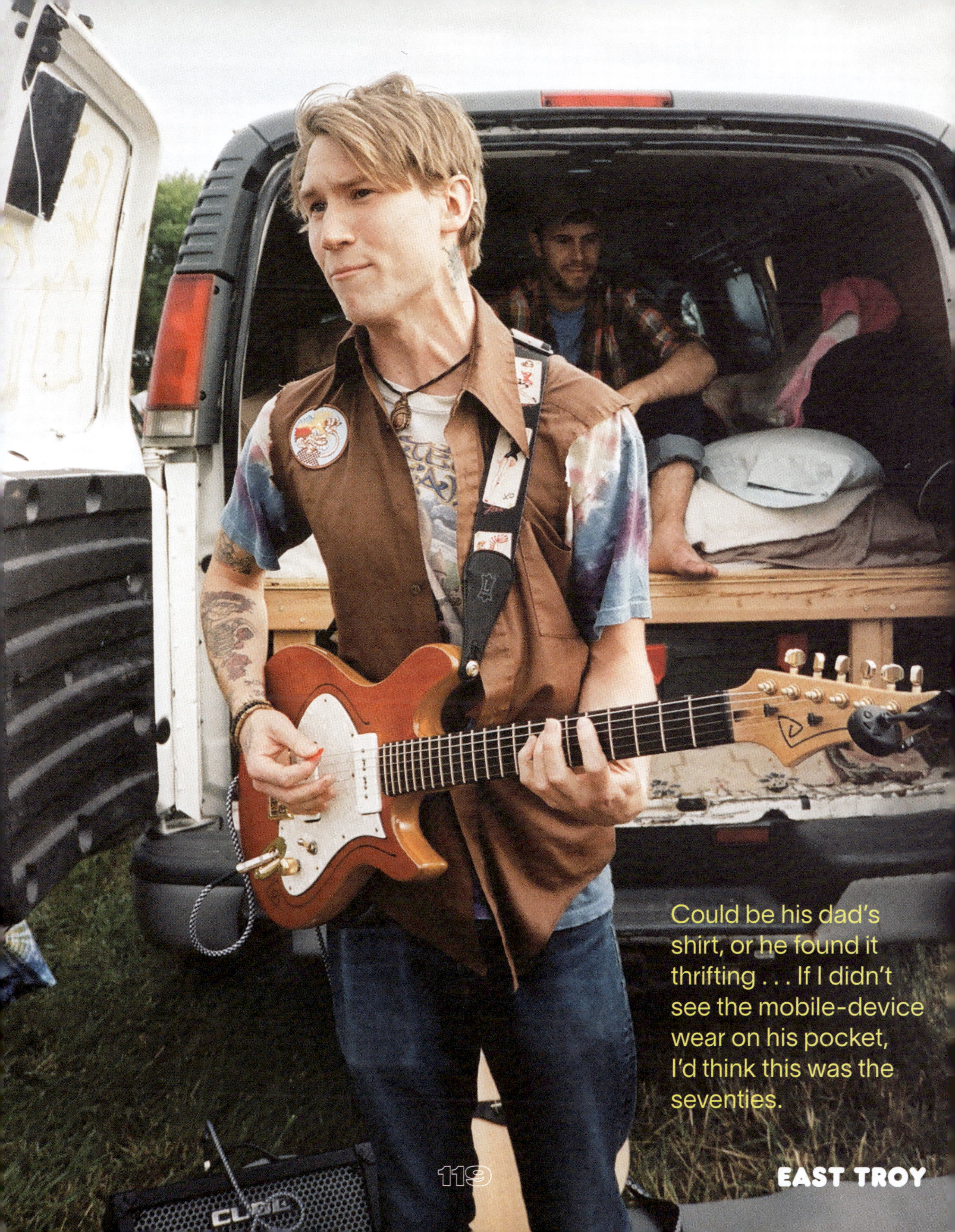

Could be his dad's shirt, or he found it thrifting . . . If I didn't see the mobile-device wear on his pocket, I'd think this was the seventies.

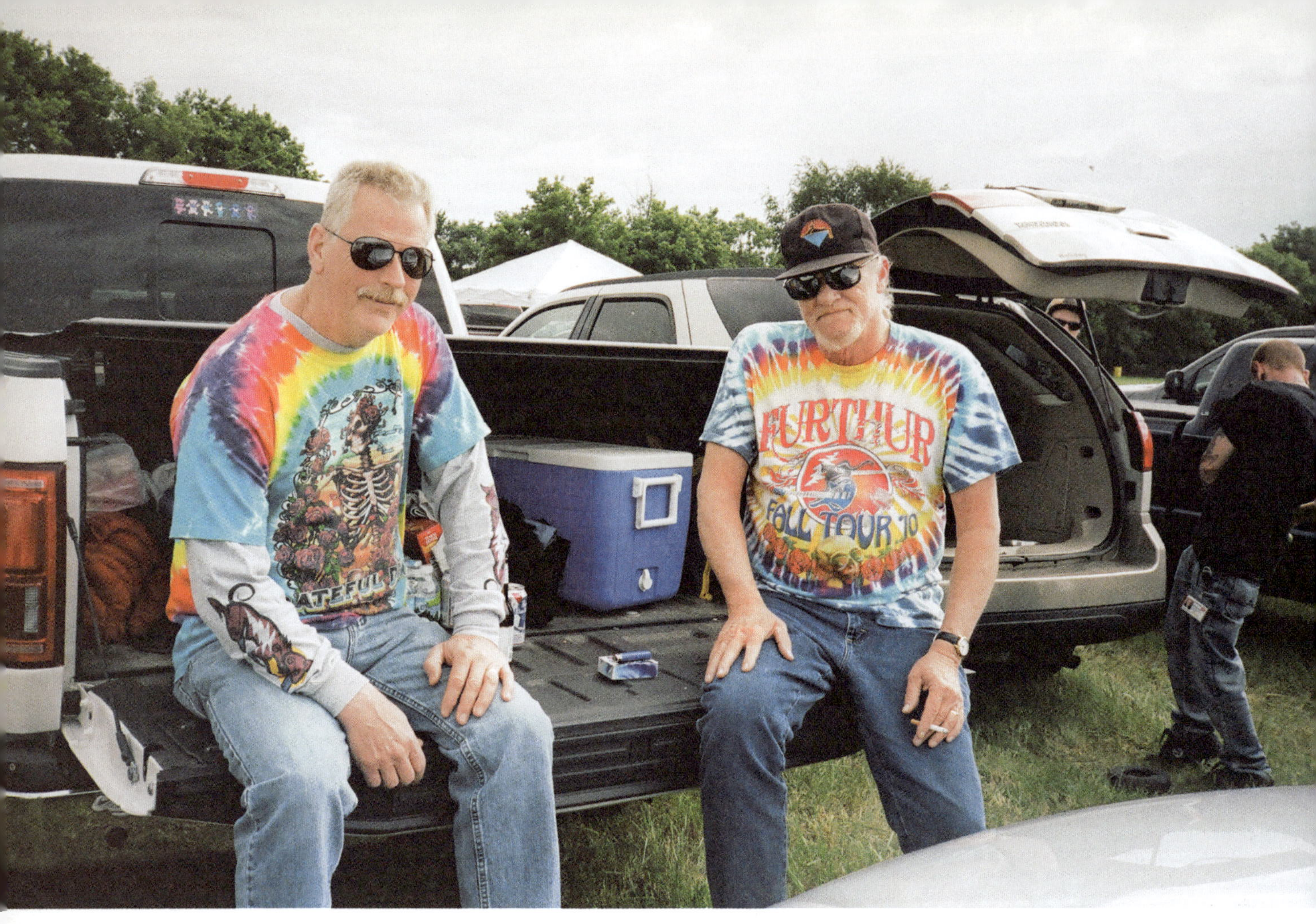
FURTHUR
FALL TOUR '10

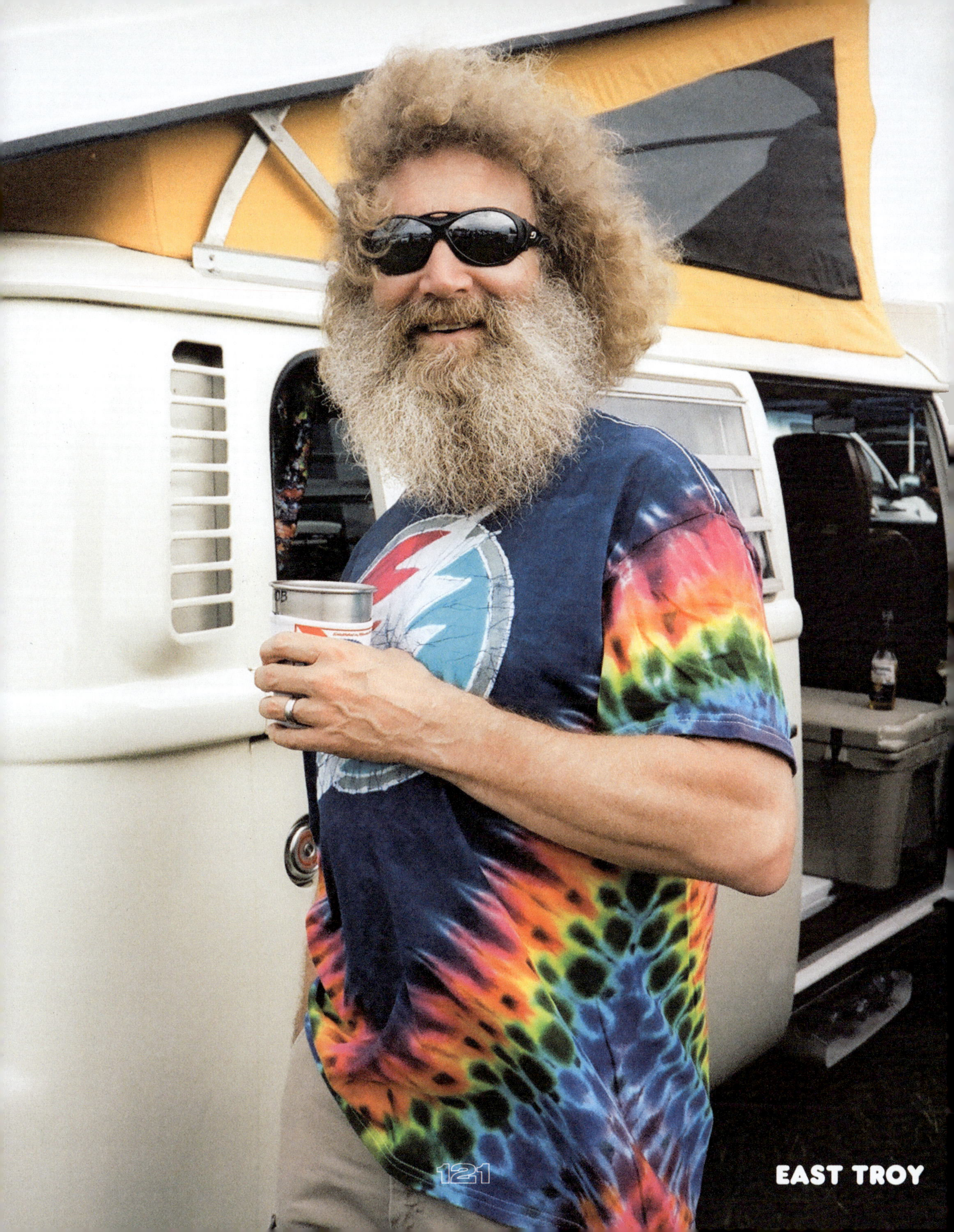

EAST TROY

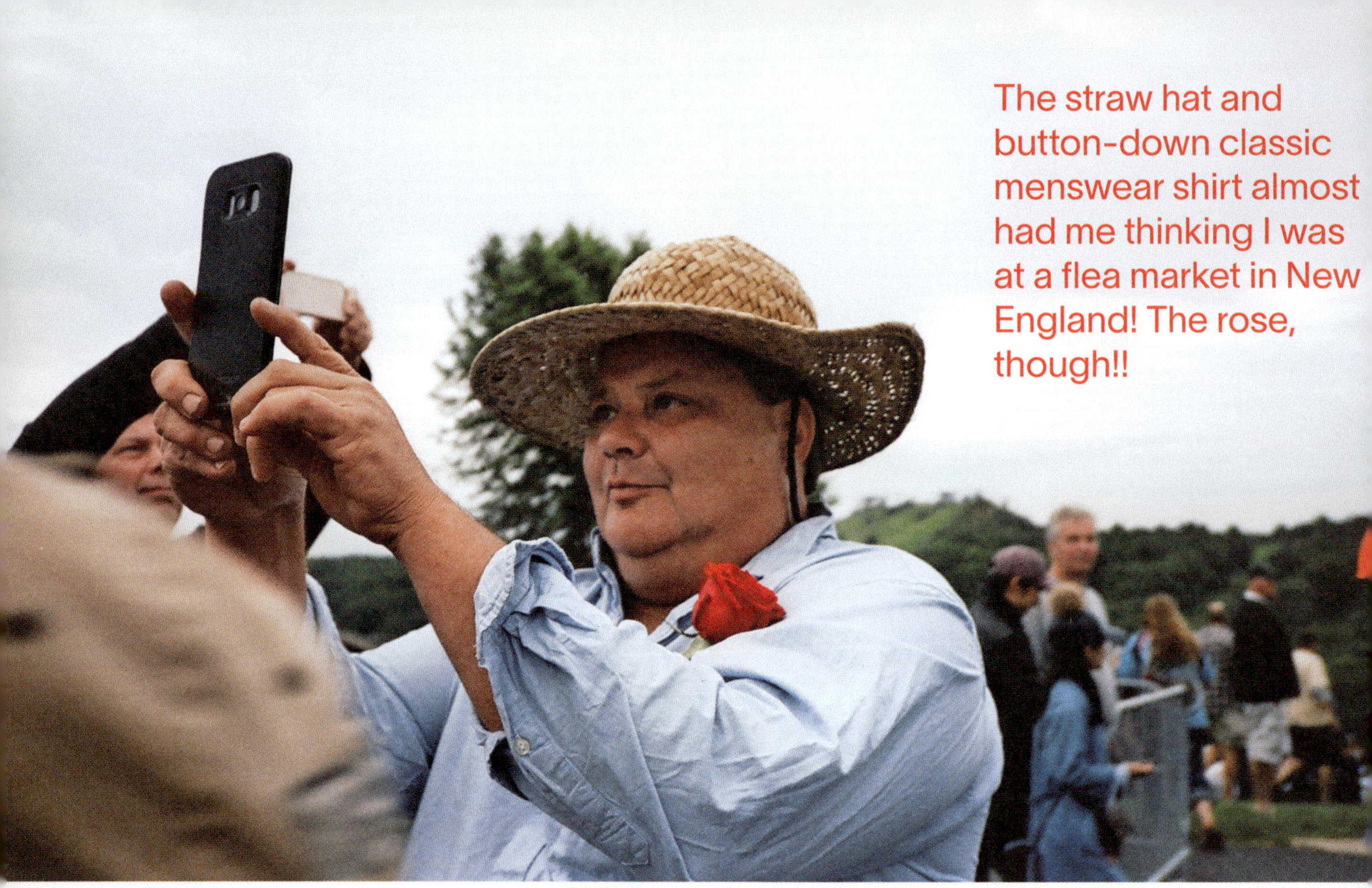

The straw hat and button-down classic menswear shirt almost had me thinking I was at a flea market in New England! The rose, though!!

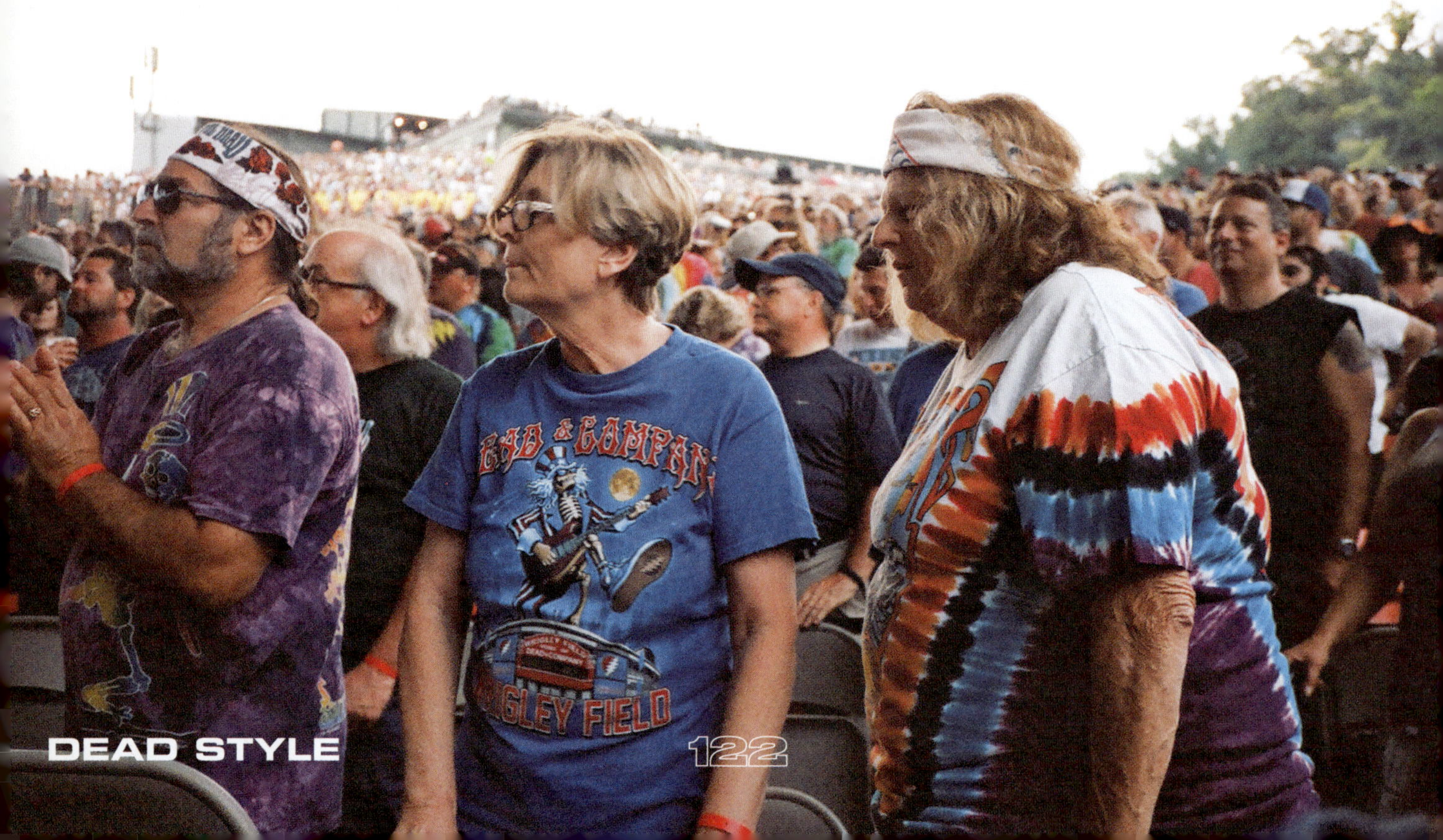

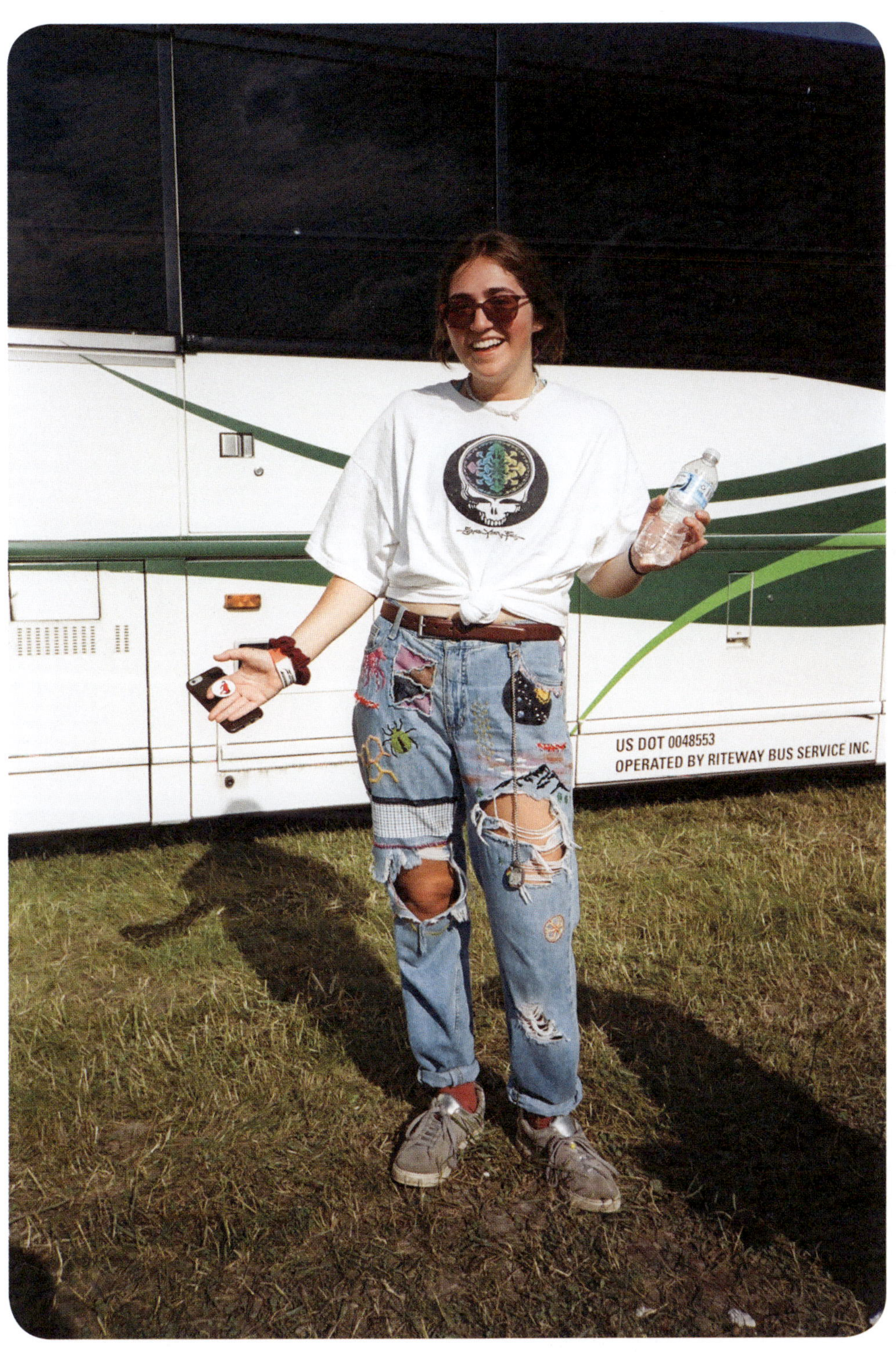
US DOT 0048553
OPERATED BY RITEWAY BUS SERVICE INC.

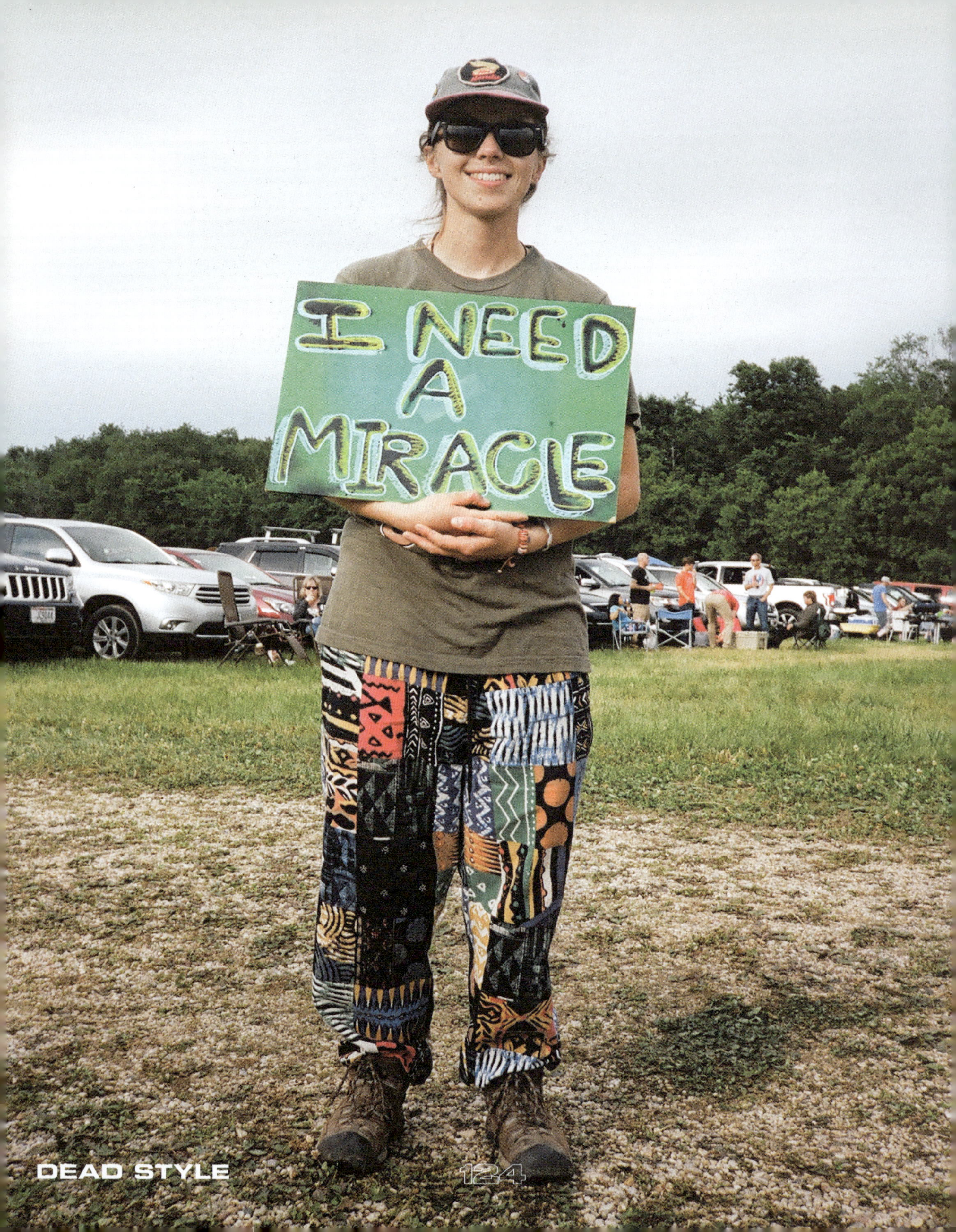
I NEED
A
MIRACLE

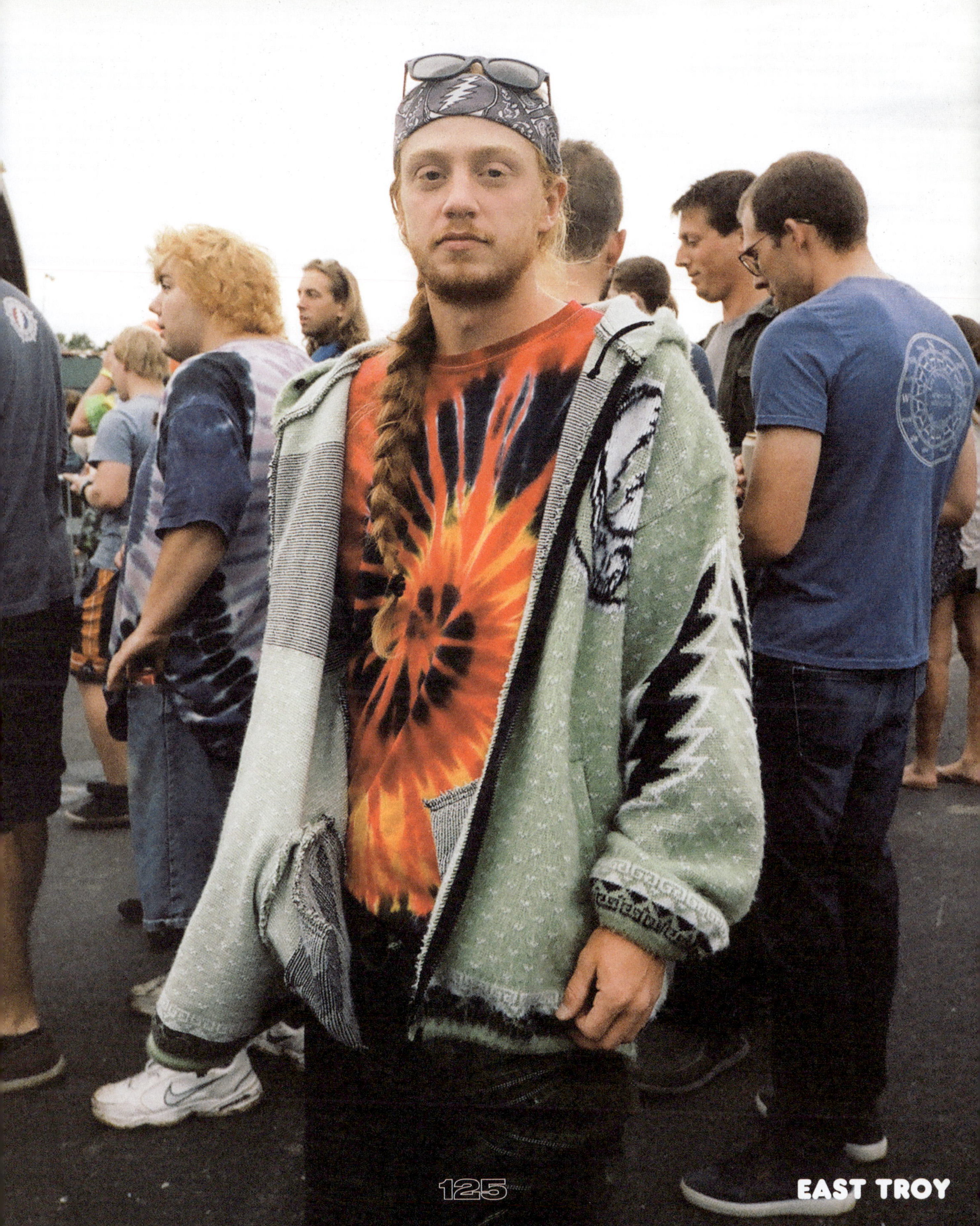

EAST TROY

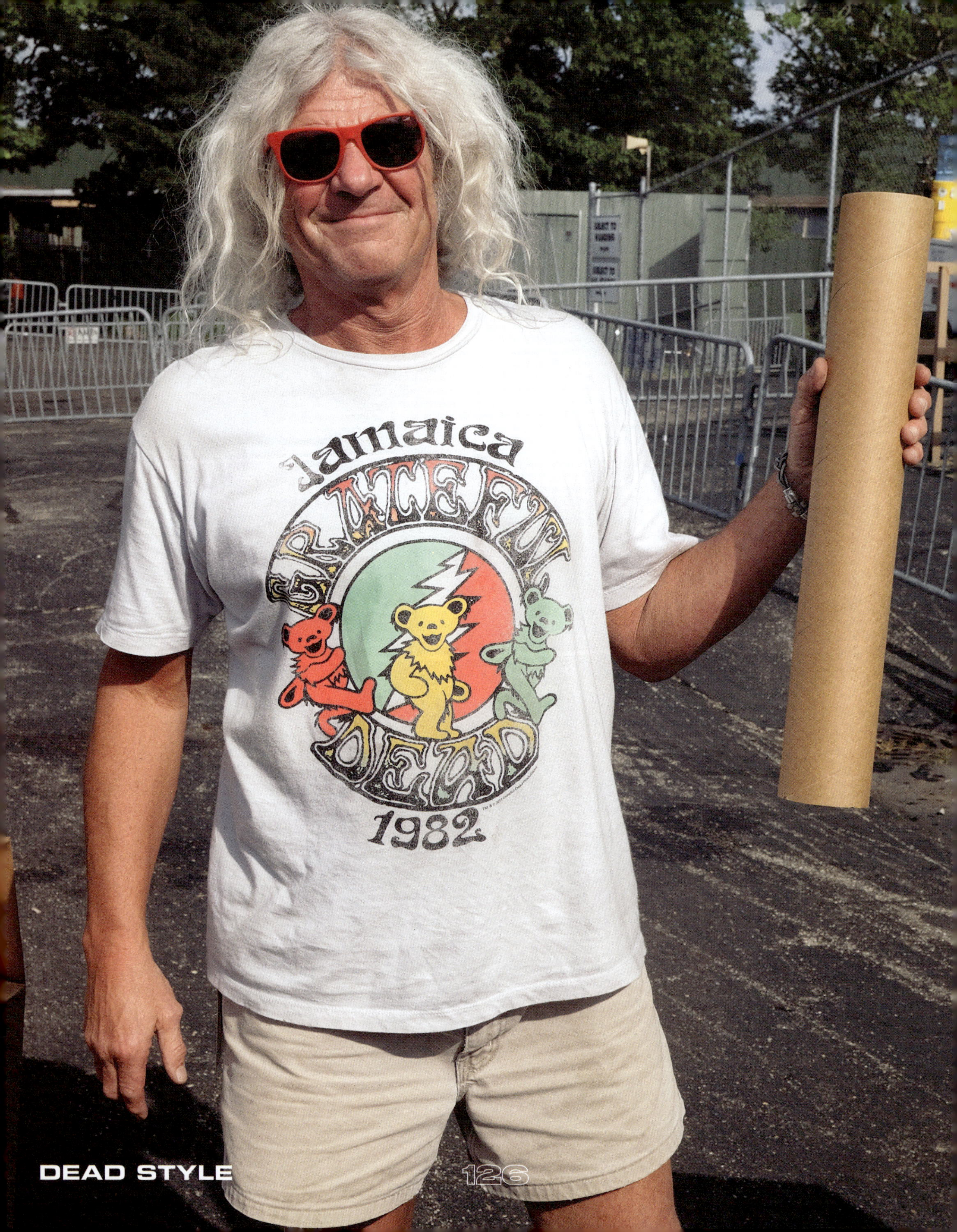
Jamaica
1982

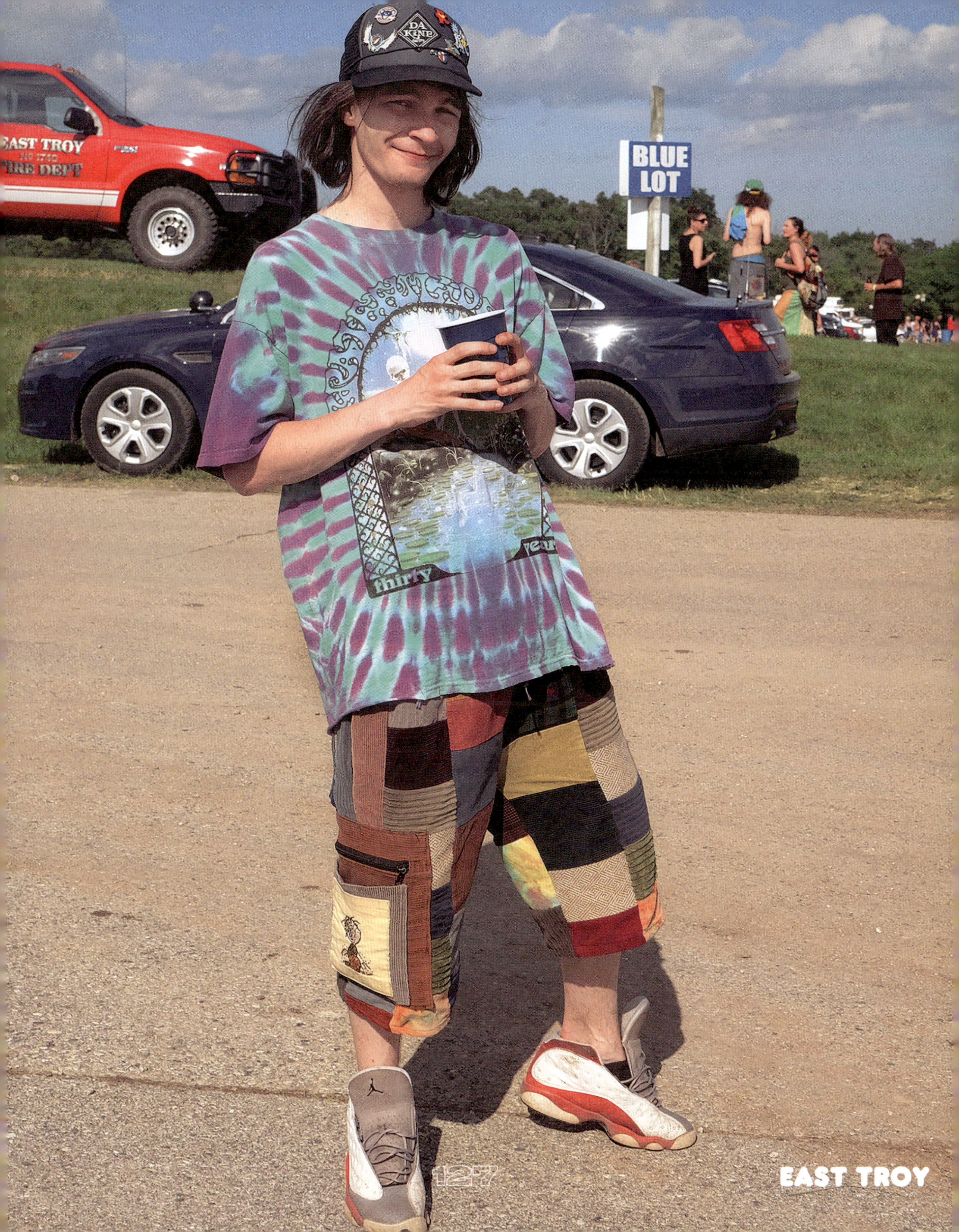
EAST TROY
NO 1740
FIRE DEPT
BLUE
LOT
thirty
years

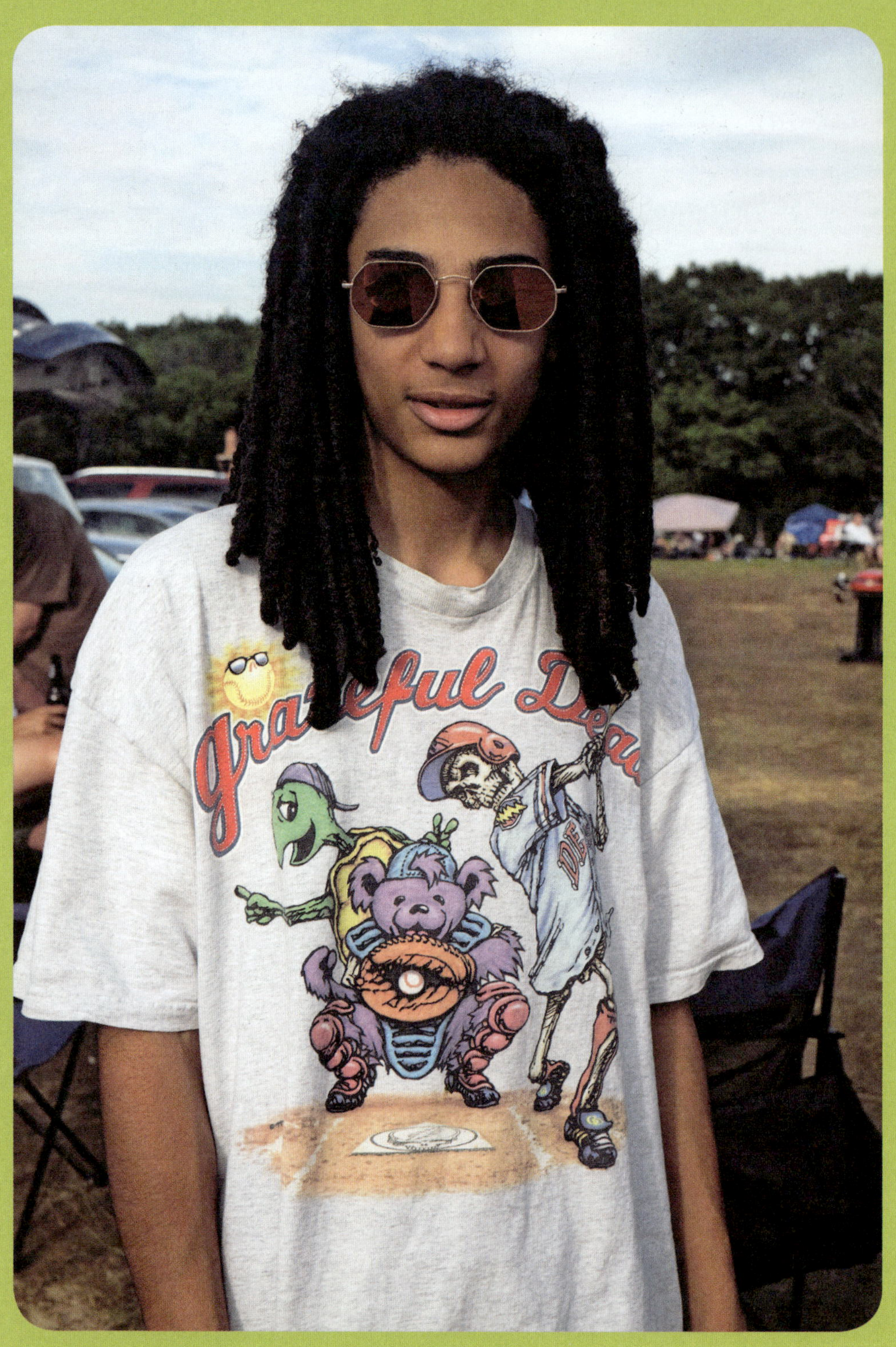

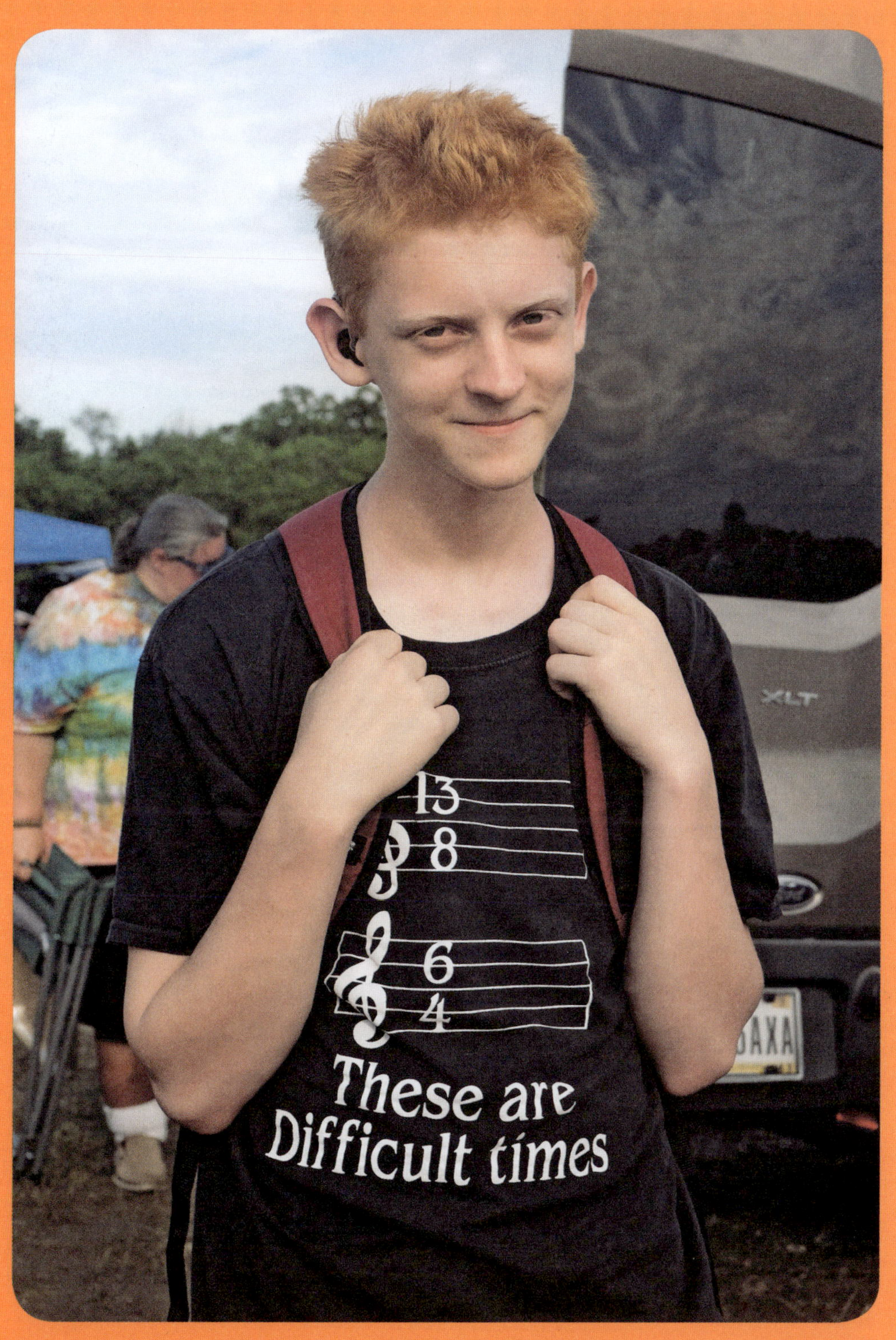
13
8
6
4
These are
Difficult times
XLT

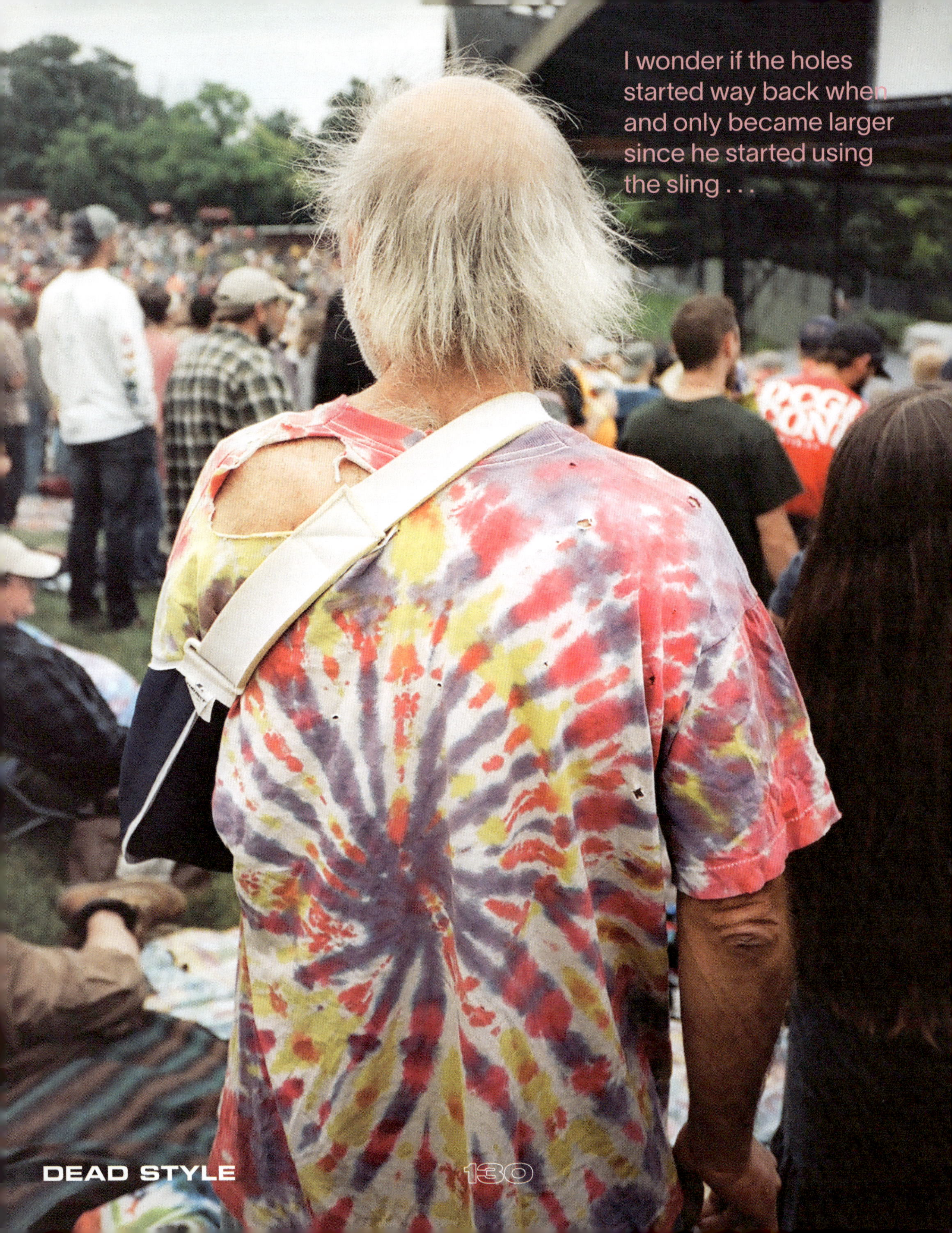

I wonder if the holes started way back when and only became larger since he started using the sling . . .

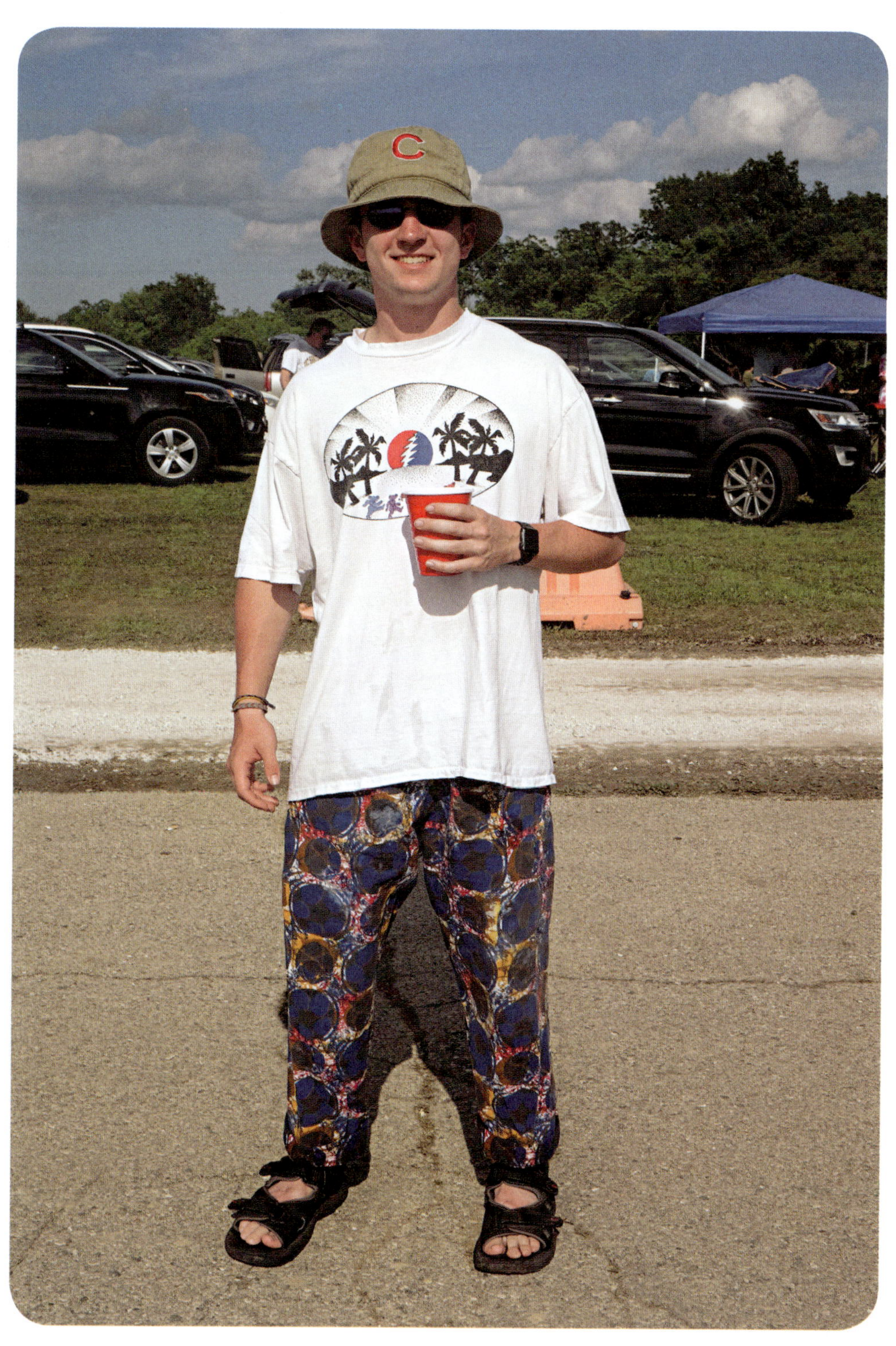

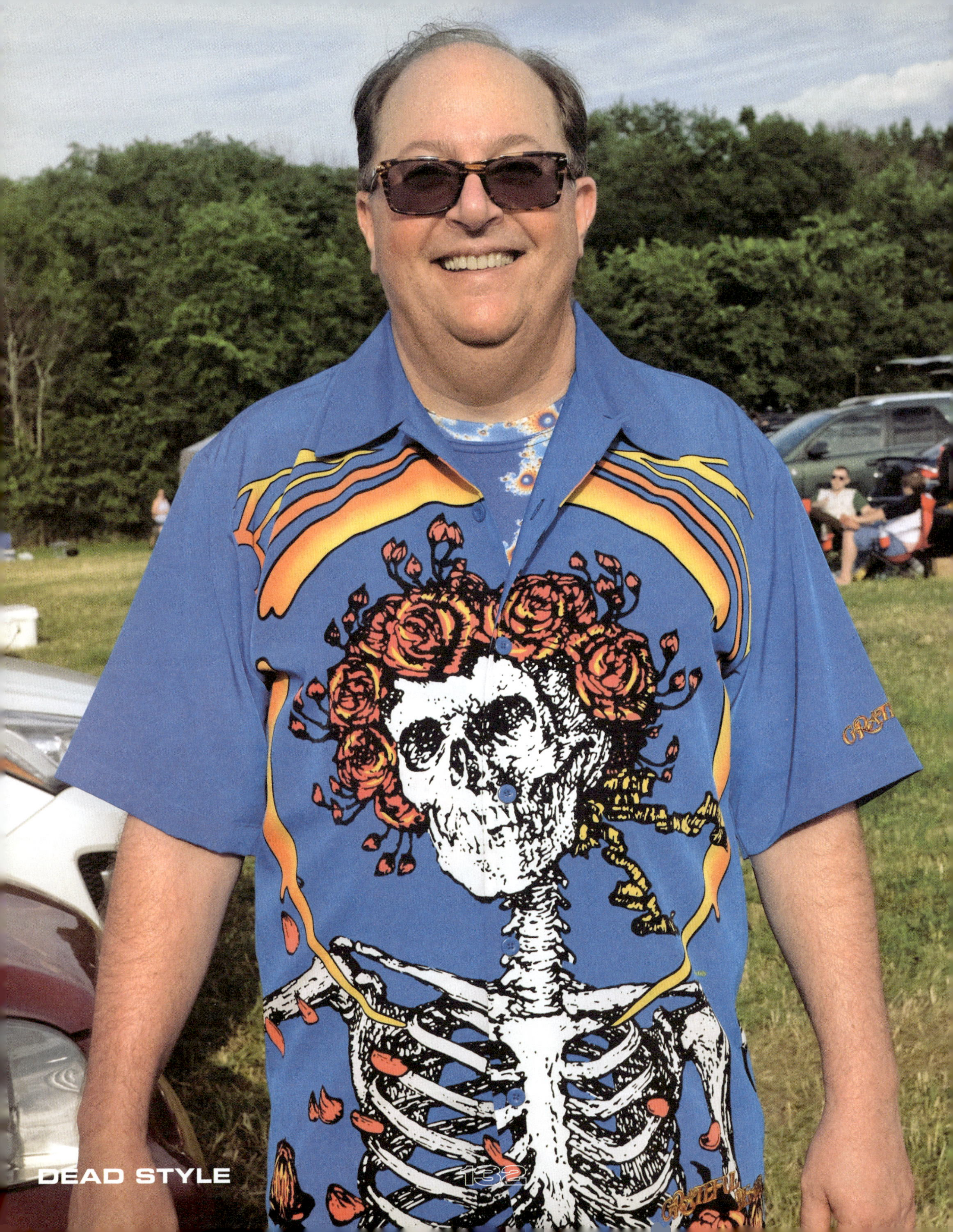

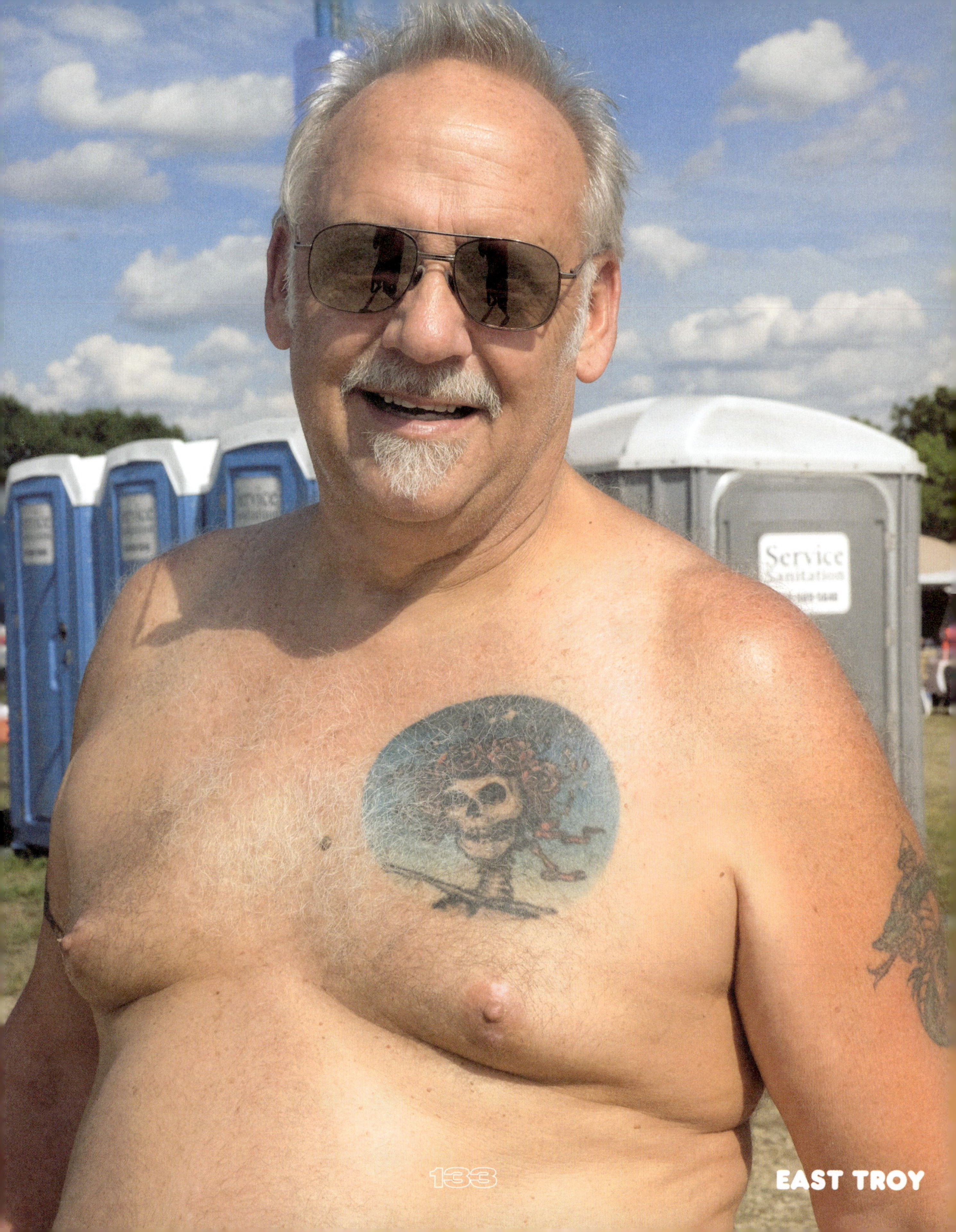

EAST TROY

WE SEE SO MUCH TIE-DYE ON T-SHIRTS BUT VERY FEW CLASSIC BUTTON-DOWN SHIRTS!

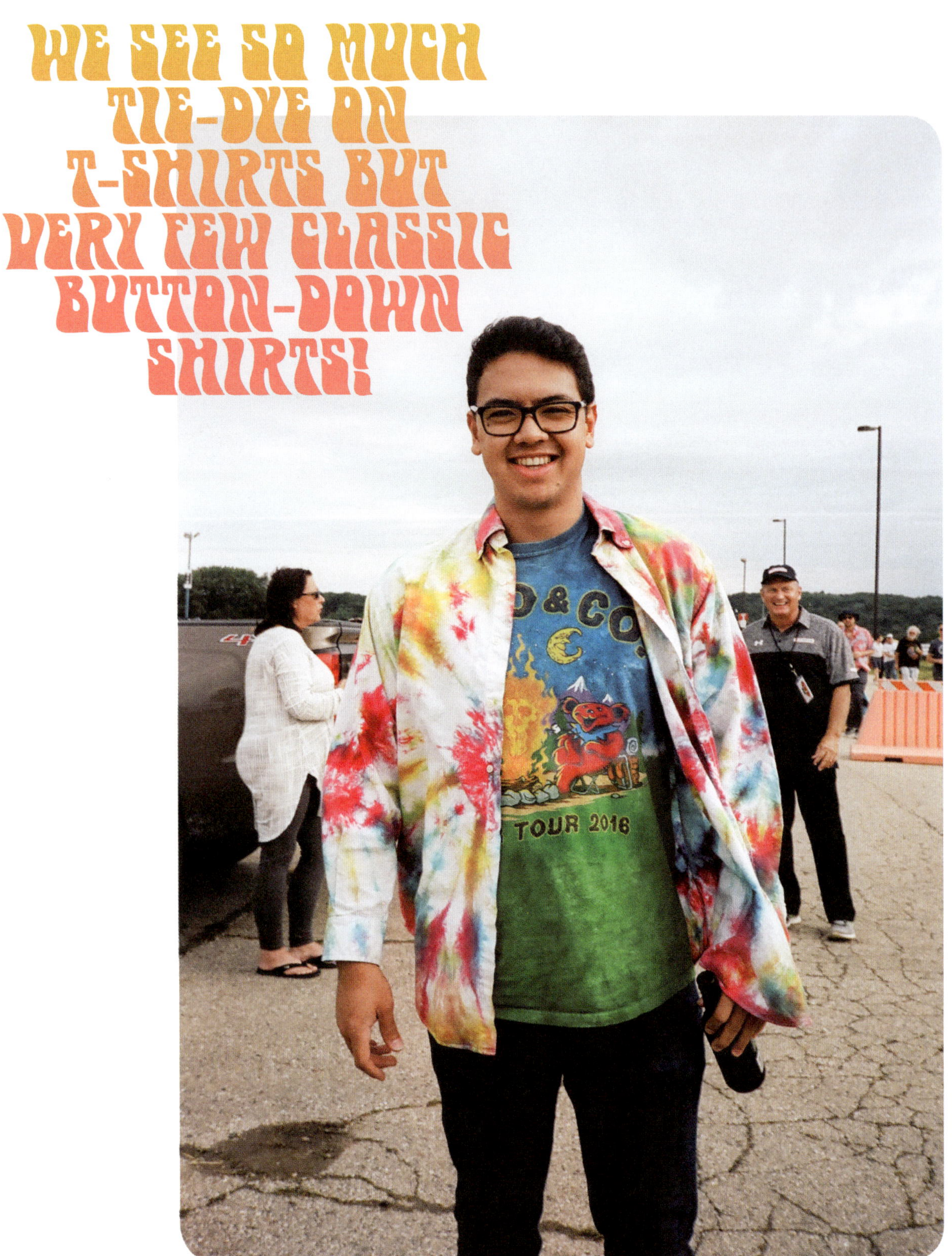

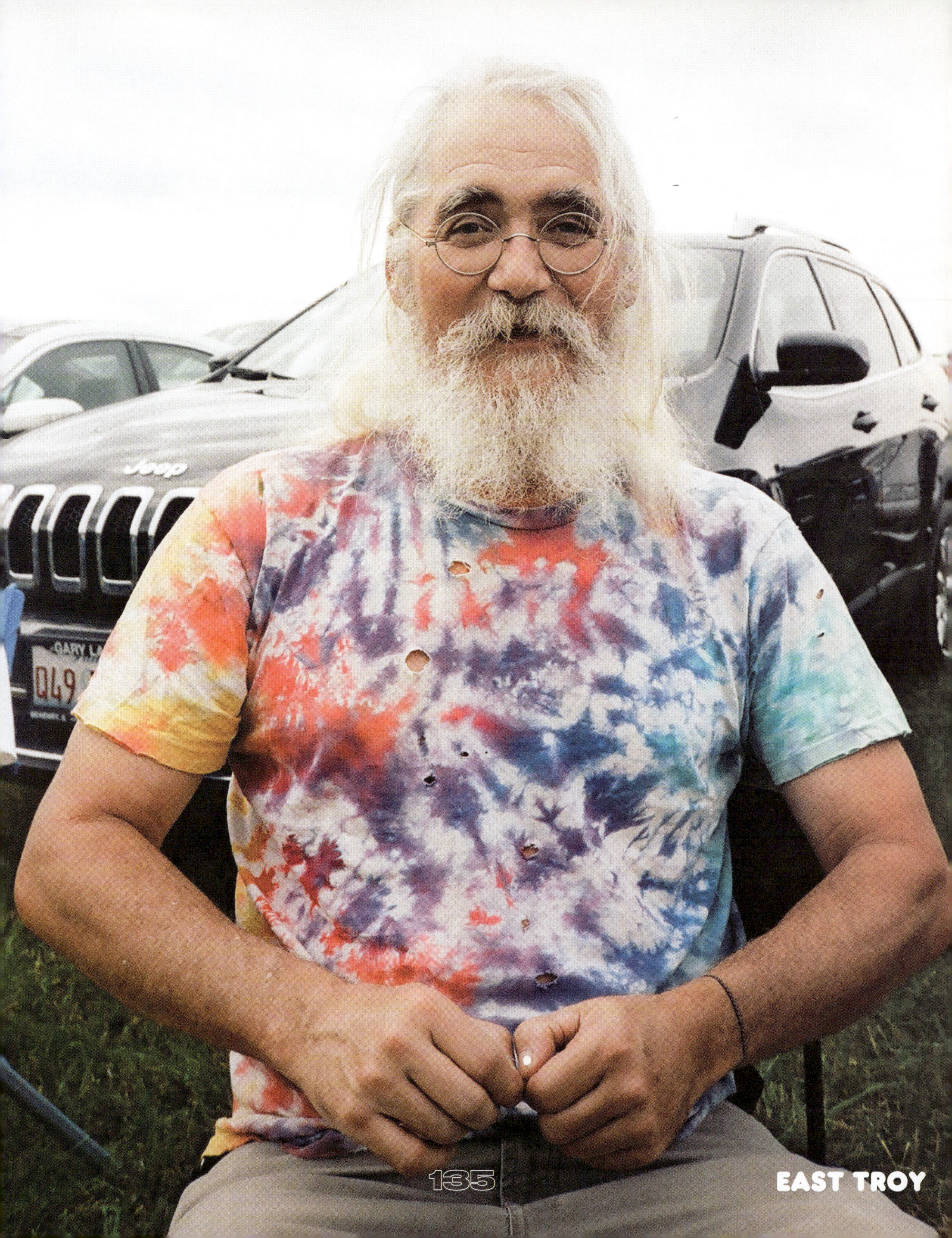

EAST TROY

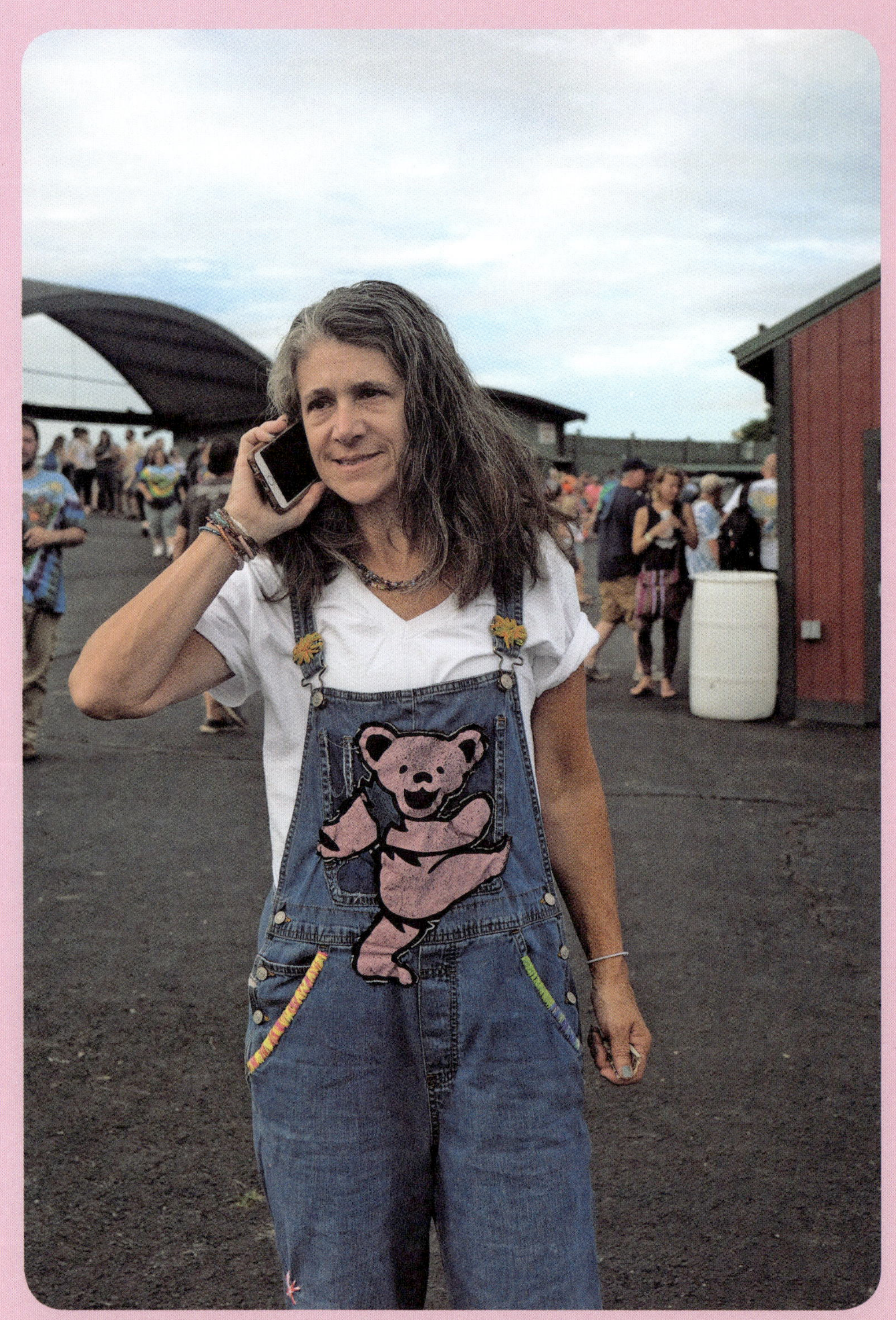

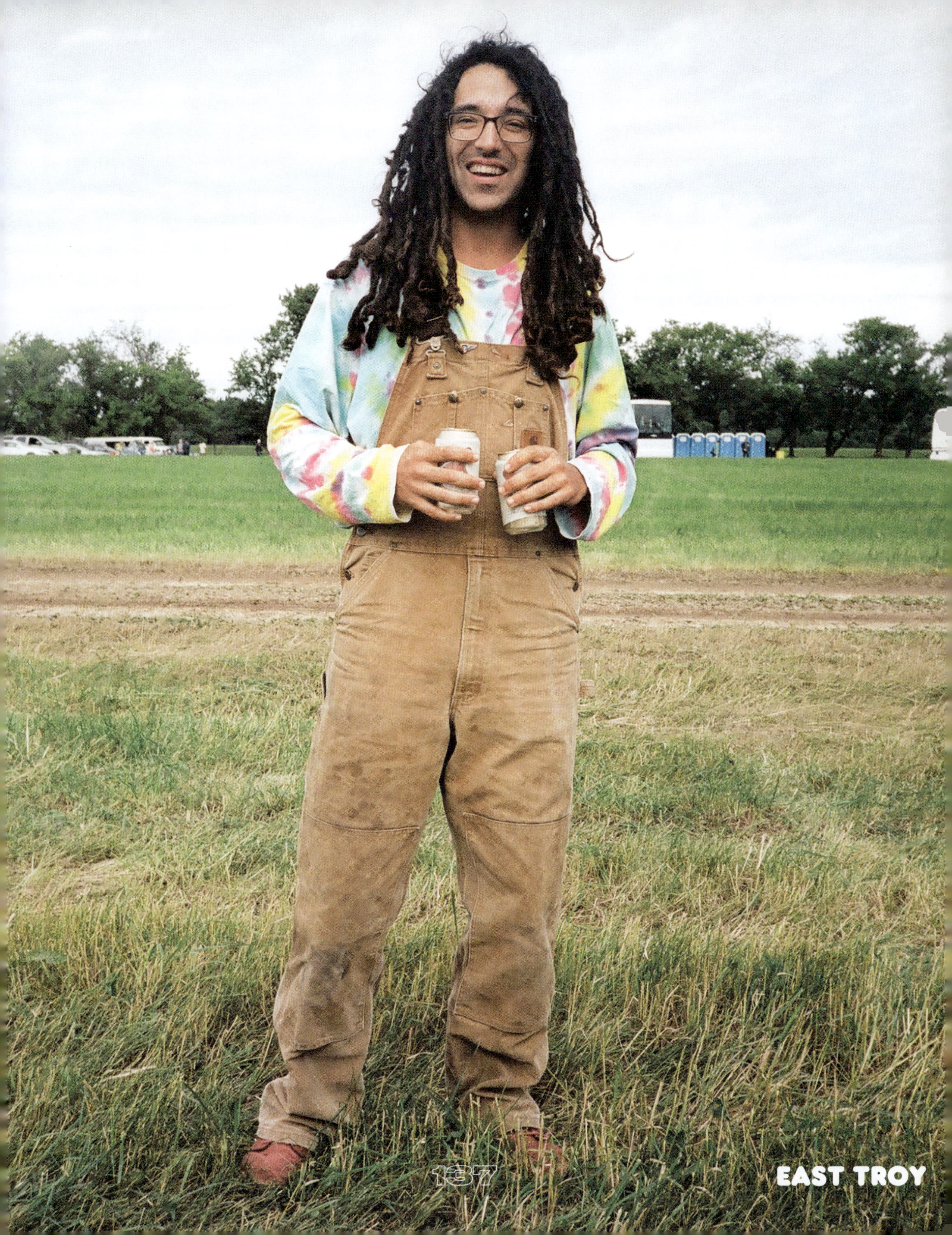

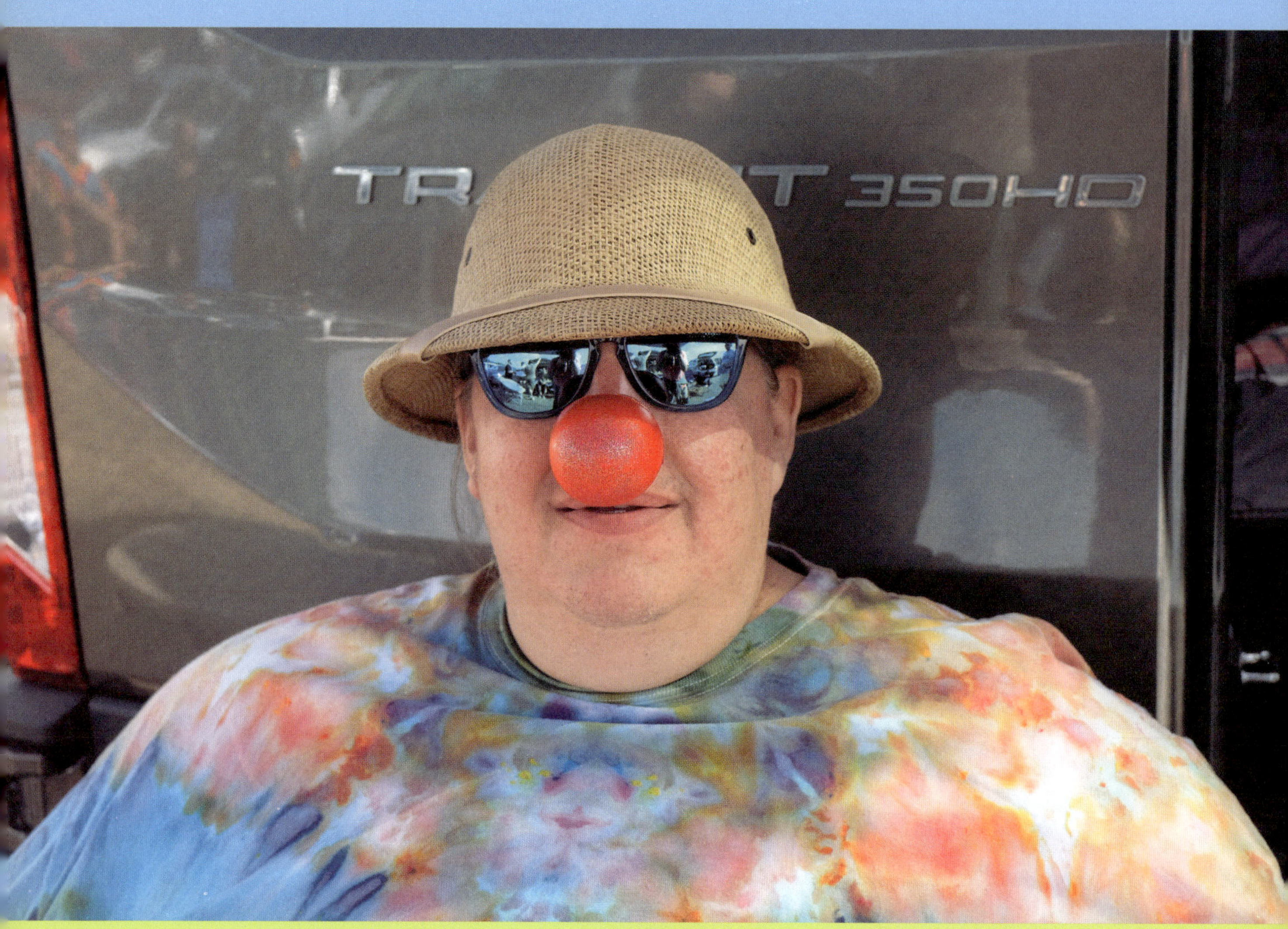
350HD

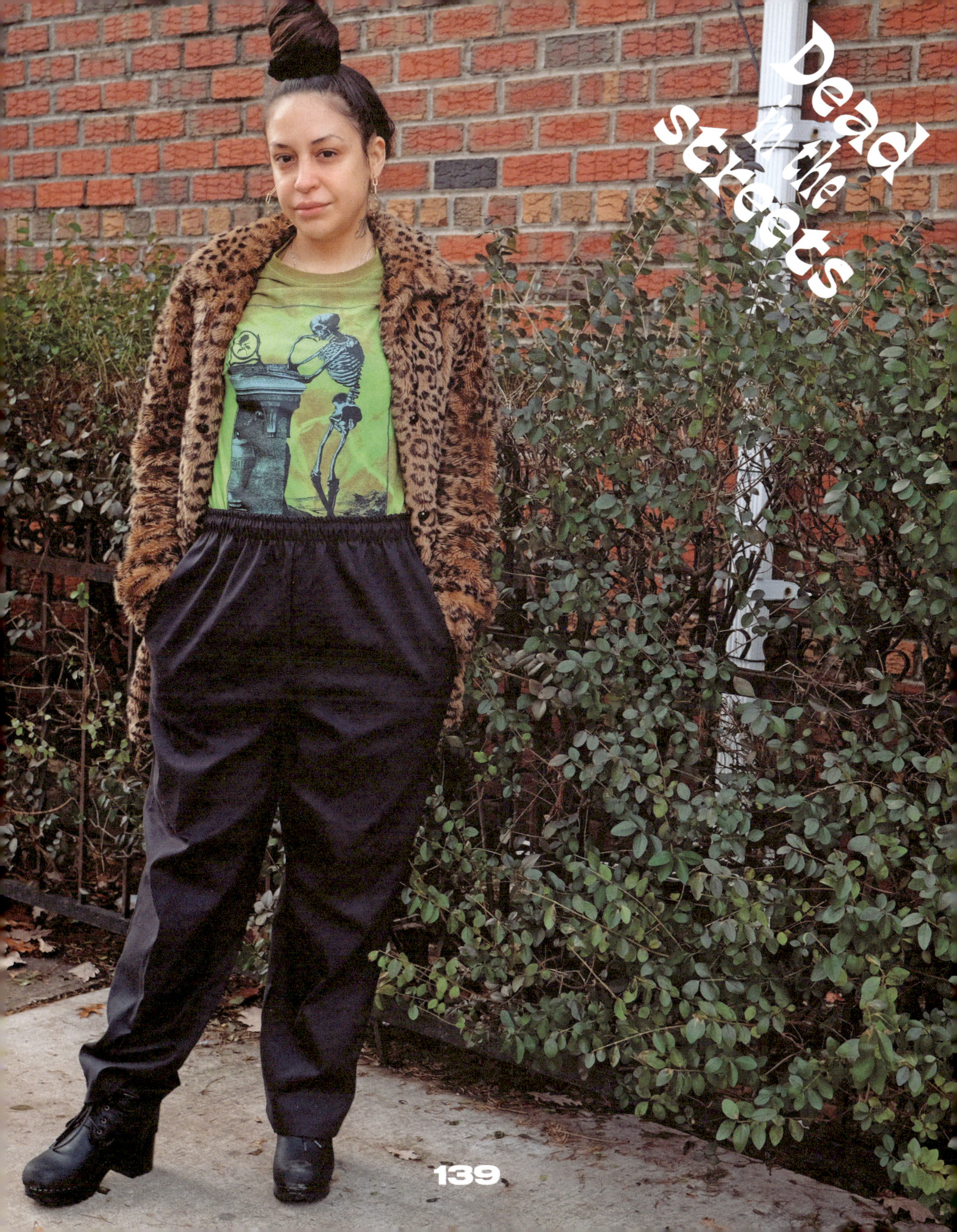

Dead in the streets

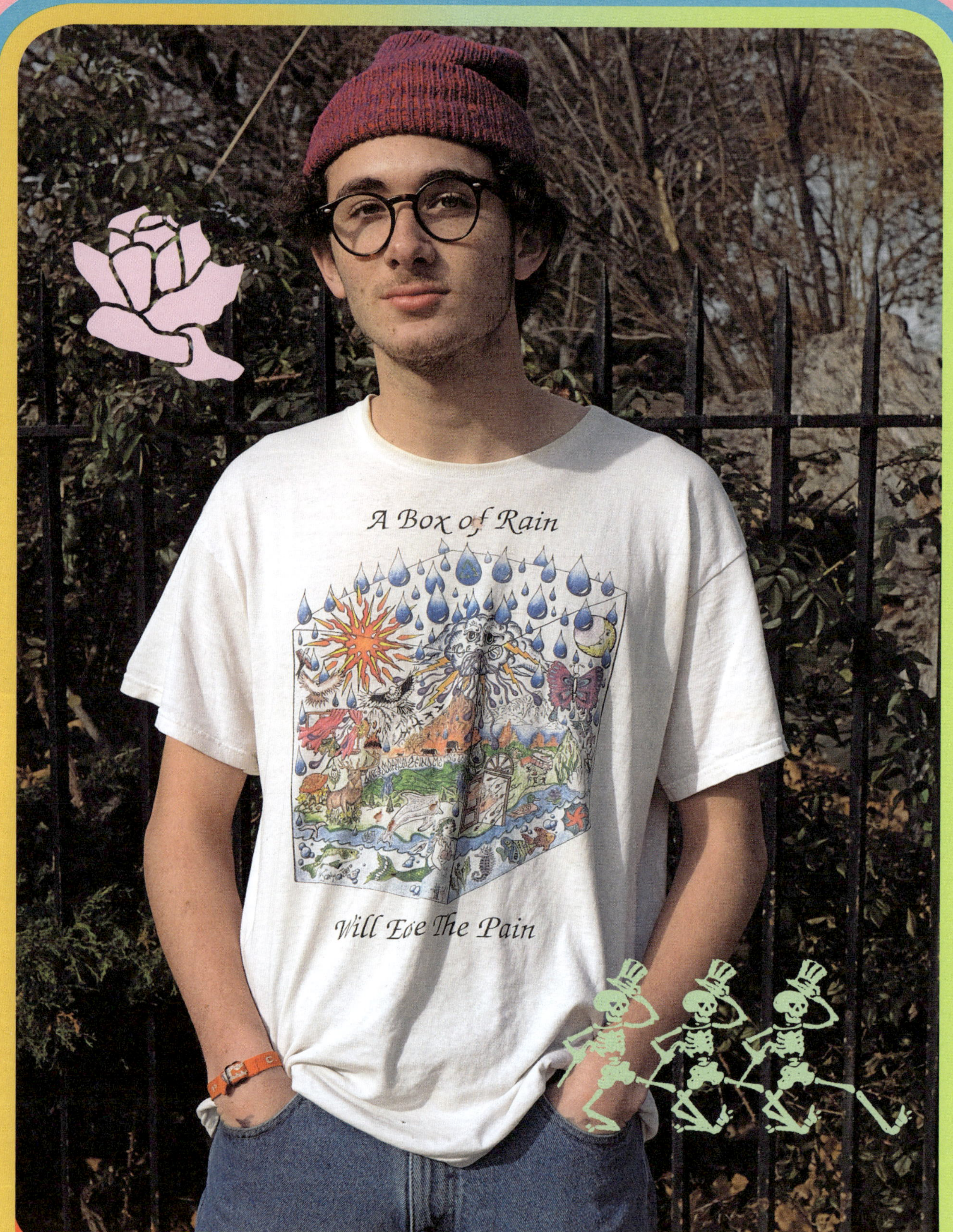
A Box of Rain

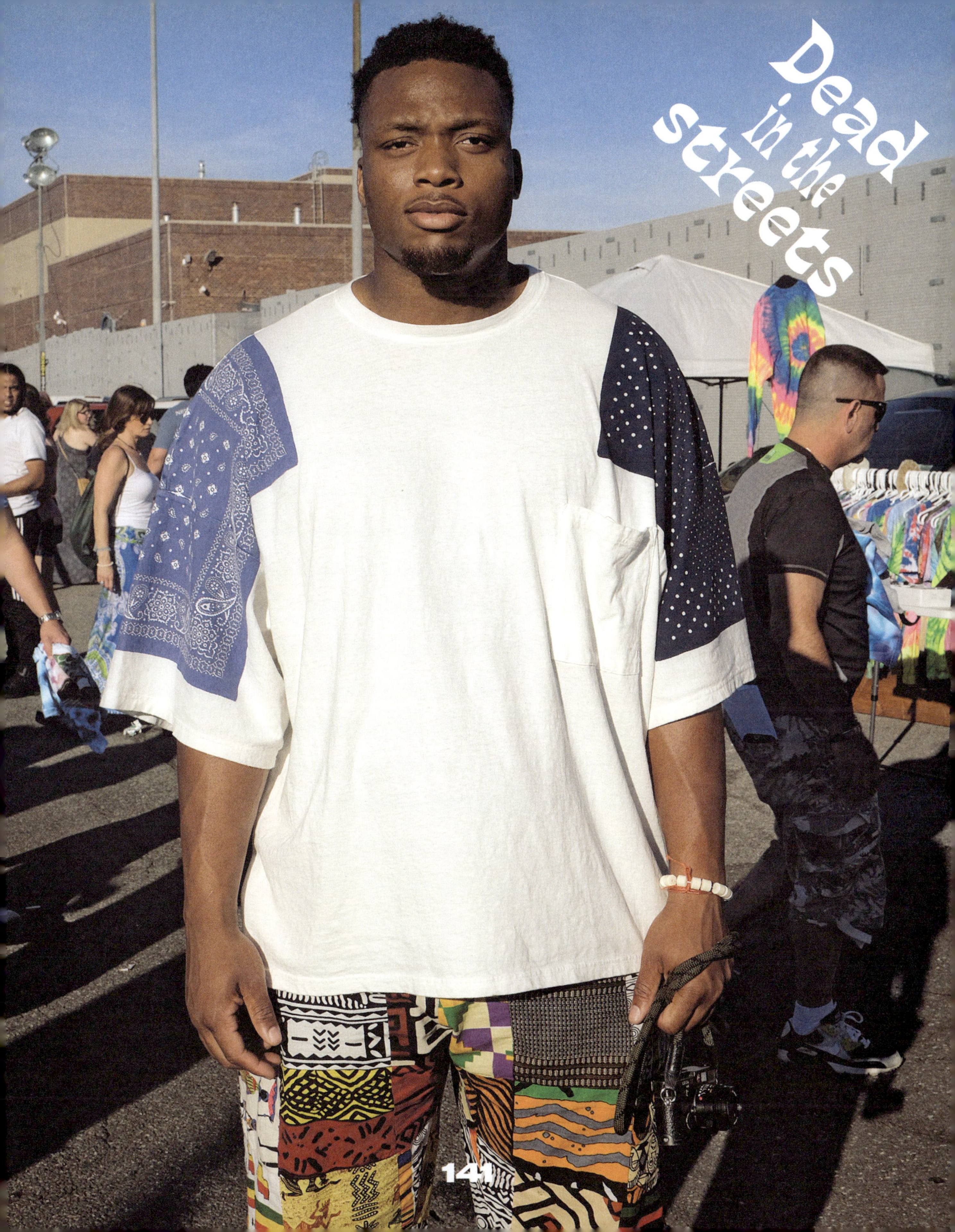
Dead
in the
streets

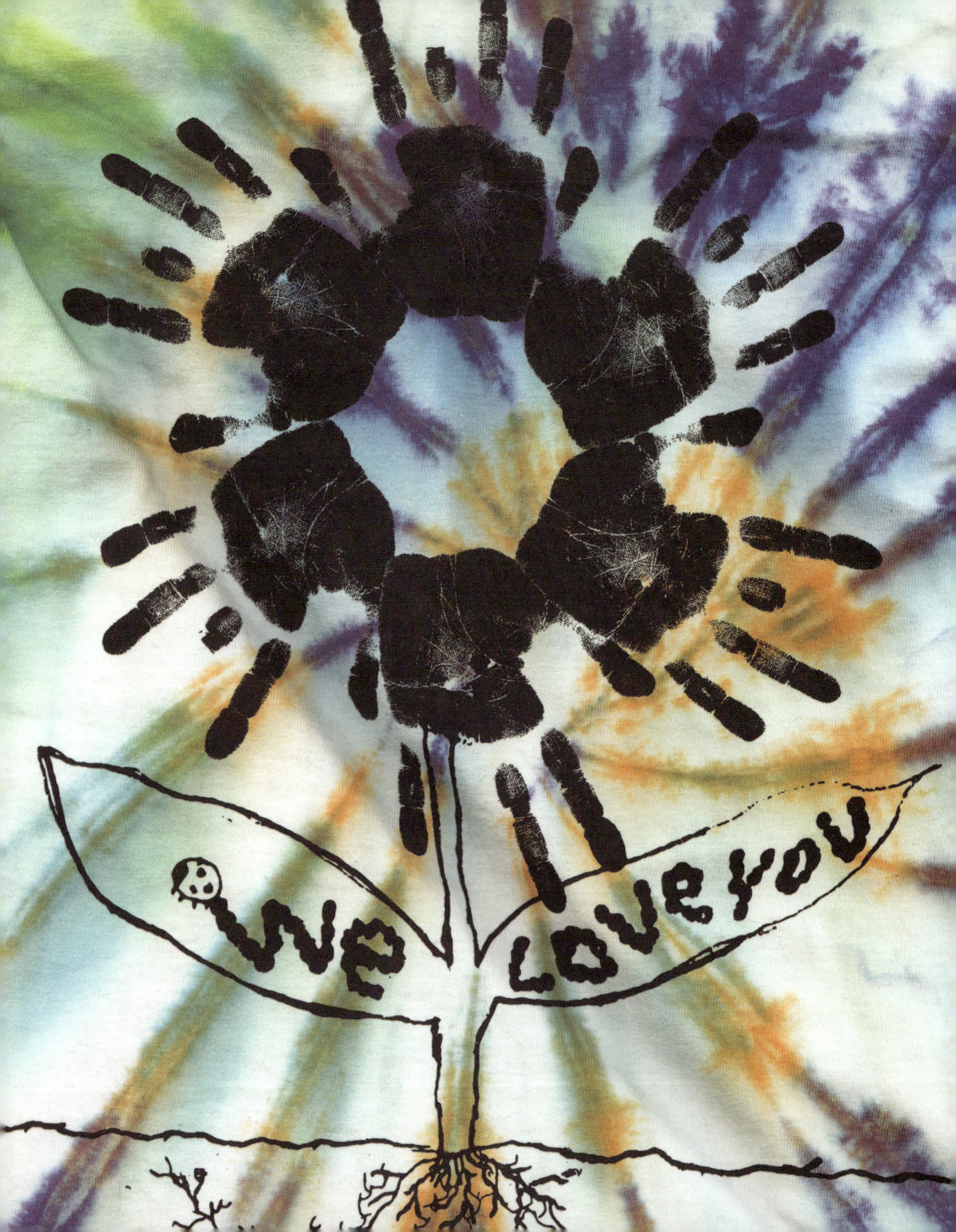
We Love you

FOLSOM FIELD

Boulder, Colorado

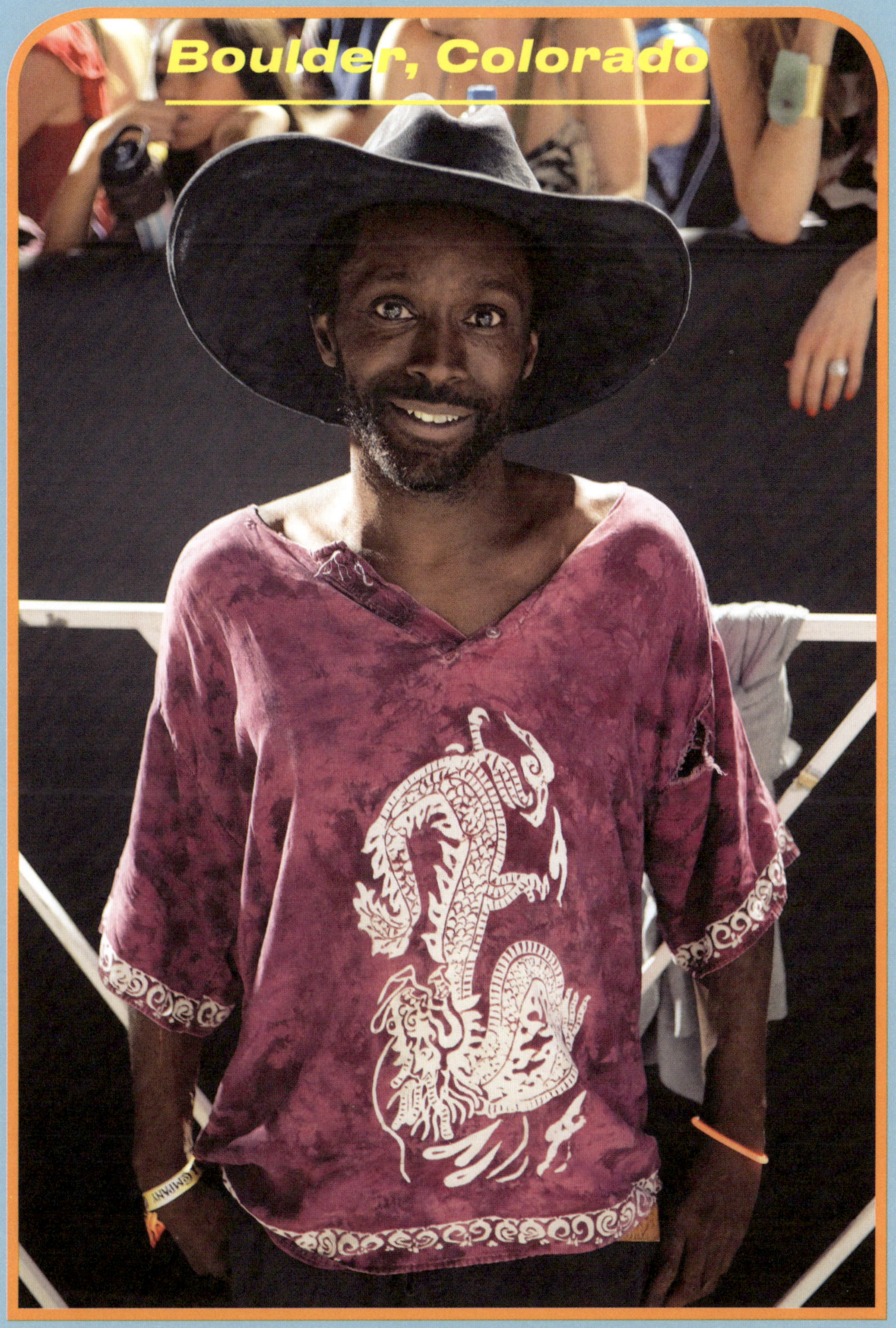

Friday, July 13th, 2018, &
Saturday, July 14th, 2018

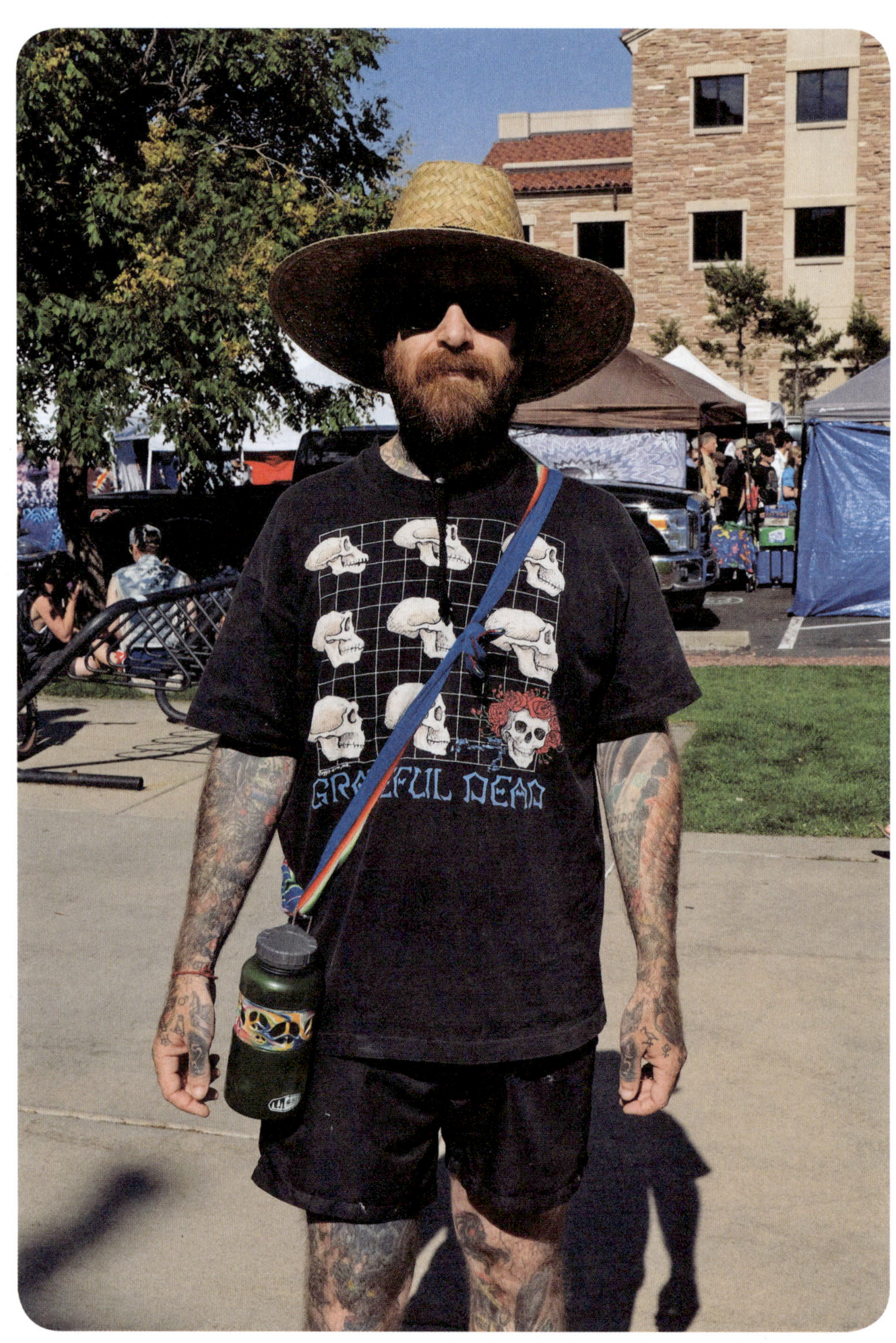

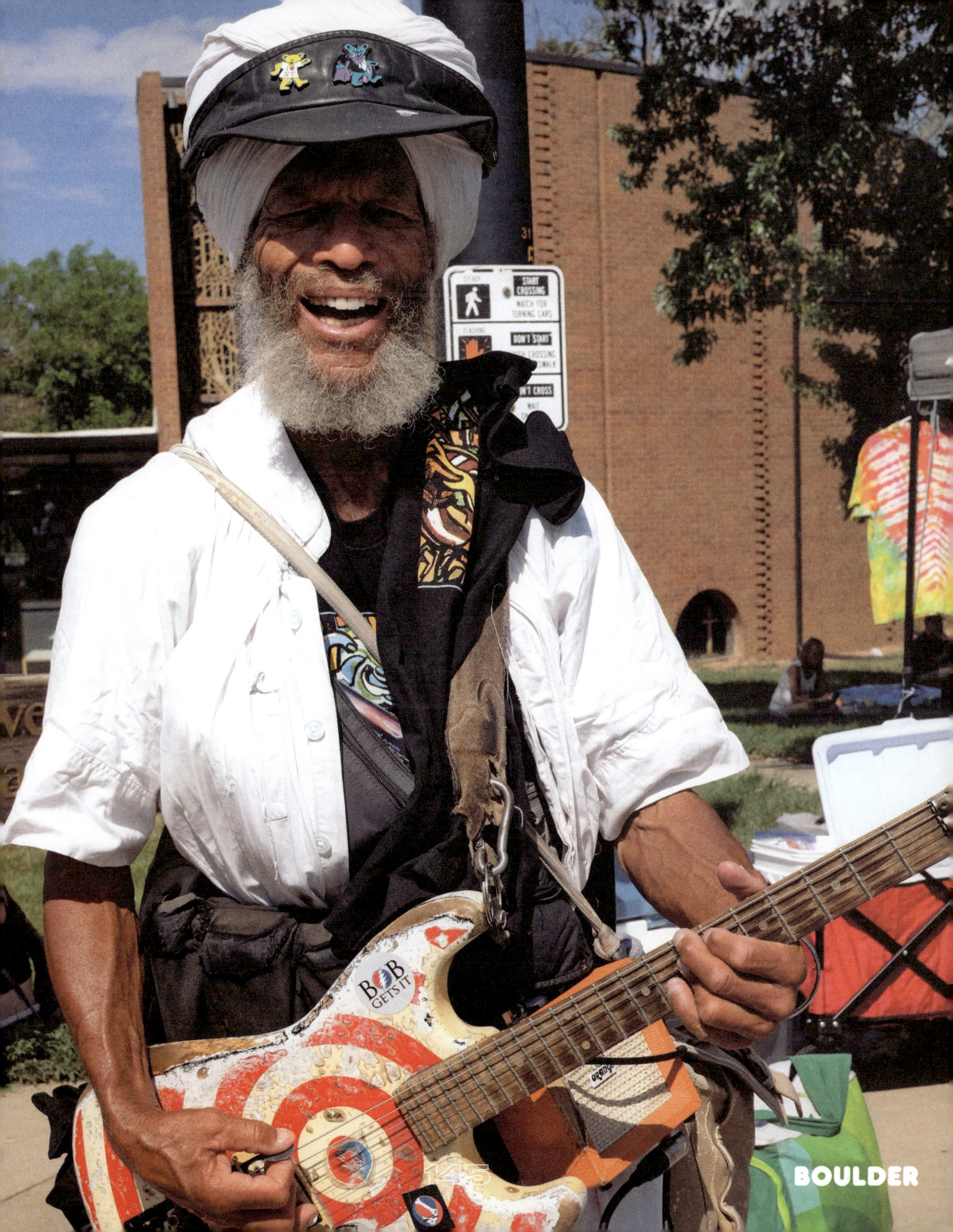
START CROSSING
WATCH FOR TURNING CARS
DON'T START
DON'T CROSS
BOB GETS IT

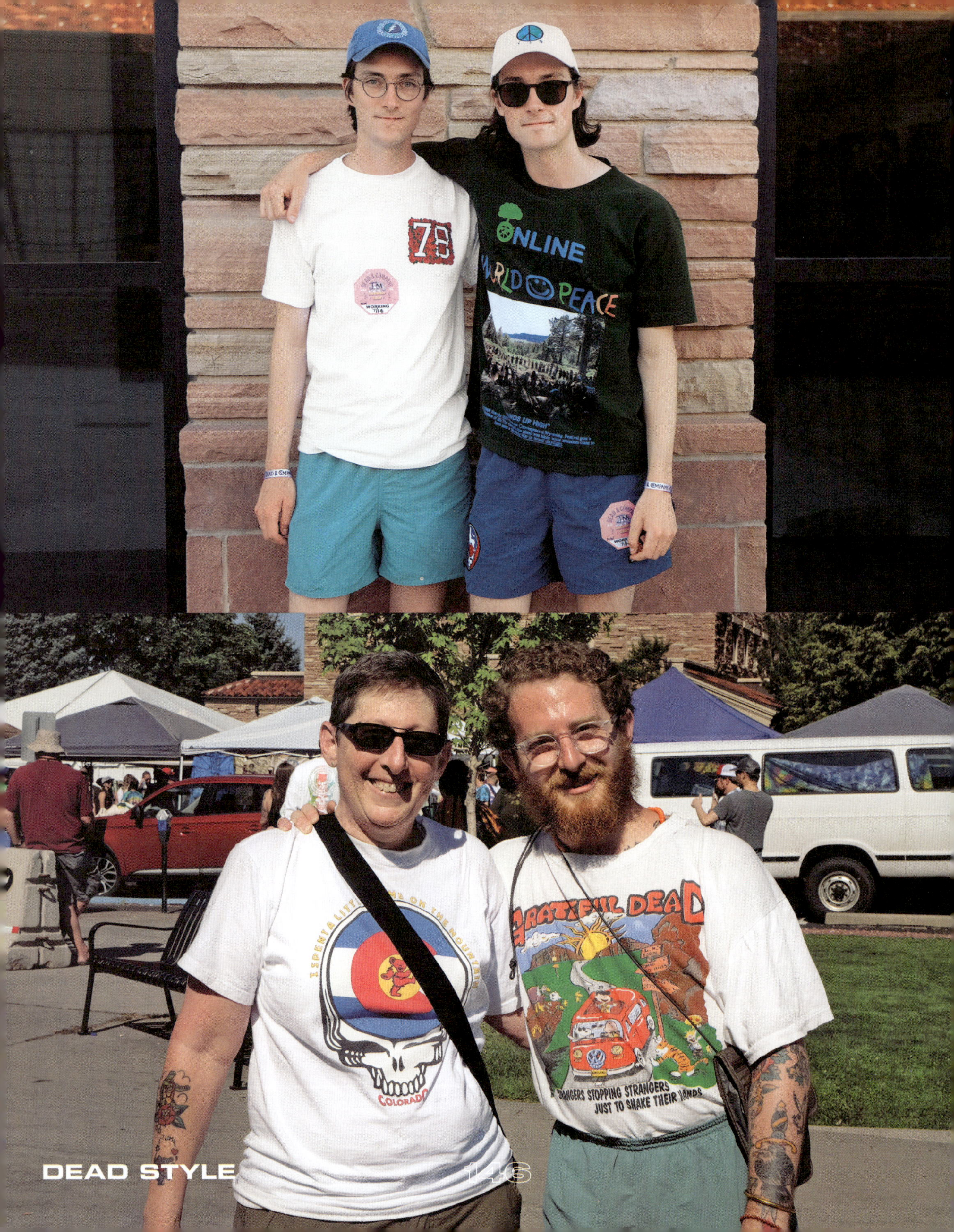
78
ONLINE
PEACE
COLORADO

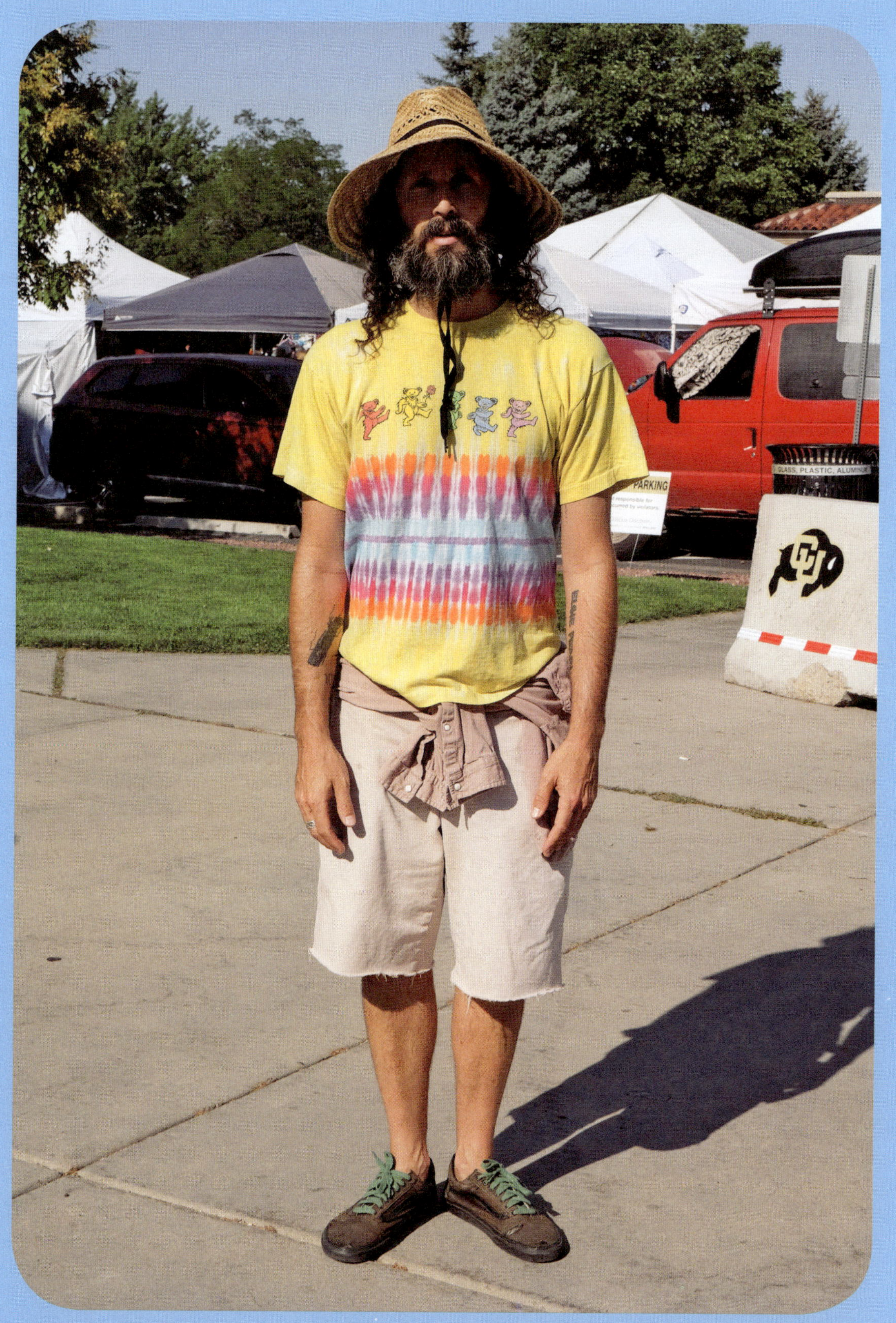
PARKING

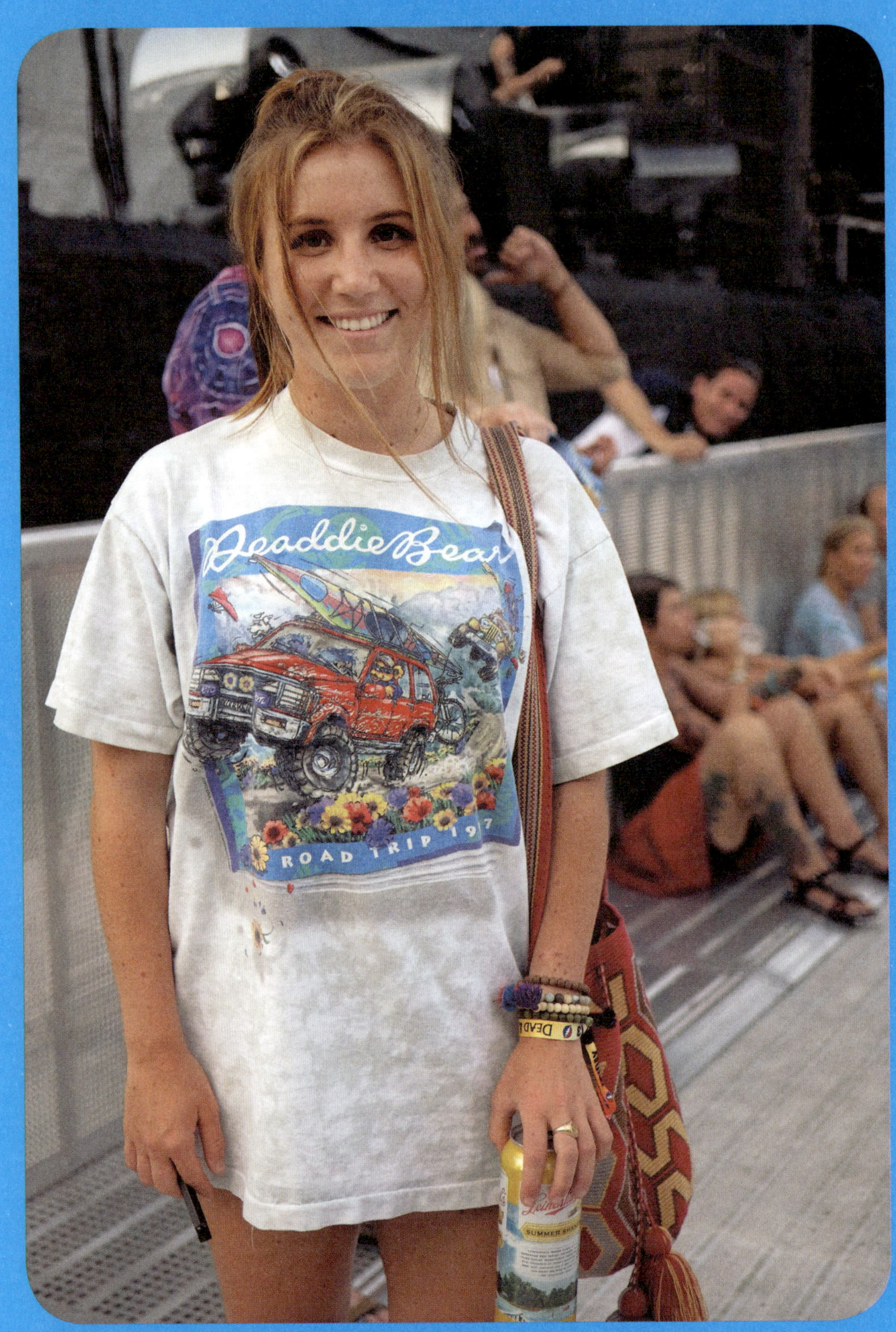
ROAD TRIP
DEAD

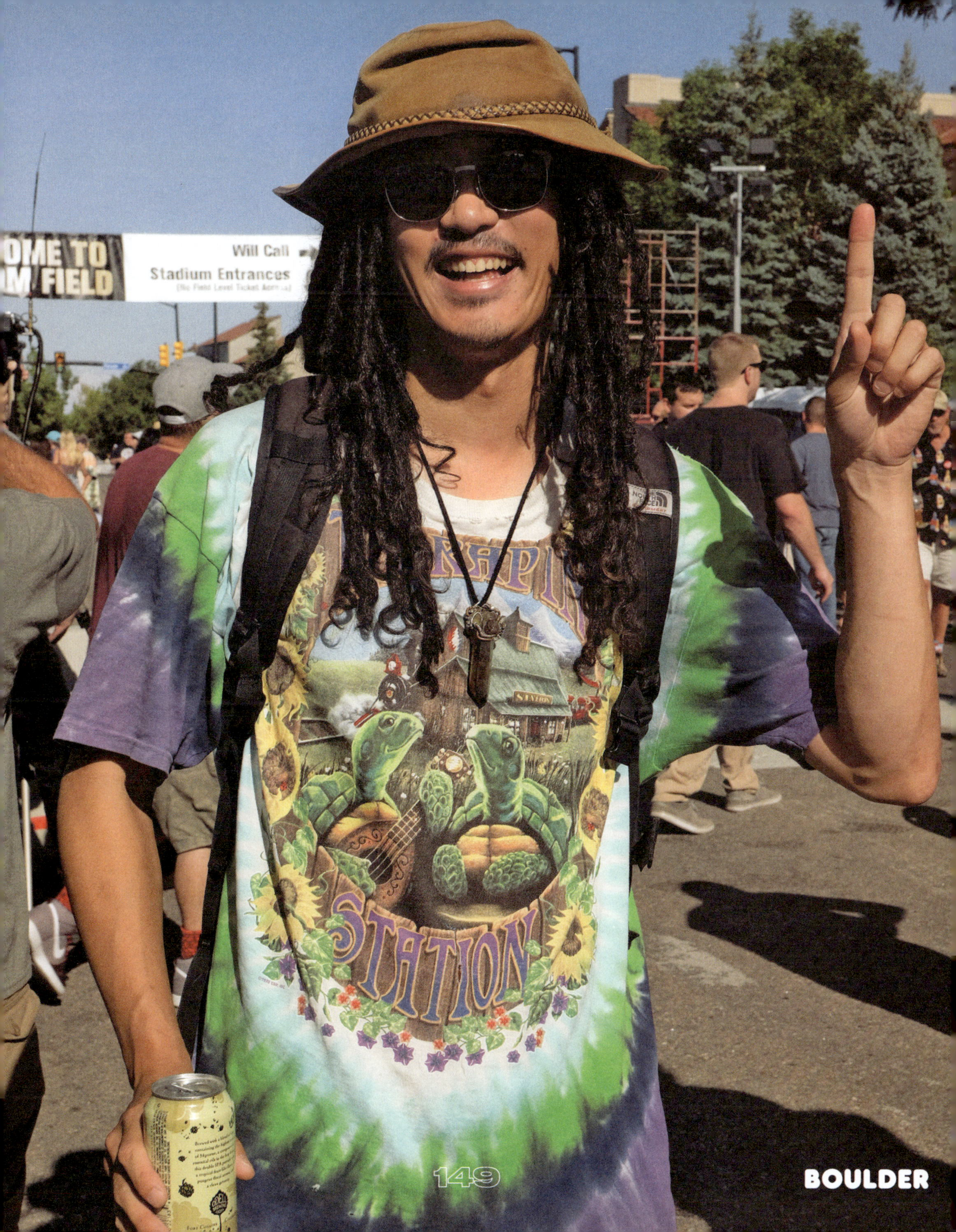
OME TO
M FIELD
Will Call
Stadium Entrances
STATION

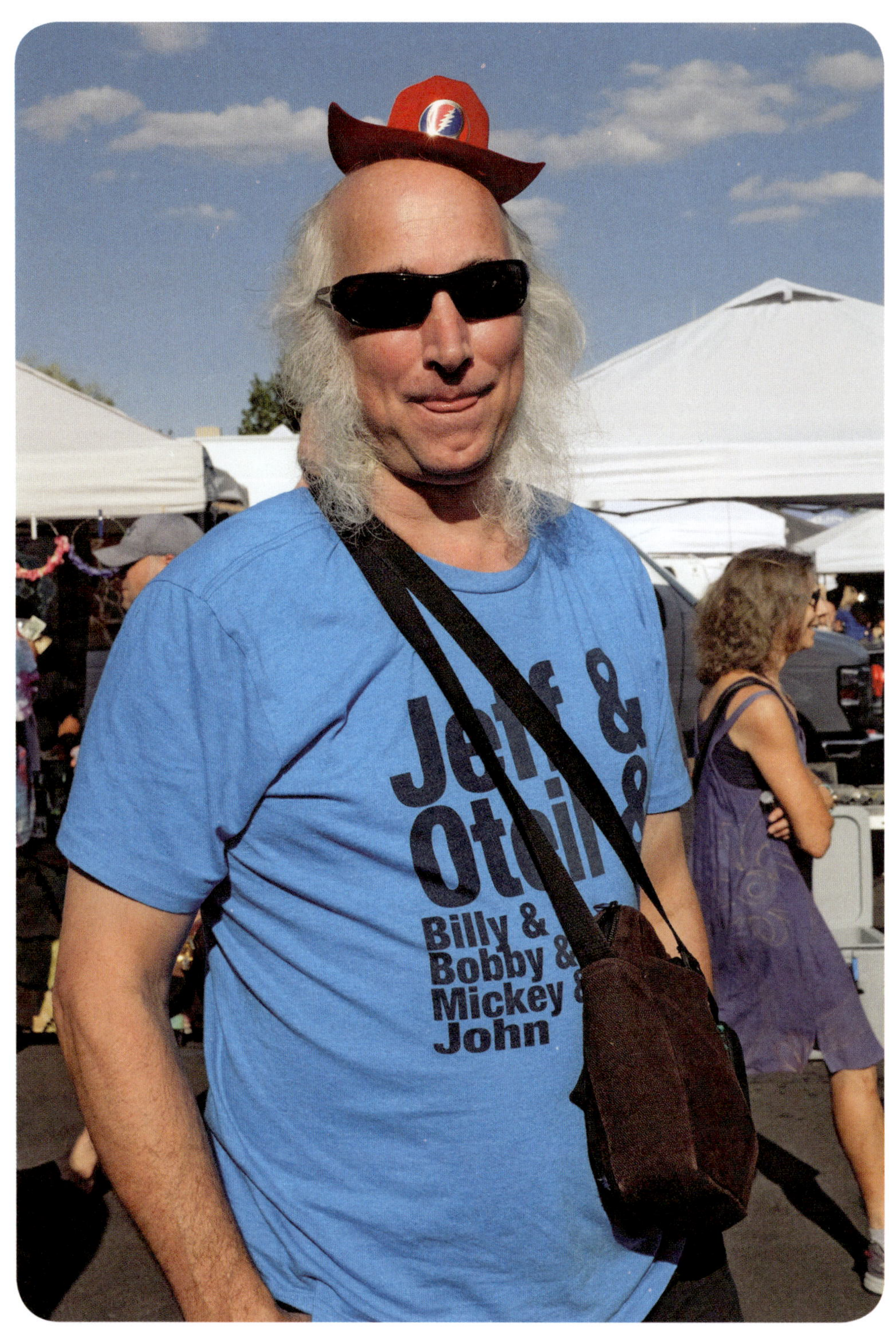
Jeff &
Oteil &
Billy &
Bobby &
Mickey &
John

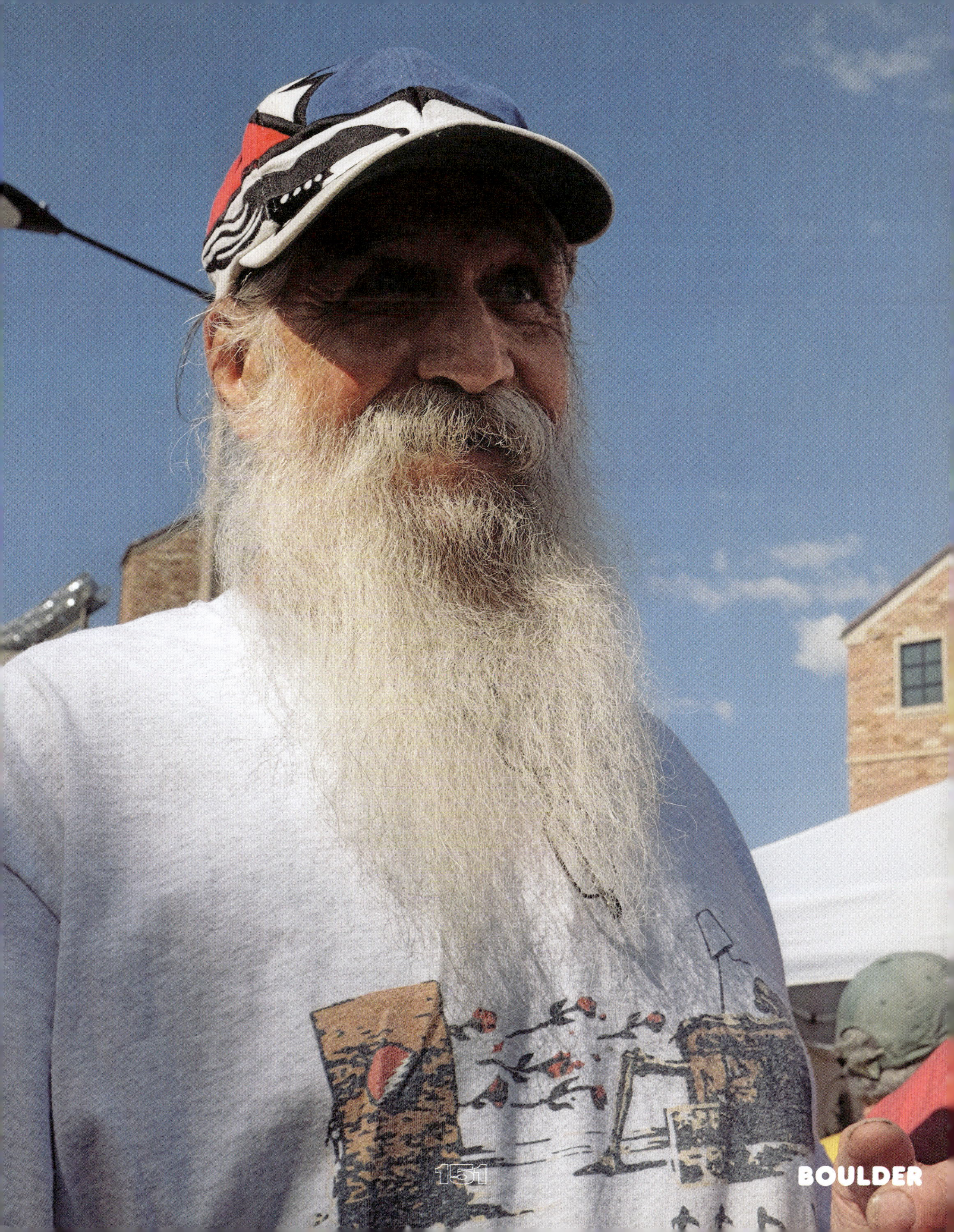

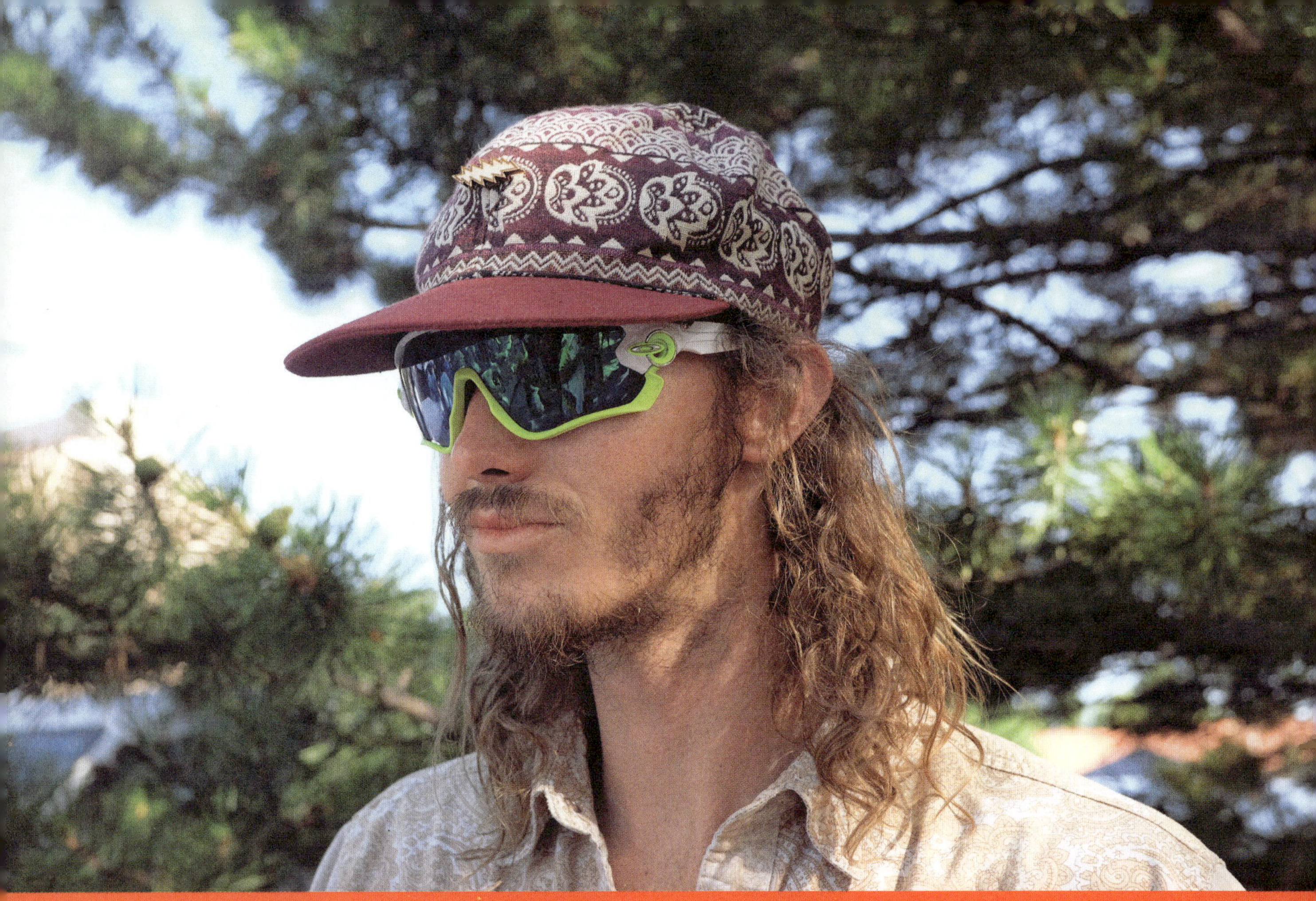

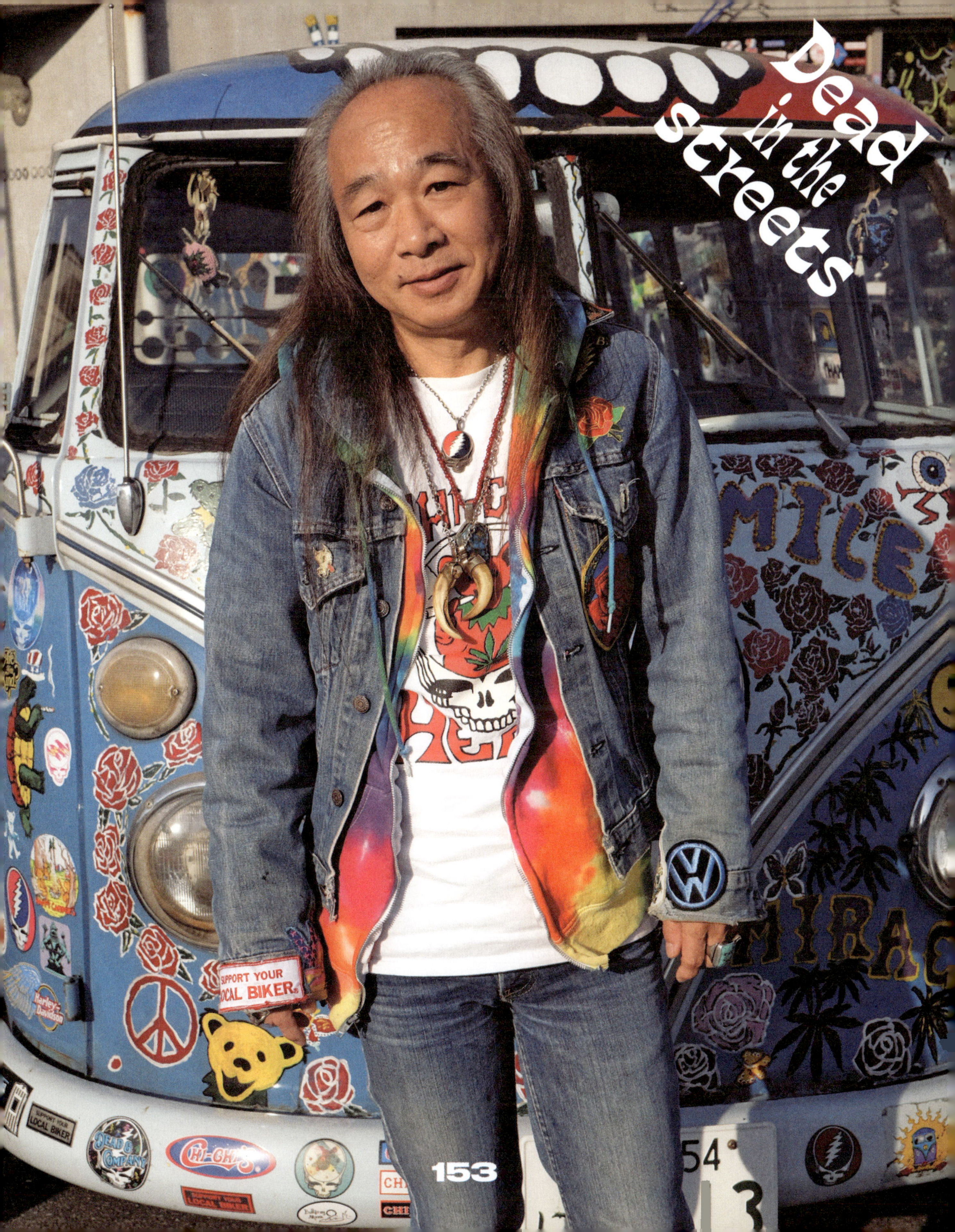

Dead in the streets

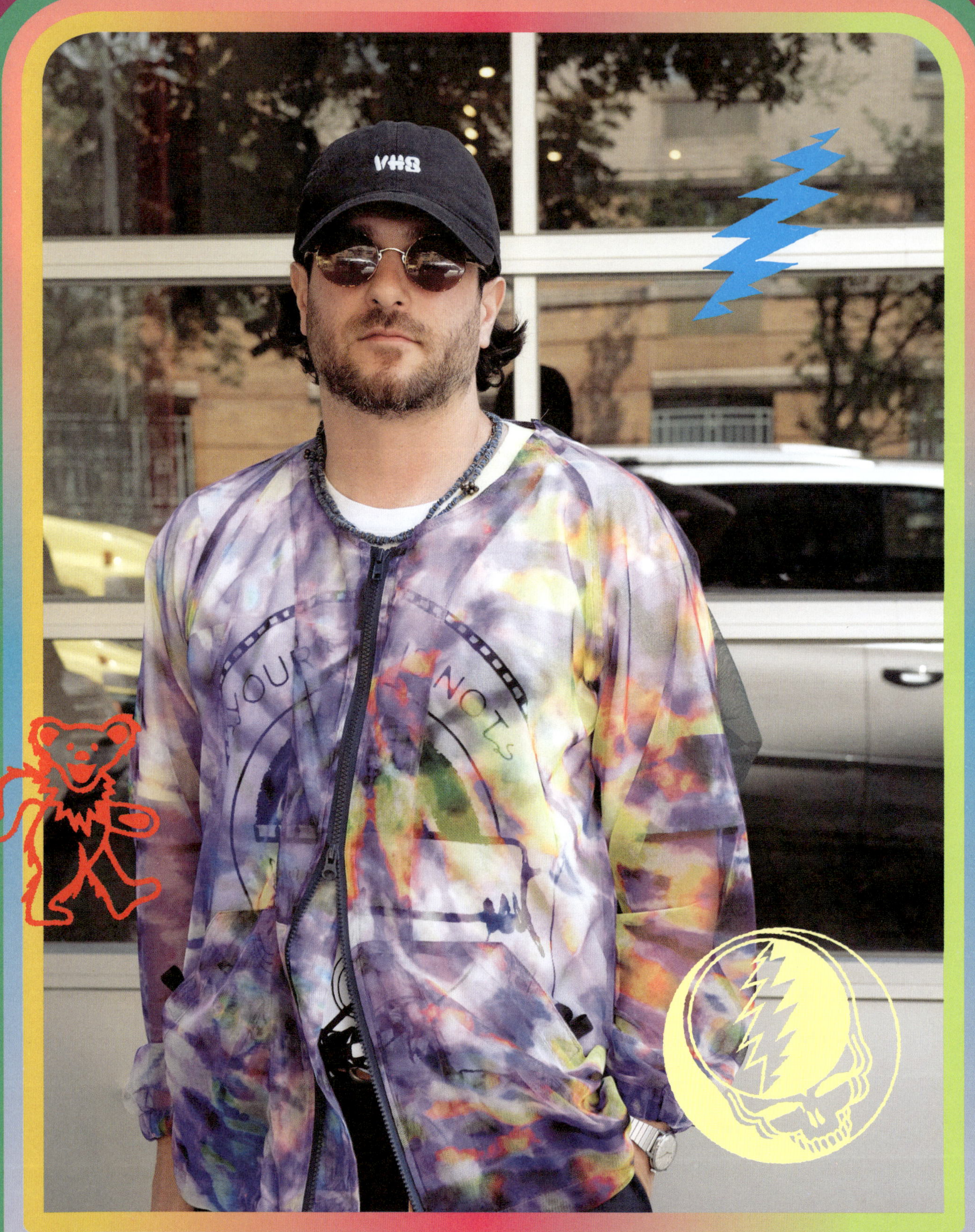

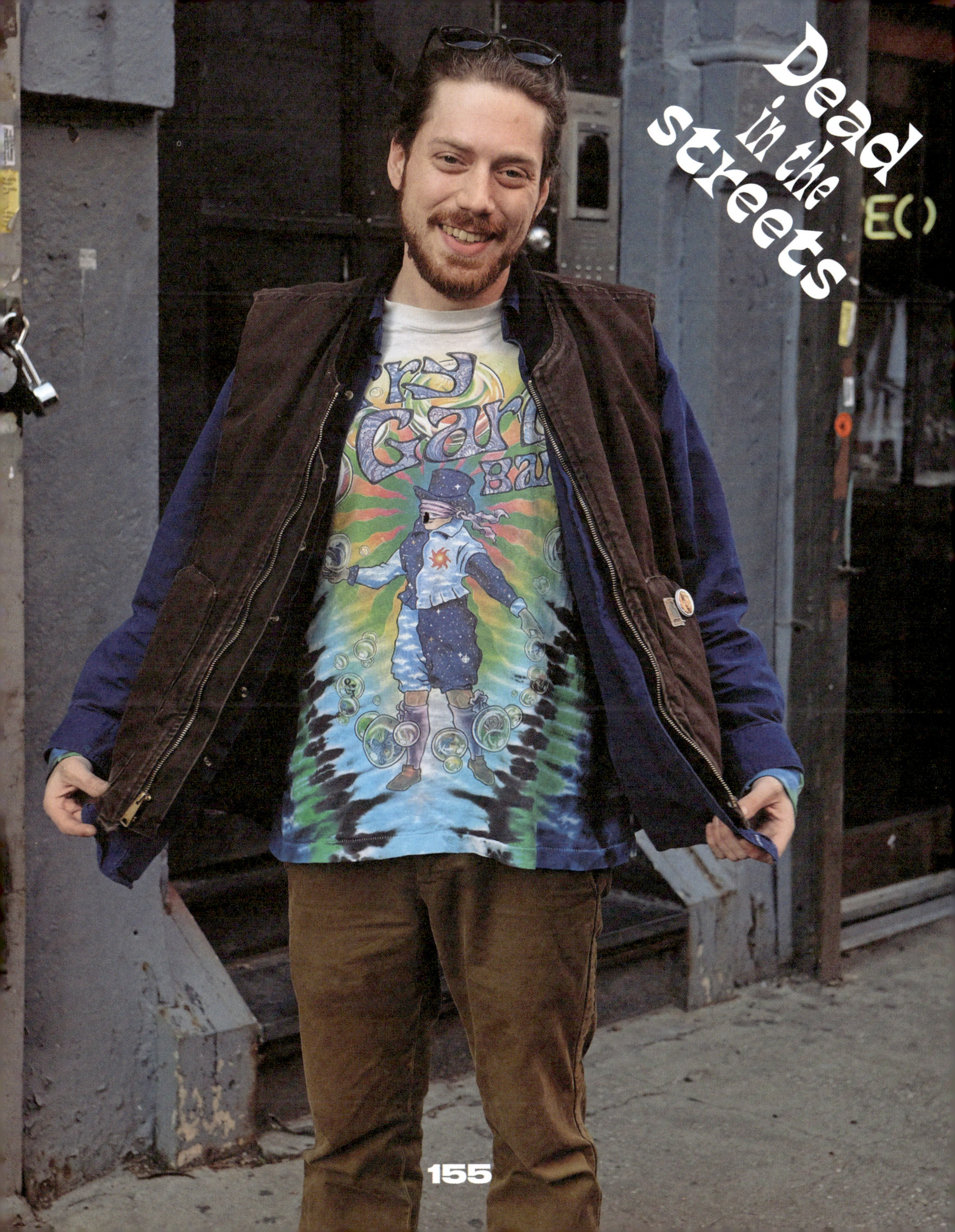

Dead in the streets

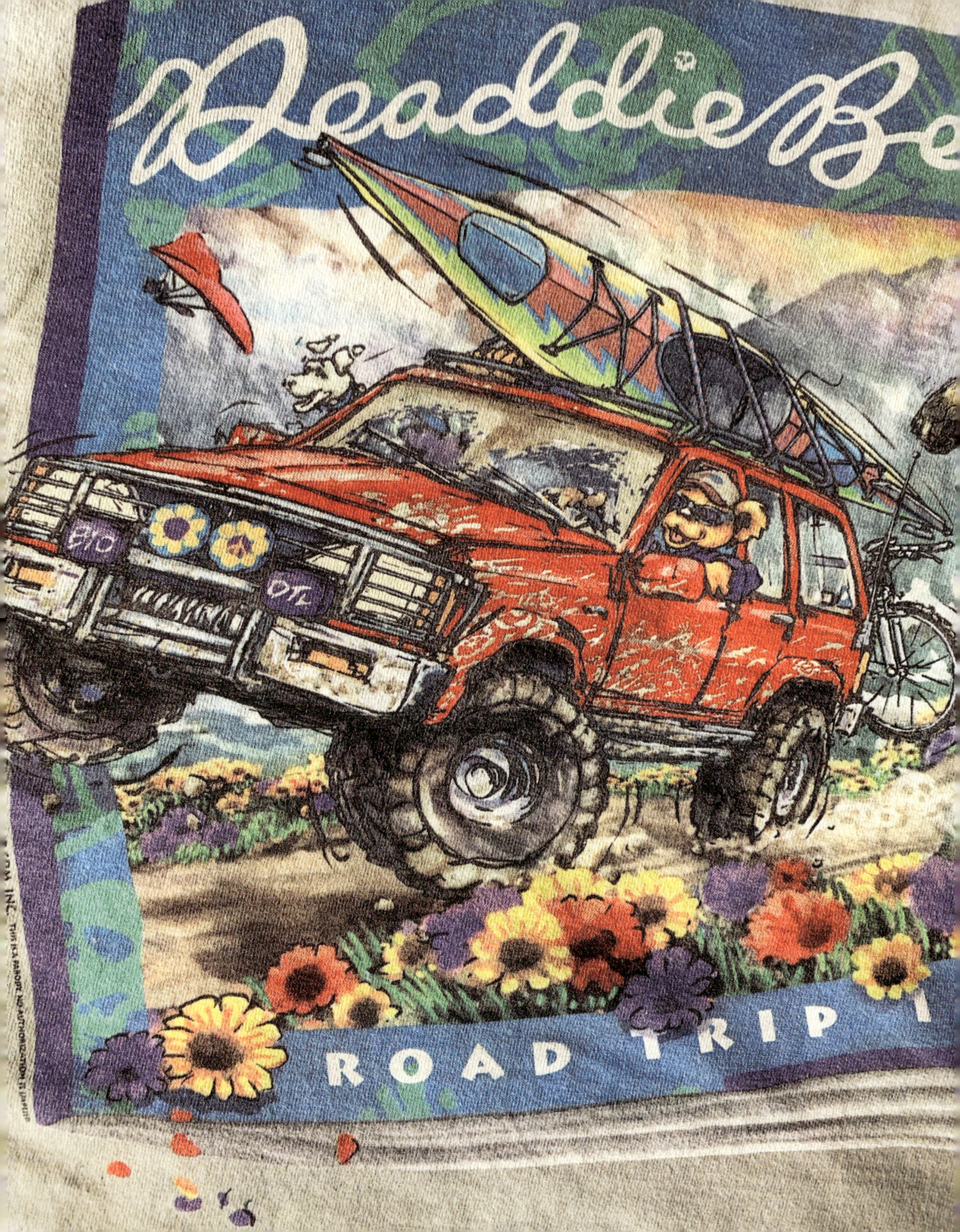
Deaddie
ROAD TRIP

THE GORGE AMPHITHEATRE

George, Washington

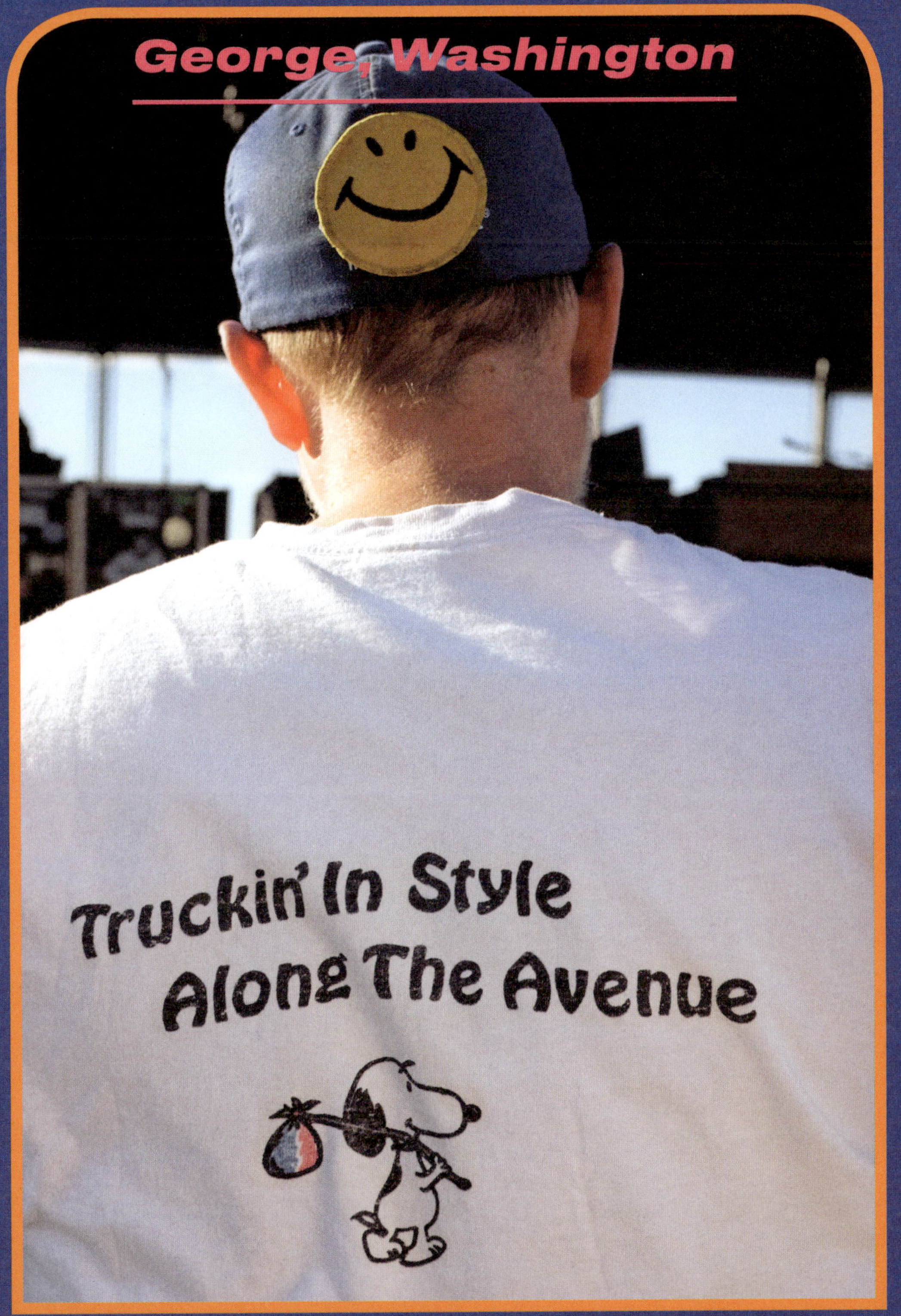

Friday, June 7th, 2019, &
Saturday, June 8th, 2019

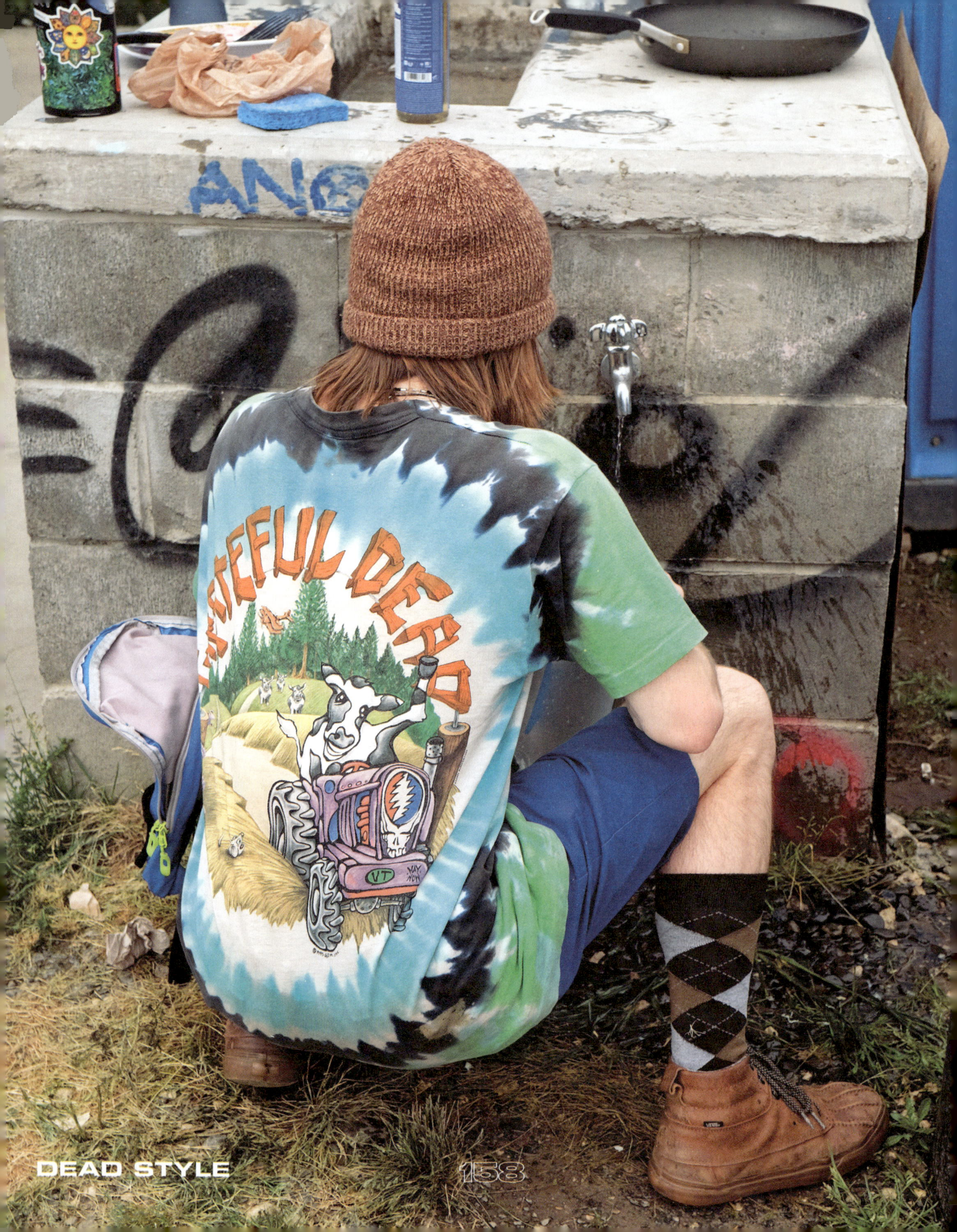

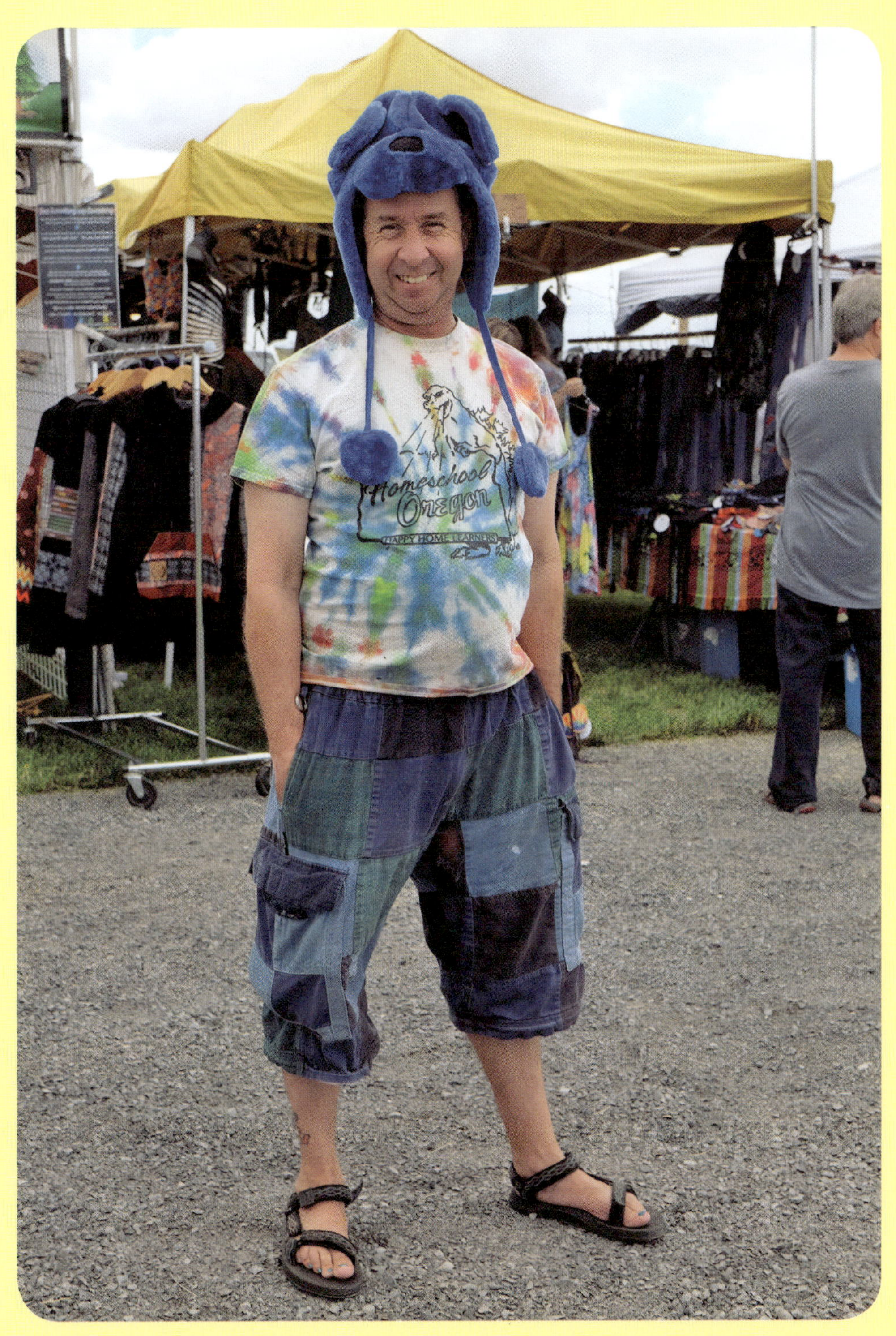

GEORGE

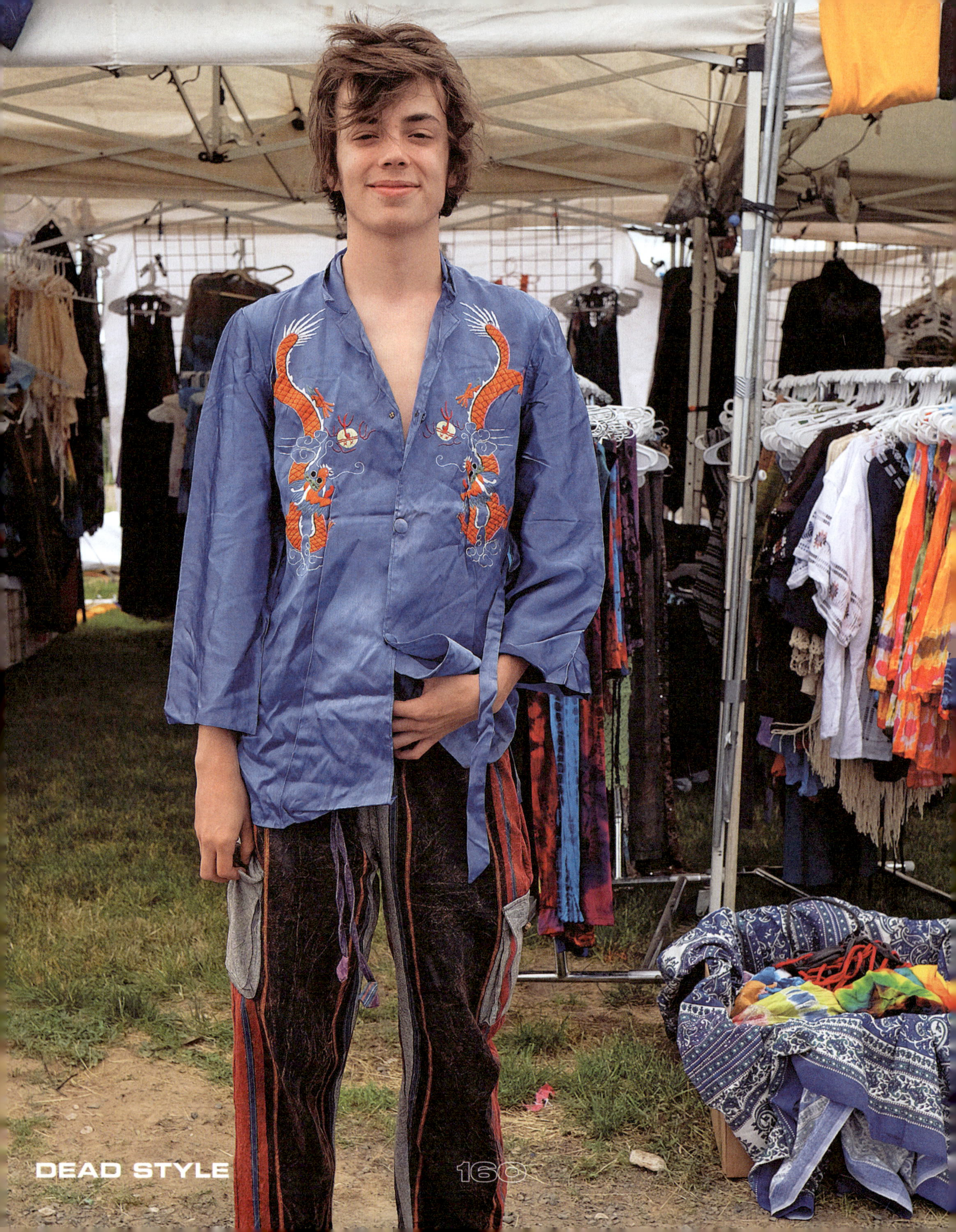

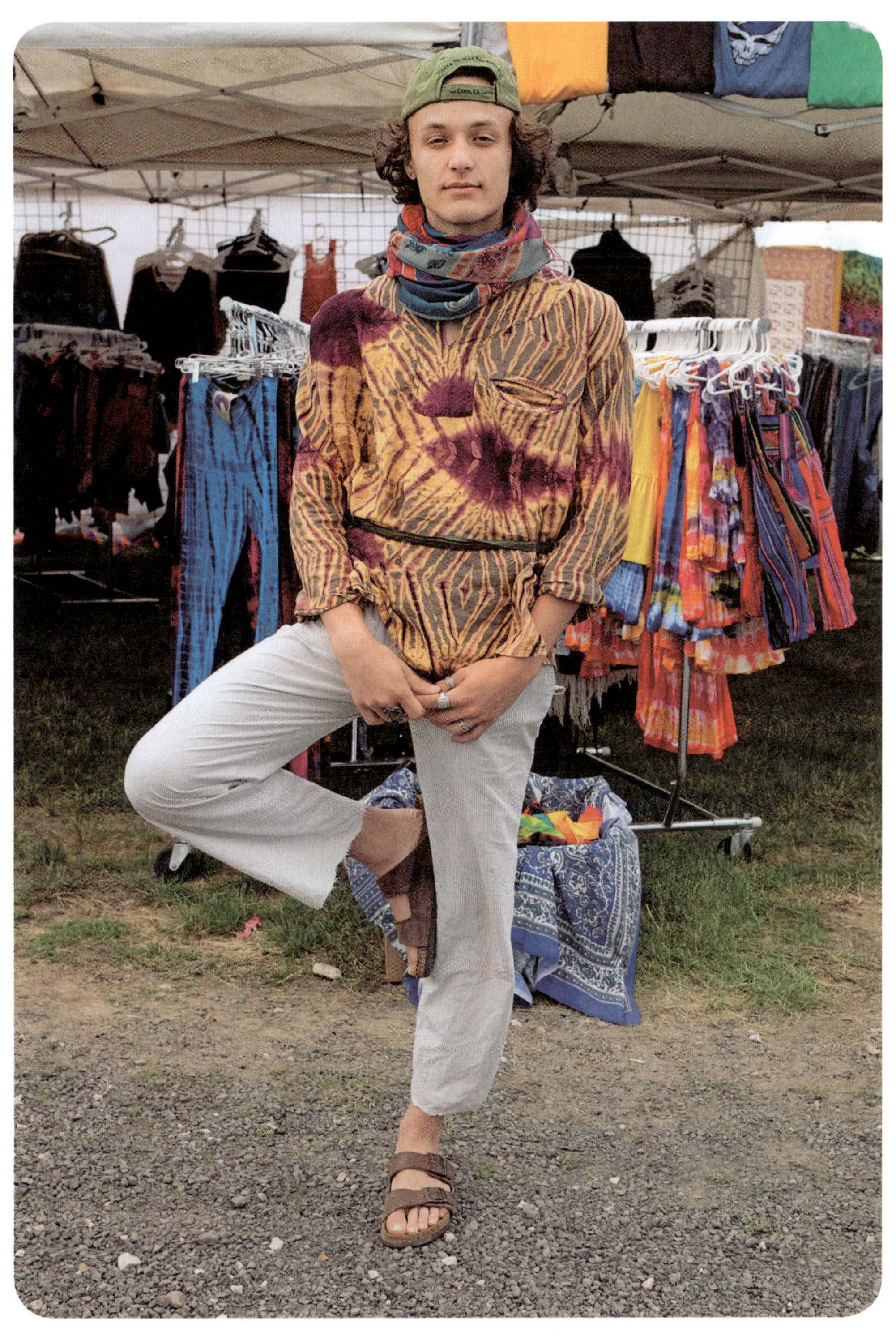

GEORGE

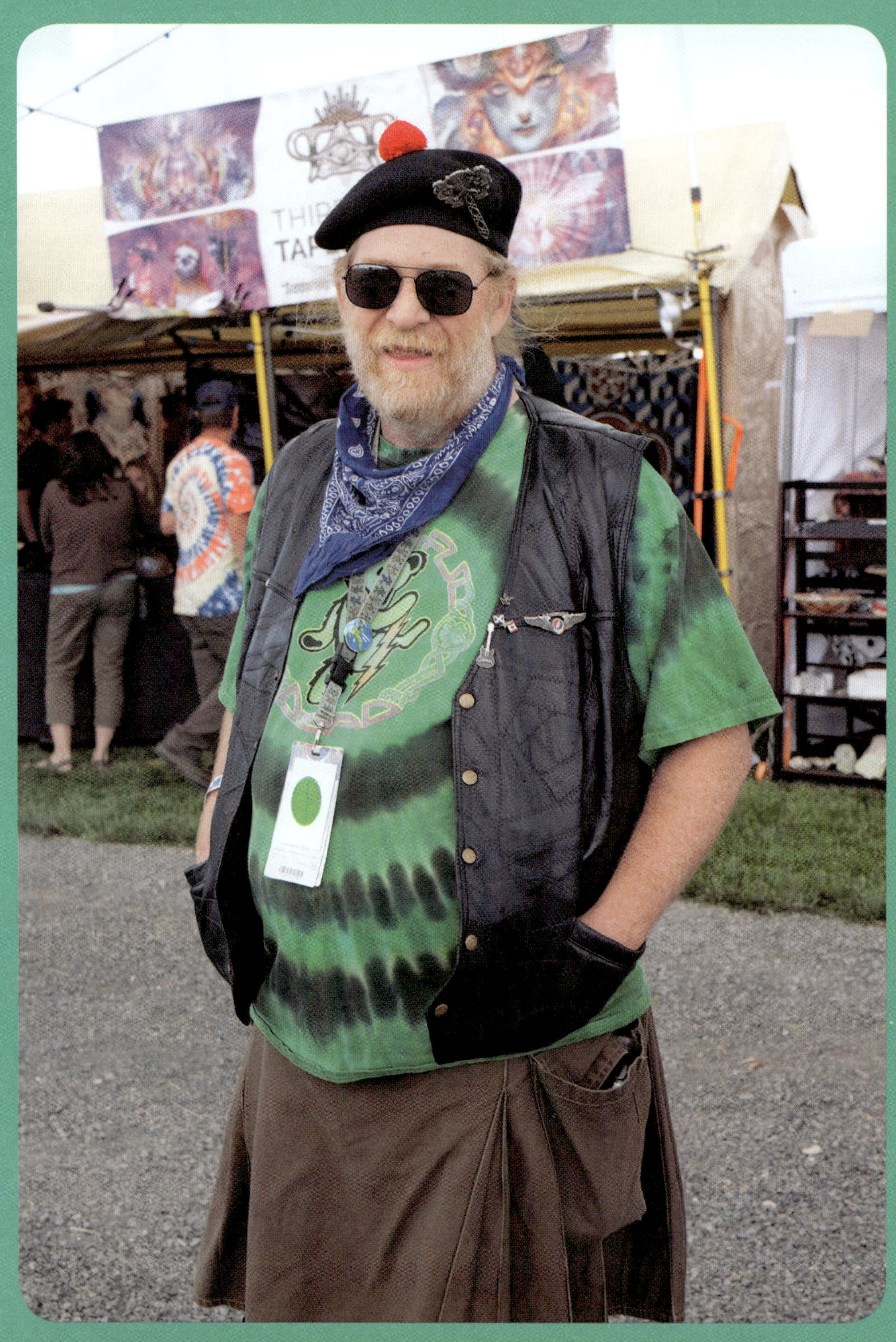

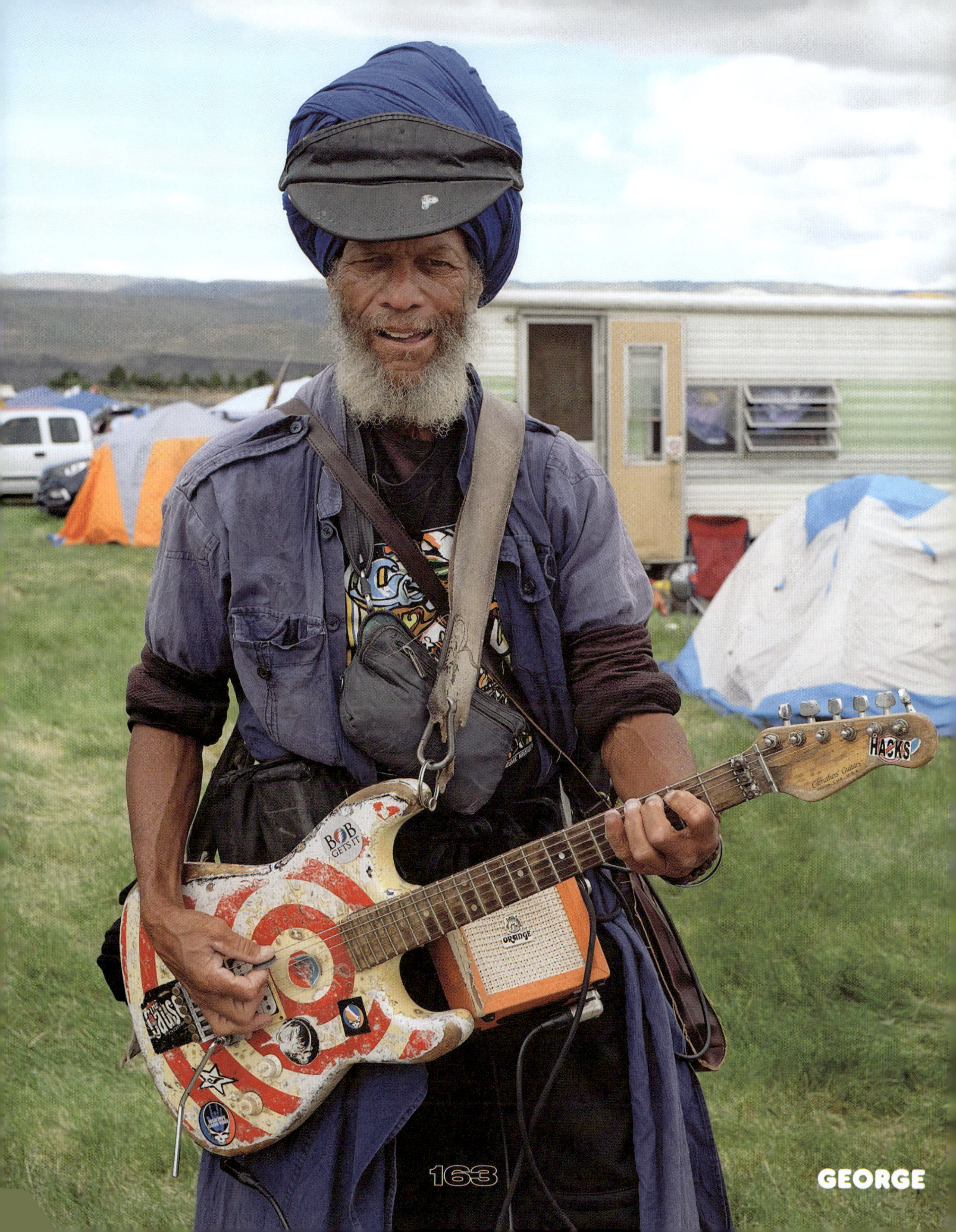

GEORGE

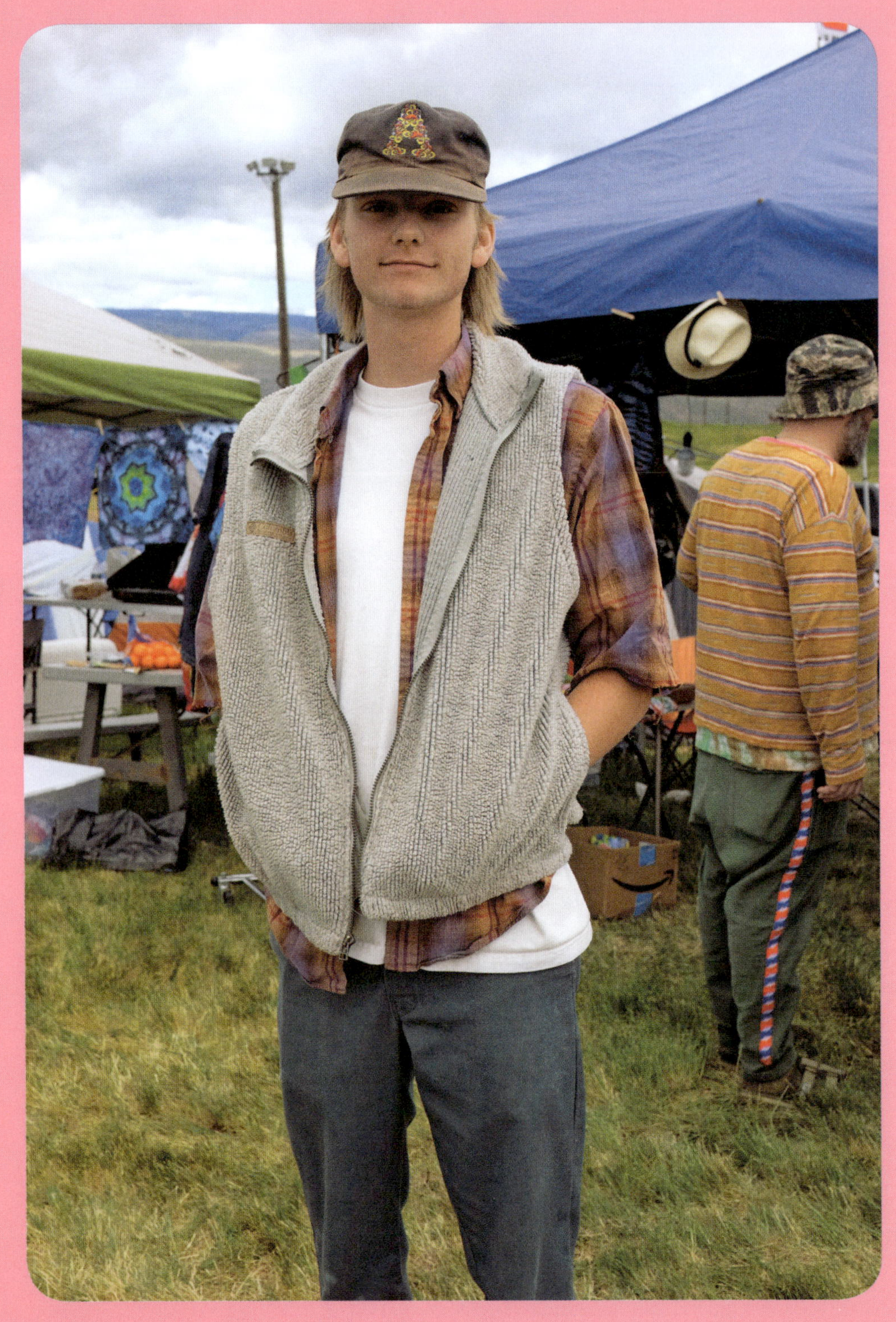

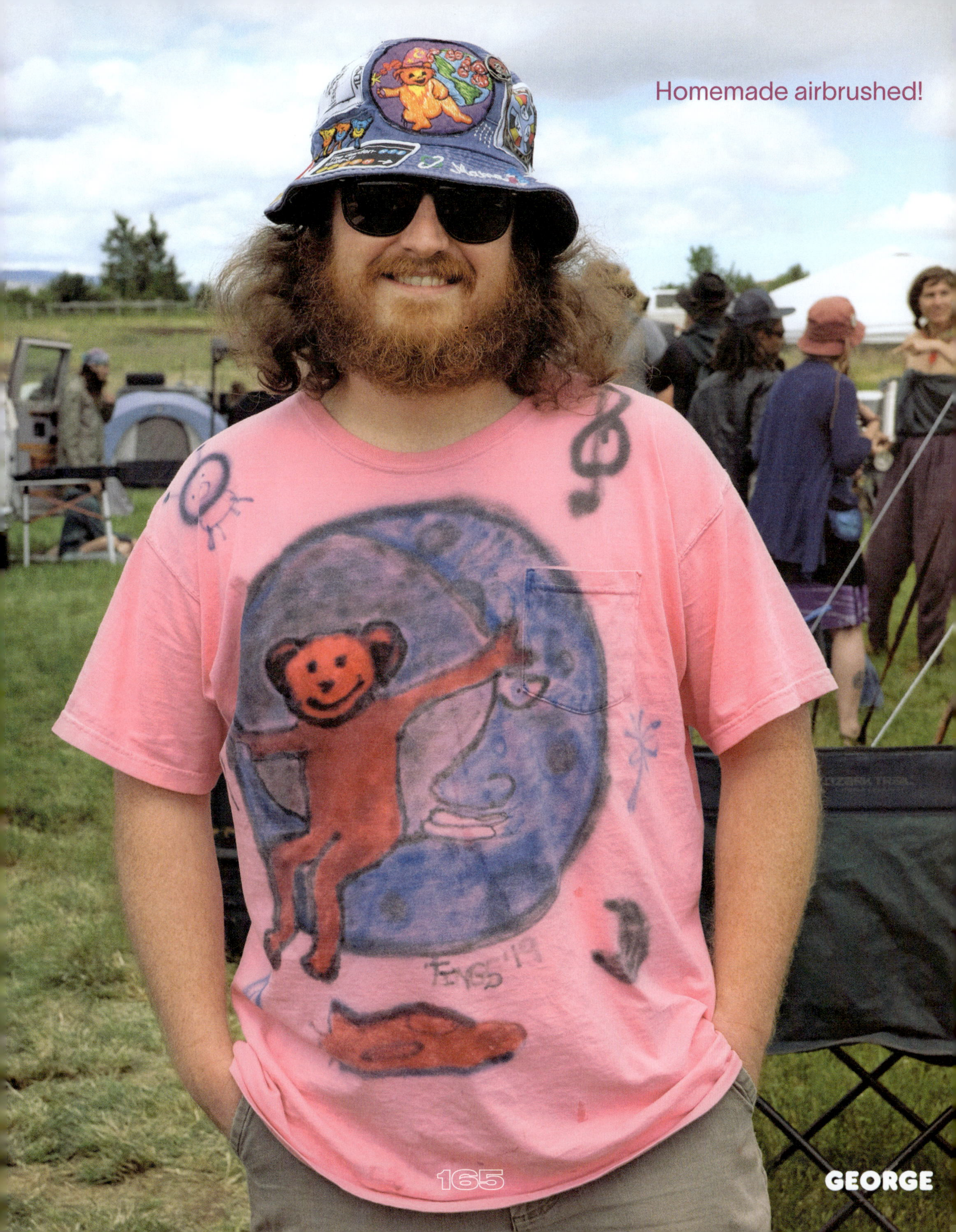
Homemade airbrushed!
GEORGE

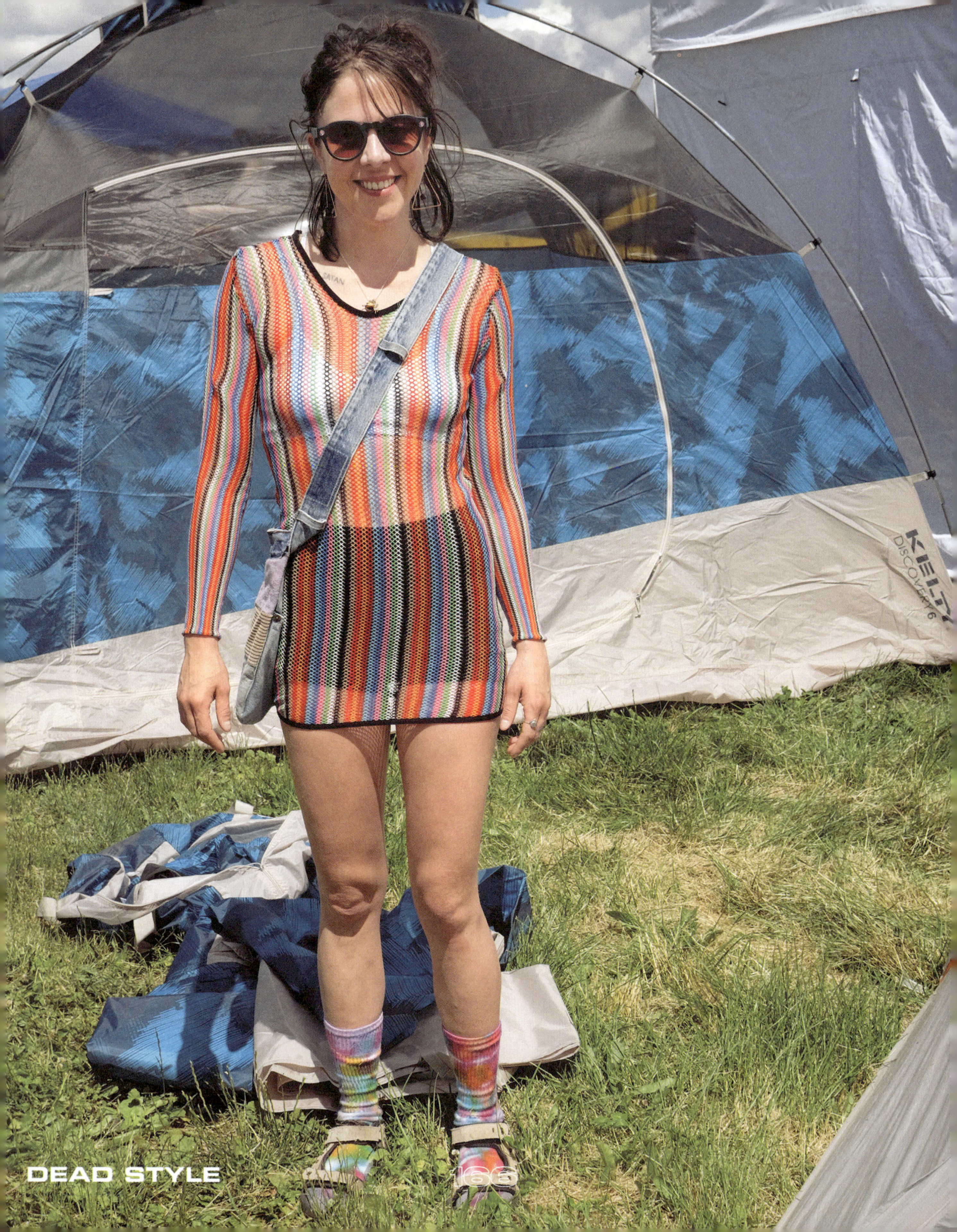

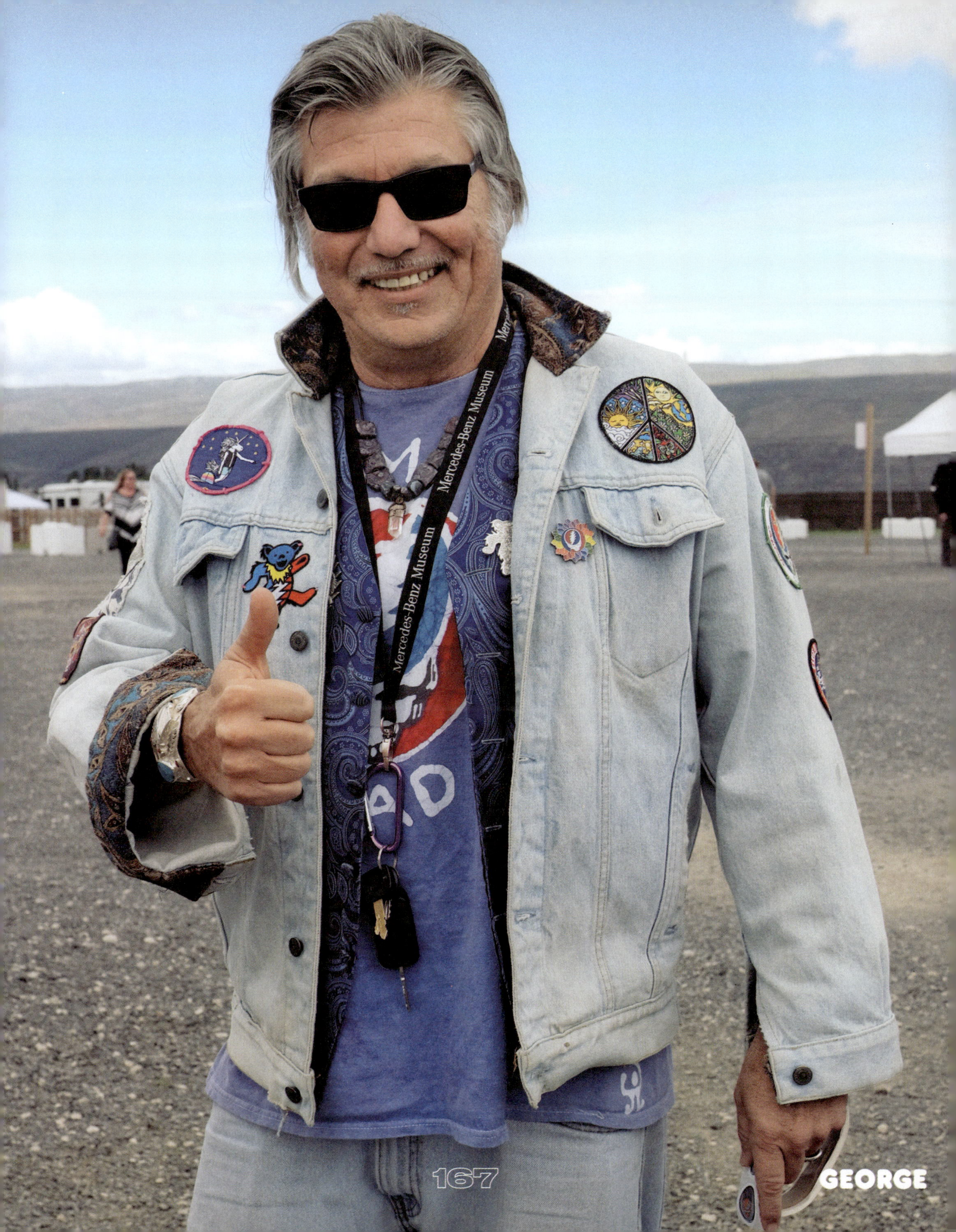

GEORGE

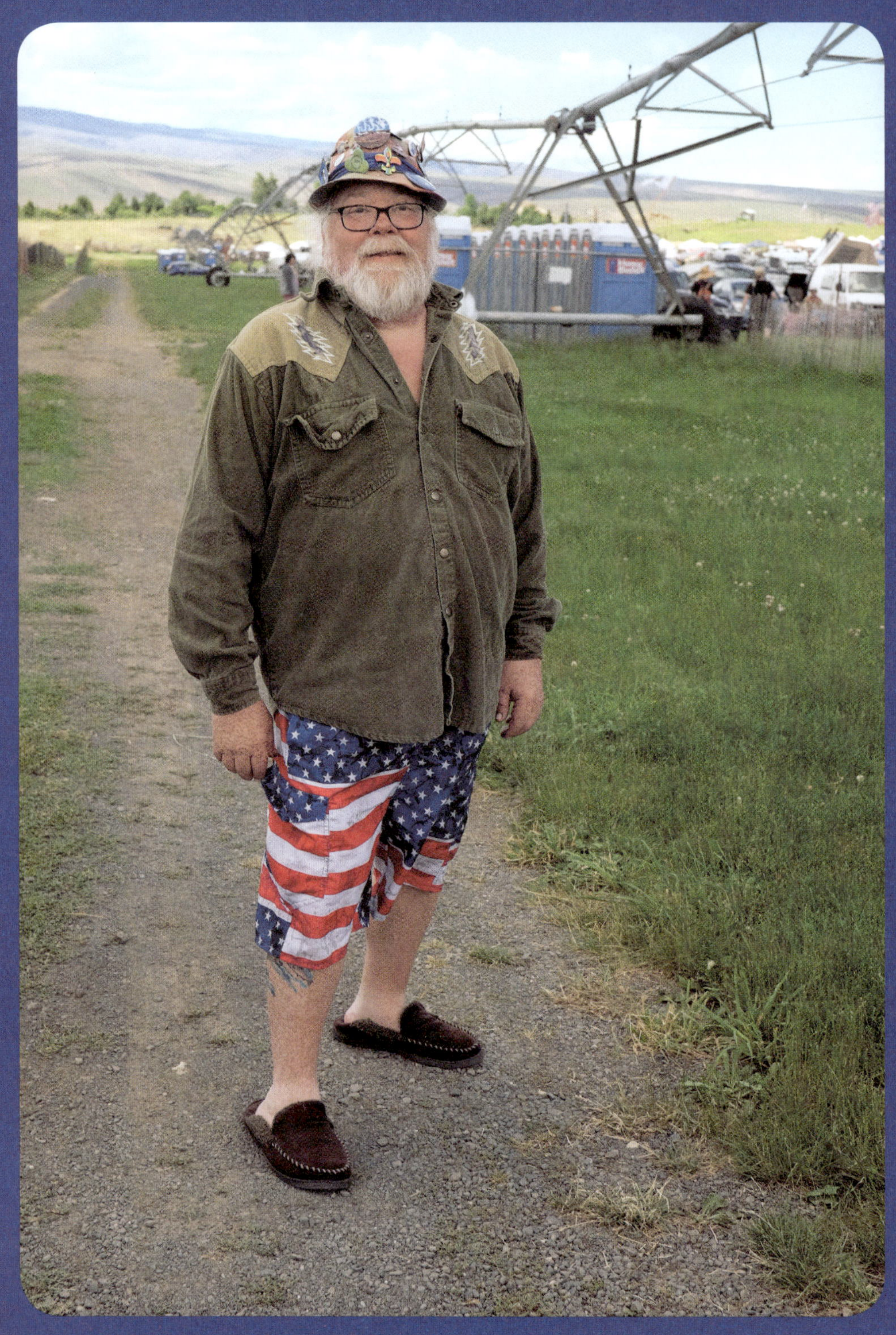

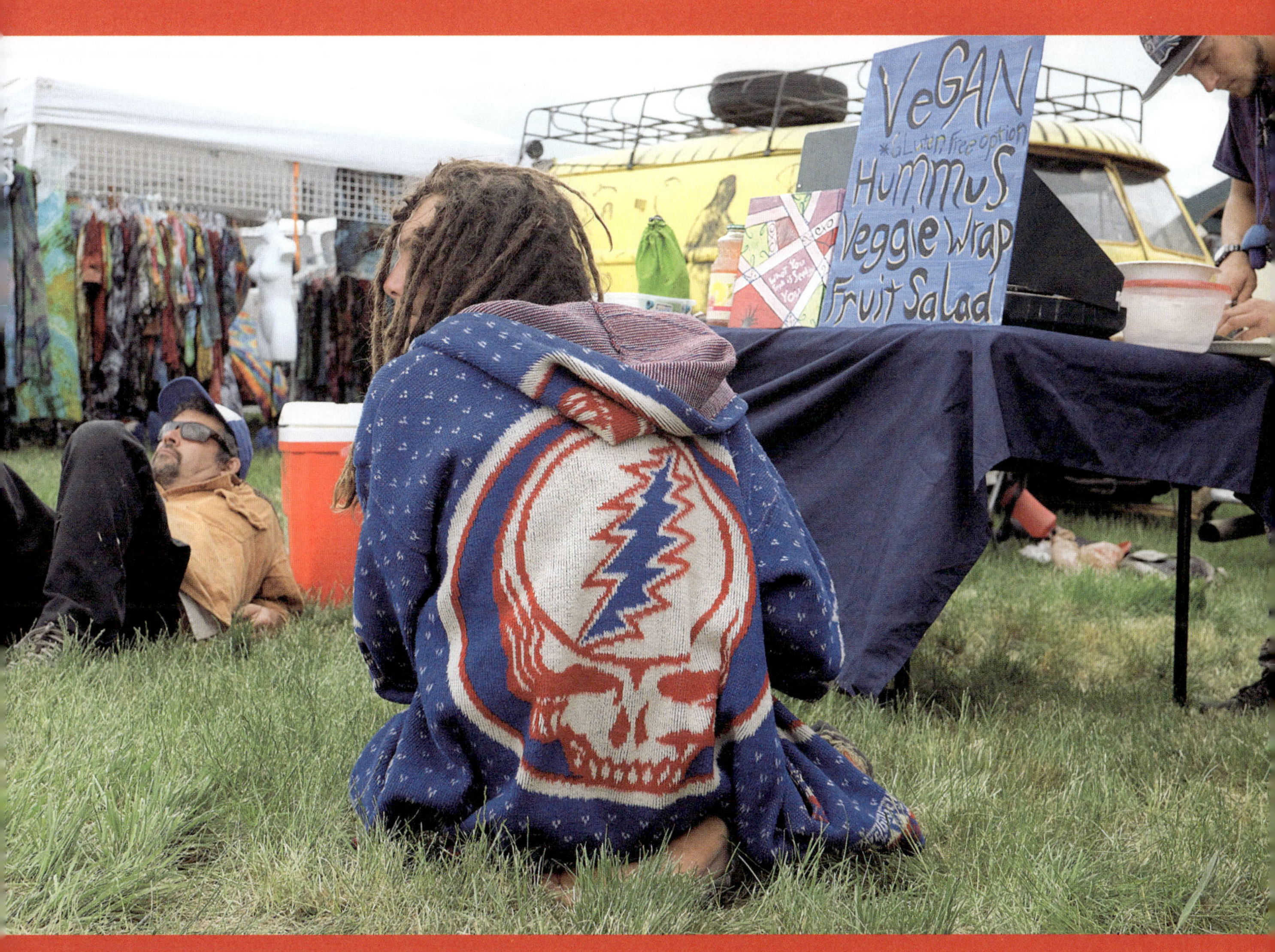
VeGAN
*Gluten free option
Hummus
Veggie wrap
Fruit Salad

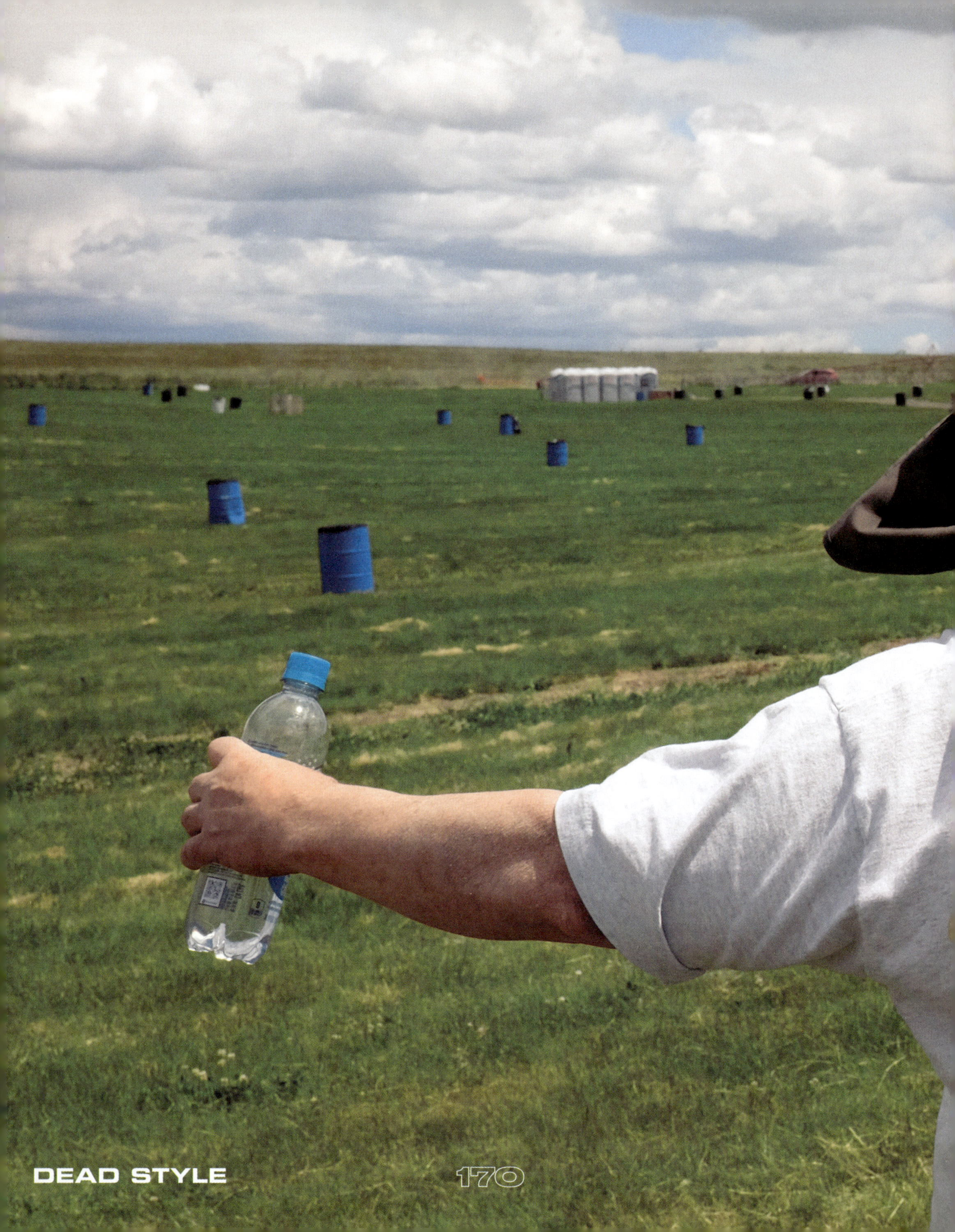

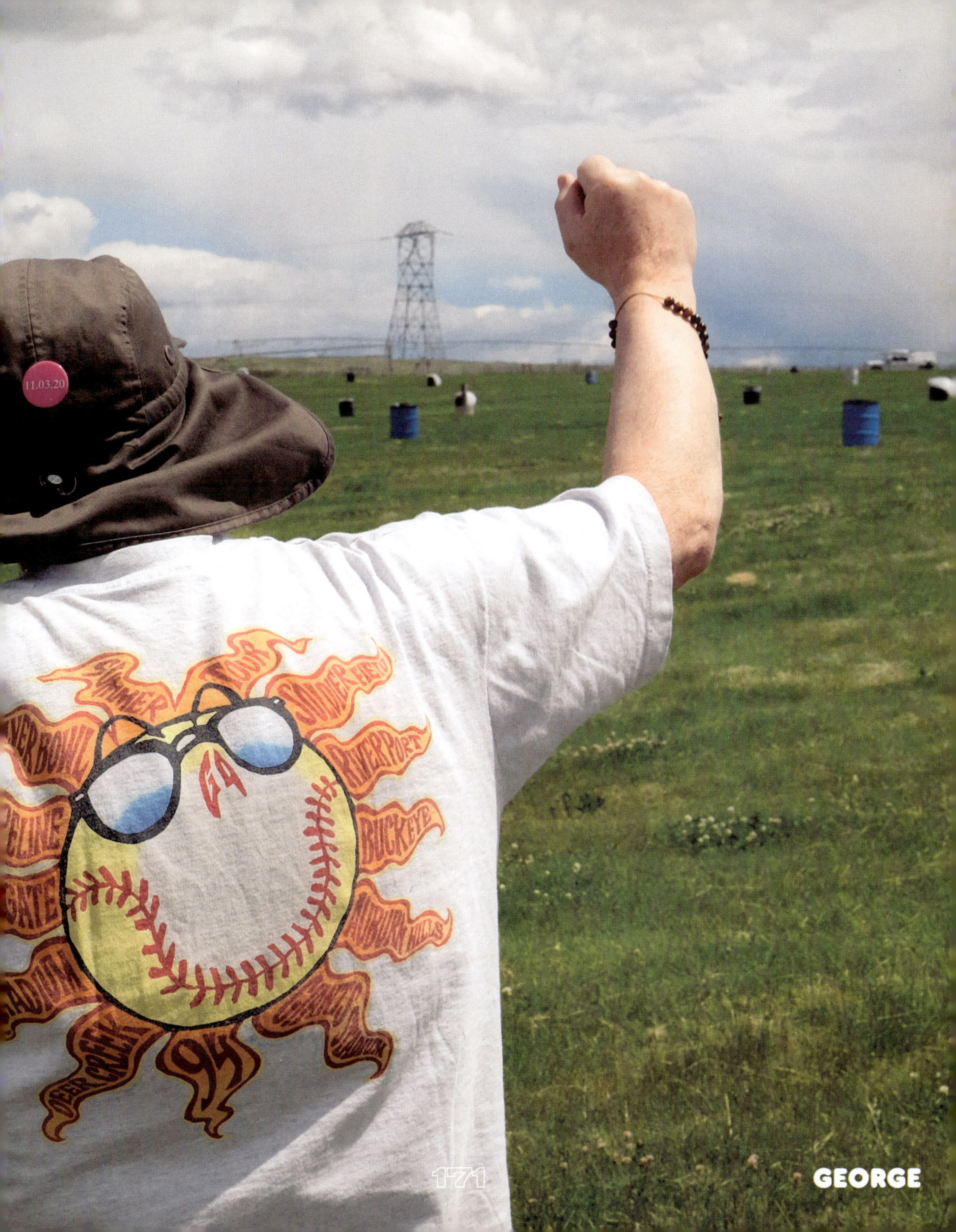
11.03.20
SUMMER
TOUR
RIVERPORT
BUCKEYE
AUBURN HILLS
DEER CREEK
94

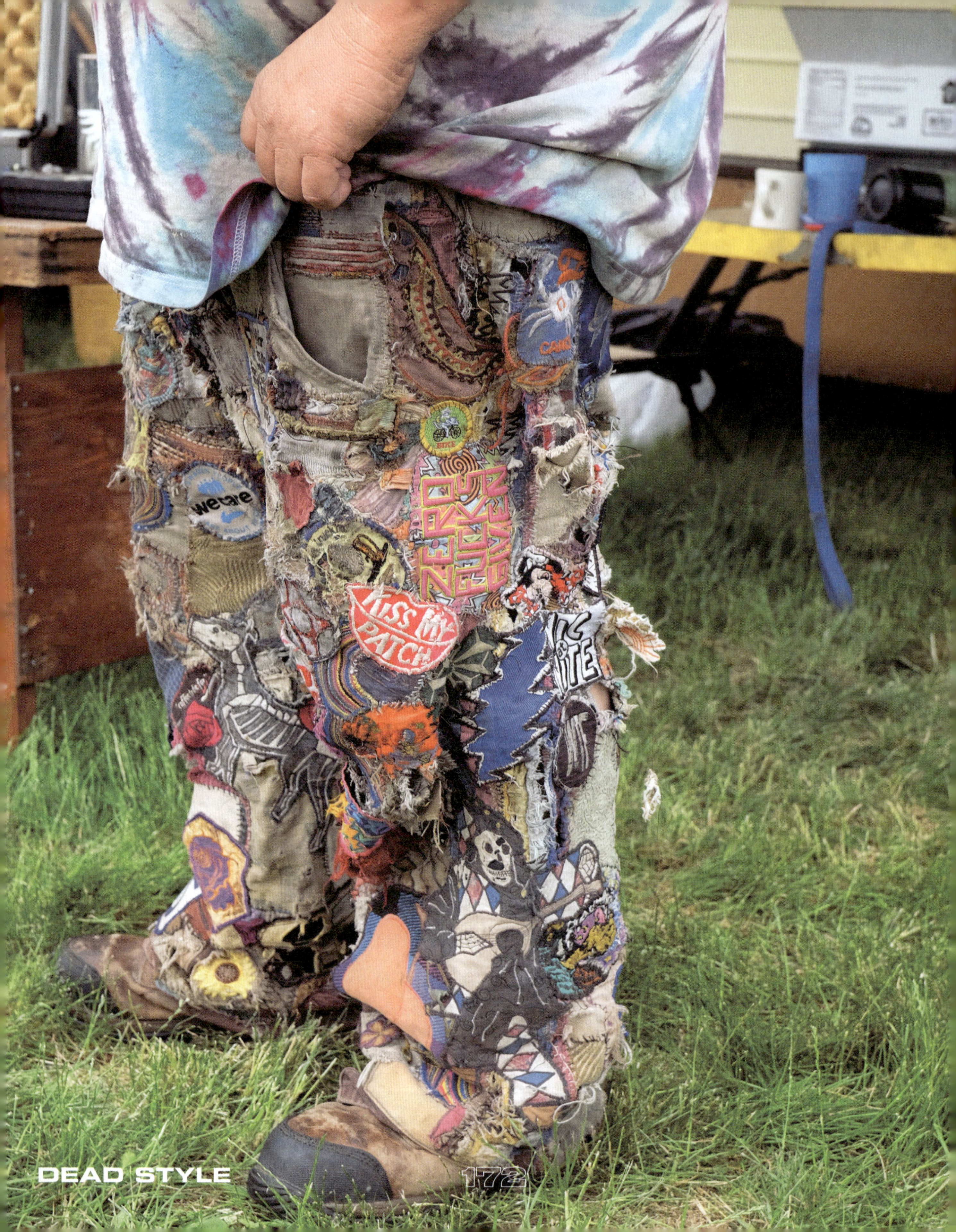
wecare
KISS MY PATCH

When I see articles of clothing like this, I just hope they never get retired. Or that when they are retired they don't end up in the trash. Coolest pants ever. No debate.

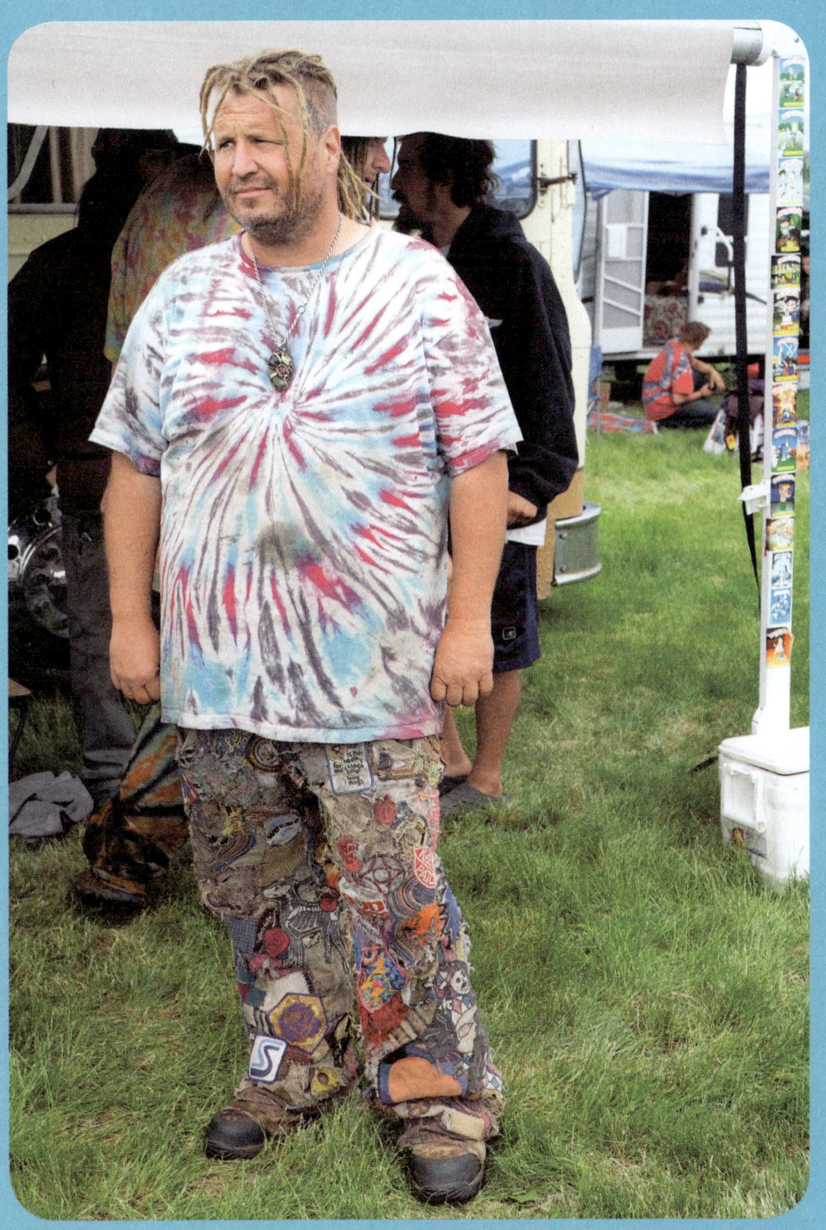

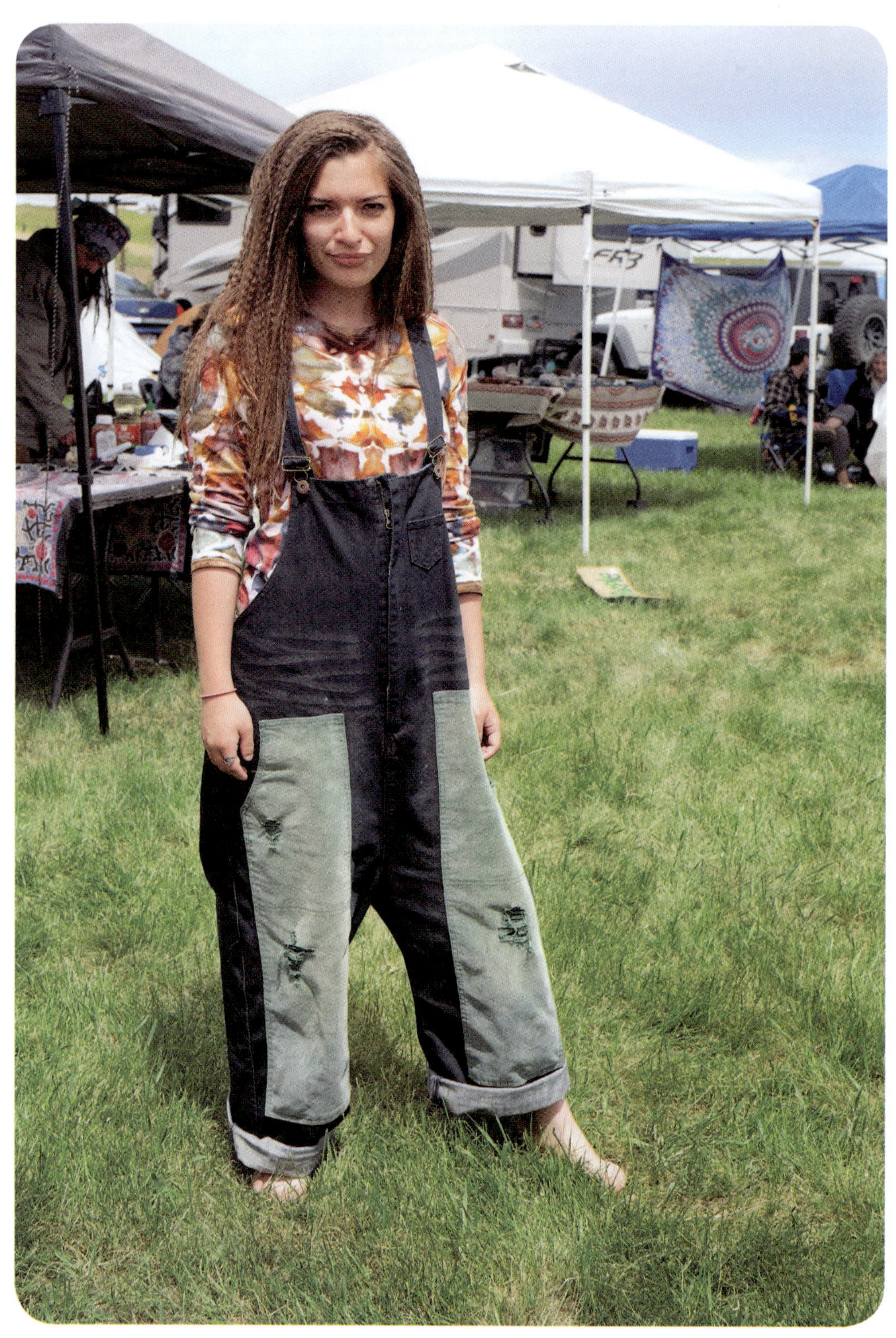

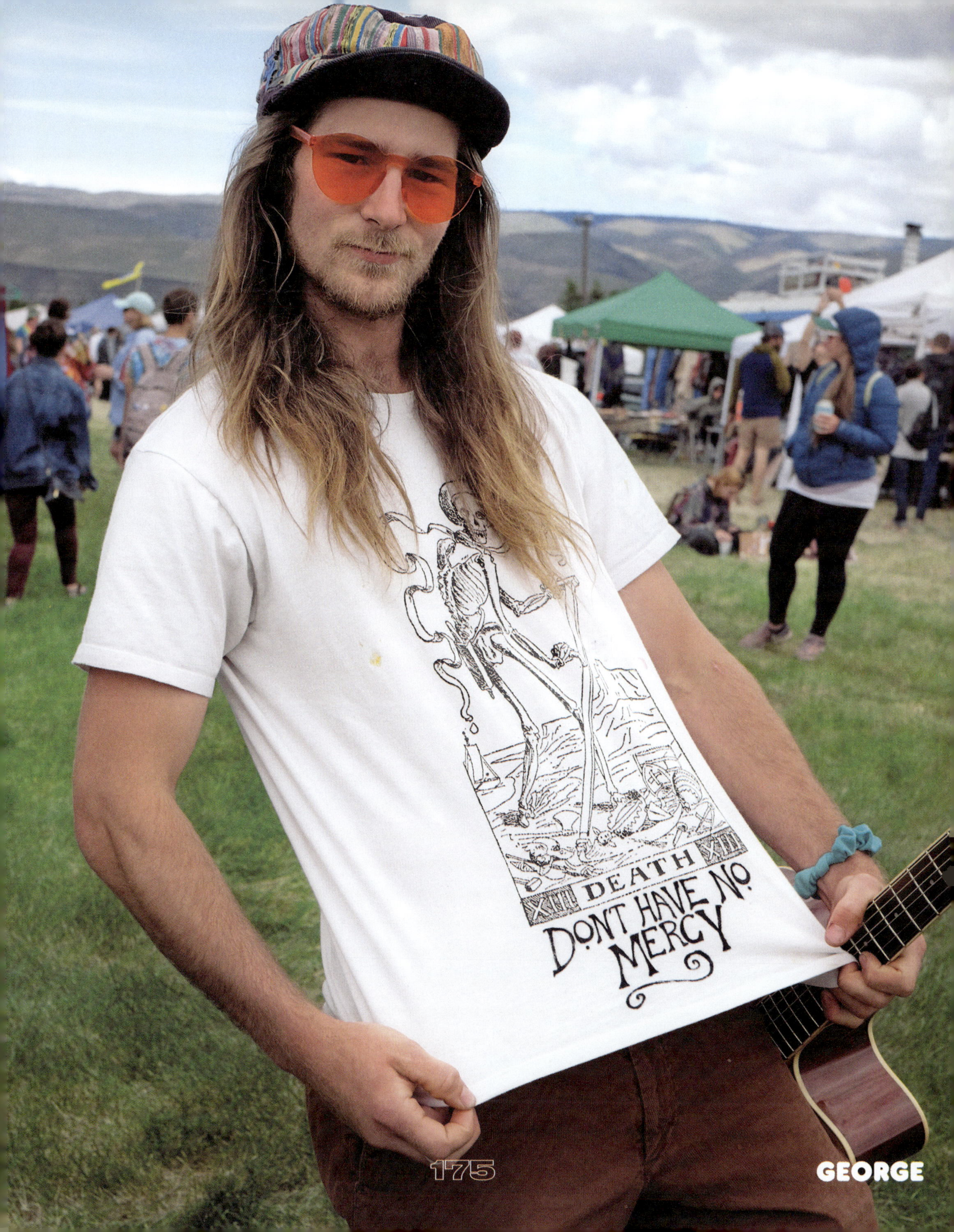

GEORGE

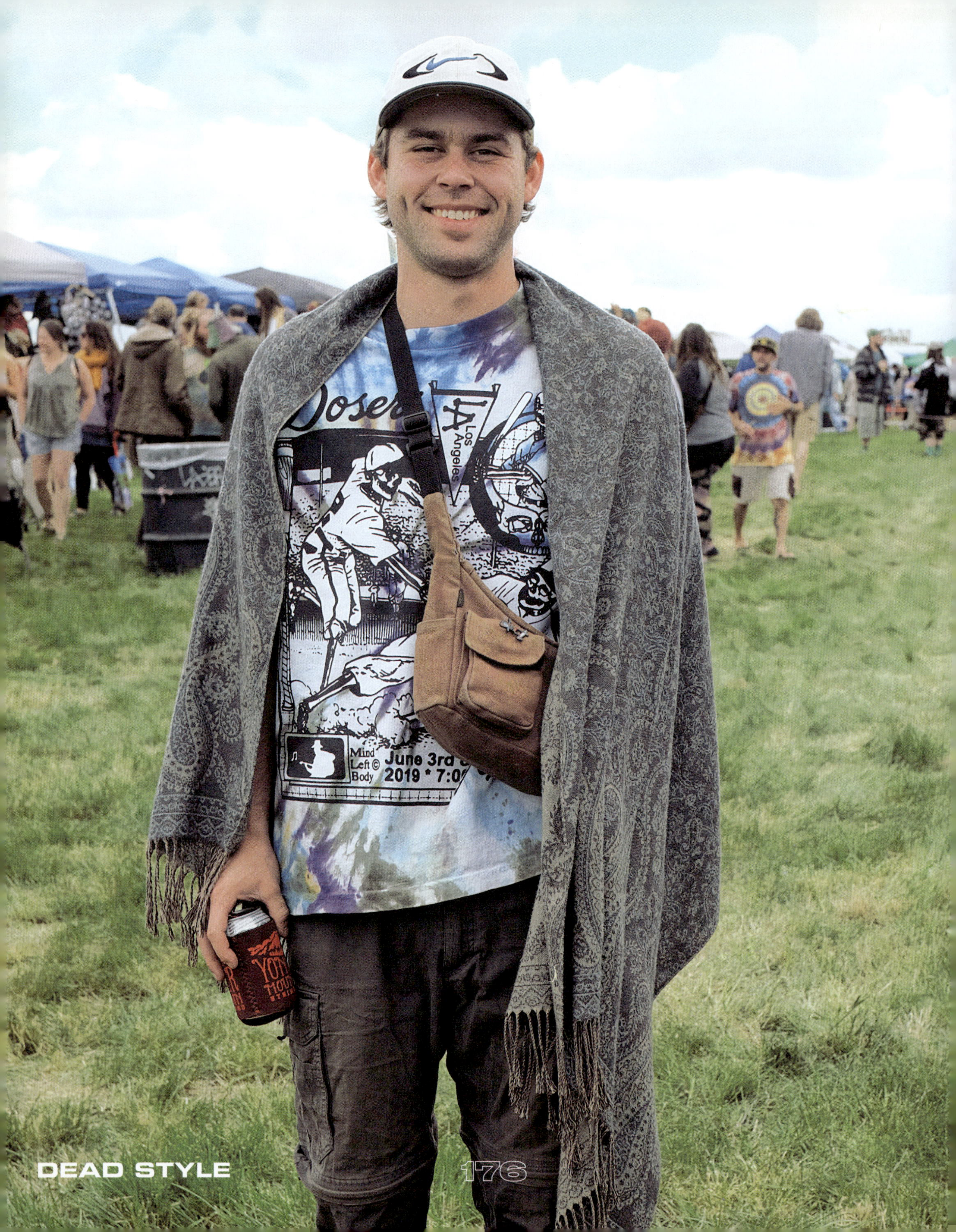
Los Angeles
Mind
Left ©
Body

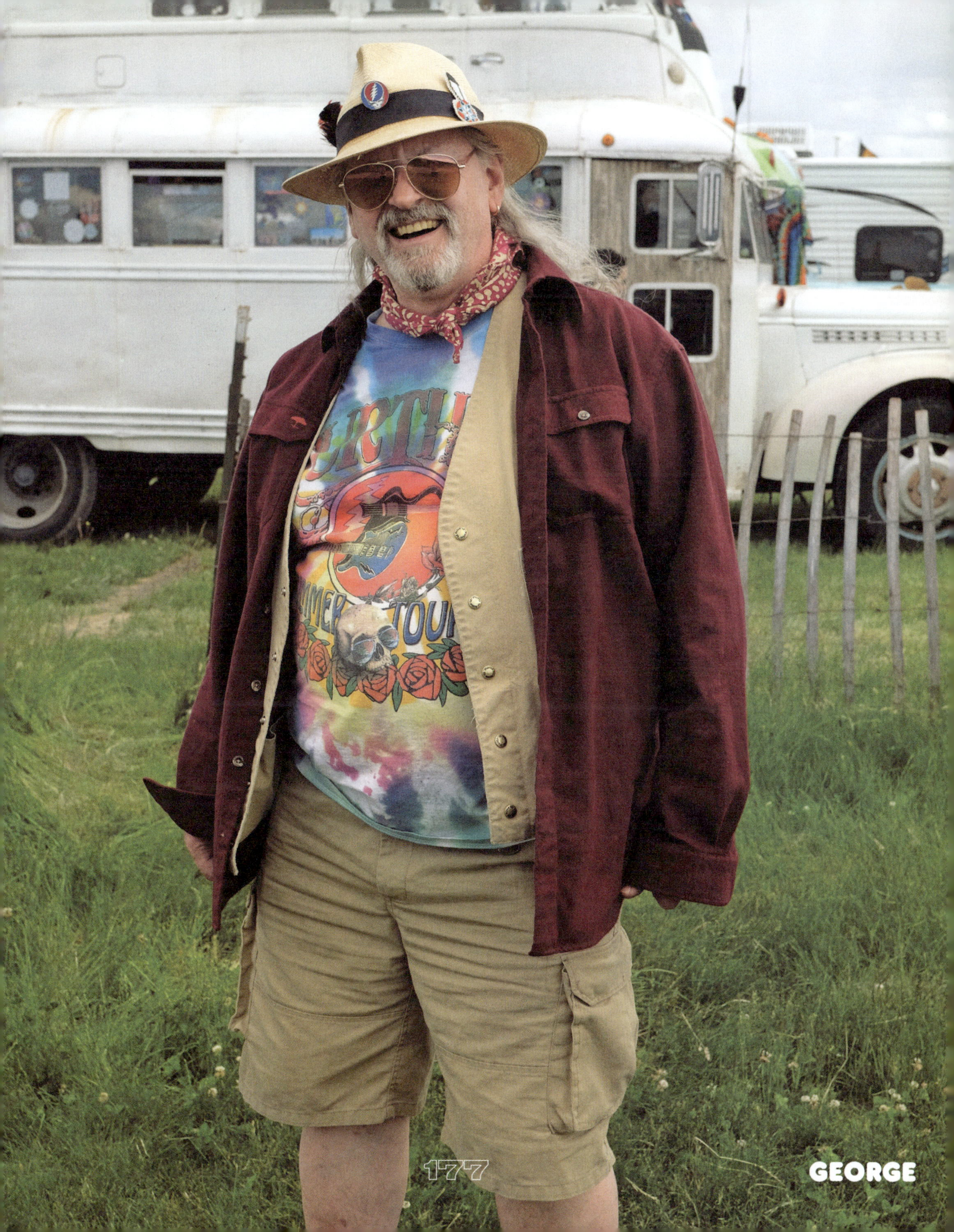

GEORGE

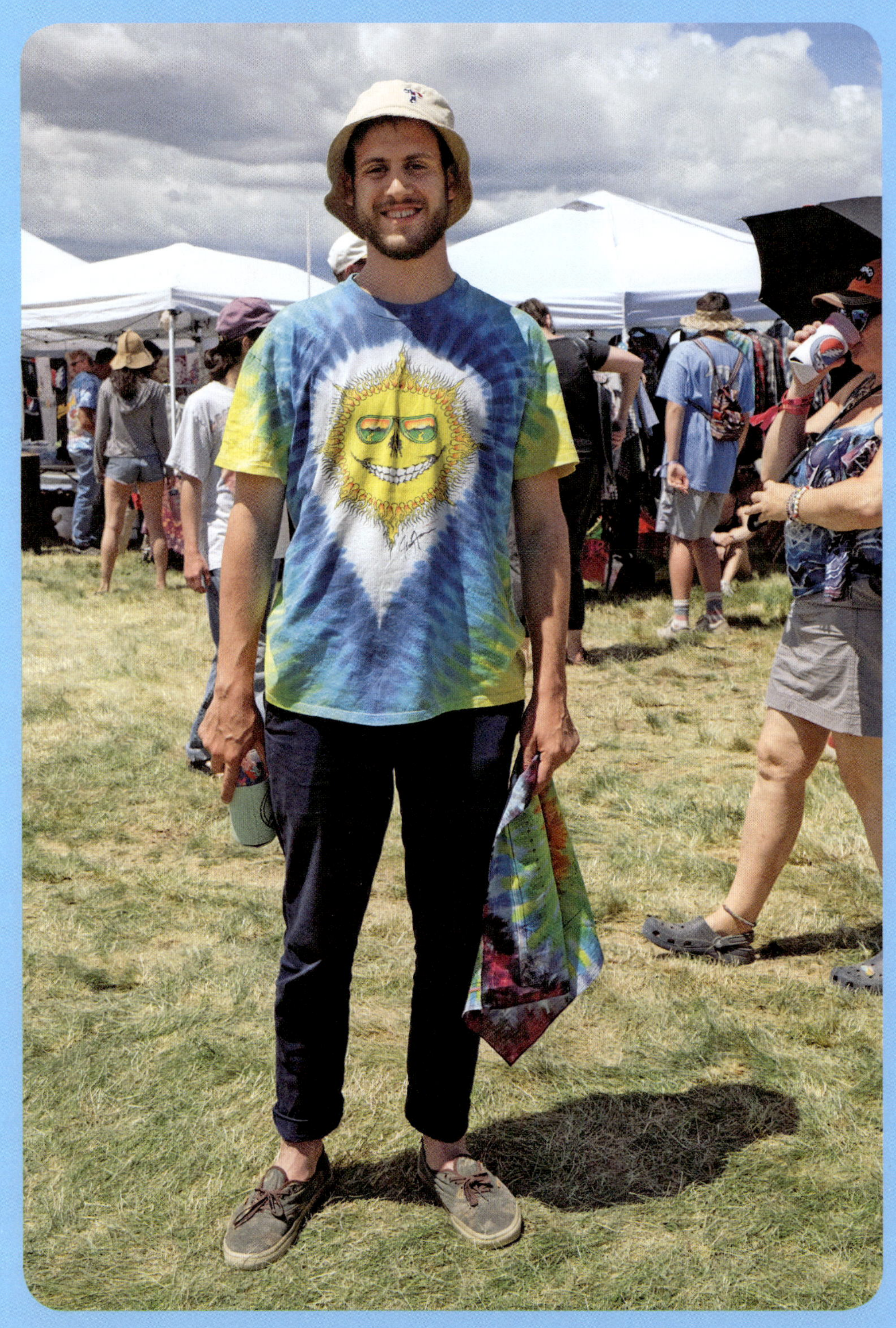

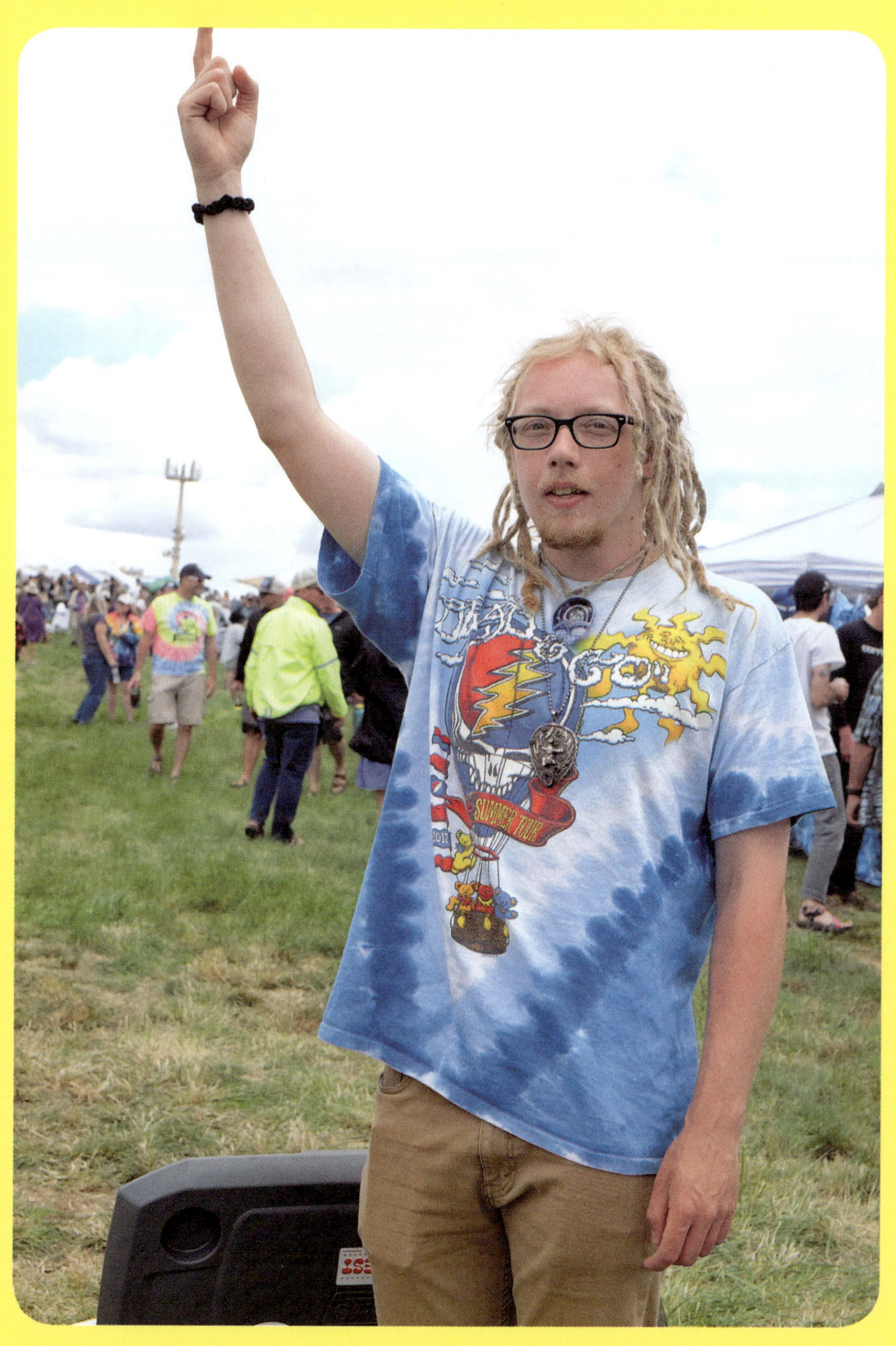
SUMMER TOUR

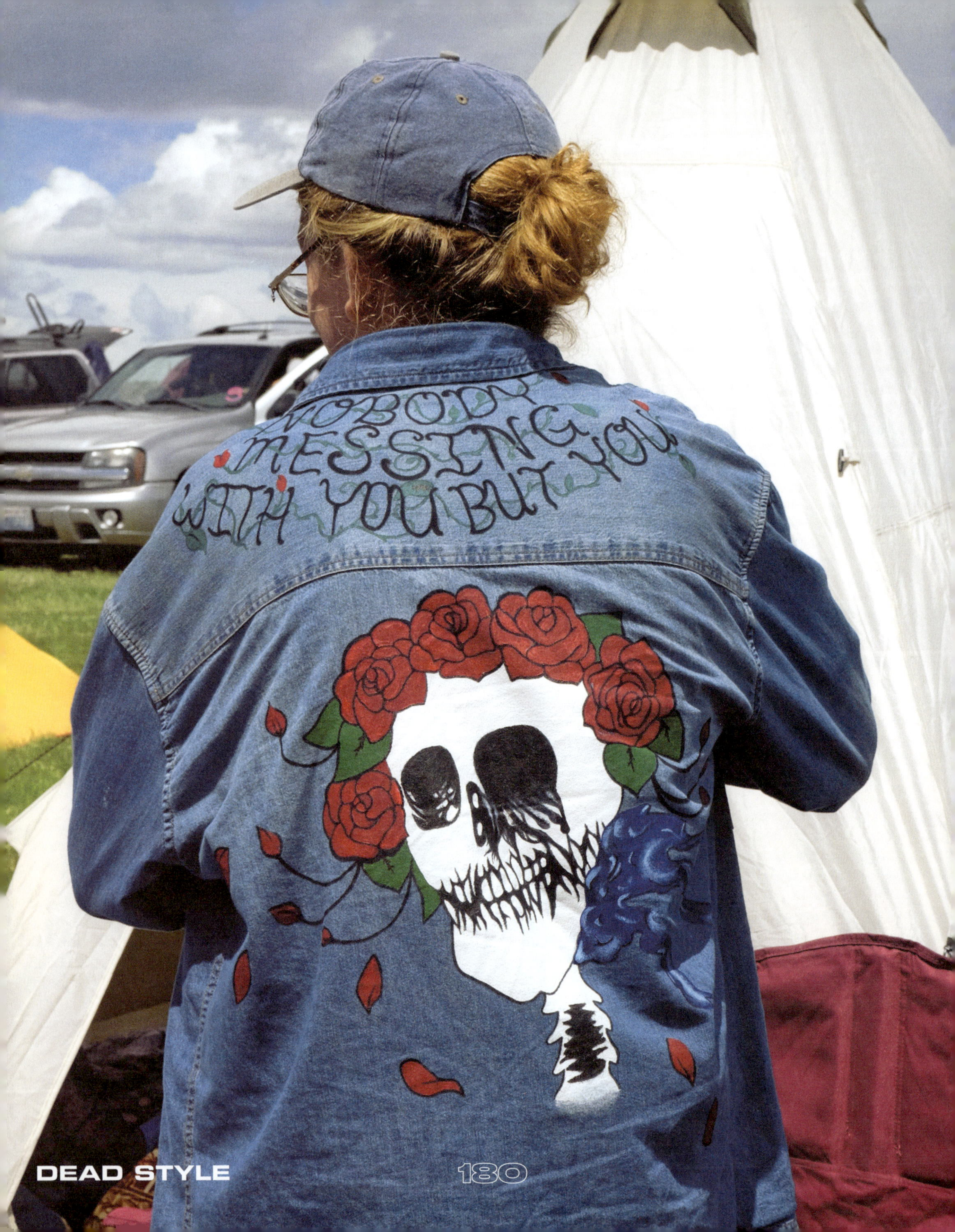
NOBODY
MESSING
WITH YOU BUT YOU

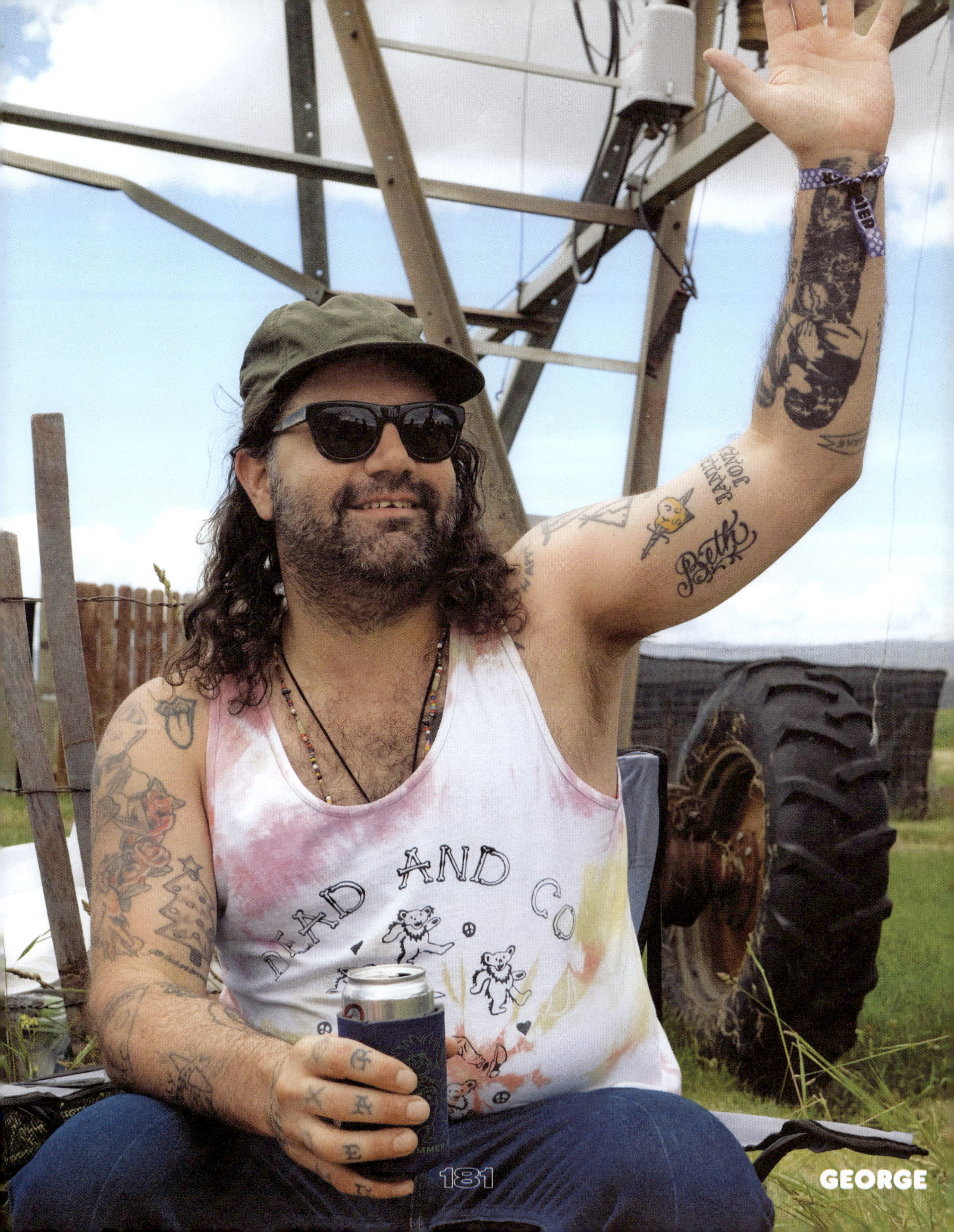

GEORGE

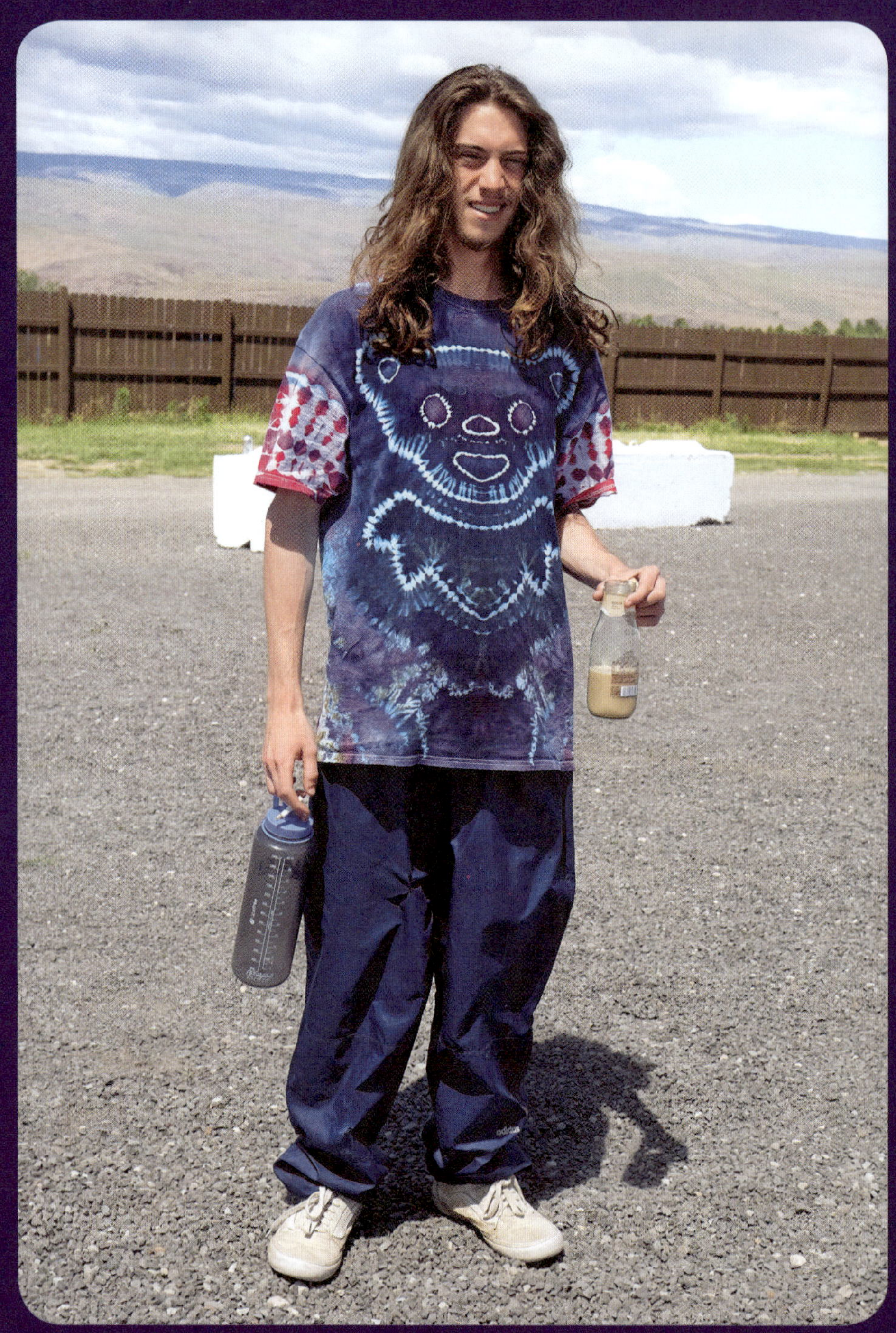

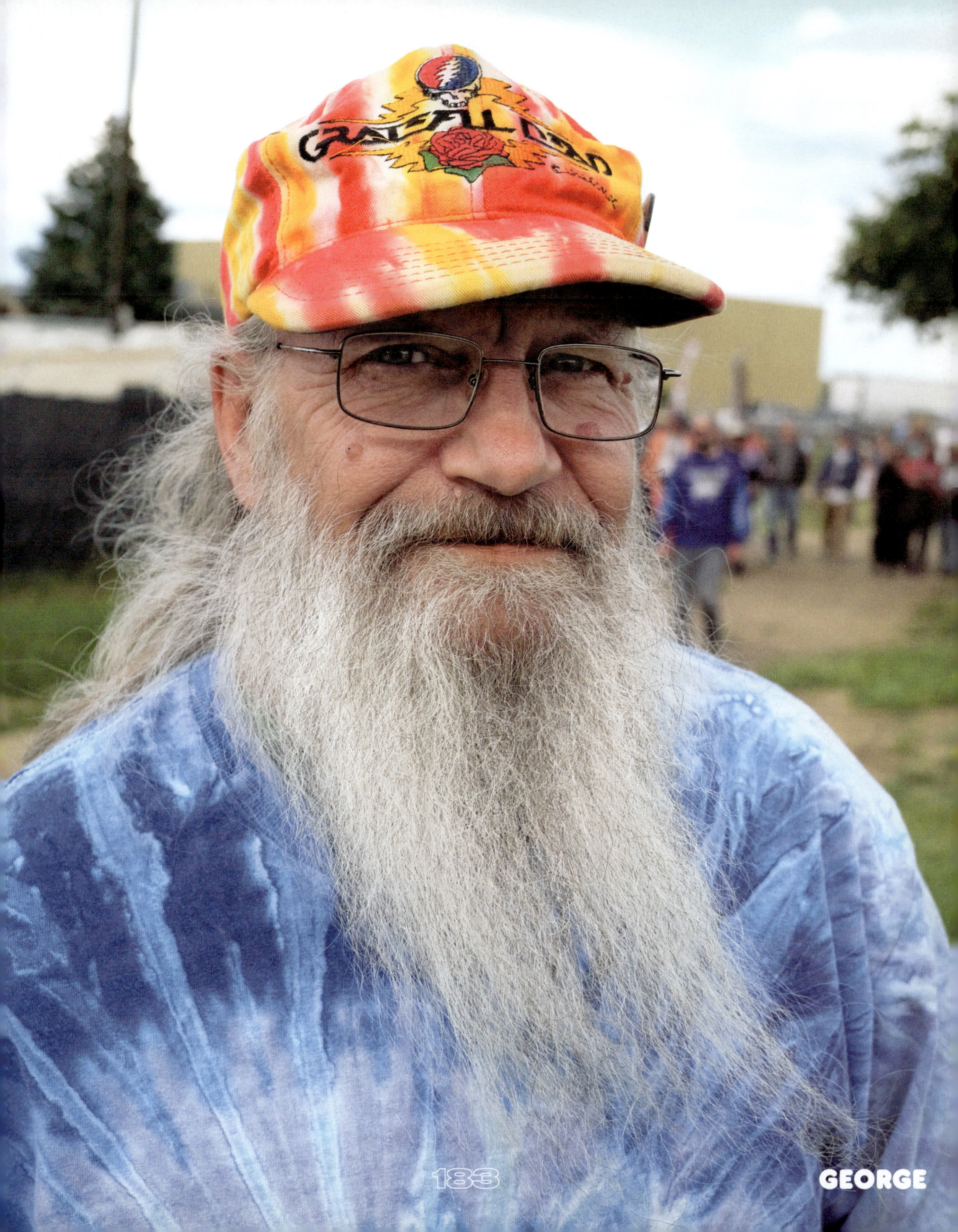

GEORGE

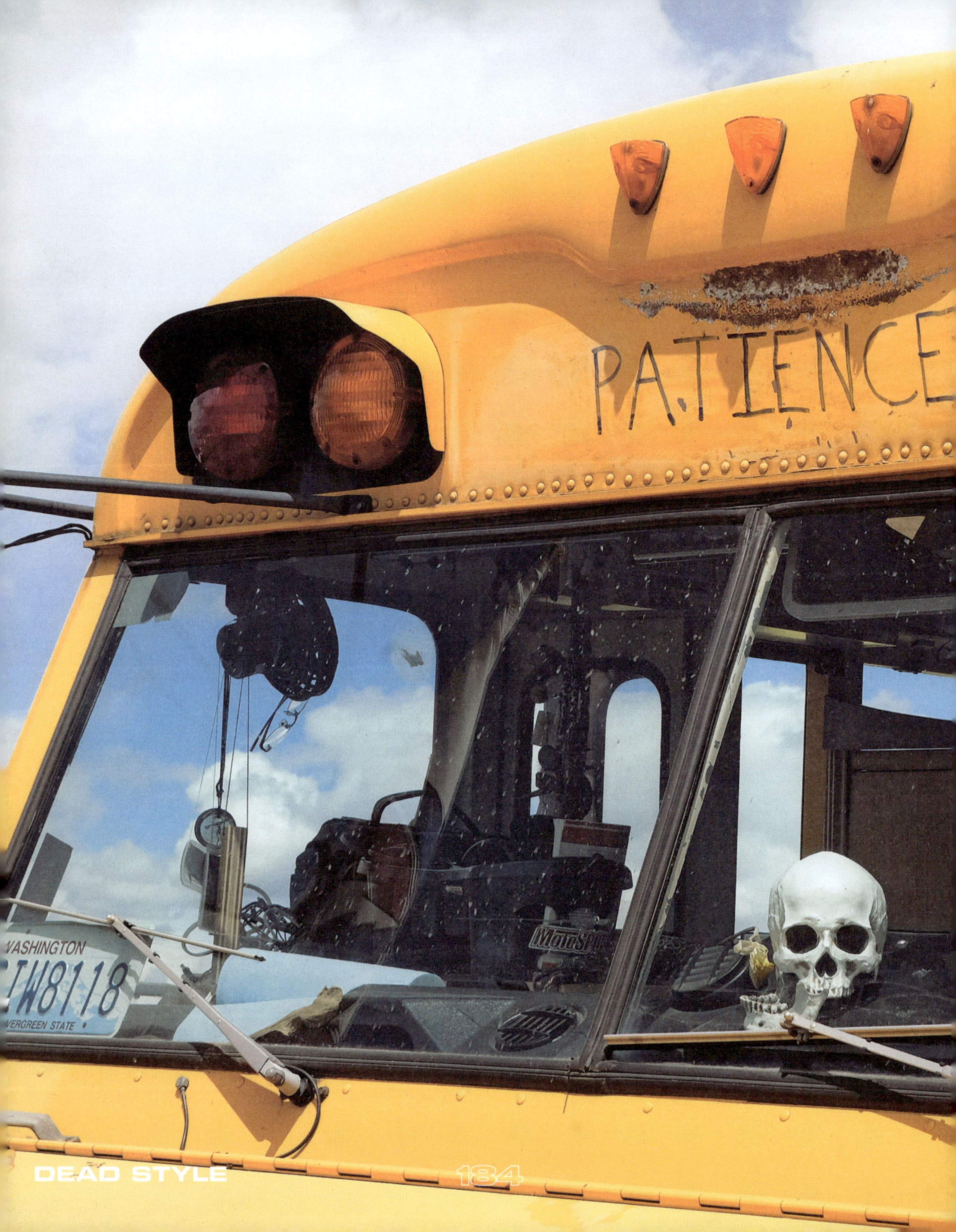
PATIENCE
WASHINGTON
TW8118
EVERGREEN STATE

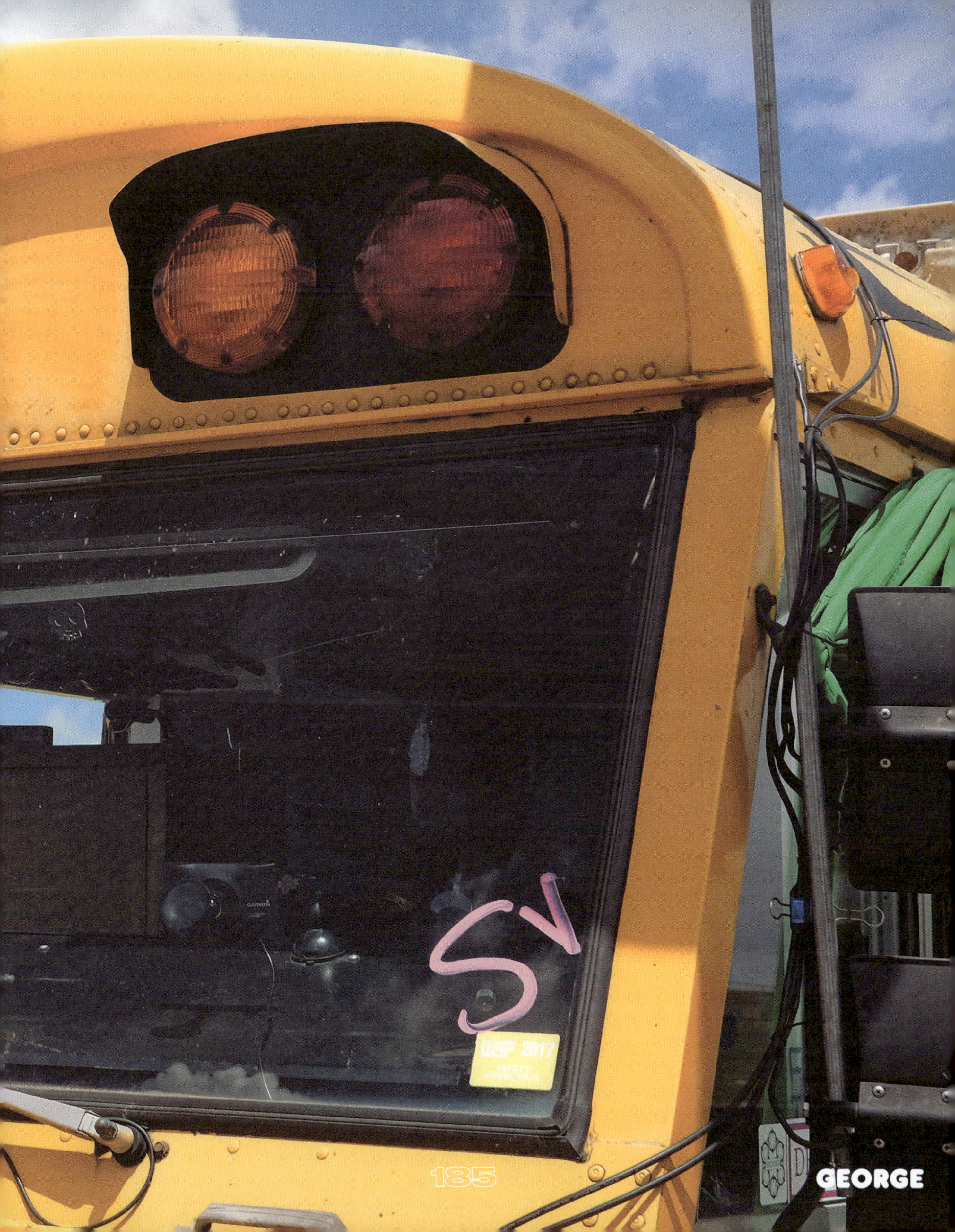
GARMIN
WSP 2017
SAFETY
INSPECTION

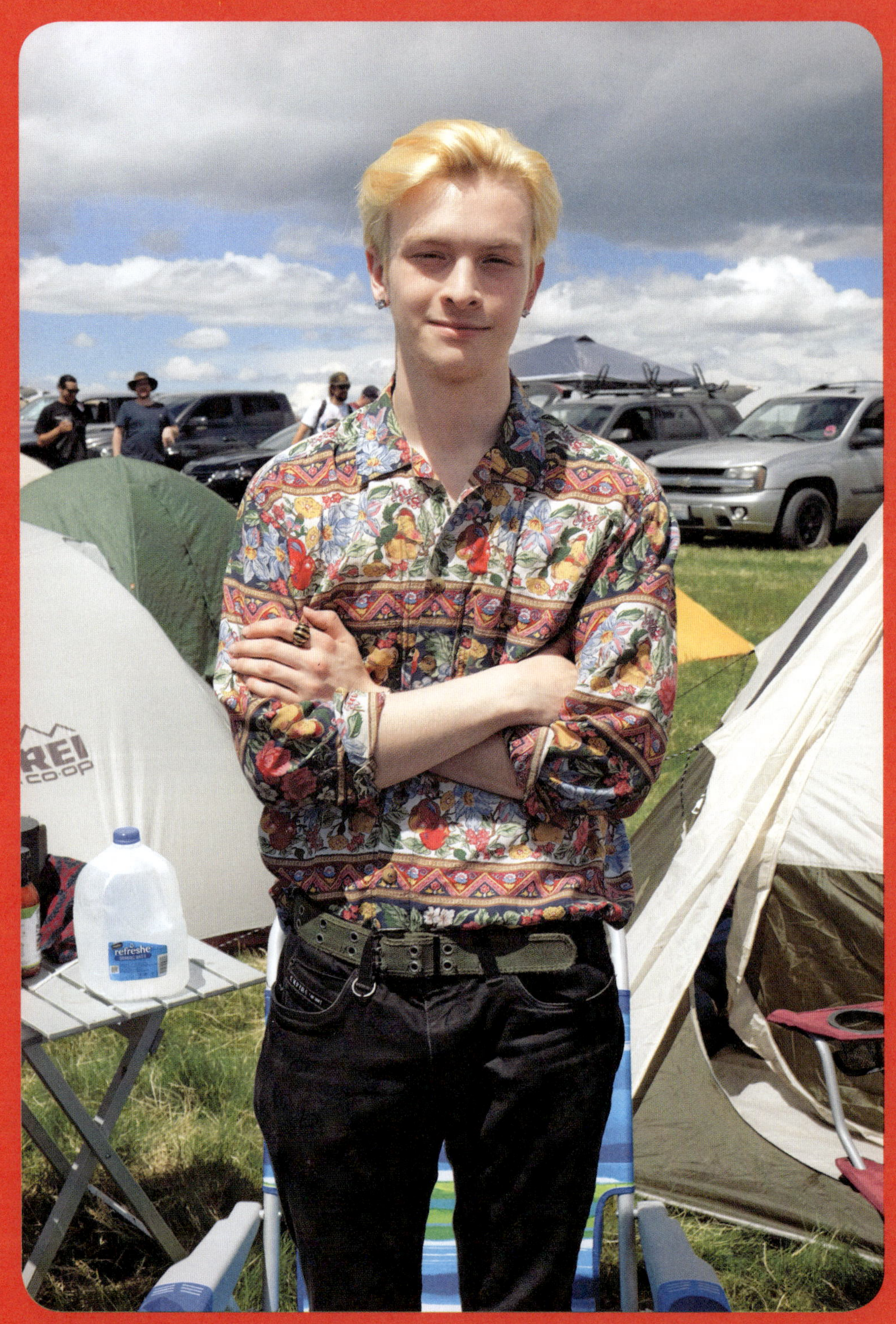
REI
CO·OP
refreshe

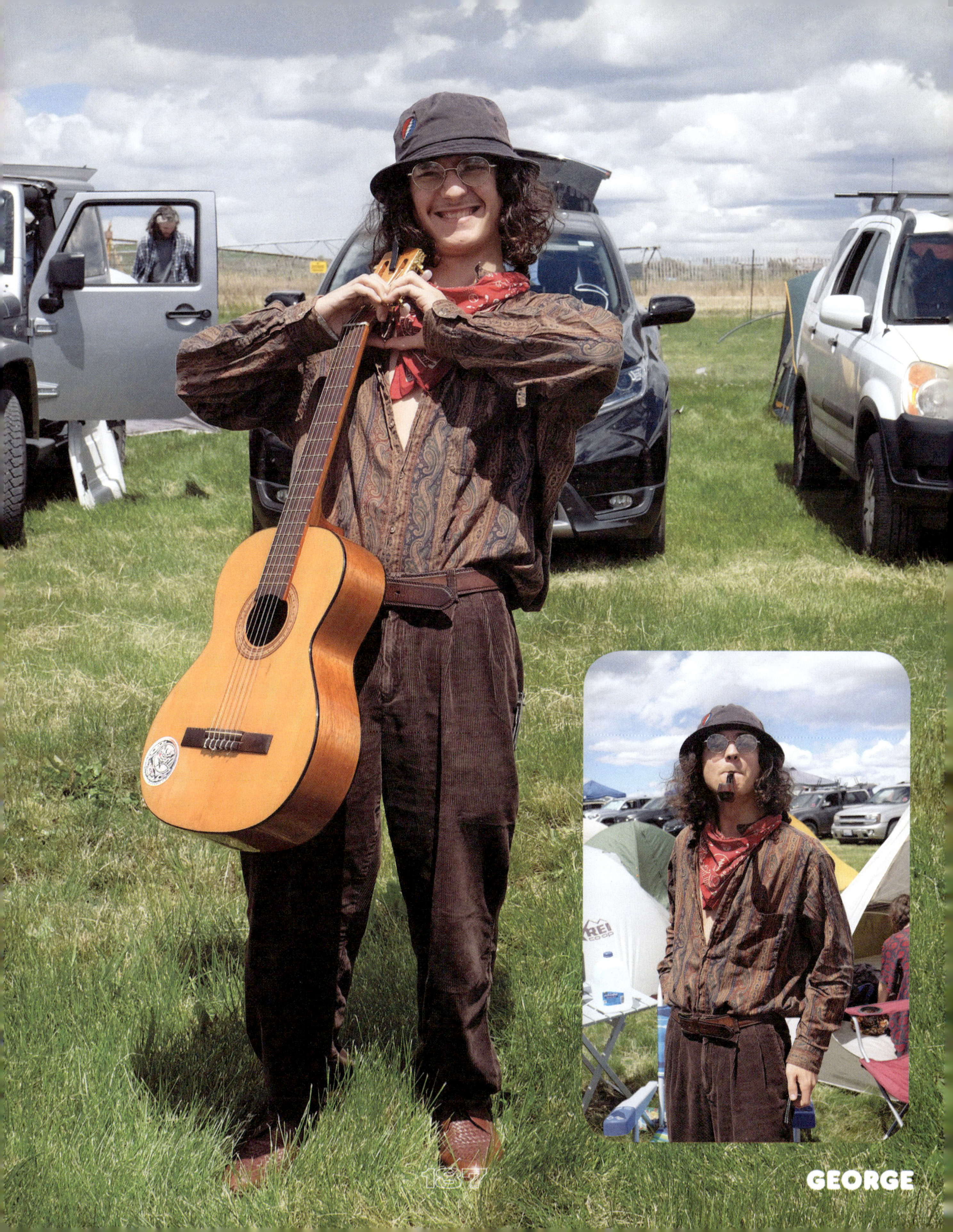

GEORGE

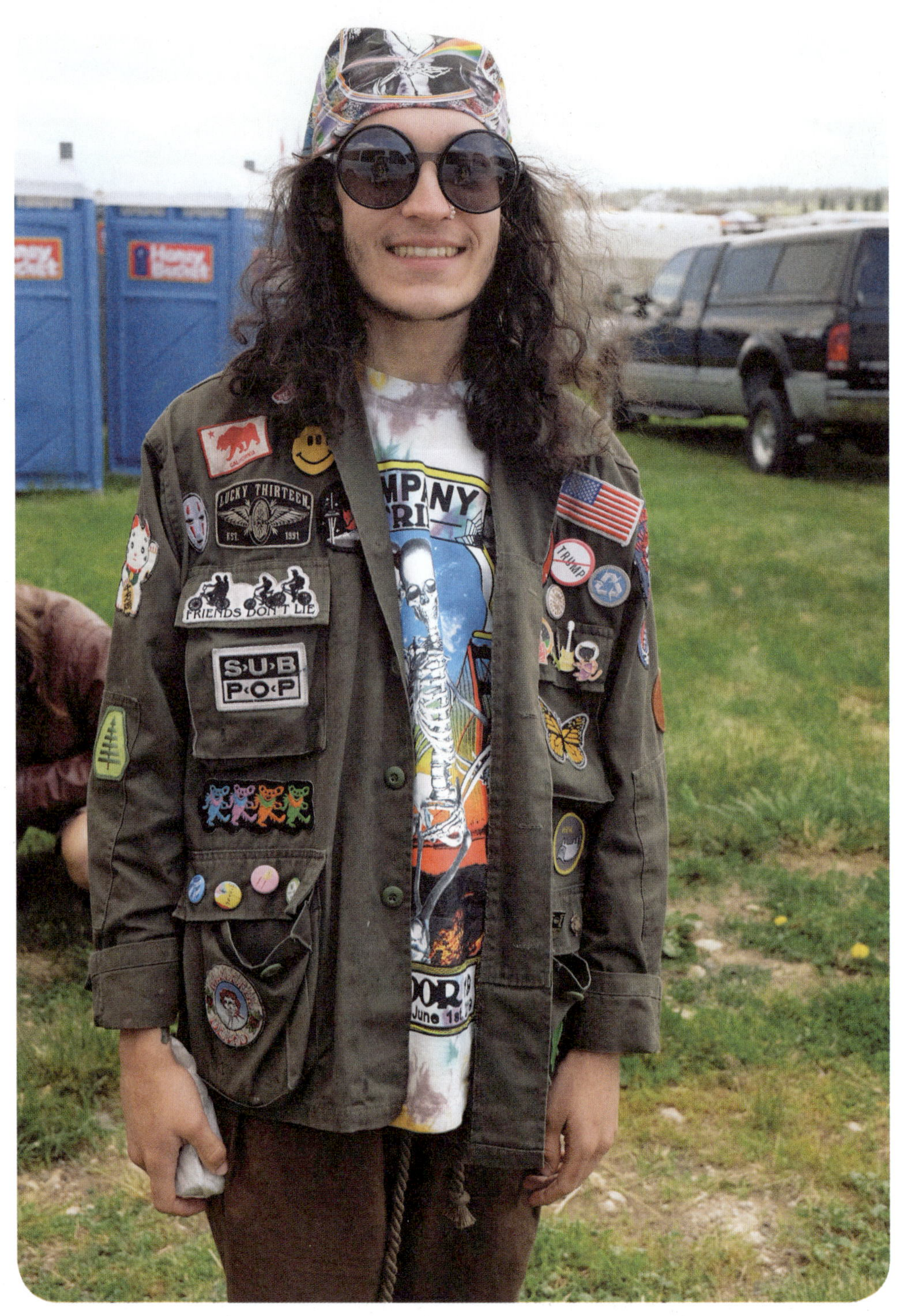
LUCKY THIRTEEN
EST. 1991
FRIENDS DON'T LIE
S·U·B
P·O·P
TRUMP

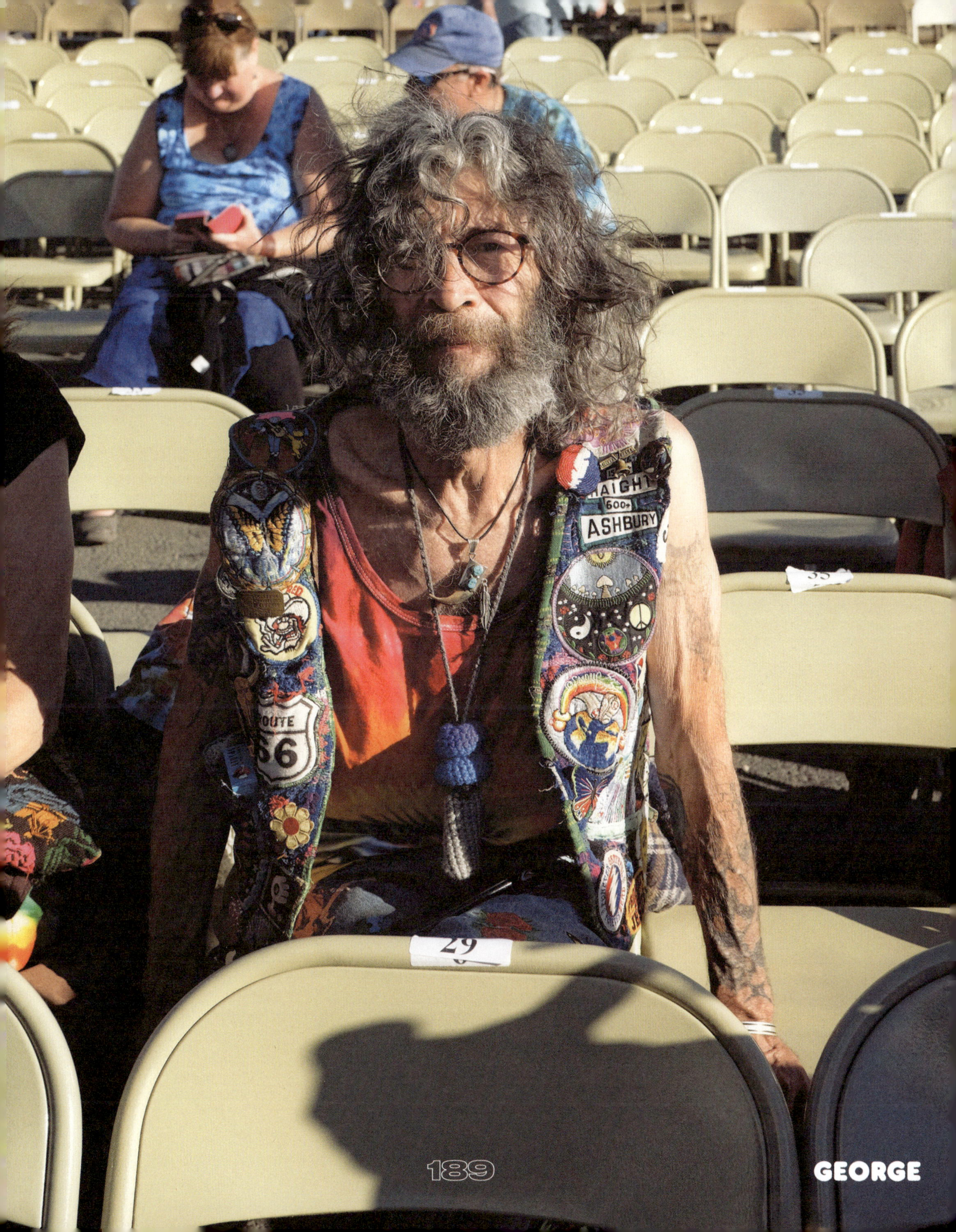

GEORGE

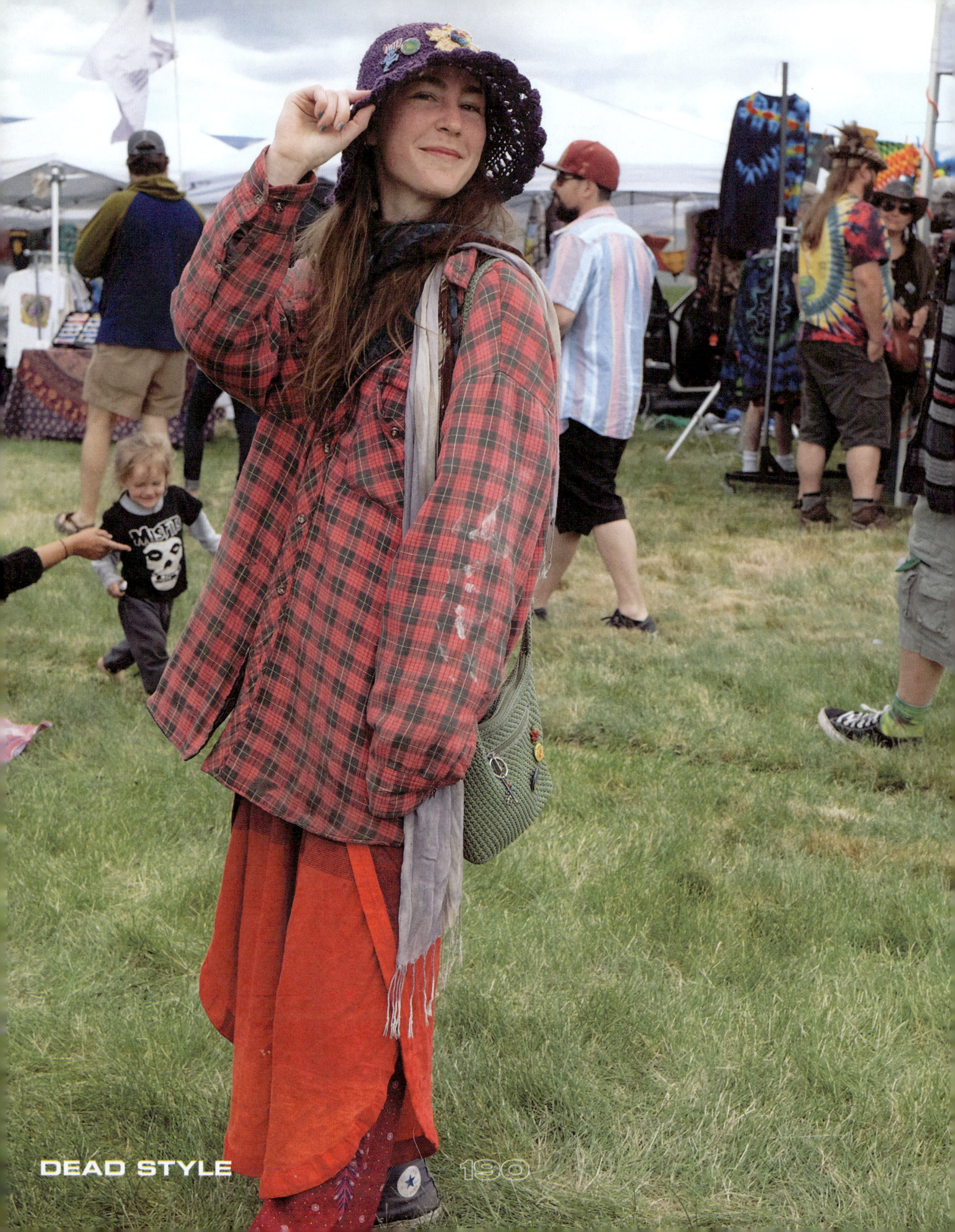

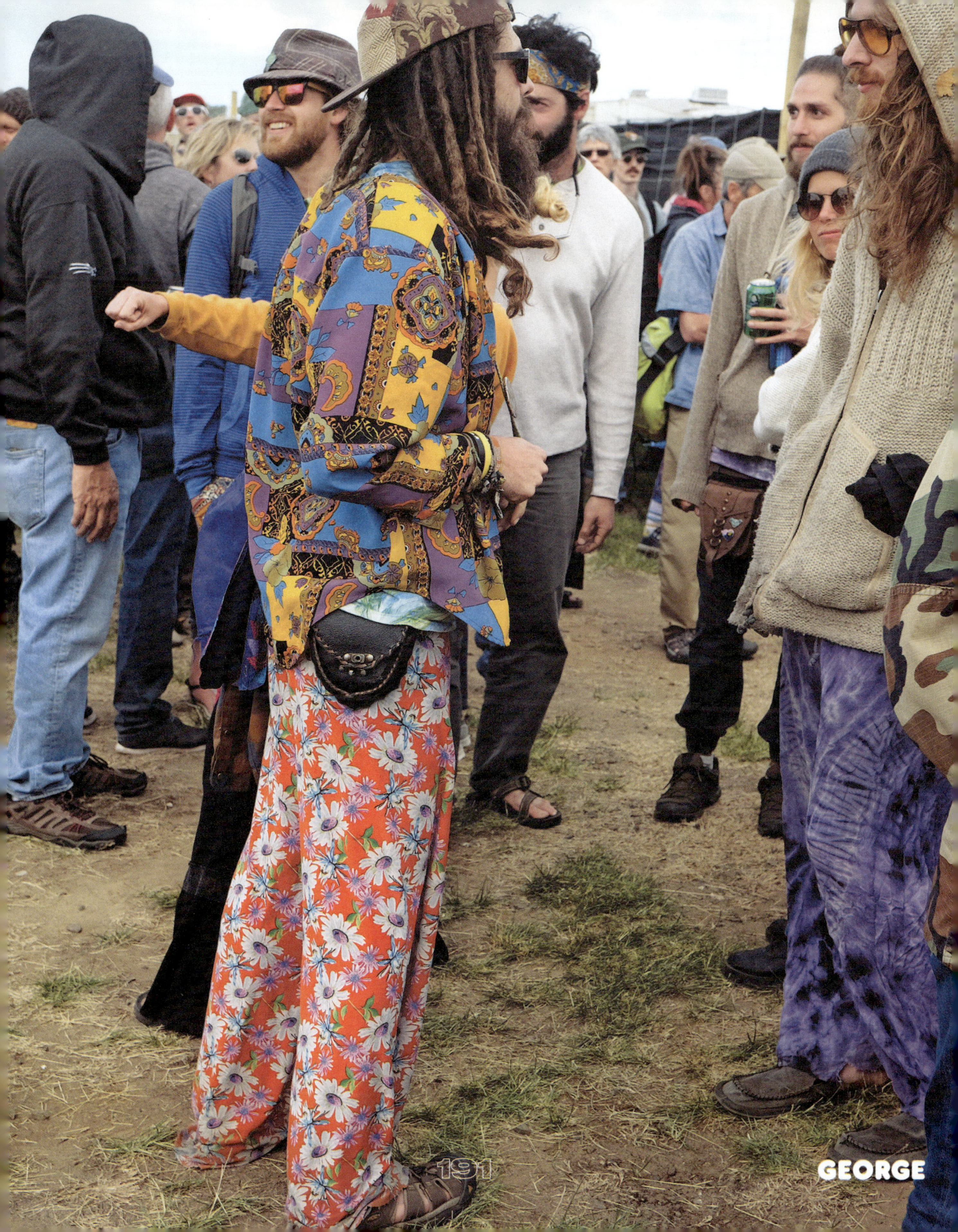
GEORGE

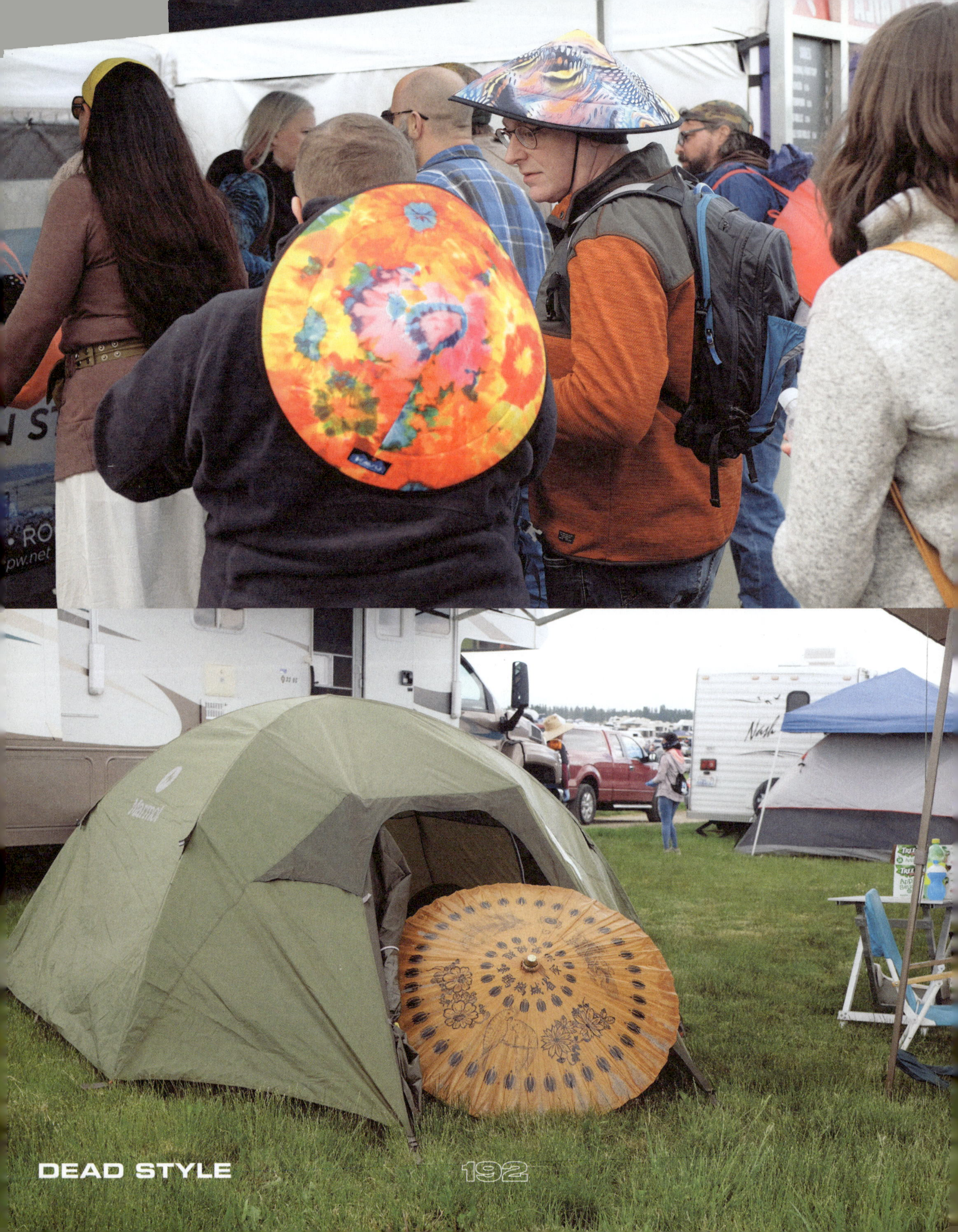

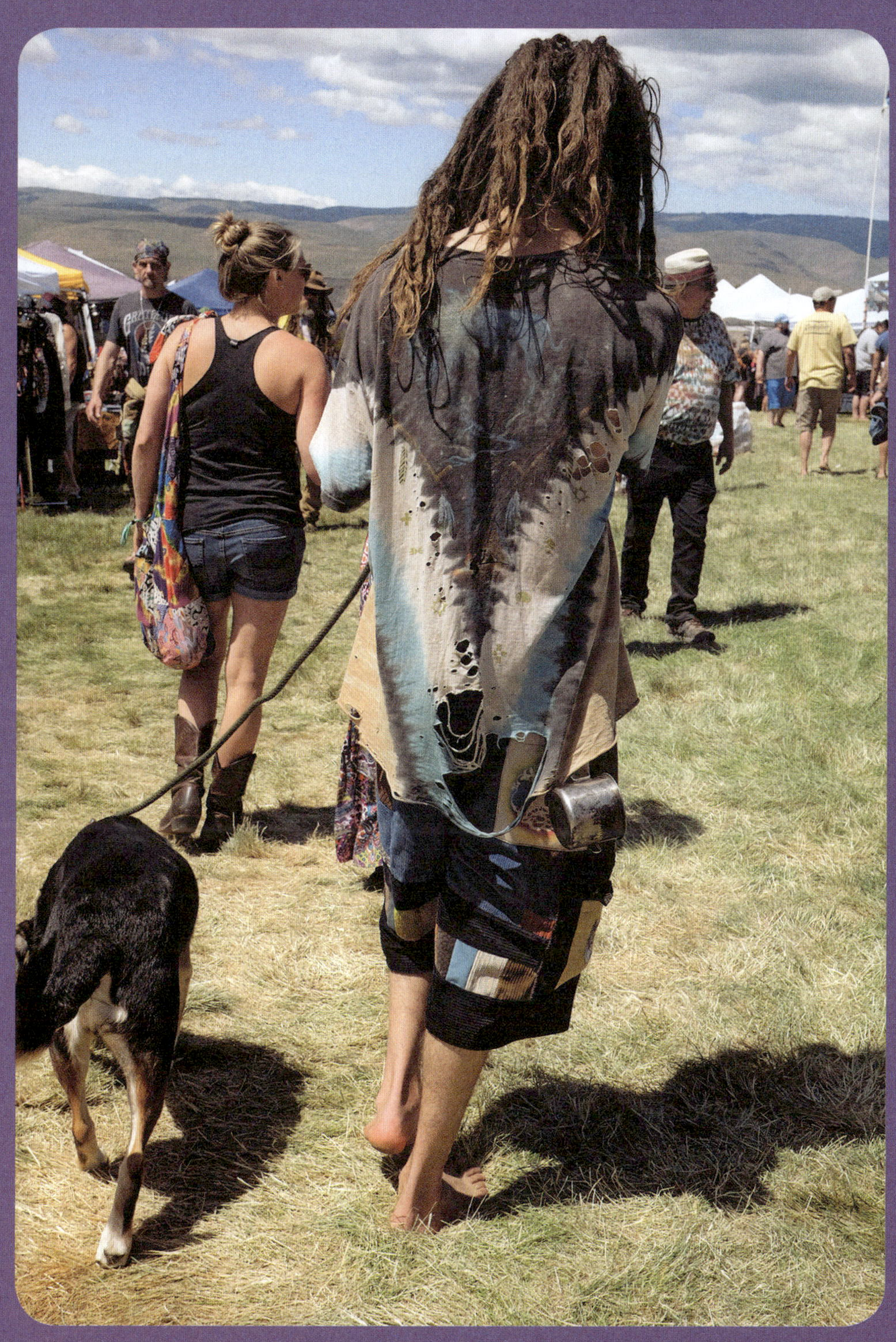

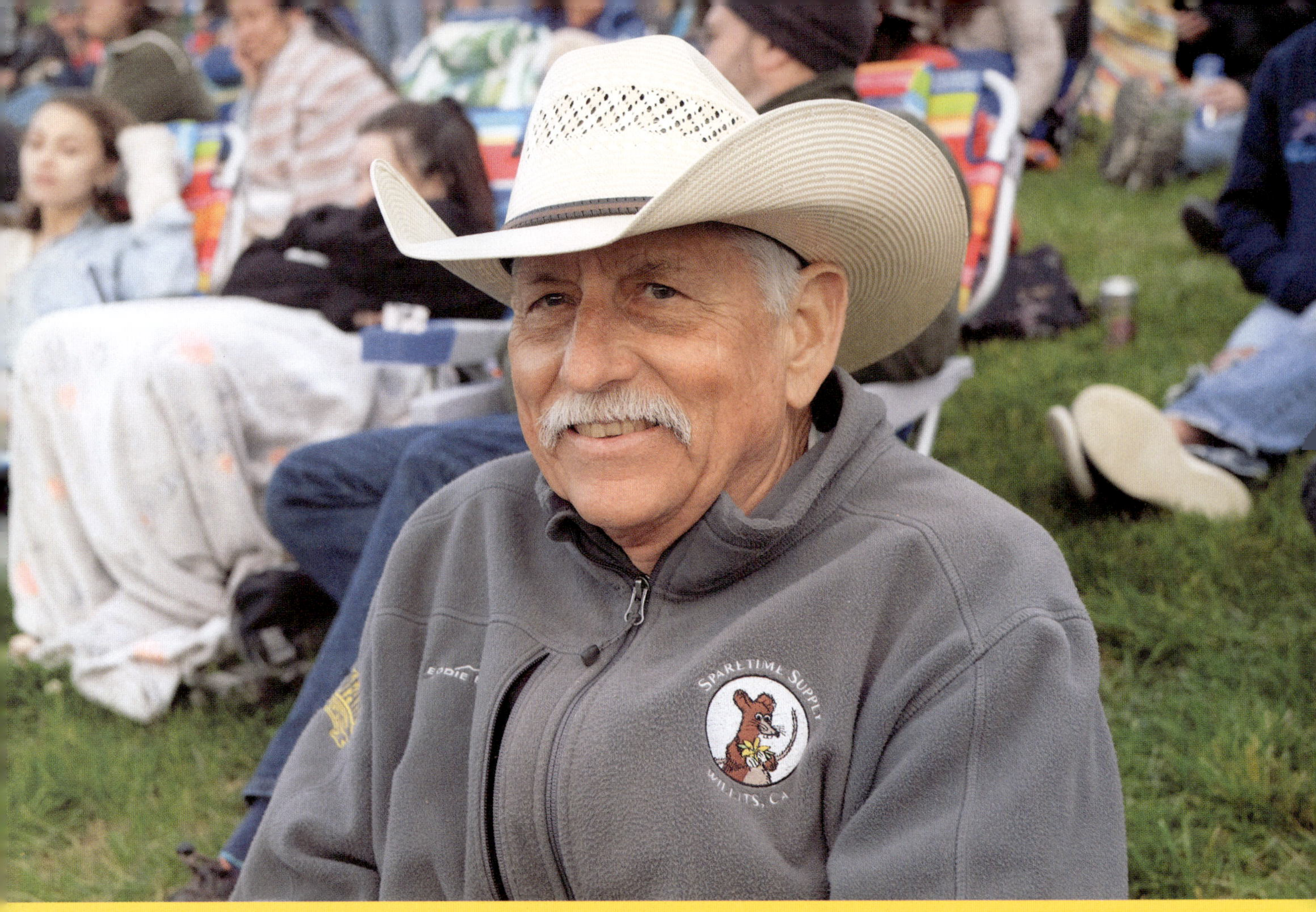
SPARETIME SUPPLY
WILLITS, CA

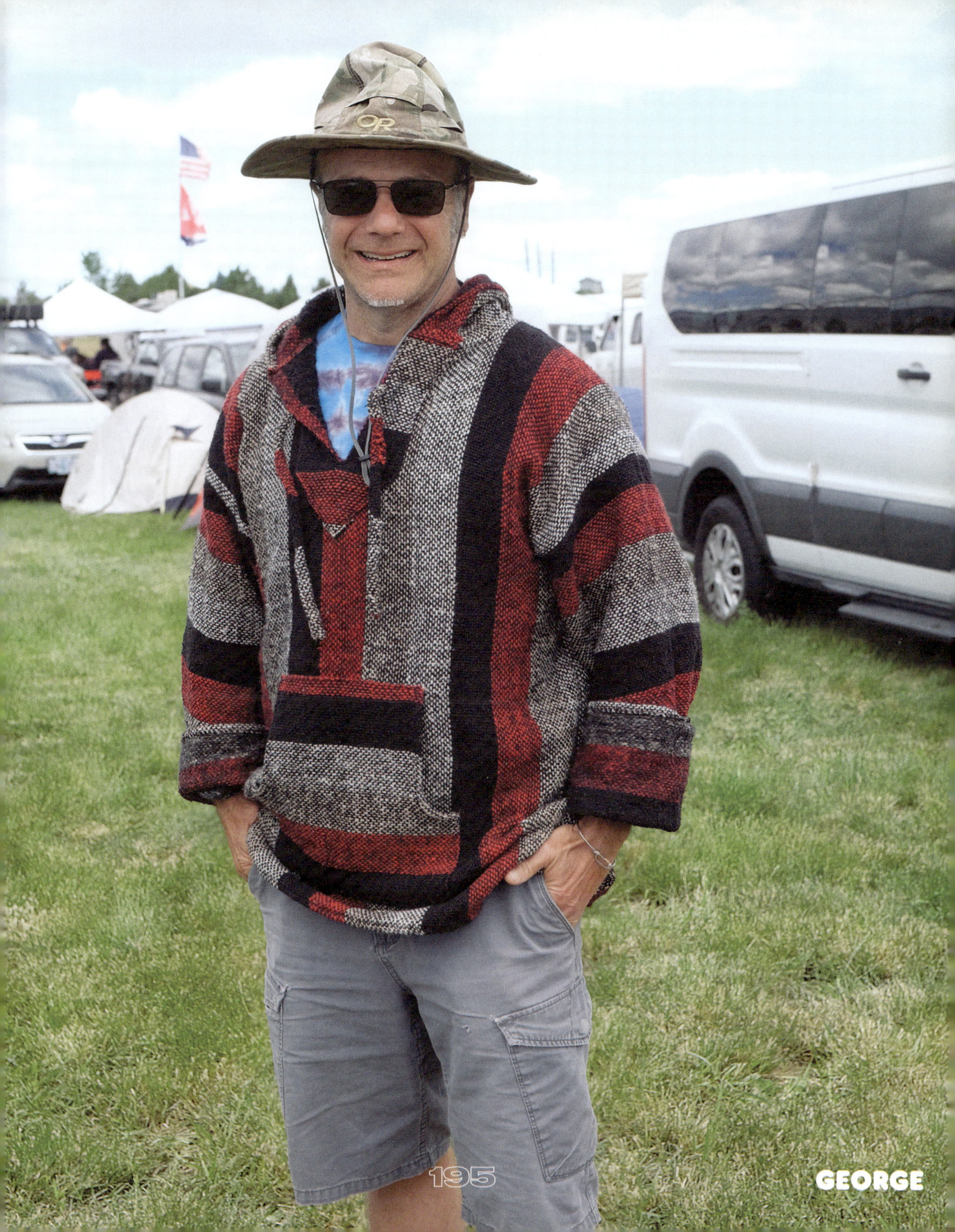

GEORGE

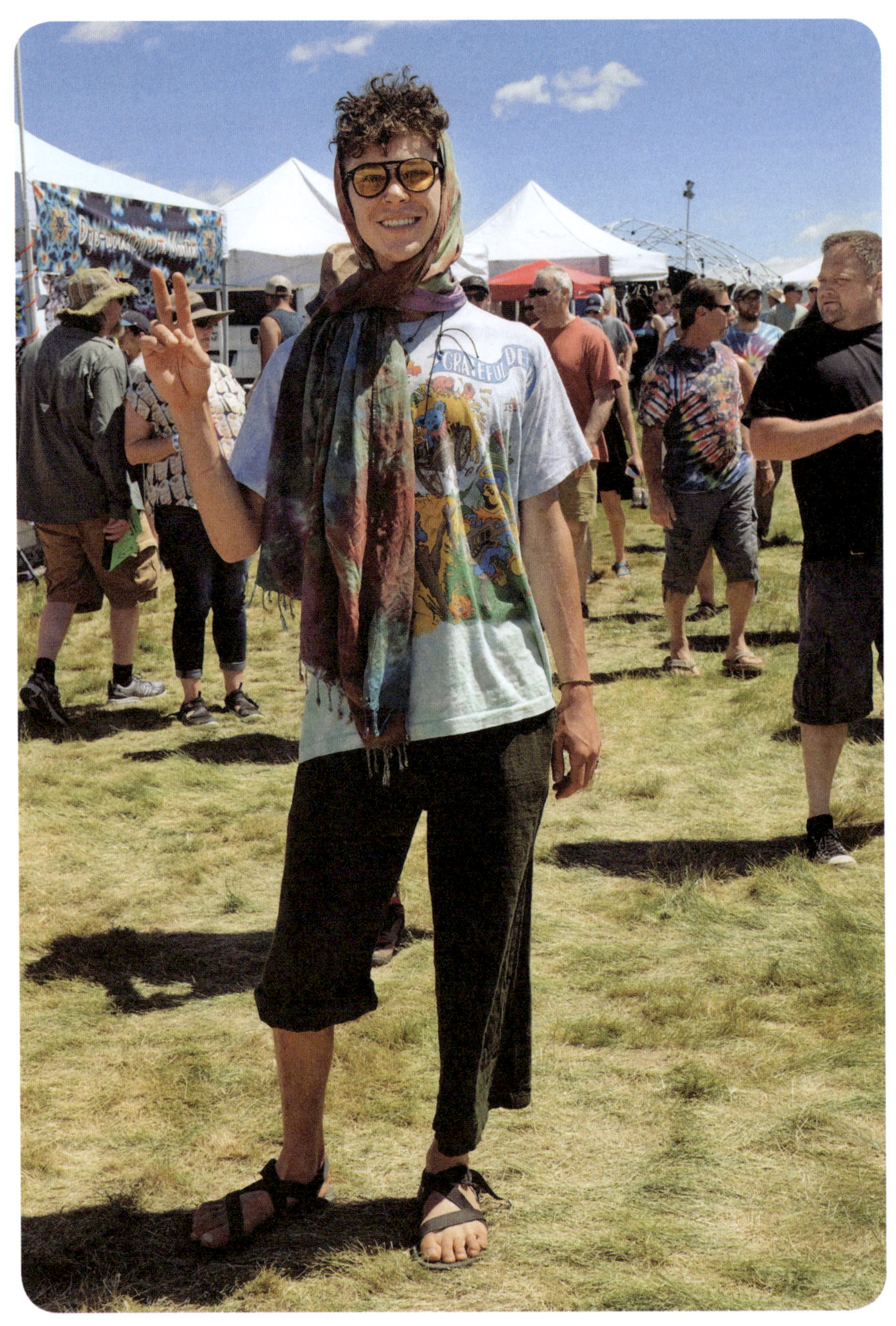

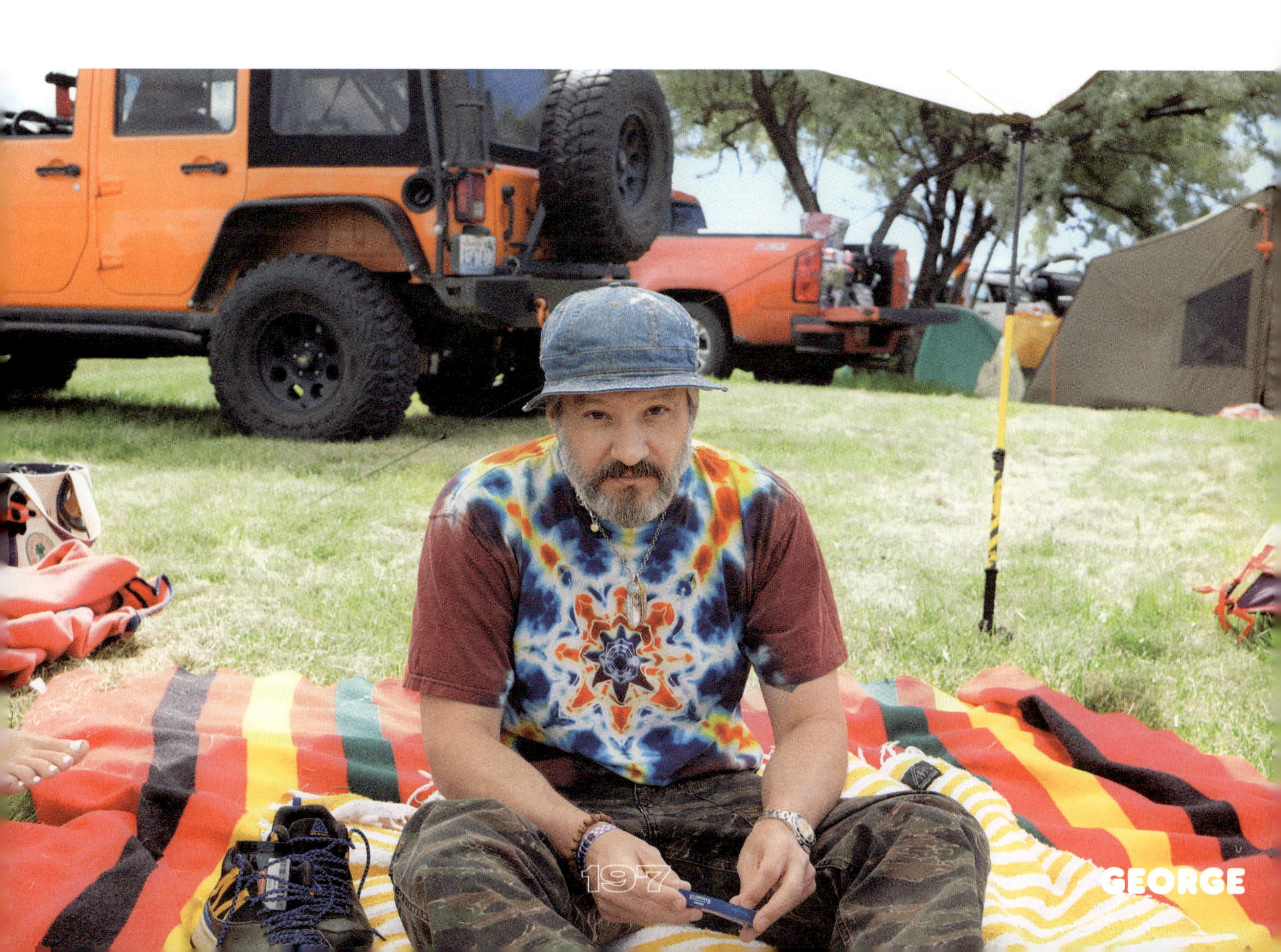

GEORGE

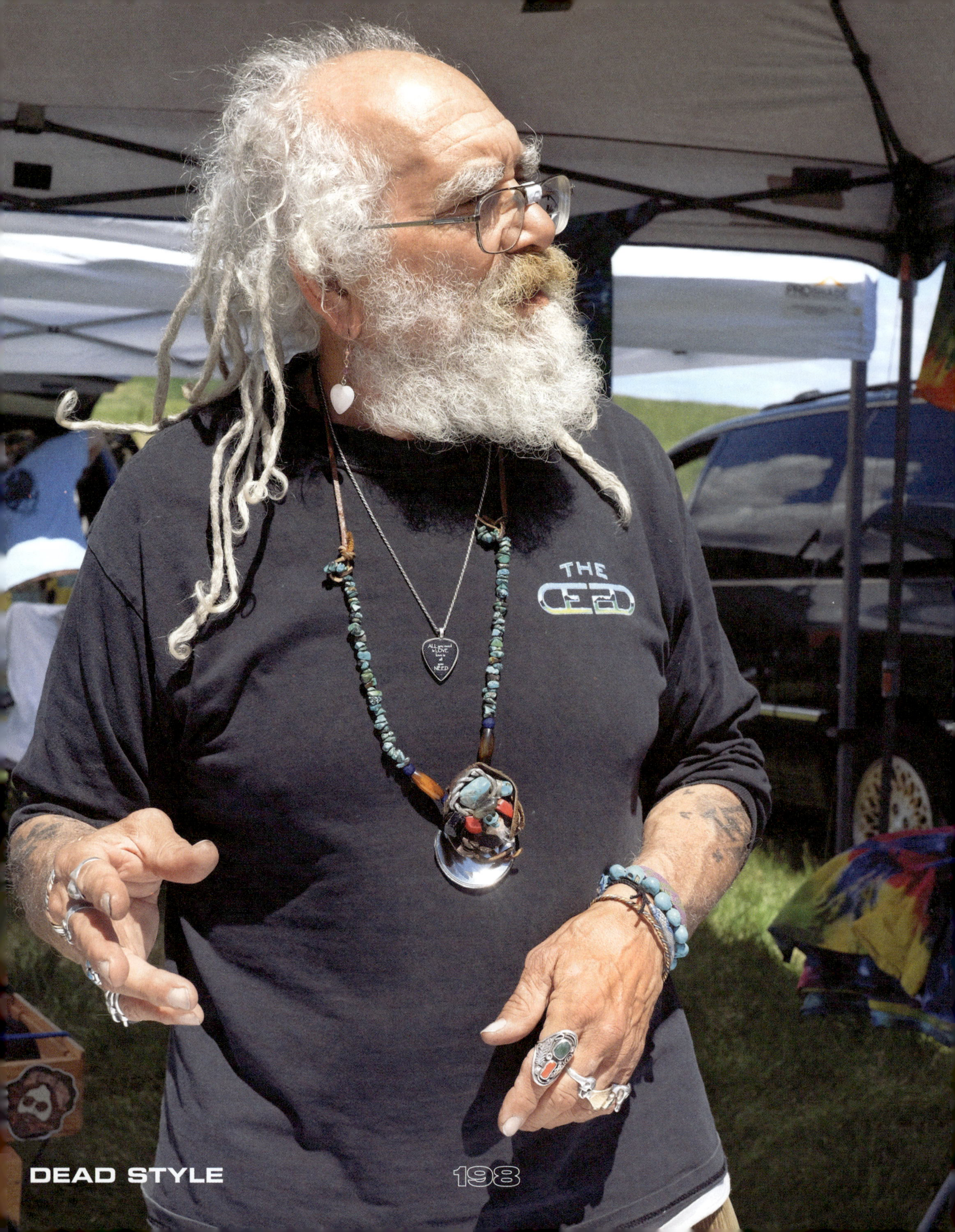
THE

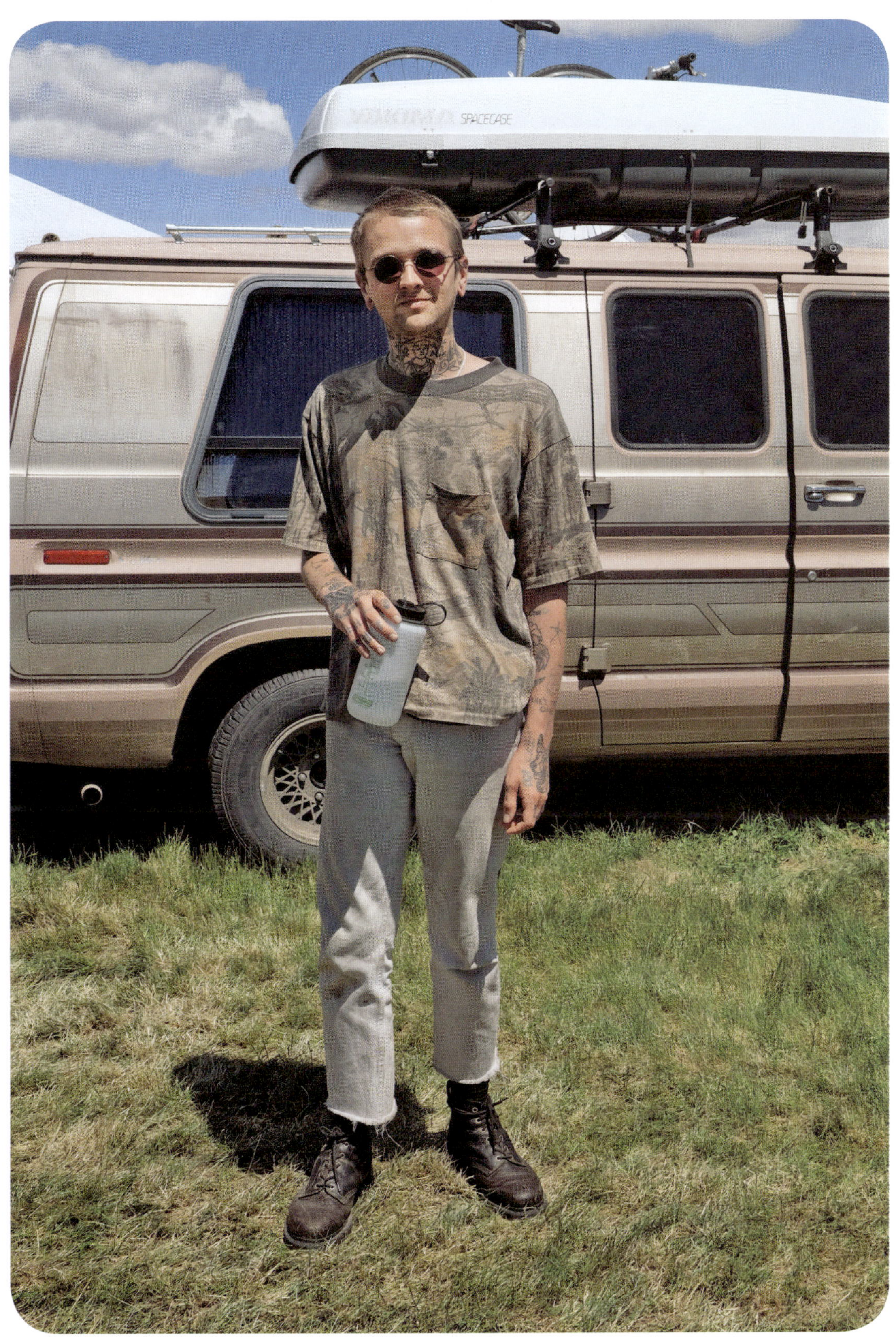

GEORGE

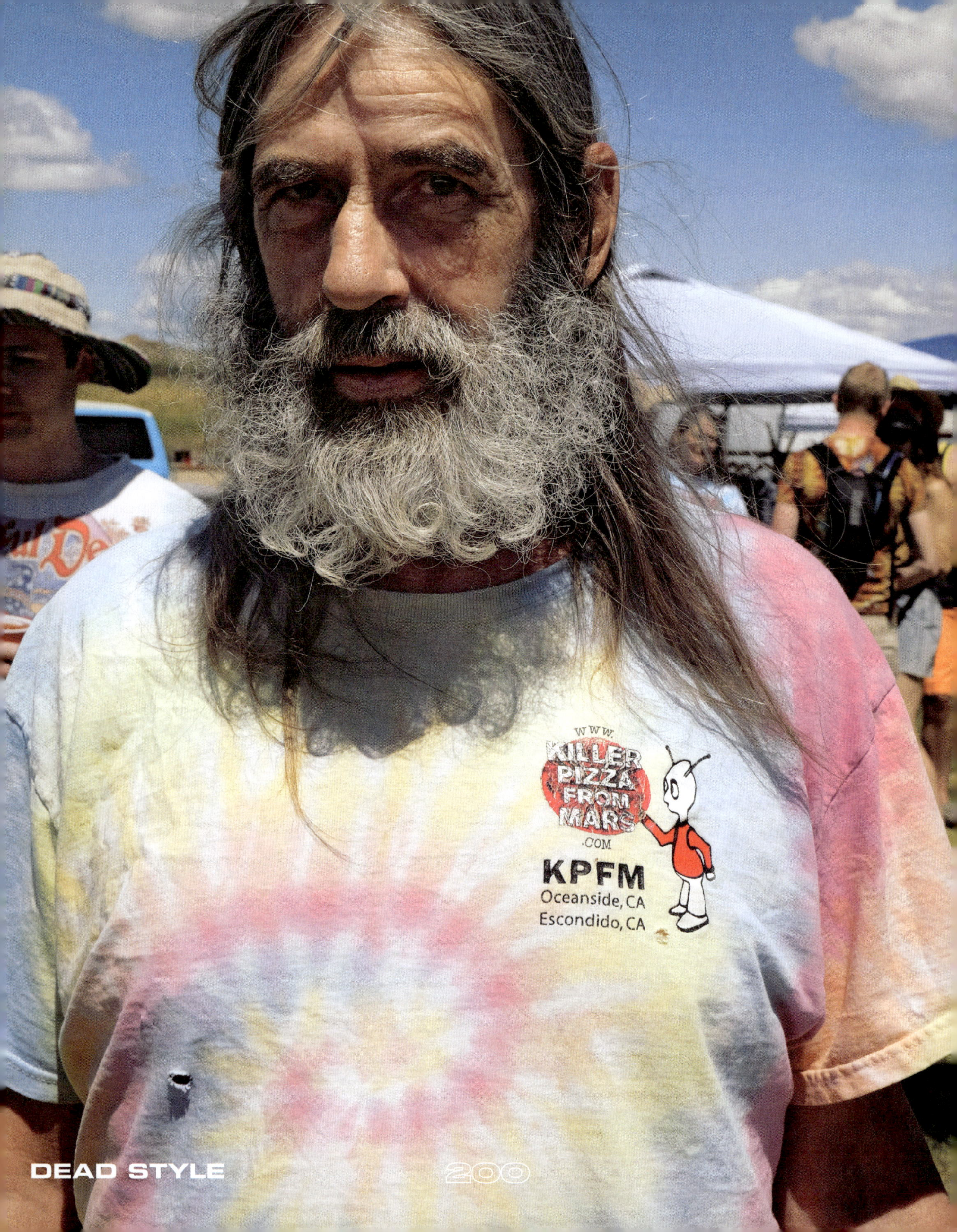
WWW.
KILLER
PIZZA
FROM
MARS
.COM
KPFM
Oceanside, CA
Escondido, CA

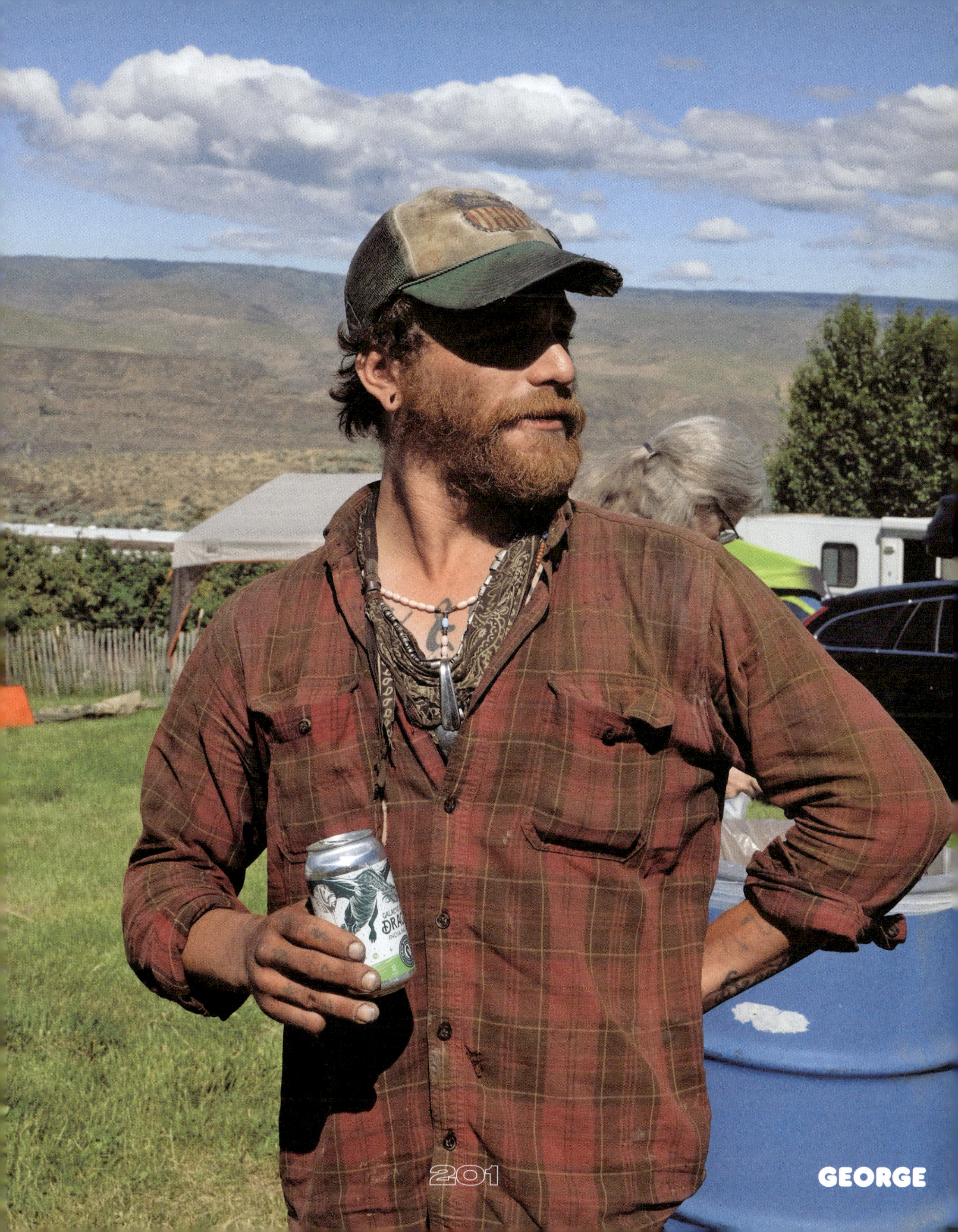

GEORGE

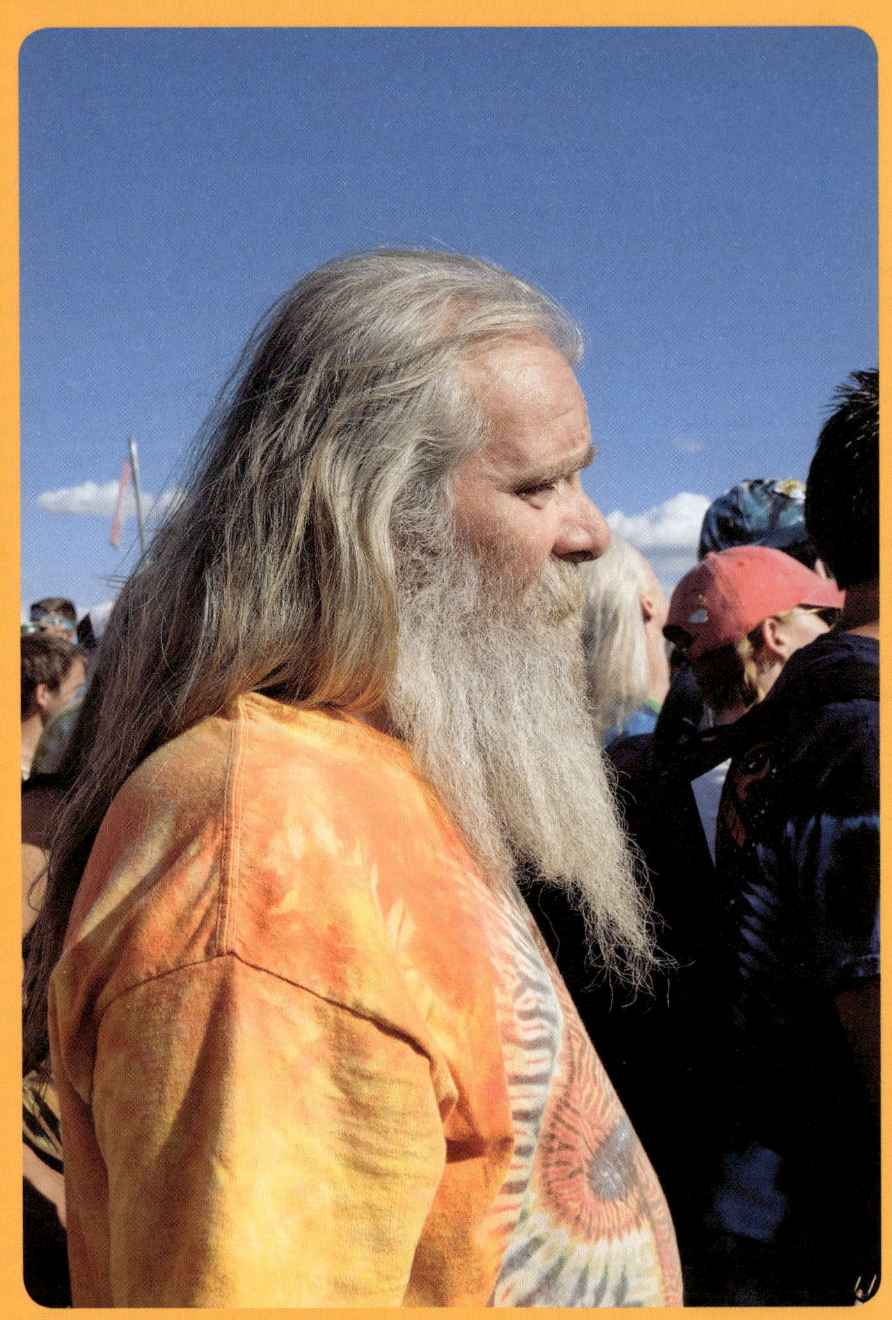

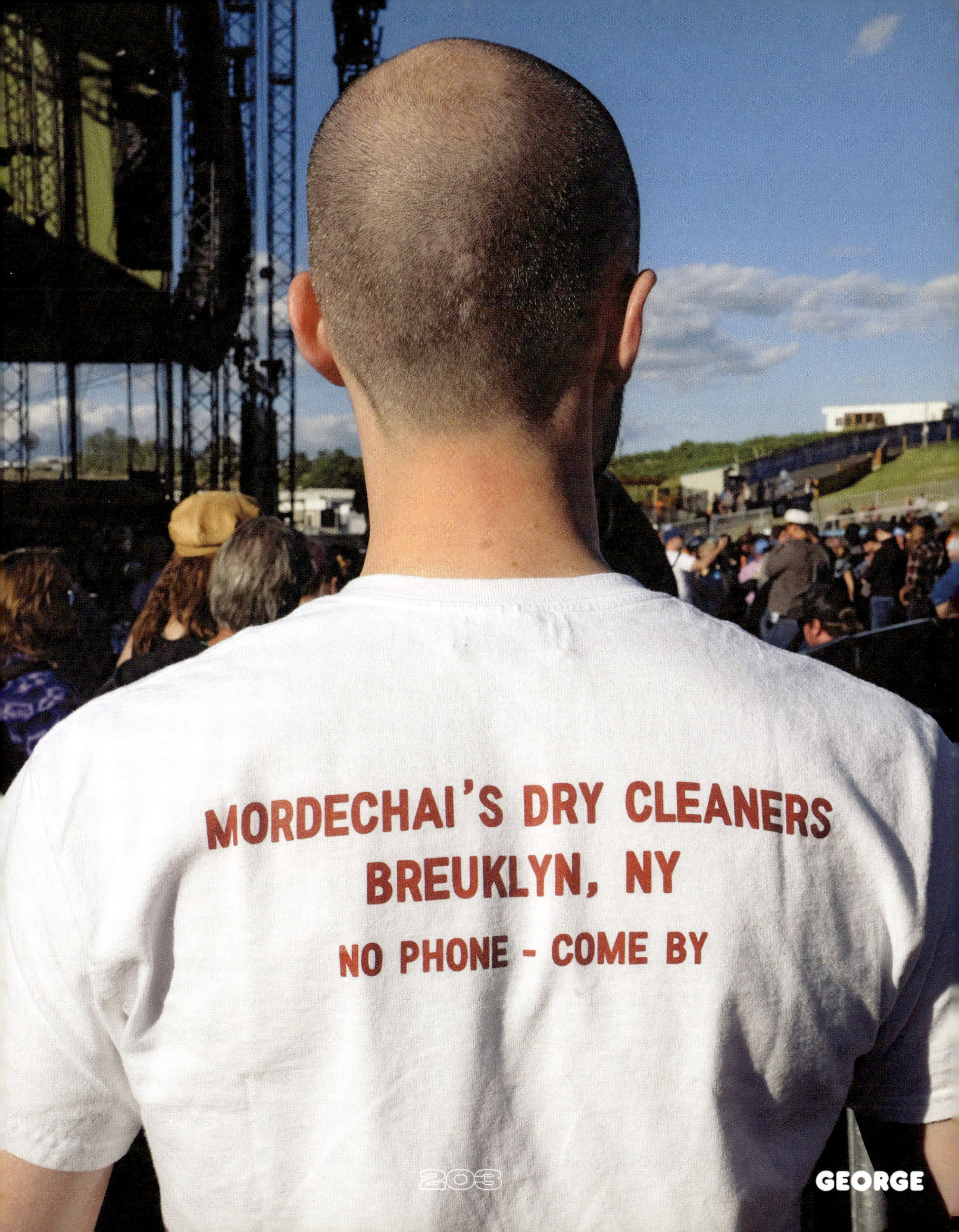
MORDECHAI'S DRY CLEANERS
BREUKLYN, NY
NO PHONE - COME BY

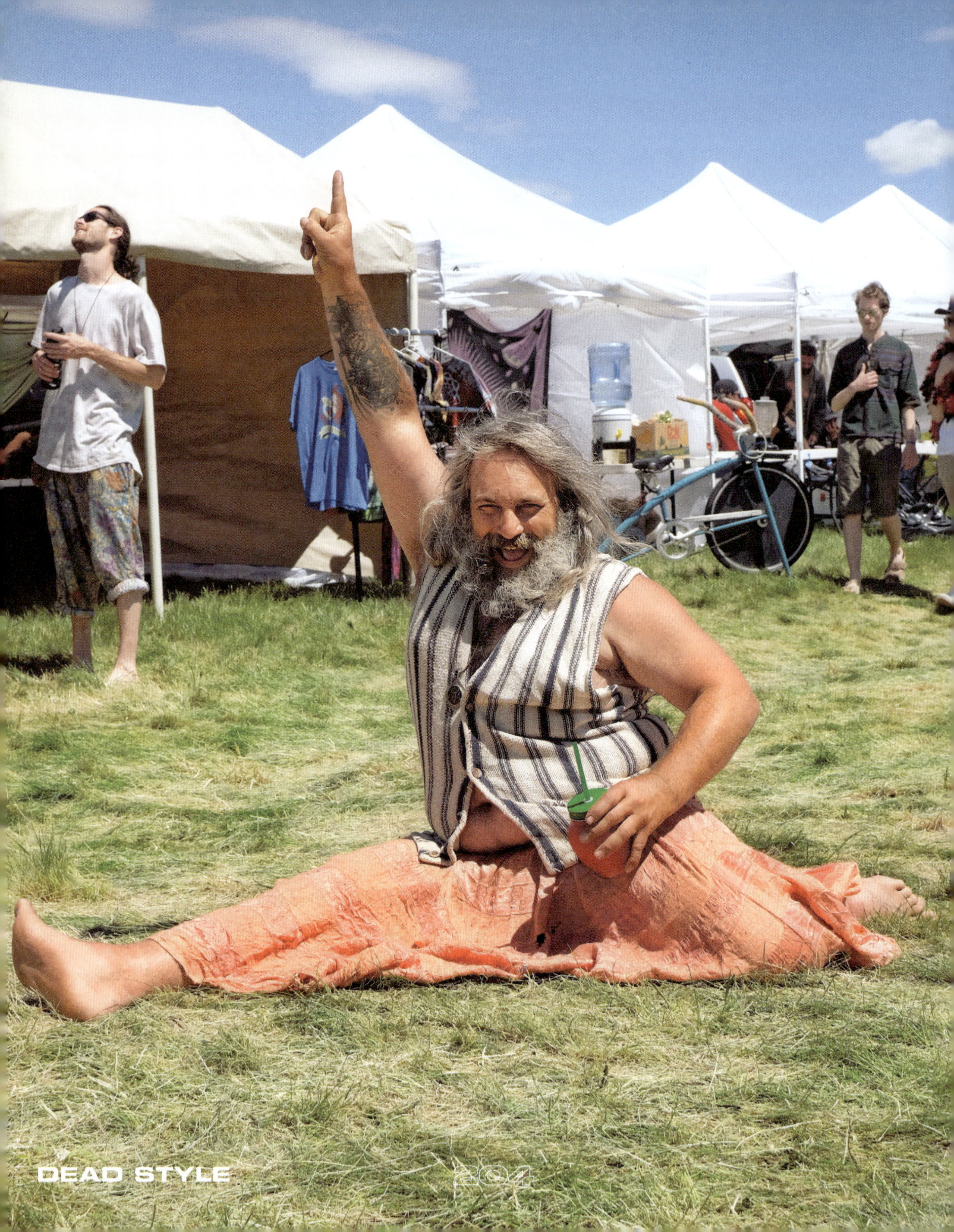

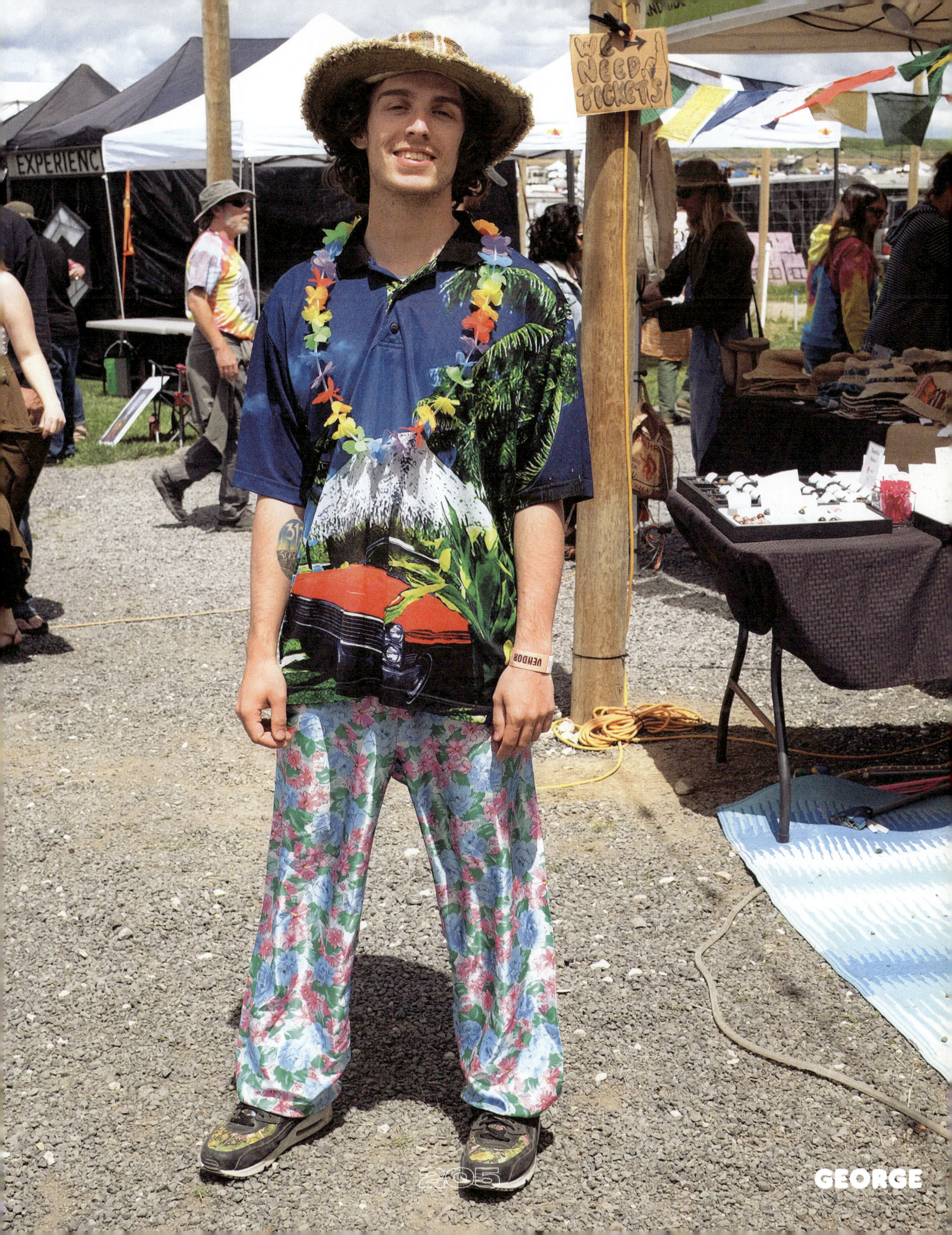

GEORGE

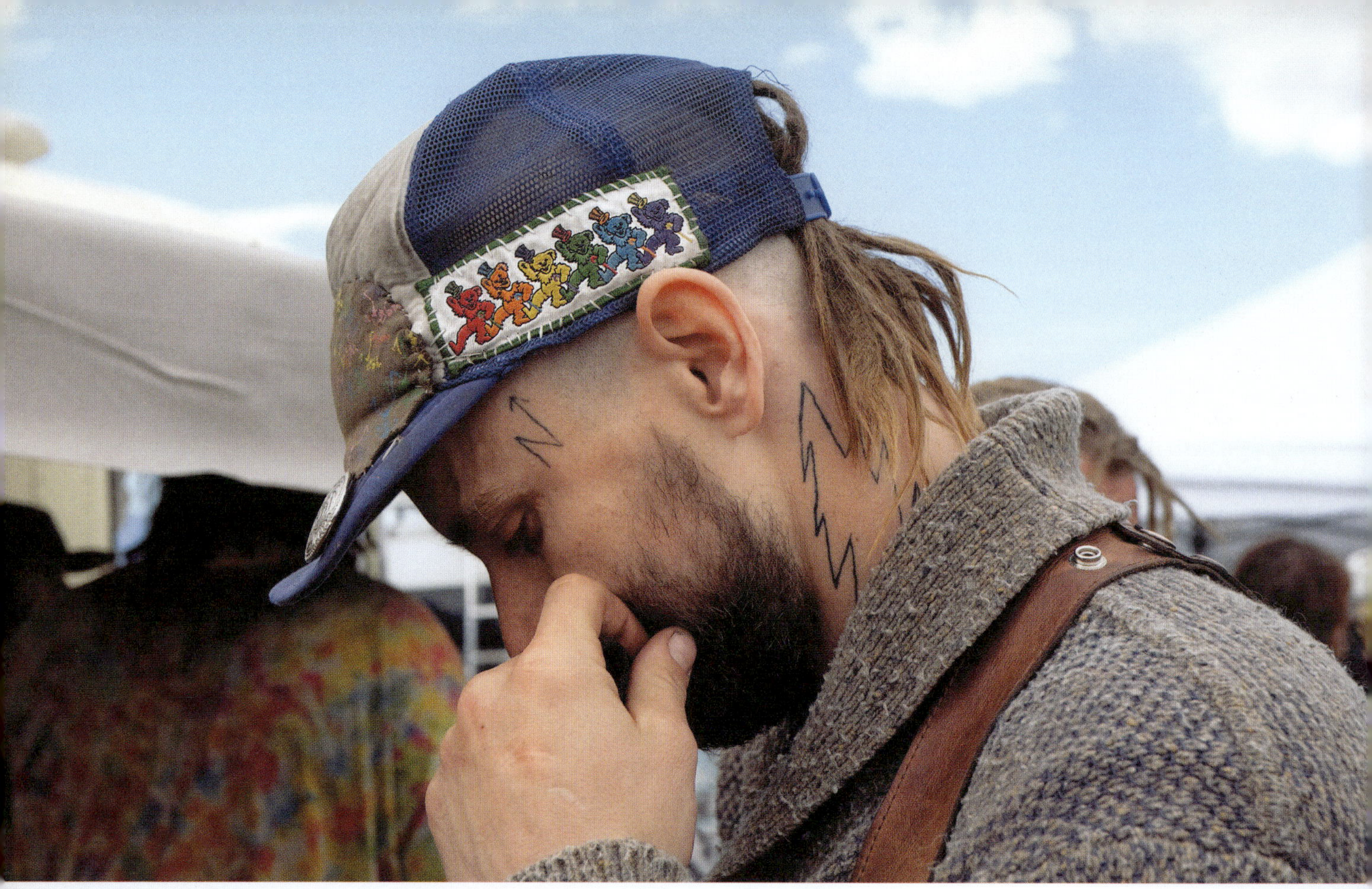

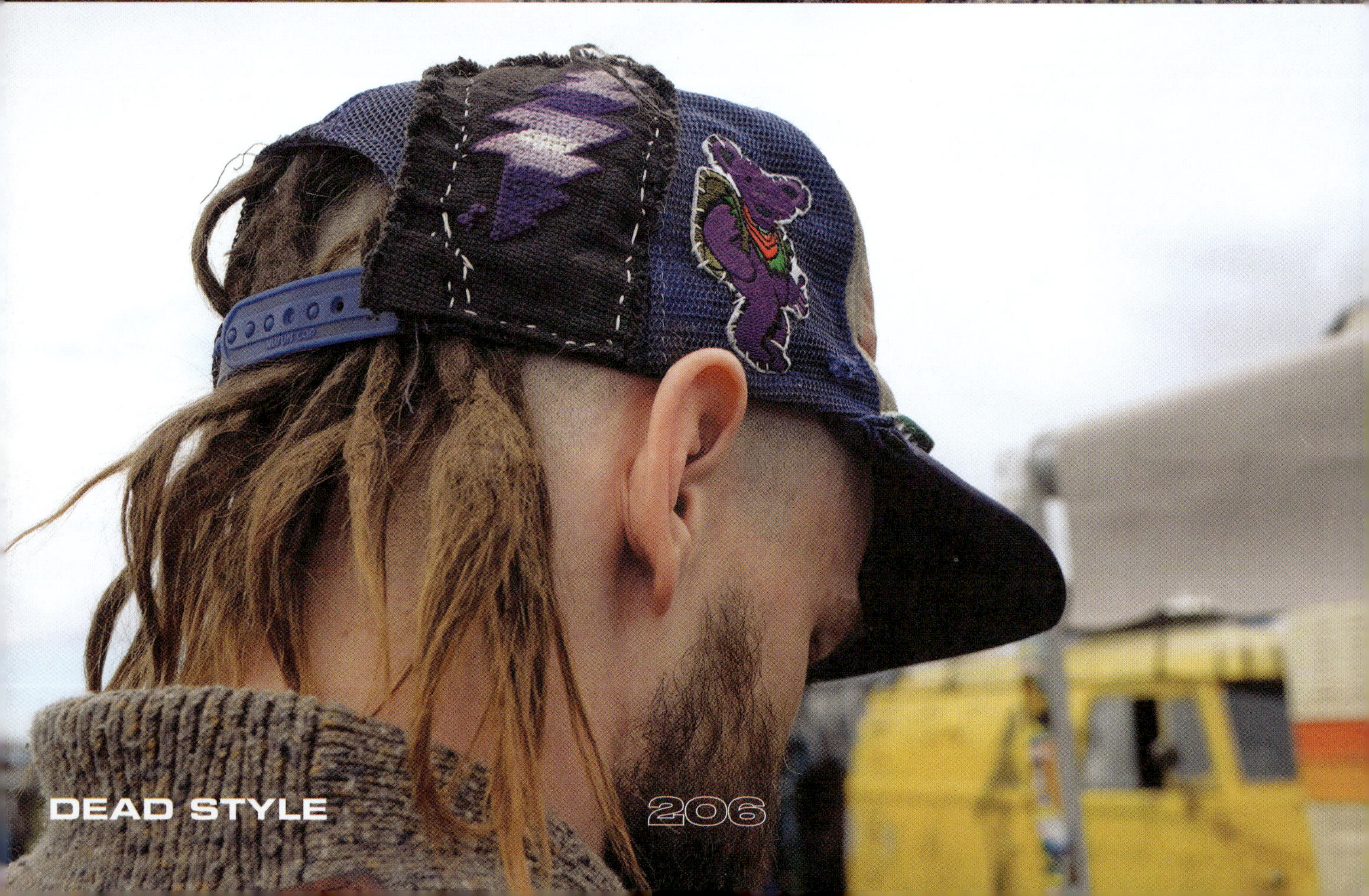

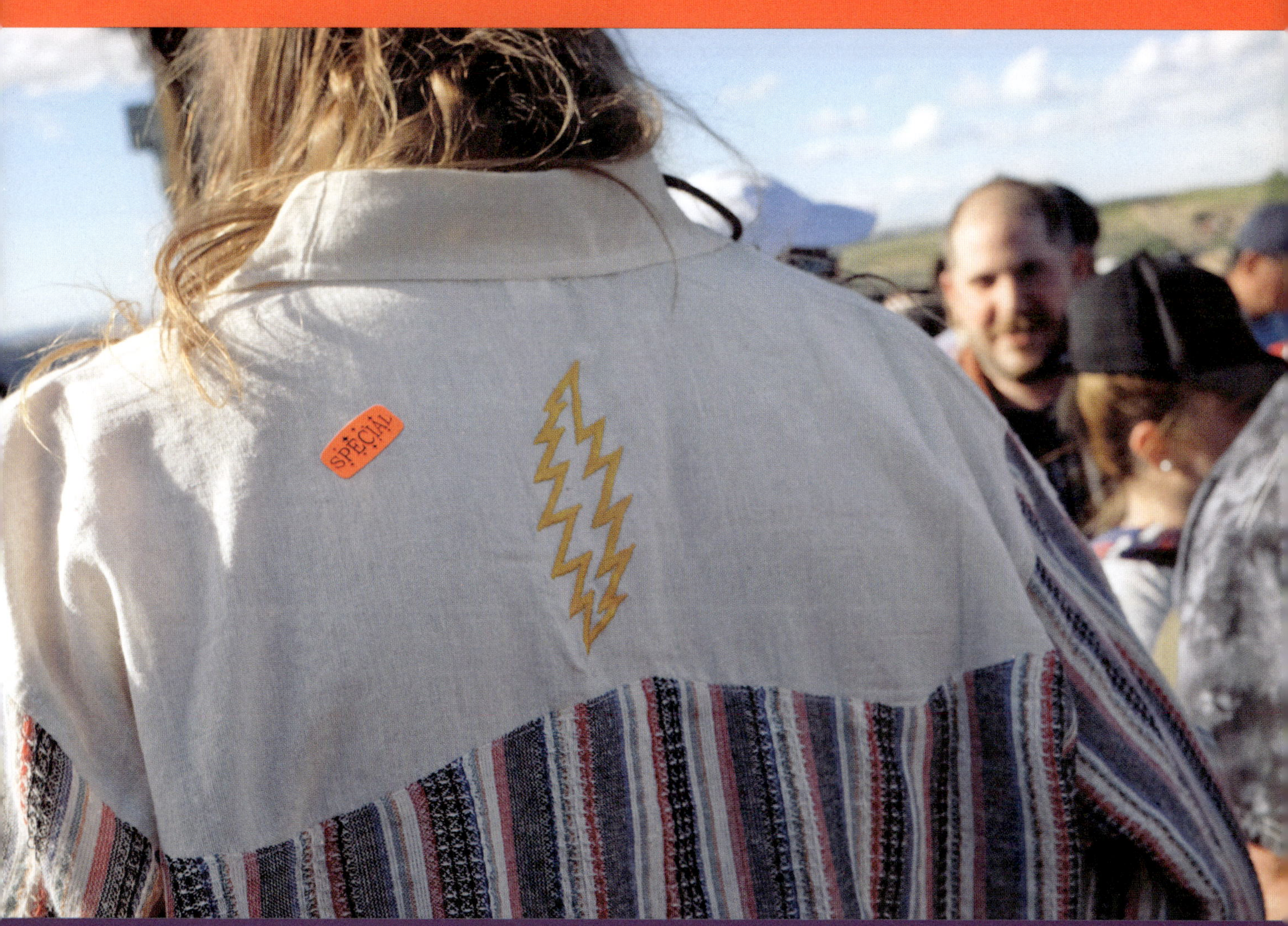
SPECIAL

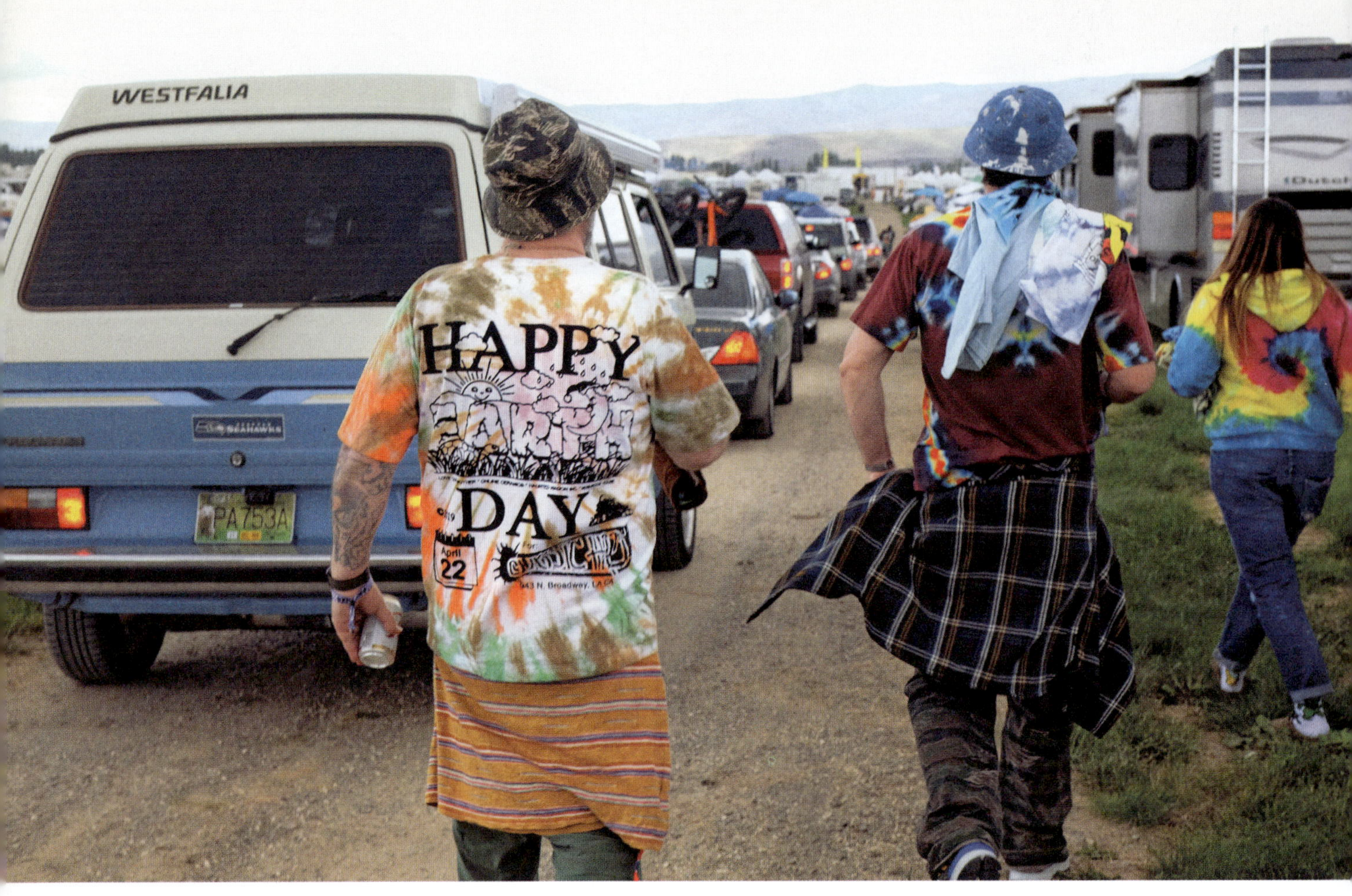
WESTFALIA
HAPPY
DAY
April
22
PA753A

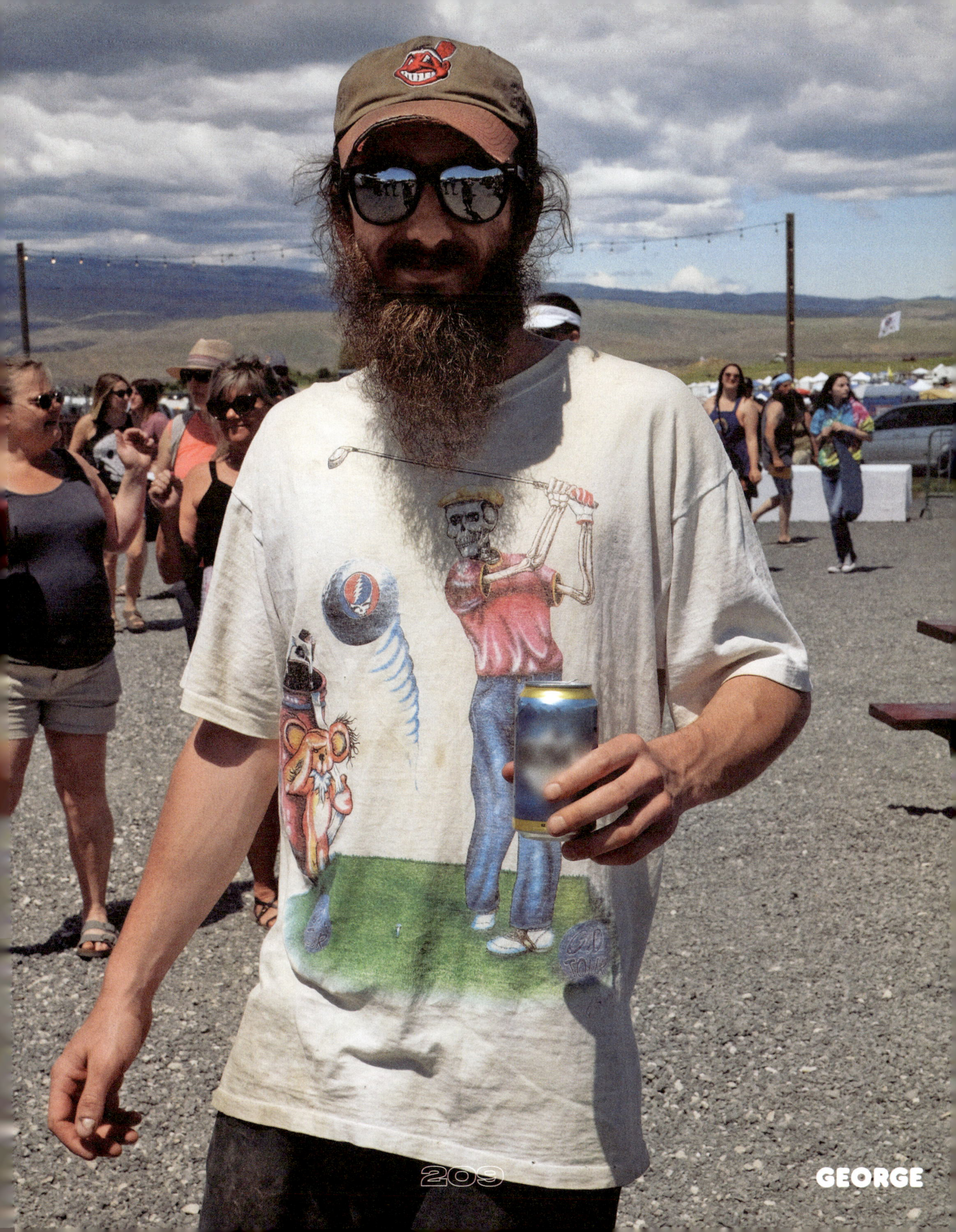

GEORGE

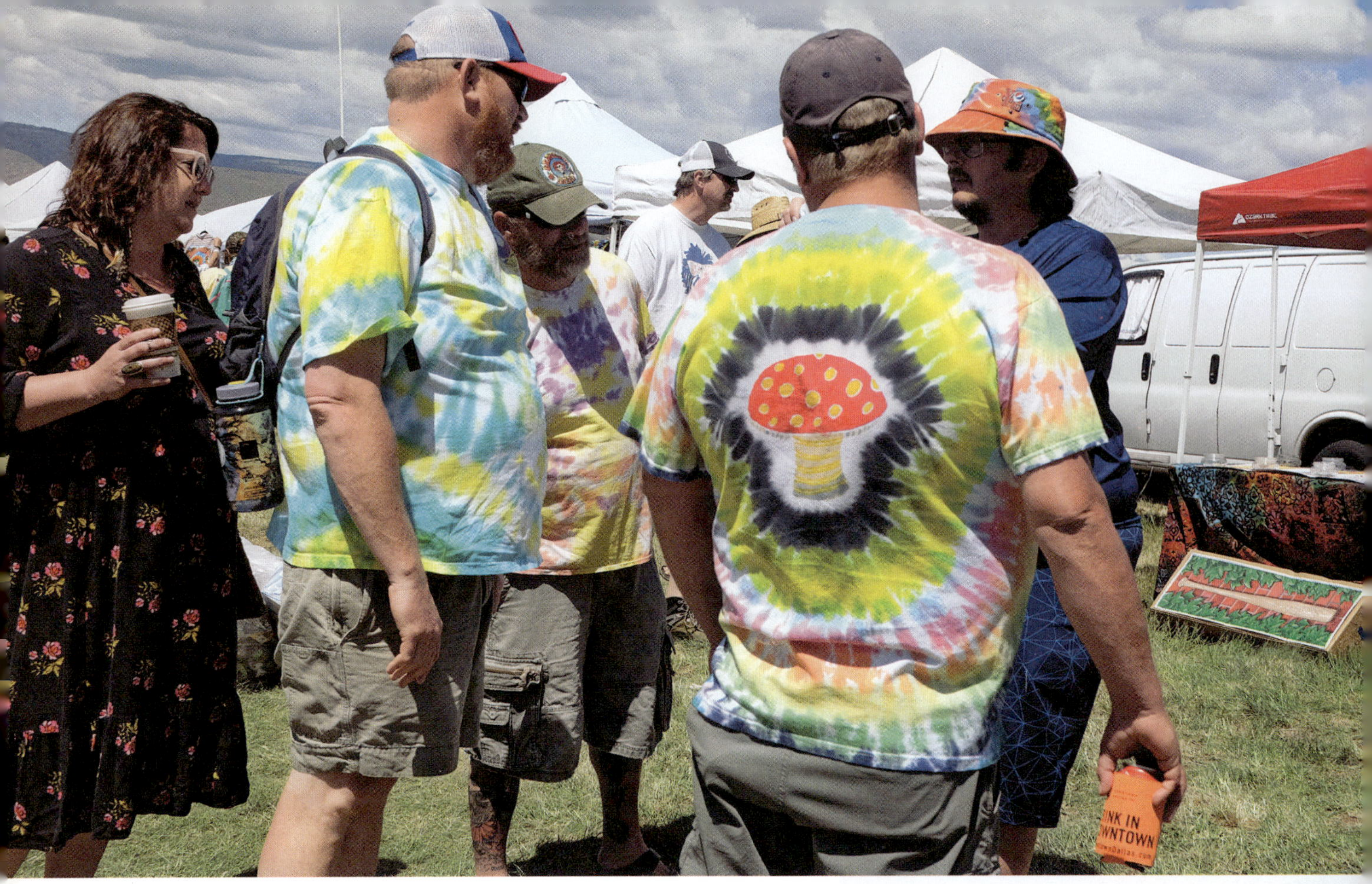

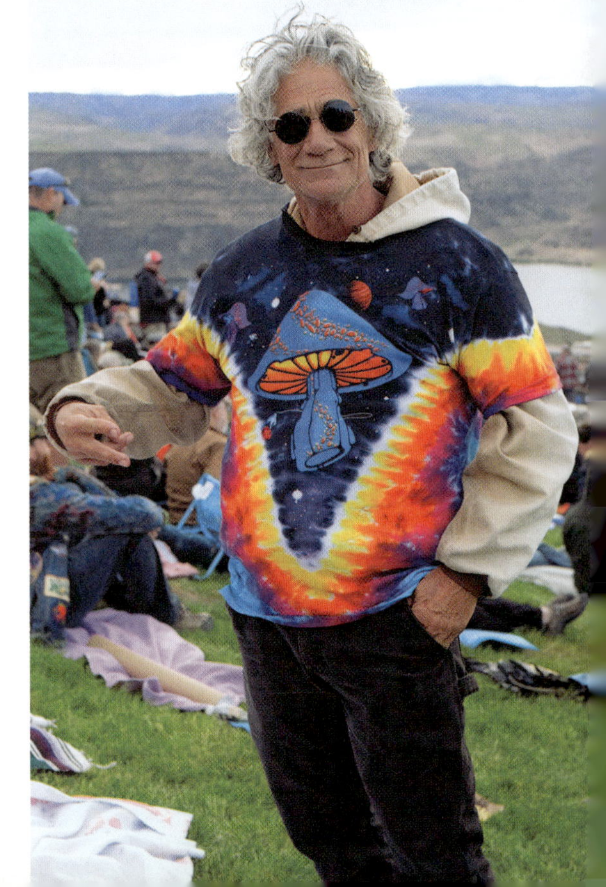

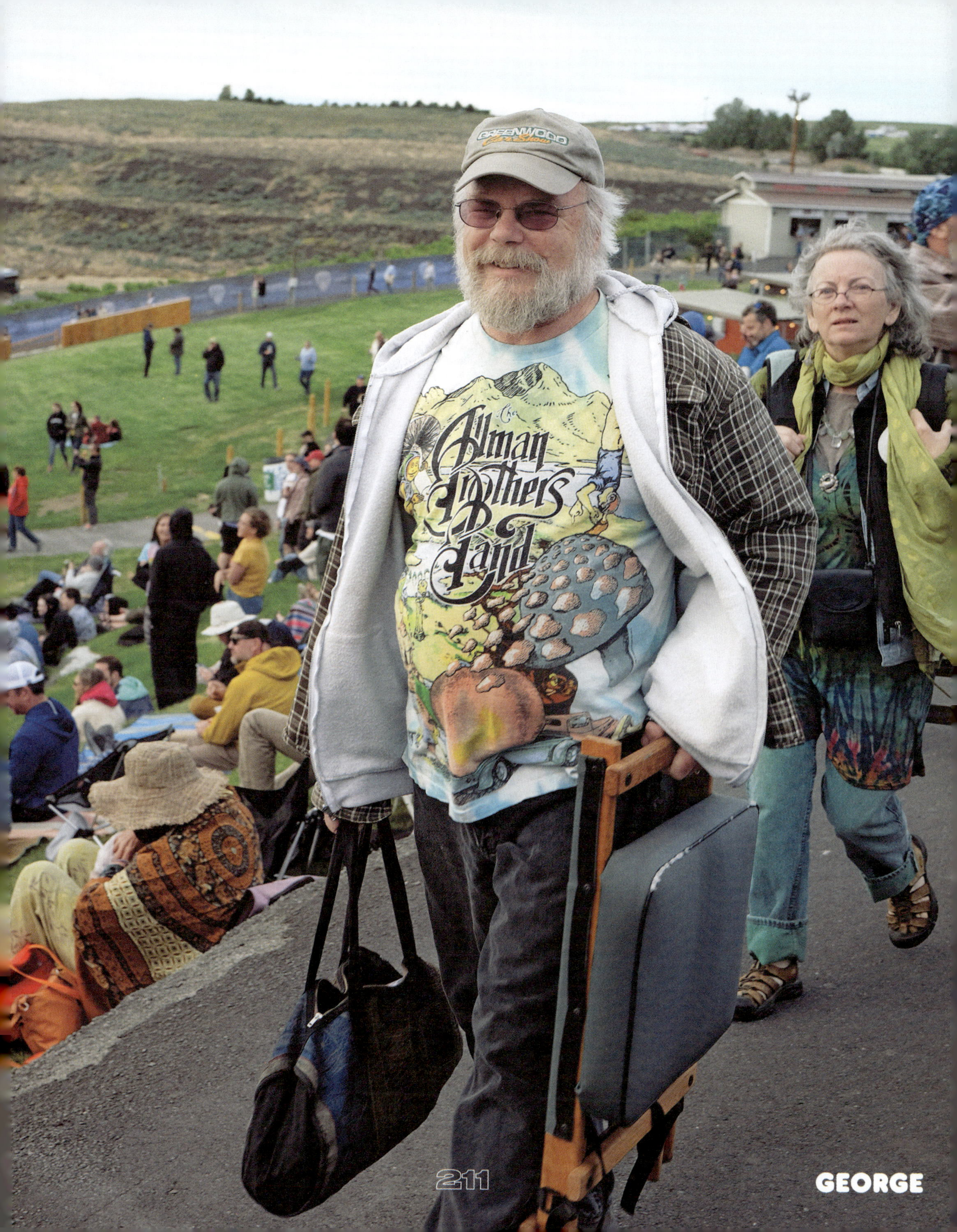
GREENWOOD
The Allman Brothers Band

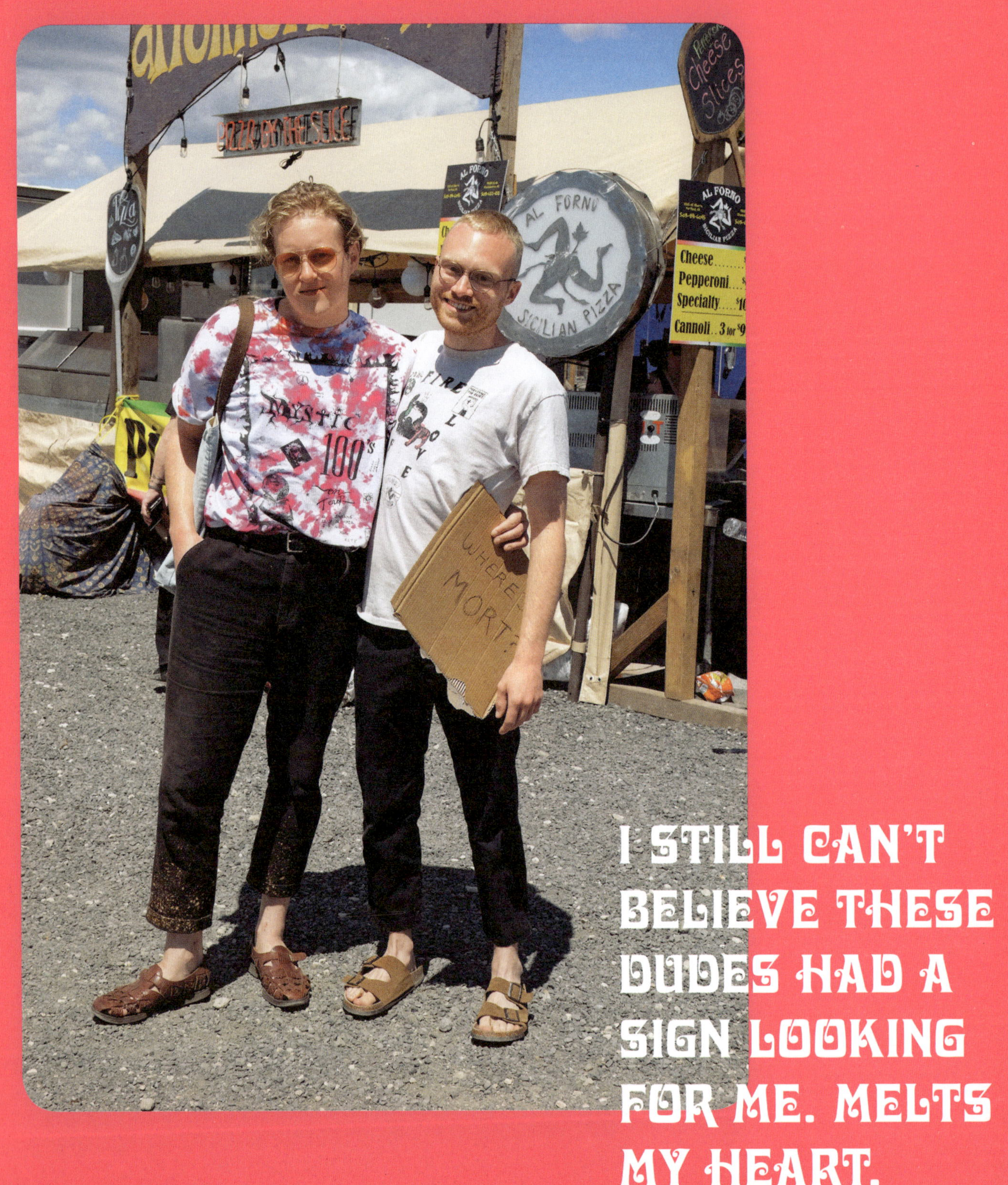

I STILL CAN'T BELIEVE THESE DUDES HAD A SIGN LOOKING FOR ME. MELTS MY HEART.

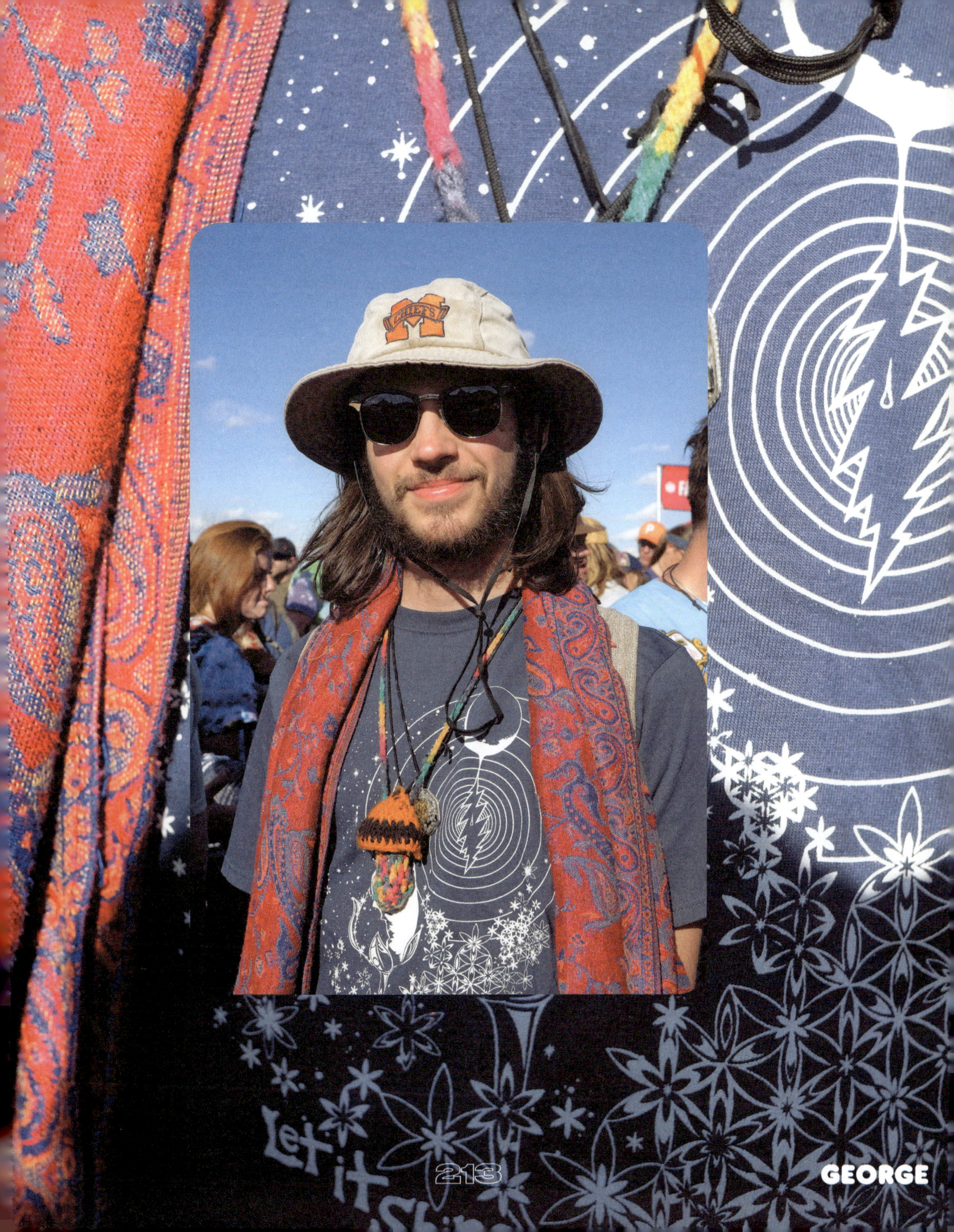

GEORGE

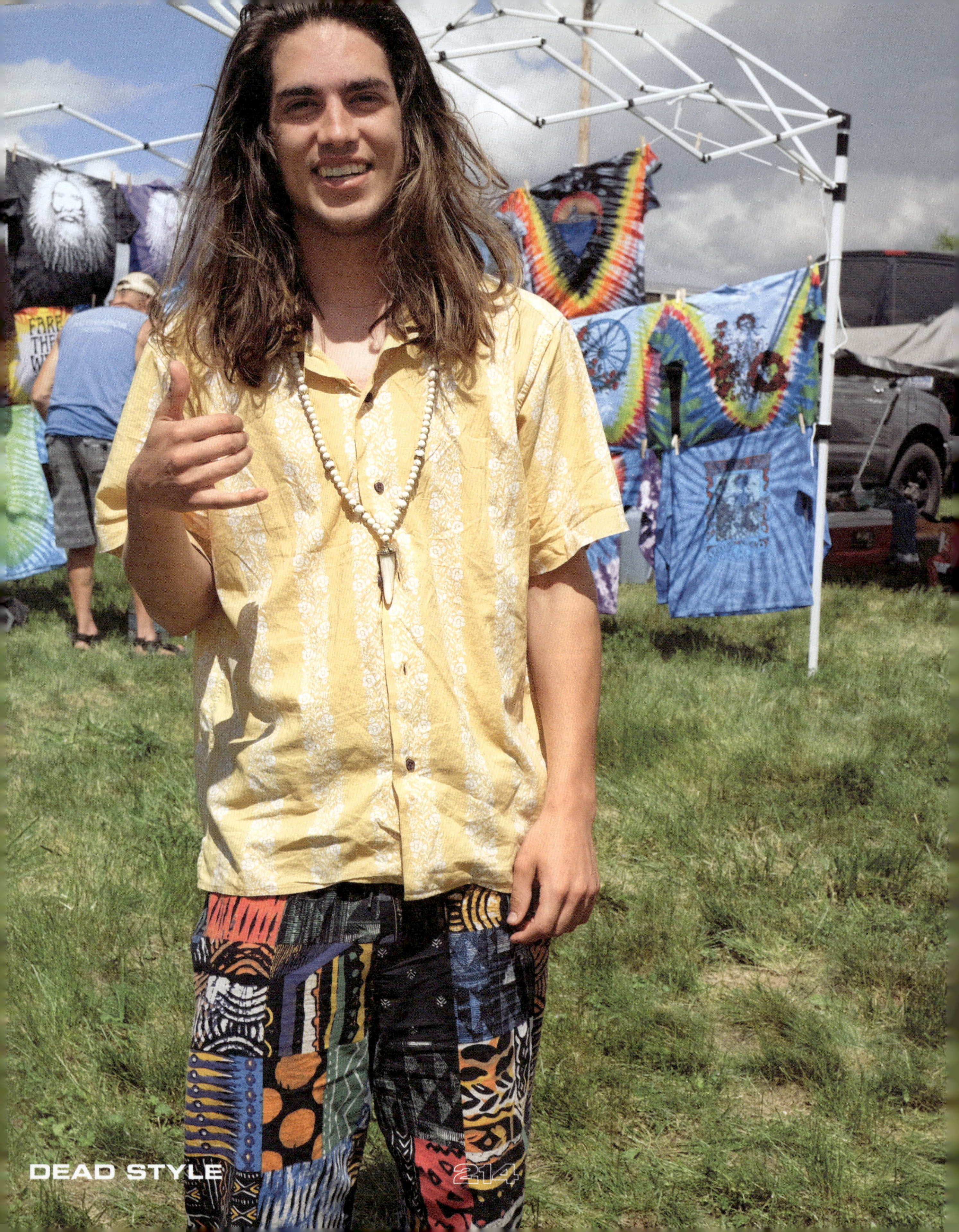

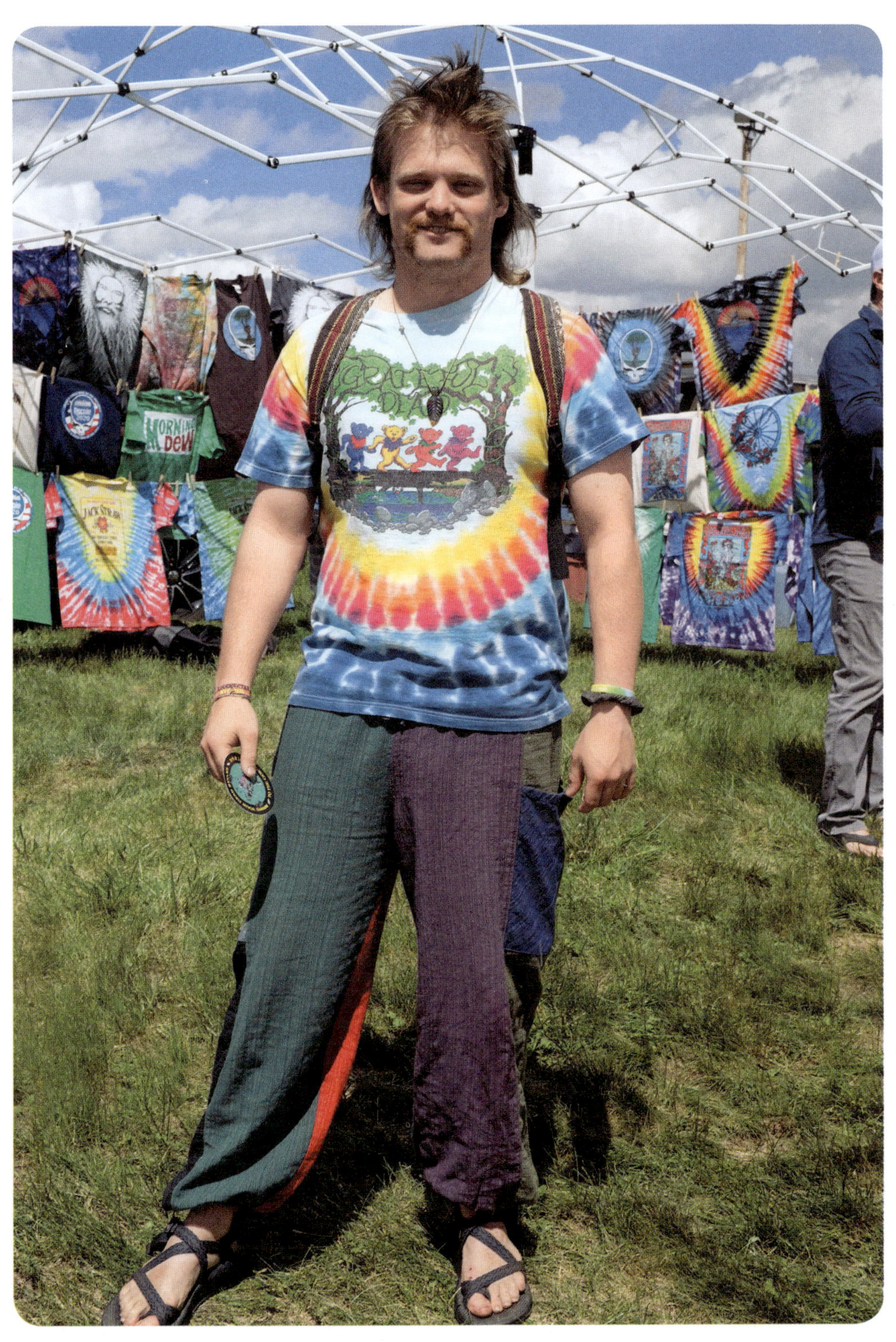

GEORGE

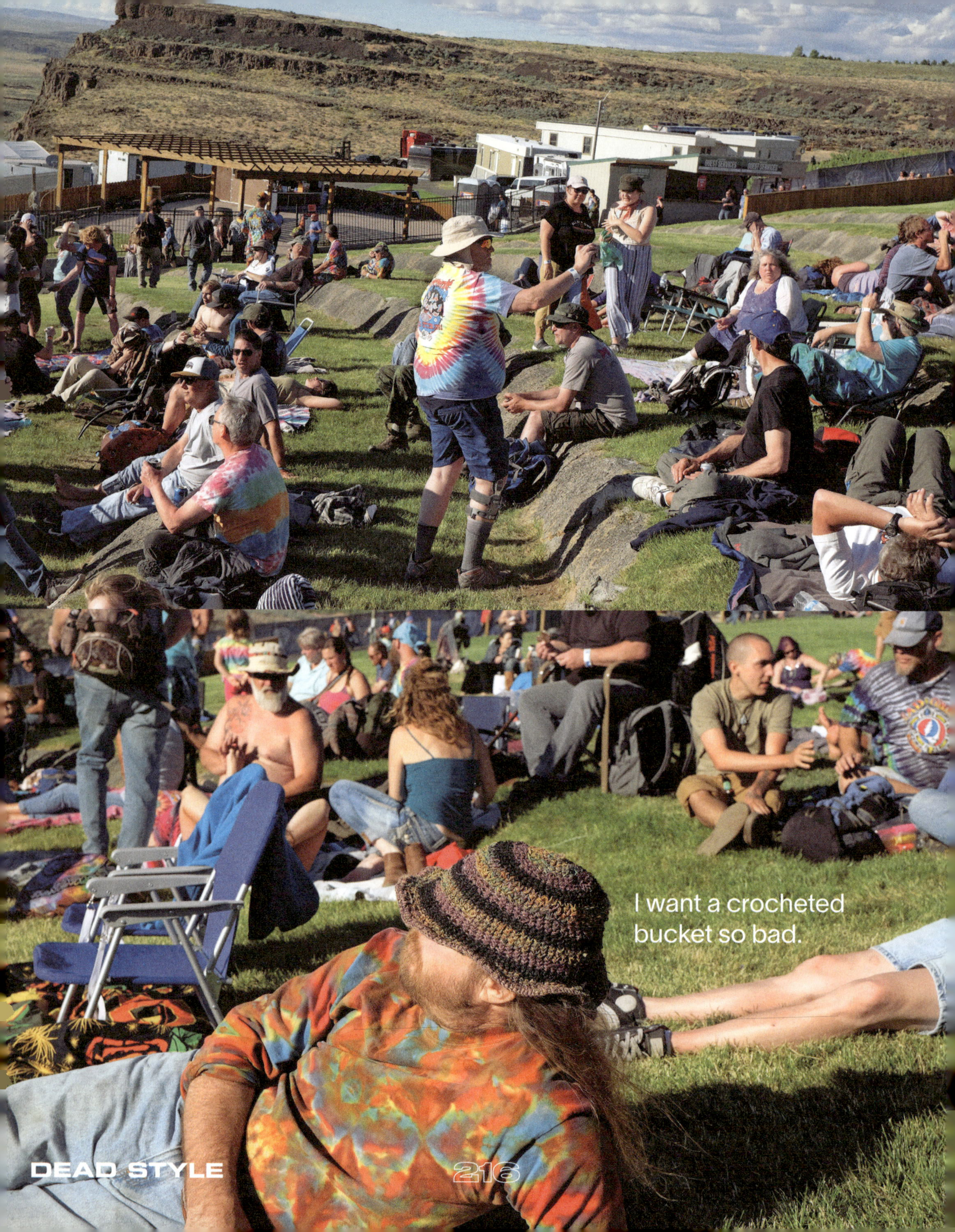

I want a crocheted bucket so bad.

IF I DIDN'T WANT TO BE ME, I'D WANT TO BE HIM.

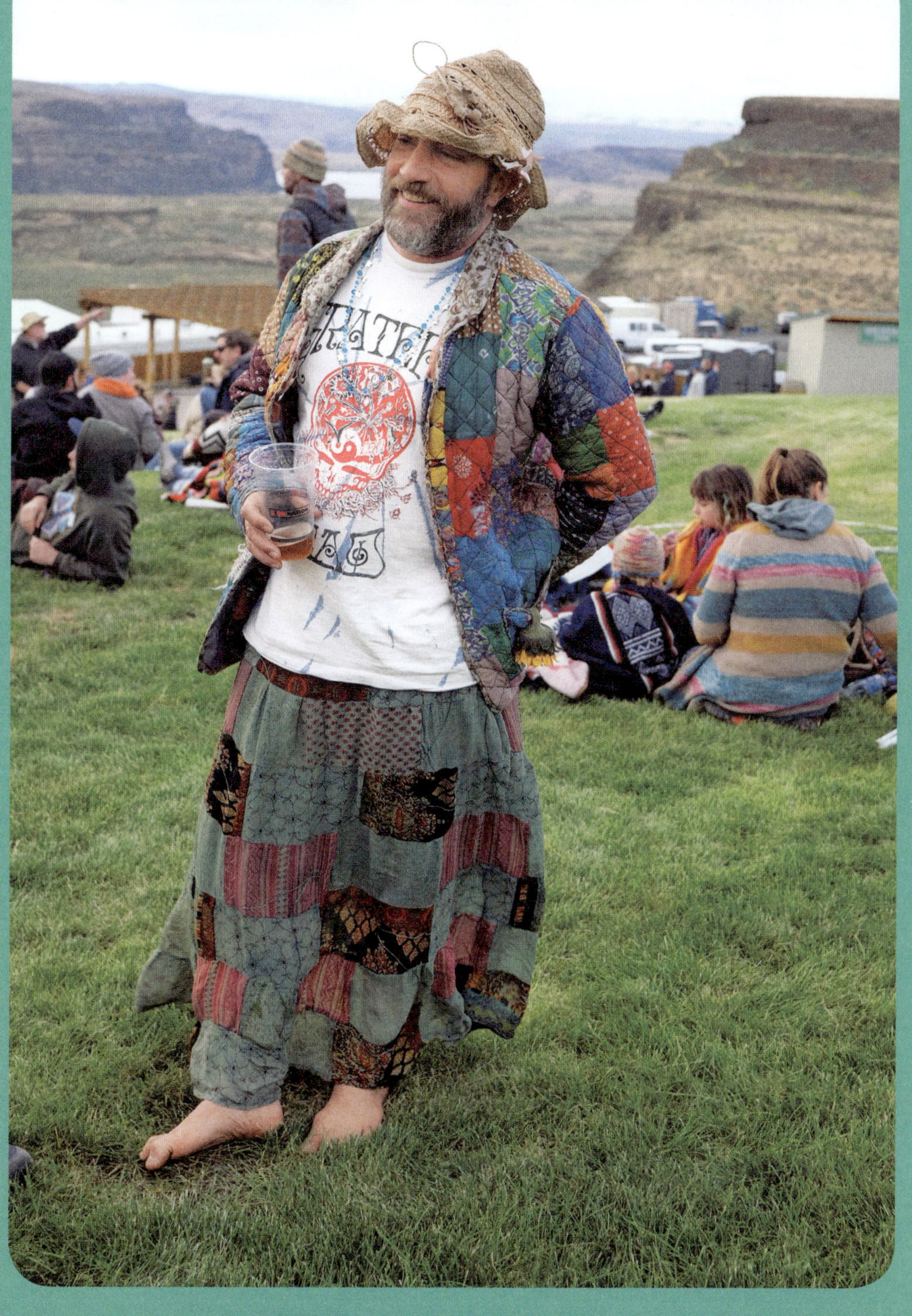

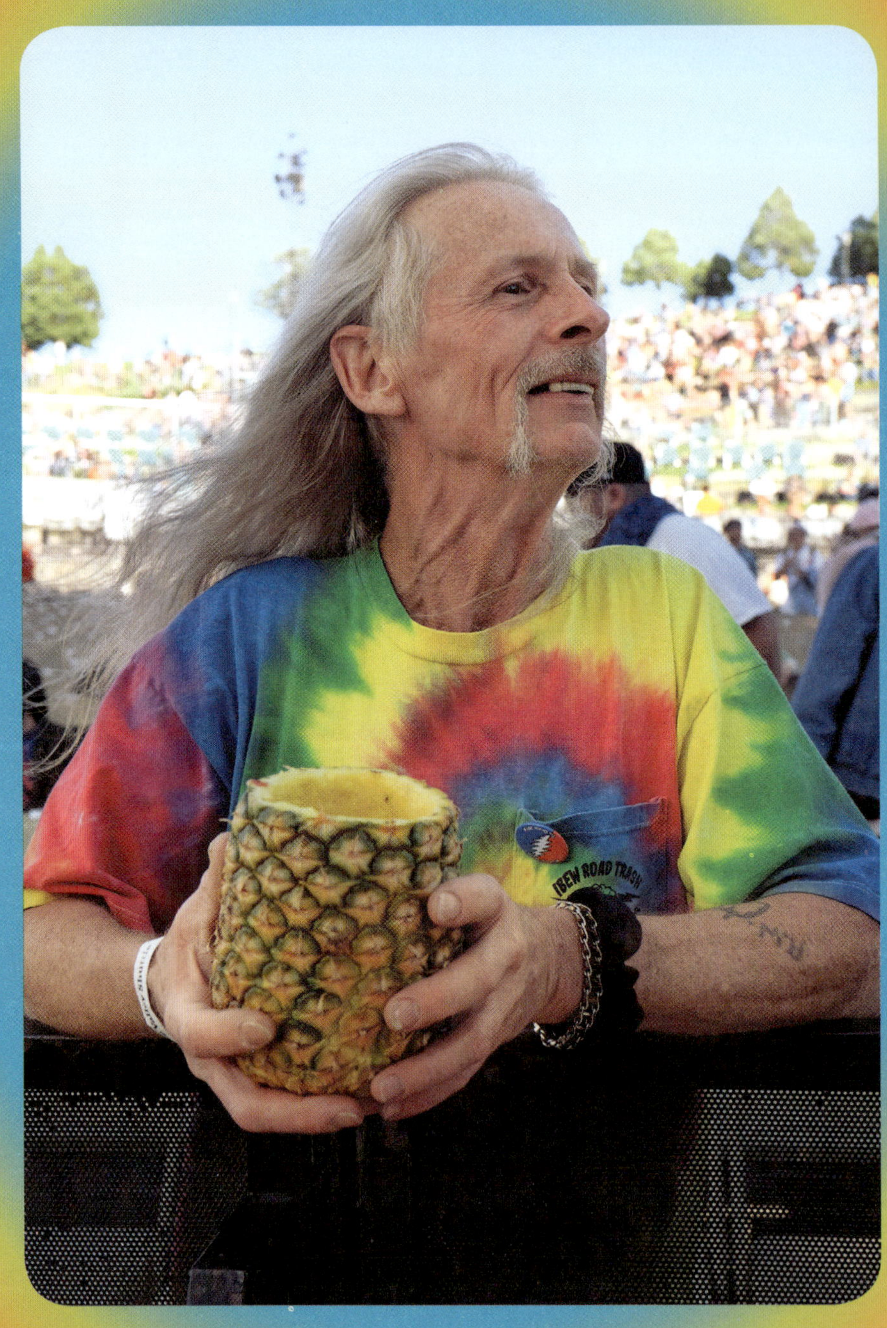
IBEW ROAD TRASH

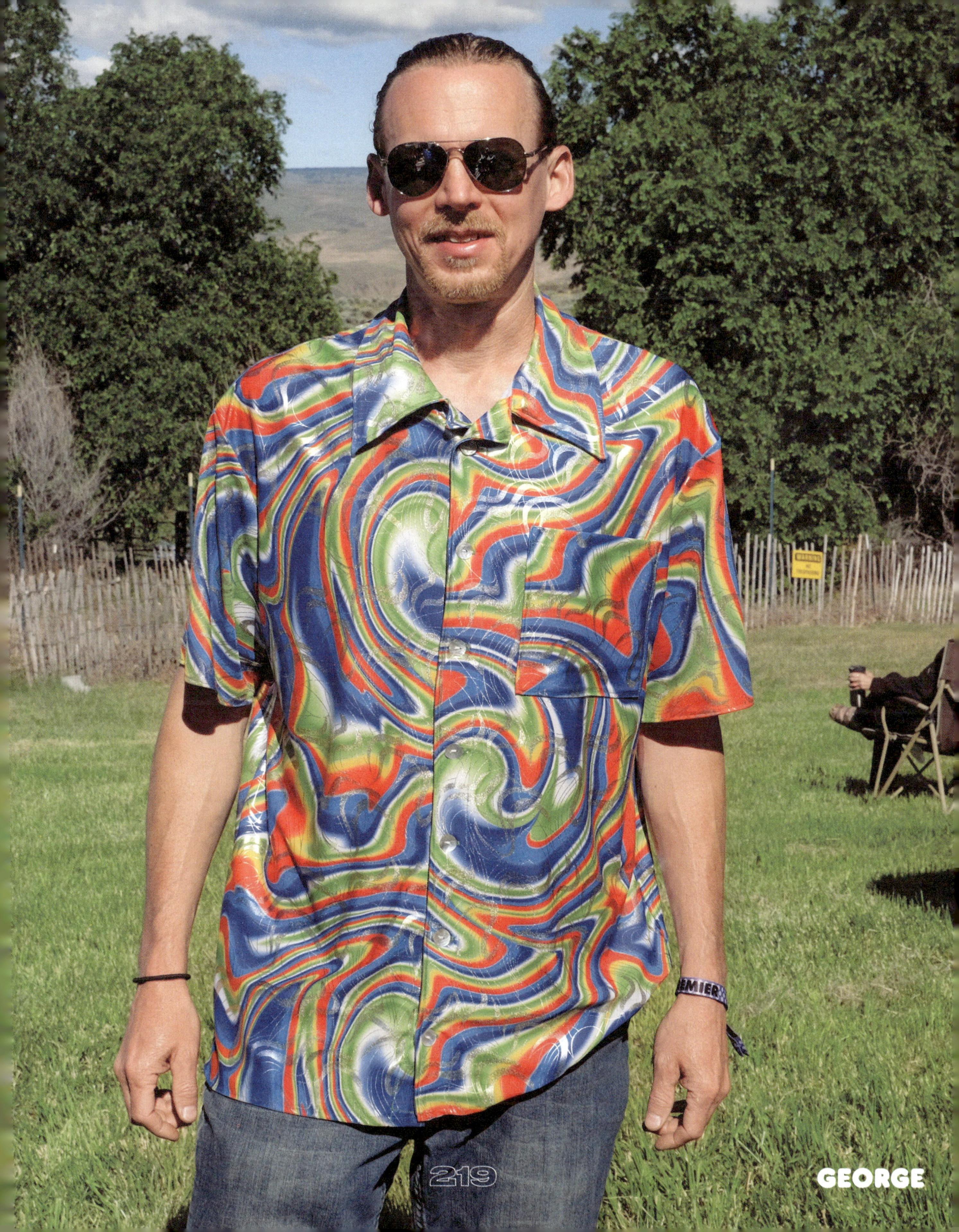

GEORGE

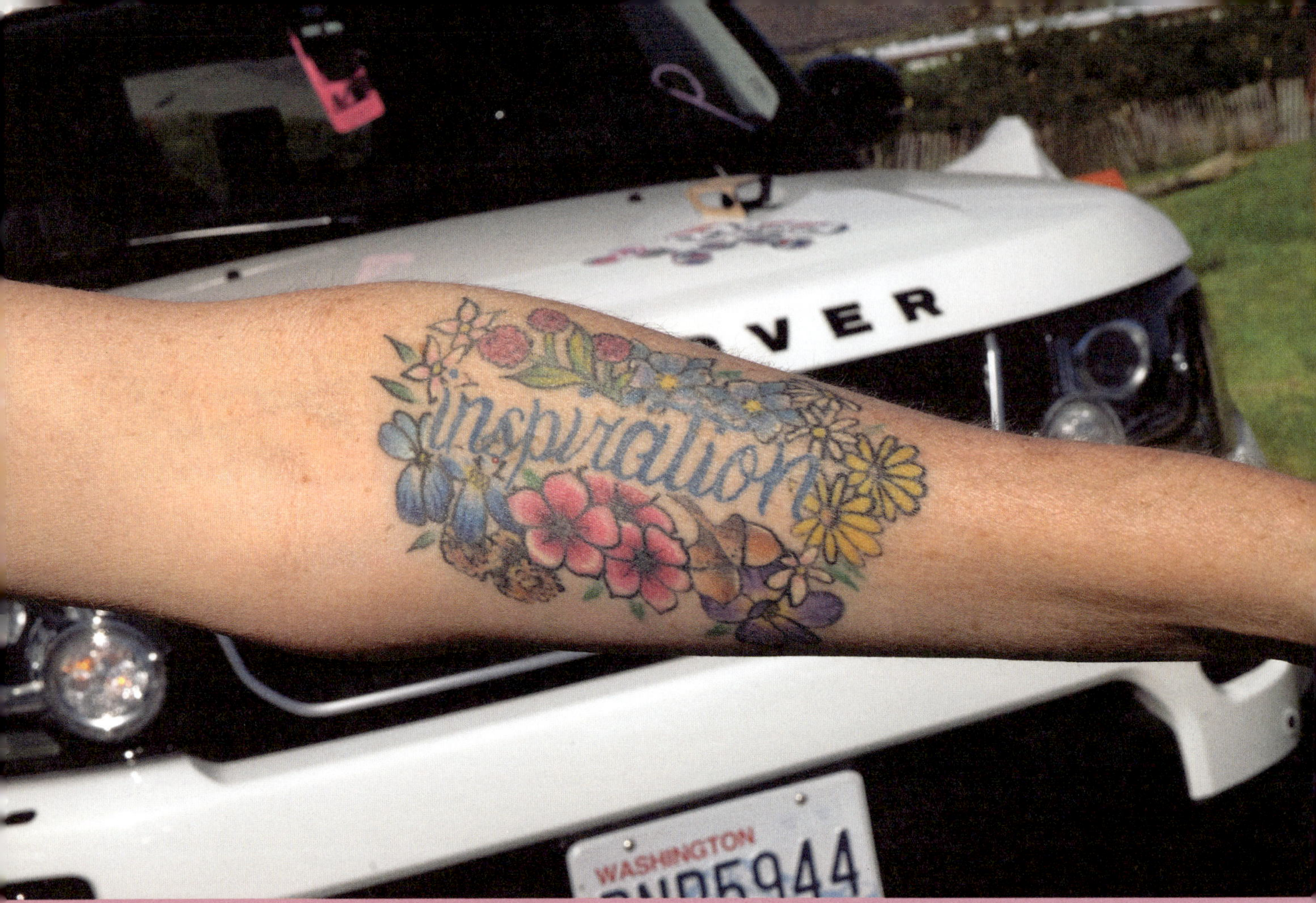
inspiration
WASHINGTON

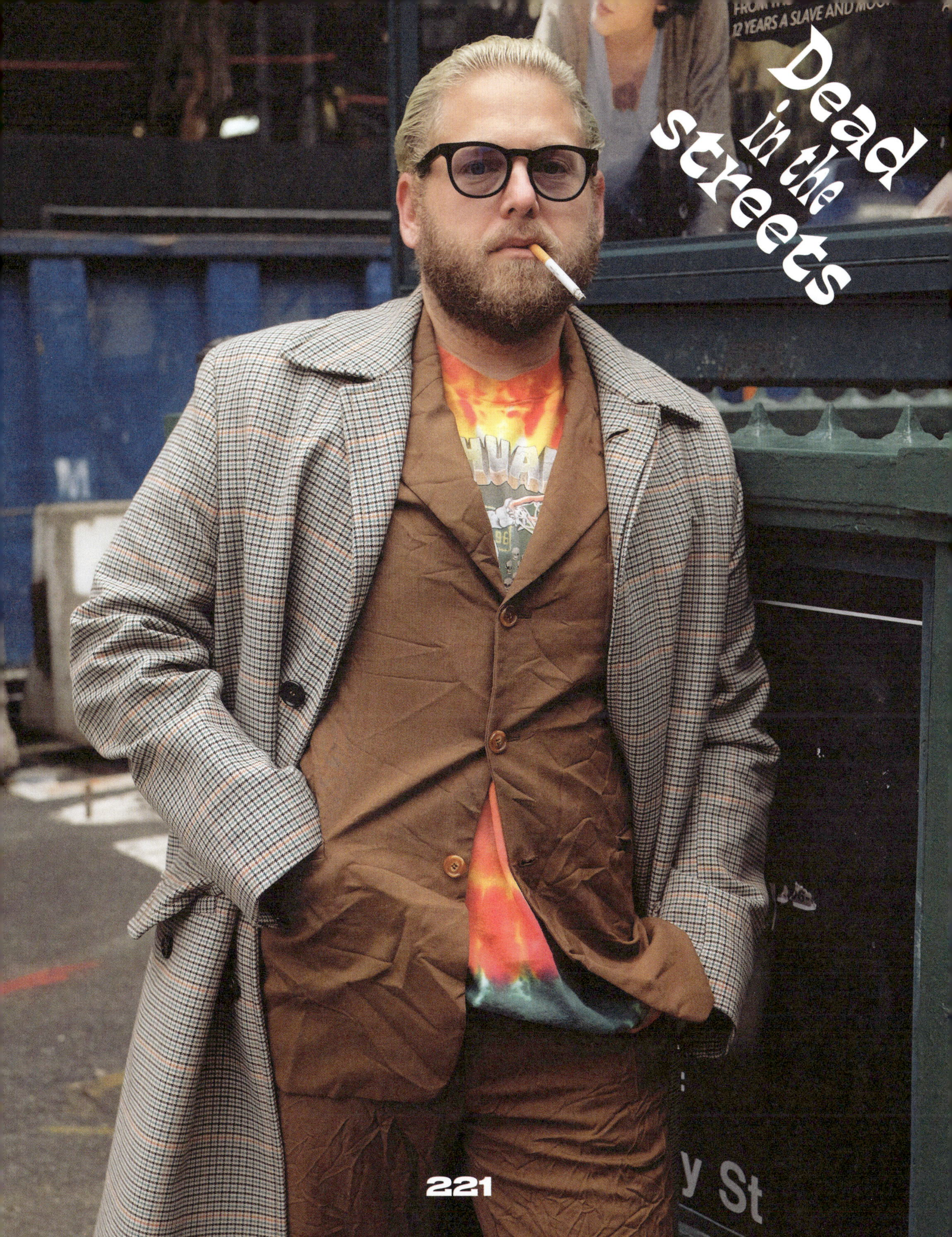
Dead
in the
streets
12 YEARS A SLAVE AND
y St

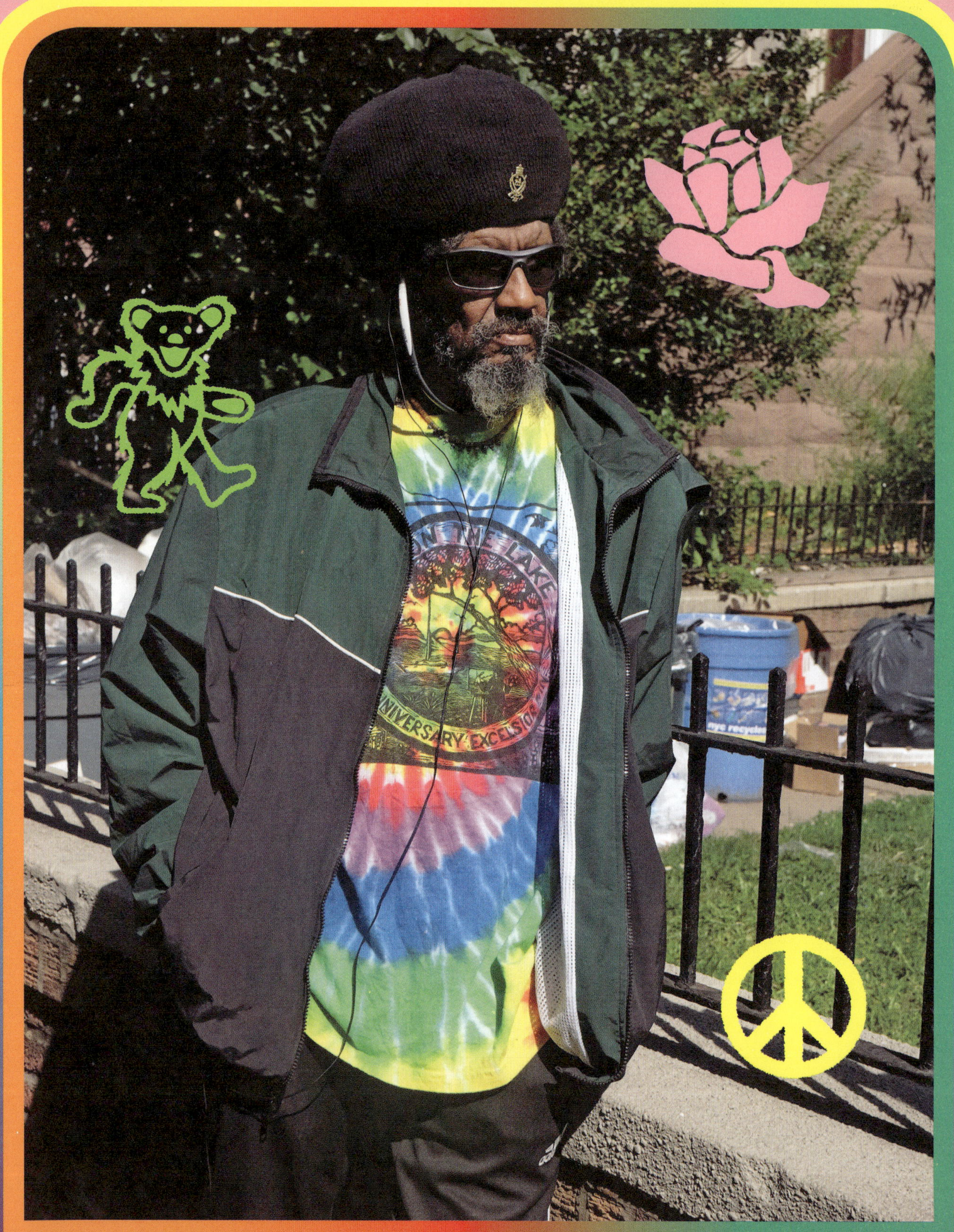
ON THE LAKE

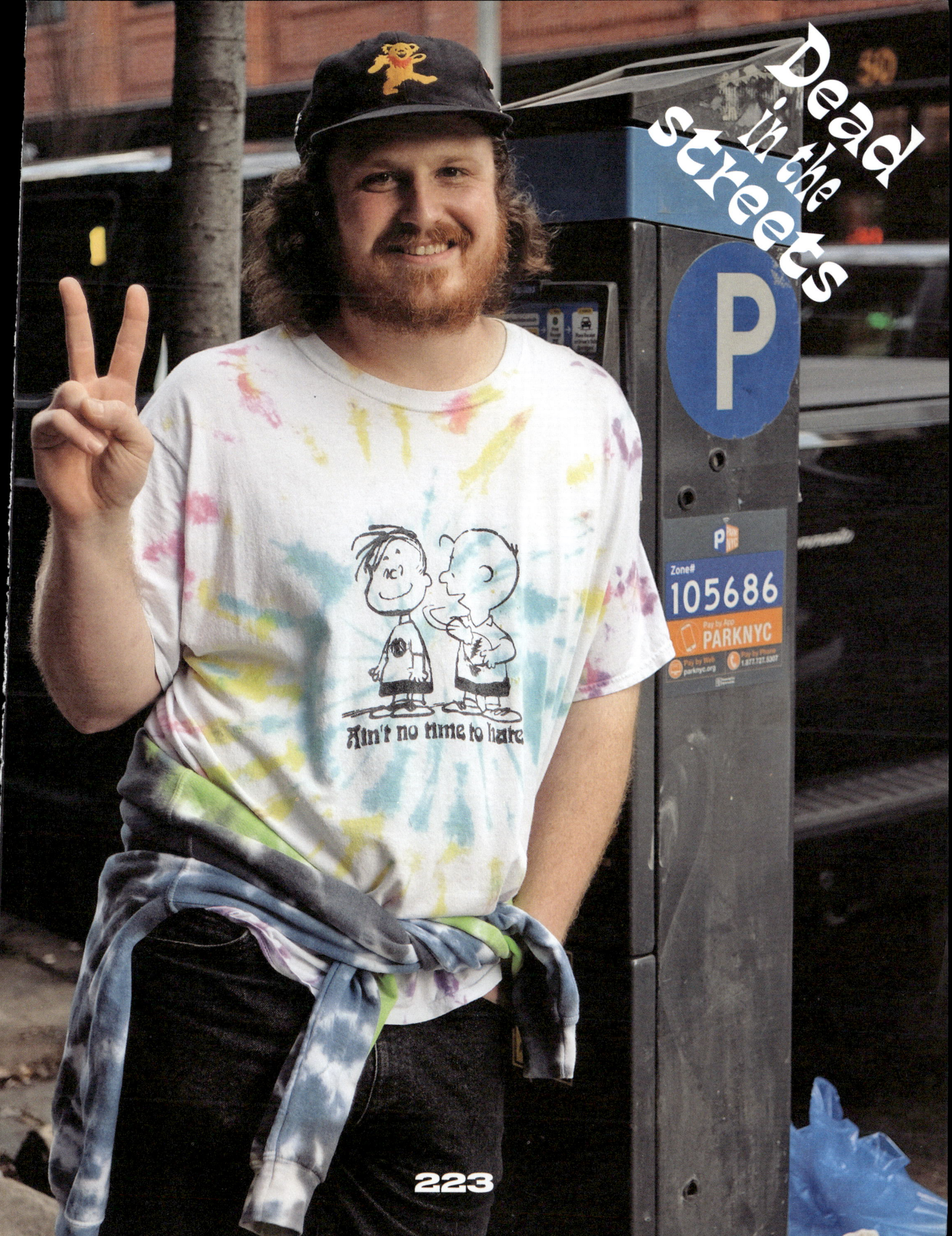
Dead
in the
streets
P
Zone#
105686
PARKNYC
Ain't no time to hate

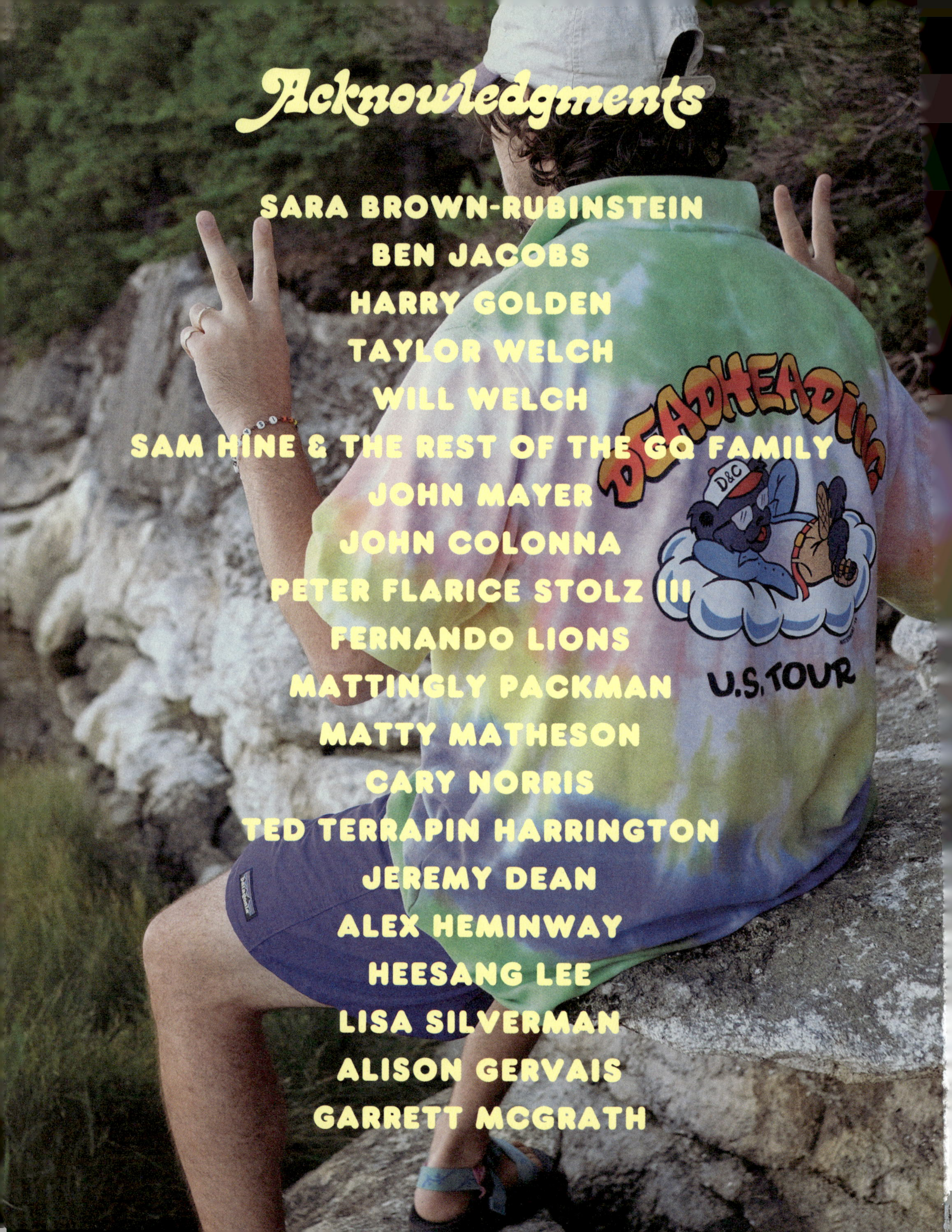

Acknowledgments

SARA BROWN-RUBINSTEIN
BEN JACOBS
HARRY GOLDEN
TAYLOR WELCH
WILL WELCH
SAM HINE & THE REST OF THE GQ FAMILY
JOHN MAYER
JOHN COLONNA
PETER FLARICE STOLZ III
FERNANDO LIONS
MATTINGLY PACKMAN
MATTY MATHESON
CARY NORRIS
TED TERRAPIN HARRINGTON
JEREMY DEAN
ALEX HEMINWAY
HEESANG LEE
LISA SILVERMAN
ALISON GERVAIS
GARRETT MCGRATH